THE SCIENCE AND TECHNOLOGY OF BUILDING MATERIALS

THE SCIENCE AND TECHNOLOGY OF BUILDING MATERIALS

Henry J. Cowan · Peter R. Smith

Department of Architectural Science, University of Sydney

VAN NOSTRAND REINHOLD COMPANY

New York

Printed in the United States of America

Van Nostrand Reinhold Company Inc.
115 Fifth Avenue
New York, New York 10003

Van Nostrand Reinhold Company Limited
Molly Millars Lane
Wokingham, Berkshire RG11 2PY, England

Van Nostrand Reinhold
480 La Trobe Street
Melbourne, Victoria 3000, Australia

Macmillan of Canada
Division of Canada Publishing Corporation
164 Commander Boulevard
Agincourt, Ontario M1S 3C7, Canada

16 15 14 13 12 11 10 9 8 7 6 5 4 3 2 1

Library of Congress Cataloging-in-Publication Data

Cowan, Henry J.
    The science and technology of building materials.

    Includes index.
    1. Building materials.   I. Smith, Peter R.
II. Title.
TA403.C649   1988   691   87-14010
ISBN 0-442-21799-4

To
Dr. Warren Julian
Dean of the Faculty of Architecture
in the University of Sydney

Preface

This book deals with the physical and chemical properties of building materials, and the influence which these properties have on their use in the design of buildings. It does not assume any knowledge of physics or chemistry beyond elementary high school science. Concepts such as metallurgical phase diagrams, geological formations, and polymer formation are explained in the text where they are first needed. Chemical notation has been used throughout this book in addition to the English names of the chemical compounds, as it is a convenient shorthand, and $CaSO_4.2H_2O$ is clearer to some readers than calcium sulfate dihydrate. A short *Note on Chemical Formulas* has been included for the benefit of readers who are unfamiliar with chemistry. This should suffice for reading almost the entire book, except for short sections on the chemistry of cement and of plastics, which include some more complex chemical formulas; these could be omitted.

The first part of the book discusses the functions which building materials are required to perform. The second part then deals with the properties of each group of materials in turn, and how these affect their functional performance.

Not merely has the number of materials available for building construction grown at an ever increasing rate, but old materials have found new uses, in which they perform functions that our ancestors would have found surprising. The days of the "cookbook" on building materials, which stated precisely what materials could be used for any one purpose, have therefore passed, except for traditional building construction which is mostly limited to small buildings. There are several excellent books on that aspect of the use of materials, and this book is not endeavoring to replace them.

While the authors wish to encourage innovation, based on a sound understanding of the properties of the materials and the functions they are required to perform, they have been at pains to point to the pitfalls. It is possible to predict that some applications of some building materials will result in failure. The opposite cannot always be predicted with certainty, particularly where durability is a problem. However, many failures could be avoided by more careful analysis, and better use of available experimental data.

Both metric SI units and the traditional British/American units (in brackets) are used throughout this book. The *Note on the SI Metric System* giving conversion from one system of units to the other is therefore not really needed, but it may be helpful to readers who consult some of the references, and find that the data are in the "wrong" units.

Chapters 4, 15, and 16 were written mainly by P. R. Smith, and the others mainly by H. J. Cowan. Unless otherwise indicated, drawings are by P. R. Smith and photographs by H. J. Cowan.

We are indebted to the following for reading all or part of the manuscript, and commenting critically on it: Prof. A. Abel, Mr. P. Fawcett, Dr. F. Fricke, Mr. S. Hayman, Prof. W. Julian, Prof. B. L. Karihaloo, Prof. G. M. Philip, and Dr. A. Radford of the University of Sydney; Prof. E. McCartney of the University of New South Wales; and Mr. G. Anderson of the National Building Technology Center.

Sydney, Australia

H. J. C.
P. R. S.

ABBREVIATIONS

1. Chemical Symbols Used in this Book

Al	aluminum
C	carbon
Ca	calcium
Cl	chlorine
Fe	iron
H	hydrogen
Mg	magnesium
N	nitrogen
Na	sodium
O	oxygen
S	sulfur
Si	silicon

2. Units of Measurement Used in this Book

Btu	British thermal unit
C	Celsius
cd	candela
db	decibel
dbA	decibel on the A-scale
F	Fahrenheit
ft	foot
Hz	hertz
in.	inch
K	Kelvin
kg	kilogram
kJ	kilojoule
km	kilometer
ksi	kilopound per square inch
lb	pound
m	meter
MJ	megajoule = 1,000 kJ = 1,000,000 joule

mm	millimeter = 0.001 meter
μm	micrometer = 0.001 mm
MPa	megapascal = 1,000,000 Pa
nm	nanometer = 0.000 001 mm
Pa	pascal (the metric SI unit for pressure and stress; it equals 1 newton per square meter)
psi	pound per square inch
s	second
W	watt
°	degree
%	percent

3. Other Abbreviations

AC	alternating current
ASTM	American Society for Testing Materials
BS	British Standard
d	thickness
DC	direct current
δ	deflection
e	strain
E	modulus of elasticity
f	stress
h	boundary layer heat transfer coefficient
k	thermal conductivity
L	span
PVA	polyvinyl acetate
PVC	polyvinyl chloride
Q	quantity of heat
R	thermal resistance
sin	sine of angle (trigonometric function)
T	temperature
U	thermal transmittance
W	load

A NOTE ON CHEMICAL FORMULAS

The authors have used chemical formulas, although they appreciate that some readers may never have taken a course in chemistry. This is not strictly necessary to understand a simple formula. Chemical formulas and equations are a convenient method for explaining in a few letters what would otherwise take several lines, and they allow the reader to comprehend the composition of chemically simple materials at a glance. The rules are few and simple.

An atom is the smallest unit of a chemical element. Its valency is the number of free bonds that it has available to combine with other atoms to form a molecule. For example, a very common material is water, which consists of hydrogen and oxygen. H is 1-valent, and O is 2-valent, so that it takes 2 H and 1 O to make the simplest molecule, H_2O. These concepts are explained in Sections 2.2 and 18.1.

Only 12 chemical elements are mentioned in the formulas used in this book. Their names, chemical symbols, and valencies are as follows:

Chlorine (Cl), hydrogen (H), and sodium (Na) have a valency of 1.

Calcium (Ca), magnesium (Mg), and oxygen (O) have a valency of 2.

Aluminum (Al) has a valency of 3.

Carbon (C) and silicon (Si) have a valency of 4.

Iron (Fe) can have a valency of 2 or 3. Materials that have 2-valent iron are called *ferrous*, and materials that have 3-valent iron are called *ferric*.

Sulfur (S) can have a valency of 2, 4, or 6, and nitrogen (N) can have a valency of 3 or 5, but they occur only in very few formulas in this book.

The more complicated-looking chemical formulas occur in Chapter 13, dealing with cement, and in Chapter 18, dealing with plastics. Let us look at the meaning of these formulas.

Two of the raw materials used for making portland cement are alumina and silica. Alumina consists of aluminum and oxygen, and silica of silicon and oxygen. O is 2-valent, Al 3-valent, and Si 4-valent. Therefore the simplest molecule of alumina consists of 2 Al and 3 O ($2 \times 3 = 6$ and $3 \times 2 = 6$), giving Al_2O_3. The simplest molecule of silica consists of 1 Si and 2 O ($1 \times 4 = 4$ and $2 \times 2 = 4$), giving SiO_2.

Both of these materials are derived from clay, which contains alumina and silica in the proportion of 1 to 2. It also contains some chemically combined water, as do many other materials. We therefore get the formula $Al_2O_3 \cdot 2SiO_2 \cdot 2H_2O$ for clay.

Chapters 18 and 19 deal with so-called organic compounds (the term is explained in Section 18.1). These are compounds of carbon, in which carbon atoms combine with other carbon atoms to form chains or rings. These are a little more complicated.

Ethane is a chain molecule that consists of 2 carbon atoms linked to one another with a single bond, and surrounded by hydrogen atoms linked to the carbon atoms with a single bond (Fig. N.1). Each carbon atom has 4 bonds, but one is taken up by the link between them. Thus, each carbon atom has 3 links available for hydrogen atoms, so that they can combine with $2 \times 3 = 6$ hydrogen atoms, and the chemical formula of ethane is thus C_2H_6.

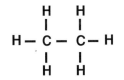

Fig. N.1. Chemical structure of ethane.

The carbon atoms could also be linked by two bonds (Fig. N.2) which leaves only two bonds for hydrogen atoms, so that the 2 carbon atoms can combine with $2 \times 2 = 4$ H, and the chemical formula is C_2H_4, which is ethylene.

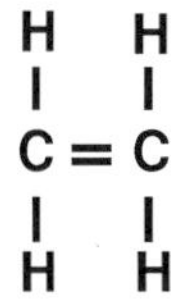

H H
| |
C = C
| |
H H

Fig. N.2. Chemical structure of ethylene.

Six carbon atoms can be linked as a continuous ring, with two bonds and one bond between these carbon atoms alternating (Fig. N.3). These links take up 3 of 4 available bonds, so that one is left for linking to hydrogen atoms, and the formula for this material (called benzene) is C_6H_6.

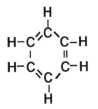

Fig. N.3. Chemical structure of benzene.

If we now take away one hydrogen atom from ethylene, we are left with C_2H_3, which has one vacant bond. Similarly, if we take one hydrogen atom from benzene, we are left with C_6H_5, which also has one vacant bond. These two can combine to form $C_2H_3 \cdot C_6H_5$ (called styrene). We do not add up all the C's and H's, because the structure is clearer that way. The full stop (·) denotes a single bond between the two parts; a colon (:) is used to denote a double bond between two parts.

Contents

THE SCIENCE AND
TECHNOLOGY OF
BUILDING MATERIALS

1

An Historical Introduction

Our construction methods for the use of timber and brick on the domestic scale do not differ greatly from those used in Ancient Rome, as the remains of Herculaneum, buried by an eruption of Mount Vesuvius two thousand years ago, illustrate. We rarely make use today of the sculpted natural stone that figures so prominently in buildings inherited from earlier centuries, however, because of the high labor costs involved.

The mortar and plaster, the paint, and the glass used today are different materials from those used prior to the nineteenth century. The greatest change, however, has occurred in the use of metals, which were only minor building materials prior to the eighteenth century. The adoption of steel-frame and reinforced-concrete construction have caused major changes in traditional construction practices.

1.1 MASONRY, CONCRETE, TIMBER, AND CANVAS

Building materials are among the oldest human artifacts, but today's materials differ appreciably from those used prior to the nineteenth century. Superbly sculpted buildings of natural stone, built several thousand years ago, survive to prove that the skill is of very ancient origin (Fig. 1.1.1). Even civilizations that lacked metal tools succeeded in working stone with remarkable precision (Fig. 1.1.2). These were exceptional buildings even in their own time, however, the most common building materials in the Ancient World, and in the developing countries until recently, being timber (or bamboo or reeds) and sun-dried bricks (or pisé). These

readily available materials were, and are, nondurable, but simple buildings using them could, and can, be erected quickly and cheaply (Fig. 1.1.3).

Hard-burnt bricks have been found that are 10,000 years old. The amount of fuel needed to produce such durable building blocks, however, limited their use prior to the days of the Roman Empire, at which time they became a common building material; they have remained so in the Middle East.

In Western Europe during the Middle Ages, brick was considered a more expensive material than stone and was used almost exclusively in regions where natural stone was not available. In the thirteenth century, bricks became more common, and by the eighteenth century brick was increasingly substituted for stone to reduce costs (see Chap. 15).

This substitute brick was stuccoed or plastered and then painted with "joint" lines to imitate stone. These lines were eventually omitted, but it is still common practice to plaster external brick walls in European regions where natural stone was commonly used in the past. In the traditional "brick regions" of Europe, external brick walls, using face bricks, are usually left unplastered.

Concrete was invented by the Romans in the first century B.C., and it became the most common material for major public buildings during the Roman Empire. Falling into disuse in the fifth century A.D., it was rediscovered only in the eighteenth century as a result of a systematic scientific investigation (see Sec. 13.3).

Wood is, and probably always has been, the most common material for buildings on the domestic scale

1

Fig. 1.1.1. King Zoser's Mortuary Complex at Saqqara, Egypt.
Built about 2600 B.C., this is one of the oldest stone buildings in existence. The columns shown here consist mostly of original masonry; the walls between are restored work.

(Chap. 16). It has also been used for very large and important buildings in all countries that have a good supply of timber. Until the end of the nineteenth century, most of the important buildings in China and Japan were built from timber (Fig. 1.1.4).

Canvas was the principal material of nomads' tents, but it has also been used since antiquity for temporary cover. For example, the Romans used it for sun awnings in their open-air theatres; these were installed before the performance and removed afterwards (Ref. 1.3).

1.2 MORTAR AND PLASTER

It is much easier to lay blocks and bricks with mortar joints than to cut them to fit precisely with dry joints (Fig. 1.1.2). Today, mortar is usually made from sand, portland cement, and some additives, but, prior to the late nineteenth century, mortar usually consisted of sand and lime. Since lime is water-soluble, the mortar joints were a common source of weakness in stone and brick structures.

The Romans, as already mentioned, discovered materials with cementing properties (see Sec. 13.3), and used them to build very strong brick walls, many of which have survived to the present day, particularly in buildings later turned into churches. Nevertheless, they also built some stone structures with dry joints. The Greeks always used dry joints for their stone temples.

Gypsum was used as mortar in Egypt, and naturally occurring bitumen in Mesopotamia. In very important structures, the stone was sometimes set in molten lead—for example, in the Aya Sofya, the great By-

Fig. 1.1.2. Squared masonry from Cuzco, capital city of the Incas in the Peruvian highlands.
These stones were carefully fitted by prolonged rubbing with sand since the Inca civilization did not have metal tools. The joints are so tight that it is impossible to push a razor blade between the stones. No mortar was used. Because of the man-hours and precision required, this is a very expensive form of construction. It was used in Greek temples. One of the rare uses in modern times was in the Morgan Library (1903), where the multimillionaire Pierpont Morgan insisted on a revival of the Greek method to achieve perfect durability (Ref. 1.1).

zantine church built in Istanbul in the sixth century A.D.

Plastering has a similar purpose. It produces smooth surfaces on walls that would otherwise be rough. Many plastered walls in important buildings were decorated with pictures from the time of Ancient Greece to the eighteenth century. Fresco painting was done on wet lime plaster, and the paints dried and set with the plaster.

Modern plaster is usually made with portland cement, but gypsum plaster and lime plaster were used until the early years of this century (see Chap. 13).

1.3 PIGMENTS

When Greek architecture was rediscovered in the eighteenth century, it was admired particularly for the austere whiteness of its marble and limestone temples. This is still a widely held view of classical architecture, but we know today that most of the marble was painted; the paint has merely disappeared through weathering.

Paintings of the Ancient World survive in Egyptian tombs (see Fig. 19.1.1) and in buildings buried by volcanic action in the Greek island of Thera, in the fifteenth century B.C. (Ref. 1.4), as well as in Pompei and some villas nearby that were buried in the first century A.D.

Some of these paintings have high artistic merit in spite of the limited range of colors available in Egypt and Minoan Greece. White was made from lime, and black from soot. Yellow, red, and brown were made from earth pigments containing iron ore. Blue was obtained from various copper salts, and green by mixing blue with yellow. The Romans had a wider range of colors because they were able to import pigments from the various parts of their empire. Vitruvius described them in detail (Ref. 1.5). Green could be produced directly from malachite. A particularly good blue was imported from outside the empire (Armenia). There were several shades of red to supplement the earthy red ochre. Vermilion was manufactured from mercury, and purple was obtained from a shellfish. Vitruvius also described several substitute pigments for less important work which were cheaper; for example, blue was obtainable by dying chalk with woad.

The Middle Ages and the Renaissance added further to the range of pigments, but some were very expensive; for example, ultramarine blue was produced by grinding lapis lazuli, a semiprecious stone. In the Middle Ages, the cost of a painting depended more on the cost of the pigments than the wages of the painter.

Most of the pigments and the vehicles in which they are dispersed are today made synthetically, this being one group of building materials that has been radically transformed by modern technology (see Chap. 19).

1.4 GLASS

Glass was already made in ancient Egypt for use in jewelry. It did not become a major building material, however, until the Middle Ages. Although a few glass panes have been found, the Romans usually left their windows strictly as openings, or they covered them with transparent parchment. For some important buildings, thin, translucent slabs of alabaster or marble were used (see Fig. 12.6.4).

Medieval glass let in much more daylight than these stone slabs, but it was not transparent because of the many imperfections and air bubbles. *Sheet glass* was made from cylinders blown from liquid glass. The ends were cut off and the cylinder opened up into a flat sheet in an oven, but the surface of the glass was damaged by contact with the oven floor.

The other traditional process—*crown glass*—was perfected in the late Middle Ages. The liquid glass was blown into a rough globe and then spun until, by centrifugal force, it attained a wheel-like shape (see Fig. 17.2.2). This was then cooled and cut into panes. Since the glass did not touch any surface while soft, it was perfectly clear; however, only relatively small panes could be produced. The brilliantly clear, slightly curved crown-glass panes that were introduced into

Fig. 1.1.3. Circular hut in the Highlands of New Guinea, made of bamboo tied together with vegetable fibers.
The walls are woven mats and the roof is thatch. The hut can be erected by two people in a single day, if they have previously collected the materials from the surrounding countryside, cut the poles to length, and woven the mats.

England in the seventeenth century are one of the characteristics of the buildings of that period.

Glass is today produced by entirely different, improved, and cheaper processes developed in the twentieth century (see Sec. 17.2).

1.5 METALS

Metals played only a minor role in building construction prior to the eighteenth century. The Romans used lead extensively for water pipes and for roof covering, and they also used copper for these purposes. Copper is still used as a high-quality roofing material, but lead became too expensive in the early years of this century.

Wrought iron, copper, and copper alloys have been used since the Middle Ages, and possibly earlier, for door hinges and locks and sometimes for entire doors. Lead was used for joining the small panes of glass in medieval windows, and the assembled windows were then strengthened with iron bars.

The Greeks and Romans used bronze and iron for dowels and clamps to join blocks of stone laid without mortar (see Sec. 1.2). In Byzantine, and later in Muslim, arches and domes, the horizontal thrust was often absorbed by timber or metal bars, this being the earliest use of metal as a structural material. In the Renaissance, iron chains were used instead to absorb the outward thrust of domes (Ref. 1.6).

During the eighteenth century as new and cheaper processes were developed for the manufacture of iron, this metal came to be used extensively for machines and also for load-bearing beams and columns in the factories that housed the new machines.

During the nineteenth century, iron, and later steel (see Sec. 10.1), was increasingly employed for the structural parts of buildings. In the 1860s, reinforced

Fig. 1.1.4. Timber dome of the Temple of Heaven in Beijing, China. The dome is supported on huge circular timber columns; built in 1890, it replaces a previous temple destroyed by fire in 1889 (Ref. 1.2).

concrete was invented, and it became a major building material in the twentieth century.

The adoption of structural steel and reinforced concrete caused major changes in traditional construction practices. It was no longer necessary to use thick walls of stone or brick for multistory buildings, and it became much simpler to build fire-resistant floors. Both these changes served to reduce the cost of construction. It also became possible to erect buildings with greater heights and longer spans.

Corrugated iron was developed in the 1820s, and processes for coating it with zinc or tin for corrosion protection date from the 1830s. Because of its strength and relatively low weight, corrugated iron was exported as a roofing and walling material from Europe to its colonies and to America.

Metal (lead and later aluminum) was first used in the mid-nineteenth century in damp-proof courses (see Glossary); these had previously employed slate or other impervious stones.

Steel and aluminum windows, curtain walls, and partitions are developments of the present century.

1.6 MATERIALS ARE NOT ALWAYS WHAT THEY APPEAR TO BE

The ethics of using construction that imitates more expensive materials has been argued from time to time. Structural honesty was one of the tenets of many neo-Gothic theorists in the late nineteenth century, although John Ruskin was prepared to accept gilded wood on the ground that everybody knew it was not solid gold. Similar tenets were espoused by the Modern Movement, particularly in the 1950s and 60s.

It may also be argued that to produce construction that looks precisely like a more expensive one, and that fulfills the same purpose, is a mark of professional skill. The criterion is then whether the substitution produces an equally good or an inferior construction. At any rate, faking of expensive materials is an ancient craft. Several examples are given by Vitruvius; the following, describing vaulting imitated by stucco work, may serve as an example:

When vaulting is required, the procedure should be as follows. Set up horizontal furring strips at intervals of not more than two feet apart, using preferably cypress, as fir is soon spoiled by decay and by age. Arrange these strips so as to form a curve, and make them fast to the joists of the floor above or to the roof, if it is there, by nailing them with many iron nails to ties fixed at intervals. These ties should be made of a kind of wood that neither decay nor time nor dampness can spoil, such as box, juniper, olive, oak, cypress, or any other similar wood, except common oak; for this warps and causes cracks in work in which it is used.

Having arranged the furring strips, take cord made of Spanish broom, and tie Greek reeds, previously pounded flat, to them in the required contour. Immediately above the vaulting spread some mortar made of lime and sand, to check any drops that may fall from the joists or from the roof. If a supply of Greek reed is not to be had, gather slender marsh reeds, and make them up with silk cord into bundles all of the same thickness and adjusted to the proper length, provided that the bundles are not more than two feet long between any two knots. Then tie them with cord to the beams as above described, and drive wooden pegs into them. Make all the other preparations as above described.

Having thus set the vaultings in their places and interwoven them, apply the rendering coat to their lower surface; then lay on the sand mortar, and afterwards polish it off with the powdered marble. After the vaultings have been polished, set the impost moulding directly between them. These obviously ought to be made extremely slender and delicate, for when they are large, their weight carries them down, and they cannot support themselves (Ref. 1.7).

Vitruvius then proceeds to explain how the walls should be stuccoed and the walls and the vault prepared for fresco painting. This description of an imitation masonry vault was written just over two thousand years ago, and it presumably describes a common Roman practice, although no examples survive.

A similar technique was developed in the late Renaissance and particularly used during the Baroque era to create vaults and domes of extraordinary complexity from plaster supported by a light timber framework. This technique continued in use until the early years of the twentieth century. The famous ceilings built in Britain in the eighteenth century by Robert Adam were nearly all constructed of lath and plaster.

In our own time, a number of materials have been developed whose use has been criticized on the ground that they pretend to be something that they are not. For example, a hard-wearing laminate can be made by photographing the color and grain of a timber surface, printing it on paper, and then impregnating the paper with melamine-formaldehyde (see Sec. 18.5). This laminate can be veneered to a cheap timber base to provide a surface that has wearing properties far superior to that of timber and a surface appearance that is not significantly inferior to that of veneered timber. When these laminates were first introduced in the 1950s, they were severely criticized on the ground that they

pretended to be something that they were not. Present opinion is often more tolerant.

REFERENCES

1.1. Leland M. Roth: *McKim, Mead & White, Architects*. Thames and Hudson, London, 1984, p. 291.
1.2. Liang Ssu-Ch'Eng: *A Pictorial History of Chinese Architecture*. MIT Press, Cambridge, MA, 1984, p. 116.
1.3. R. Graefe: *Vela Erunt*. Philip von Zabern, Mainz, 1979. 221 pp. + 150 plates.
1.4. C. G. Doumas: *Thera*. Thames and Hudson, London, 1983. 168 pp.
1.5. Marcus Vitruvius Pollio: *The Ten Books of Architecture*. (transl. by M. Morgan). Dover, New York, 1960, pp. 214–221.
1.6. H. J. Cowan: *The Master Builders*. Wiley, New York, 1977. pp. 169–202.
1.7. Vitruvius: *Loc. cit.*, pp. 205–206.

SUGGESTIONS FOR FURTHER READING

H. J. Cowan: *The Masterbuilders*. Wiley, New York, 1977. 299 pp.
K. D. White: *Greek and Roman Technology*. Thames and Hudson, London, 1984. 272 pp.
H. J. Cowan: *Science and Building*. Wiley, New York, 1978. 374 pp.
J. Bowyer: *History of Building*. Crosby Lockwood Staples, London, 1973. 275 pp.

Part I

The Function of
Building Materials

2

Strength and Deformation

Adequate strength is a prime requirement for any building material. Adequate stiffness is an important secondary requirement.

In the discipline known as "Materials Science," materials are divided into metals, ceramics, and plastics, a classification that will be discussed in Sec. 2.3. Both the elastic and the plastic deformation of metals can be explained in terms of their crystal structure.

Since most materials under certain conditions of temperature and pressure can become ductile or brittle, ductility and brittleness are not considered as properties of a particular material. Steel and aluminum, however, are normally ductile, and concrete and brick are normally brittle.

We will define the concepts of stress and strain in this chapter and then consider the failure of materials by plastic deformation and by fracture. Finally, we will examine the procedure for testing materials.

2.1 THE IMPORTANCE OF ADEQUATE STRENGTH AND STIFFNESS

Adequate *strength* is the prime requirement for any building material. It does not matter how perfectly it fulfills its other requirements; if it collapses or breaks under the loads it is required to support, it is useless, or worse. The load to be carried in a structural member may be much greater than the weight of the structural member, but even so-called *non-load-bearing members* must be able to support their own weight and resist any restraints imposed at their supports.

Adequate *stiffness* is usually a secondary requirement. Most structural members are designed for strength and checked for *deflection* (see Glossary); if the latter is excessive, the design must be reviewed.

Deflection is limited primarily because many brittle finishing materials (*see* Sec. 2.4), particularly for ceilings, may be damaged if it is too great. Excessive deflection is also unsightly, and sagging ceilings may give the impression that a building is unsafe when it is merely lacking in stiffness. In a "flat" (i.e., slightly sloping) roof, it may interfere with roof drainage.

2.2 THE FUNDAMENTAL PARTICLES OF MATTER

The fundamental particles of matter combine to form over 100 *elements*. These can be arranged in a periodic table (Fig. 2.2.1). Each element consists of a *nucleus* (which itself consists of a number of elementary particles) and a number of *electrons*, which are negatively charged particles. The electrons revolve around the nucleus in a manner somewhat similar to the planets revolving around the sun. However, whereas each planet has a separate orbit, a number of electrons revolve around the nucleus in the same orbit. The number of electrons that can revolve in each orbit increases as we go outwards from the nucleus. The innermost orbit, or *shell*, can hold a maximum of two electrons, the next can hold a maximum of eight electrons, the next after that a maximum of sixteen electrons, and so on.

The smallest unit of an element is called an *atom*, which consists of one nucleus and the appropriate number of electrons (Fig. 2,2.2). Atoms combine to form *molecules*; for example, two atoms of oxygen (2 O) form one molecule of oxygen (O_2). Other types of molecules are possible. Three atoms of oxygen (3 O) can combine to form one molecule of ozone (O_3), a gas that differs greatly from oxygen.

The element oxygen combines readily with other elements to form oxides. For example, it can combine with iron (Fe, from the Latin word for iron, *ferrum*) in three different ways:

- Fe_3O_4: Called *ferrosoferric oxide* by chemists and *magnetite* be geologists (the latter because it has natural magnetic properties and was used as a magnetic compass by early mariners);
- Fe_2O_3: Called *ferric oxide* by chemists and *haematite* by geologists
- FeO: Called *ferrous oxide*.

Readers may be referred to any textbook on chemistry or materials science (for example, Ref. 2.1) for further examples.

Molecules may take a solid, liquid, or gaseous form. Gases become liquids and liquids become solids when they are cooled. Close to absolute zero (−273.16°C or −459.67°F), all materials are solid. Conversely, at sufficiently high temperatures, all solids and liquids become gases.

In this chapter we are concerned only with solid materials, which may be either crystalline or amorphous. *Crystals* are solids whose atoms are arranged in a definite pattern. This regular array gives rise to the characteristic crystal faces. With care and time, crystals can be grown to considerable size. This may take place in rocks over long periods of time, and precious stones are made from crystals of this sort. Most crystals are too small to be seen with the unaided eye. Ceramic crystals may or may not be transparent, but metal crystals are always opaque. "Cut crystal" is glass that is actually a *supercooled liquid* (see Sec. 17-1) and therefore not a crystal in the terminology used here. *Amorphous materials* are not crystalline,

Metals ← | → Non-metals

IA	IIA	IIIB	IVB	VB	VIB	VIIB	VIII	VIII	VIII	IB	IIB	IIIA	IVA	VA	VIA	VIIA	0
1 H 1																1 H 1	2 He 4
3 Li 7	4 Be 9											5 B 11	6 C 12	7 N 14	8 O 16	9 F 19	10 Ne 20
11 Na 23	12 Mg 24											13 Al 27	14 Si 28	15 P 31	16 S 32	17 Cl 35	18 Ar 40
19 K 39	20 Ca 40	21 Sc 45	22 Ti 48	23 V 51	24 Cr 52	25 Mn 55	26 Fe 56	27 Co 59	28 Ni 59	29 Cu 64	30 Zn 65	31 Ga 70	32 Ge 73	33 As 75	34 Se 79	35 Br 80	36 Kr 84
37 Rb 85	38 Sr 88	39 Y 89	40 Zr 92	41 Nb 93	42 Mo 96	43 Tc 99	44 Ru 101	45 Rh 103	46 Pd 106	47 Ag 108	48 Cd 112	49 In 115	50 Sn 119	51 Sb 122	52 Te 128	53 I 127	54 Xe 131
55 Cs 133	56 Ba 137	57-71 *	72 Hf 178	73 Ta 181	74 W 184	75 Re 186	76 Os 190	77 Ir 192	78 Pt 195	79 Au 197	80 Hg 201	81 Tl 204	82 Pb 207	83 Bi 209	84 Po 210	85 At 210	86 Rn 222
87 Fr 223	88 Ra 226	89 - 101 **															

Fig. 2.2.1. The periodic table of the elements.
The elements are arranged in order of increasing *atomic weight*. Each is given a serial number, which is called the *atomic number*. The elements are also arranged in vertical columns according to their chemical behavior, which depends mainly on the number of electrons in the outer shell of the atom. Since elements with few electrons in the outer shell behave like metals, this arrangement shows the metals at table left and the nonmetals at table right. For simplicity, atomic weights are given only to the nearest whole number. The atomic weight is approximately the ratio of the weight of an atom of the element to that of an atom of hydrogen, which is the simplest element and contains only a nucleus and one electron.
The names of elements of particular interest to the study of building materials, along with their abbreviations, are as follows:

H = hydrogen; He = helium; C = carbon; N = nitrogen; O = oxygen; F = fluorine; Ne = neon; Na = sodium; Mg = magnesium; Al = aluminum; Si = silicon; P = phosphorus; S = sulfur; Cl = chlorine; Ar = argon; K = potassium; Ca = calcium; Cr = chromium; Mn = manganese; Fe = iron; Ni = nickel; Cu = copper; Zn = zinc; Se = selenium; Br = bromine; Ag = silver; Cd = cadmium; Sn = tin; Sb = antimony; I = iodine; Ba = barium; W = tungsten; Pt = platinum; Au = gold; Hg = mercury; Pb = lead.

* Elements 57–71: Rare earth elements of atomic weight 139 to 175.
** Elements 89–101: Actinium, thorium, uranium, and a number of radioactive elements which have been produced in the laboratory, but do not exist in nature; atomic weights 227 to 256.

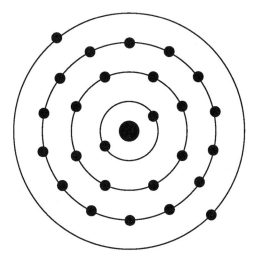

Fig. 2.2.2. Structure of the nucleus and 26 electrons of the iron atom (atomic number, 26).
The atomic weight of iron is 55.85 (hydrogen has an atomic weight of 1.008). The fact that there are only two electrons in its outer shell accounts for its metallic character.

and this category includes glass and other supercooled liquids.

2.3 METALS, CERAMICS, AND PLASTICS

In discussing their strength and deformation, it is convenient to divide materials into three categories defined as metals, ceramics, and plastics.

Metals have a characteristic "metallic" appearance; they are good conductors of heat and electricity (which may or may not be a desirable property for any particular application); and, unless formed into very, very thin sheets, they are opaque to light.

As already stated, atoms consist of nuclei and "shells" of electrons (Fig. 2.2.2). As the atomic weight increases, more electrons are added to an atom; as positions in the outer shell are filled, a new shell still further from the nucleus is formed. This outer shell may contain far fewer than the maximum possible number of electrons. If there are only one or two electrons in the outer shell, the material behaves like a metal, because the one or two "free" electrons in the outer shell are comparatively mobile in an electric field—a characteristic that gives metals their high electrical conductivity. The high thermal conductivity of metals is also associated with the mobility of the one or two outer electrons, which can transfer thermal energy from a high to a low temperature level (see Chap. 6). The opaqueness of metals is also due to the electrons in the outer shell because these readily absorb light energy.

The chemical elements with a larger number of electrons in their outer shell are the nonmetals. In the terminology used in this chapter, a *ceramic* is a compound of a metal and a nonmetal (see Ref. 2.1).

In everyday language, the word *ceramic* is used for porcelain, pottery, tiles, and bricks. All these are made from clay, which is chemically defined as hydrated aluminum silicate, that is, a compound of metal and non-metal. In Materials Science, the term *ceramic* has a wider meaning; for example, all metallic ores are classed as ceramics.

Because of their "free" electrons, metals form compounds readily. Some, like aluminum and sodium, oxidize immediately upon being exposed to air, that is, they form a ceramic skin. With the exception of gold, no metal has been found in its metallic state on the surface of the earth in significant quantities. Iron, which is today by far the most important metal, is produced from ores, most of which are various forms of iron oxide (Sec. 10.2).

In ceramics, the free metallic electrons are combined with the electrons of the nonmetal; ceramics are therefore usually poor conductors of heat and of electricity.

The importance of ceramics to the building industry lies in the fact that they are plentiful everywhere on the earth's surface and thus provide the cheapest building materials. In terms of Materials Science, not merely brick but also natural stone and concrete are considered to be ceramics.

Since many of the ceramics used for buildings are chemically stable compounds, they are not subject to corrosion. On the other hand, most ceramics—and, specifically, natural stone, brick, and concrete—are brittle and thus have poor tensile strength (see Sec. 2.5). This deficiency was a determining factor in the structural design of buildings prior to the nineteenth century, and for the following reason: Since the only durable materials available lacked tensile strength, all the long interior spans had to be designed for compression—a constraint that required curved structures, such as domes and vaults (Ref. 2.2).

The third group of materials are the *plastics*. In Materials Science, this group includes all compounds of nonmetals, not merely the materials produced by the plastics industry. Thus, all organic compounds are plastics in this terminology, and these include timber. Such materials will be discussed in Chaps. 16 and 18.

2.4 THE ELASTIC AND PLASTIC DEFORMATION OF METALS

All metals form crystals, and some ceramics also form crystals. There are three principal crystal types, and their structure can be visualized by taking a number of billiard balls of identical diameter (representing the atoms) and stacking them in various ways [Figs. 2.4.1 (a), (b), and (c)].

Let us first consider the deformation of a crystal of pure, unalloyed iron at room temperature. This is called *alpha iron* (or *ferrite*), and it has a body-centered

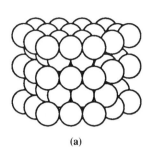

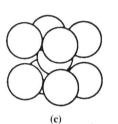

Fig. 2.4.1. Arrangement of atoms in various crystals.
(a) Hexagonal close-packed structure; (b) face-centered cubic structure; (c) body-centered cubic structure.

cubic structure [Fig. 2.4.2 (a)]. If we deform the crystal [Fig. 2.4.2 (b)], we increase the distances between some of the atoms because of the close packing of the crystal. Since the attractions between the atoms resist this deformation, force is needed to bring it about. When the force is removed, the attractions restore the original shape of the crystal. This property is called *elasticity* and the deformation involved, *elastic deformation*.

If we apply a great deal of force, however, some atoms are moved further from their original neighbors than from adjacent atoms, and the interatomic forces then cause a jump of one atomic space [Fig. 2.4.2 (c)]. This phenomenon is called *plastic deformation,* and, unlike elastic deformation, it is permanent and not recoverable when the load is removed.

We can calculate both the elastic and the plastic deformation of perfect crystals from atomic theory. The observed elastic deformation of metals agrees quite well with the theory. The force needed to produce plastic deformation in pure metals (which are not, in fact, very strong) is only a small fraction, however, of that theoretically required.

Perfect crystals can be grown at great expense in a vacuum, but they lose their perfect structure as soon as they are exposed to air. All normal metal crystals have structural imperfections (Fig. 2.4.3). These imperfections make plastic deformation much easier because of the much smaller force required for the atom at the end of a dislocation to make a new interaction (Fig. 2.4.4). In fact, very little force is needed for the plastic deformation of most pure metals. For this reason, even gold and silver are normally alloyed with another

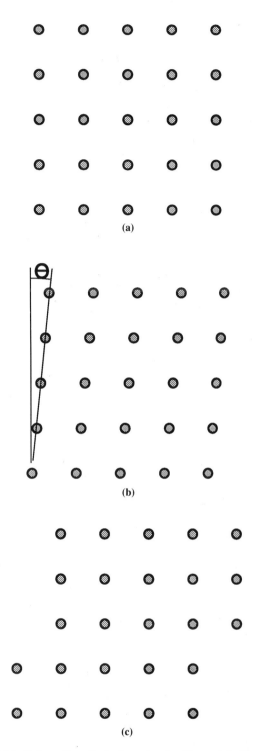

Fig. 2.4.2. Deformation of a body-centered cubic crystal of iron.
(a) Crystal before deformation; (b) elastic deformation of crystal; (c) plastic deformation of crystal.

metal, because objects made from them would otherwise be too easily deformed; sterling silver, for example, is 92.5 percent silver and 7.5 percent copper.

The most important structural metal, iron, has been used for tools for more than 3000 years. A great deal of practical metallurgy is based on old craft experience,

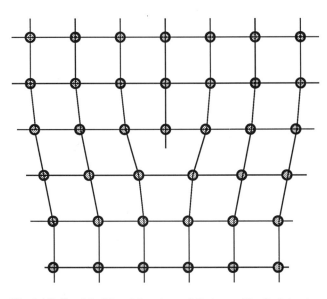

Fig. 2.4.3. Crystal with a *dislocation*, a defect caused by the intrusion of an extra line of atoms.

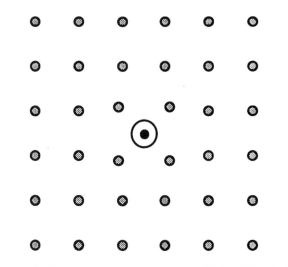

Fig. 2.4.5. Carbon atom occupying an interstitial position in the crystal lattice of iron.

and one of these discoveries is the addition of carbon to iron. Indeed, until the electric furnace was invented, the absorption of some carbon from the fuel used to smelt the ores was inevitable. A very small amount of carbon—0.1 percent, or 1 part in 1000—greatly increases the strength of iron, and this impure iron is called *steel*.

Since the atom of carbon is smaller than that of iron—it has only 6 electrons compared to the 26 in iron—it can fit into the crystal lattice of (Fig. 2.4.5). This distorts the crystal structure, however, and makes the movement of dislocations more difficult. Atoms larger than iron—for example, tungsten with 74 electrons—can also be alloyed with iron. They replace an iron atom, distort the crystal structure in the process (Fig. 2.4.6), but consequently increase the strength of

the iron by making the movement of dislocations more difficult. Thus, impure metals, or *alloys*, are much stronger than the pure metal, provided suitable alloying elements are used (see Chaps. 10 and 11).

2.5 DUCTILITY AND BRITTLENESS

Ductility is the capacity for large plastic deformations prior to rupture. *Brittleness* denotes the lack of ductility. Brittle materials rupture with little or no warning, but their strength may be higher than that of many ductile materials.

Ductile materials give warning of impending failure because of the visual demonstration of impending failure provided by the large plastic deformation. For this reason, reinforced concrete is always designed to ensure that the ductile steel fails before the brittle concrete.

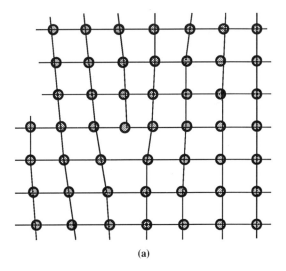

(a)

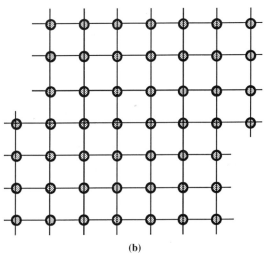

(b)

Fig. 2.4.4. Plastic deformation at a dislocation.

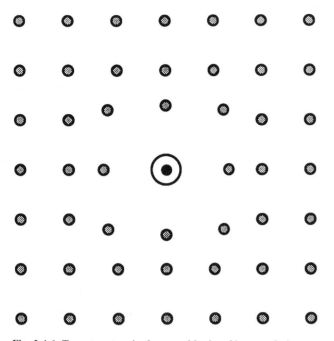

Fig. 2.4.6. Tungsten atom in the crystal lattice of iron, replacing one of the iron atoms.

Ductile materials can also absorb local stress concentrations without failure. The stress concentrations cause local plastic deformation, but the material as a whole is not damaged. In a brittle material, the crack caused by the local overstress may propogate to cause a major failure. Thus, when a sheet of glass is scratched with a glass-cutter, it will easily break along the scratch line because of the large local stress concentrations produced. A sheet of steel cannot be broken along a scratch line because the stress concentrations merely cause local plastic deformations.

Nevertheless, we make extensive use of brittle materials. They usually have good compressive strength, they are often hard and abrasion-resistant, and they are often the cheapest materials that fulfill the functional requirements.

Ductility and brittleness are not inherent properties of a particular material. Rock is a brittle material at normal temperature and pressure; flint, for example, splits with a clean cleavage so sharp that its edge was in the Stone Age used for tools and weapons. Rocks can be deformed plastically, however, as the geological record shows on rock faces exposed naturally in mountains or in cuttings made for roads (see Fig. 12.2.2). The folds and bends in rock layers could only have been produced by plastic deformation under the action of great heat and pressure.

Metals that deform plastically in normal practice become brittle if they are cooled sufficiently, for example, if they are dipped into liquid nitrogen. During World War II, a number of ships with welded steel

hulls were sent to Russia through the icy region near the North Pole. Several ships were lost because of brittle fracture of the steel, partly induced by the welding (see Sec. 10.11) and partly by the low temperatures.

It is not posssible to cause a material to fail by compressing it equally in three mutually perpendicular directions, for example, by lowering it to the bottom of the ocean where the hydraulic pressures are very high. In a porous material, the pores would be permanently compressed, but a solid material would merely compress elastically and recover its shape when brought to the surface. Materials do fail, however, in compression that acts in only one direction. In a ductile material, failure occurs by plastic deformation along a plane at 45 degrees to the direction of the compression (Fig. 2.5.1). In a truly ductile material, the test piece is eventually flattened (Fig. 2.5.2).

The same type of failure occurs if the ductile test piece is pulled, or subjected to tension. Plastic deformation again occurs along a 45-degree plane, but in this case the cross-sectional area of the test piece is reduced. Eventually it becomes so small that the reduced cross section fails in tension in a brittle manner. (Figs. 2.5.3 and 2.5.4).

In a brittle material subjected to tension, failure occurs not by shearing (sliding), but by tension across

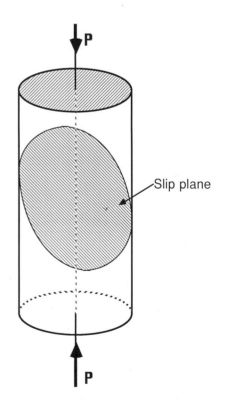

Fig. 2.5.1. Slip plane for a ductile material in compression. The test piece is subjected to a compressive force, but the material is subjected to internal shear (or sliding) stresses.

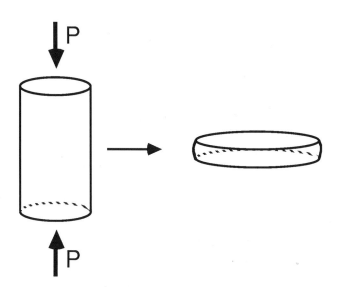

Fig. 2.5.2. Ductile test piece for compression test before and after test.

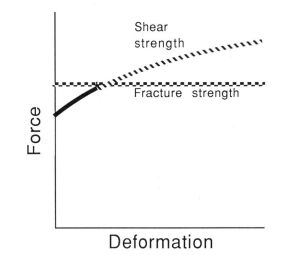

Fig. 2.5.4. The failure of a ductile material in tension is initially by sliding along slip planes controlled by its shear strength. As its cross-sectional area is reduced, its fracture strength is reached, and the material fails in a brittle manner in tension.

the test piece (Fig. 2.5.5). This is so because the shear strength of the material is higher than its fracture strength and is thus never reached (Fig. 2.5.6).

In compression, a brittle material also fails along a plane at 45 degrees to the direction of compression, but the shear stresses along this plane cause the test piece to break into two or more parts. Thus, the failure of a brittle material in tension due to fracture (or tensile stress) is quite different from its failure in compression due to a shear stress at 45 degrees to the direction of the compression.

The strength of a ductile material is approximately

Fig. 2.5.3. Ductile test piece in tension initially fails by plastic deformation at 45 degrees to the direction of the tension. Eventually its cross-sectional area is reduced to an extent that brittle fracture occurs at right angles to the direction of tension.

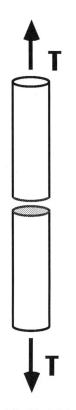

Fig. 2.5.5. A brittle material subjected to tension fails by fracture across the test piece at right angle to the direction of tension.

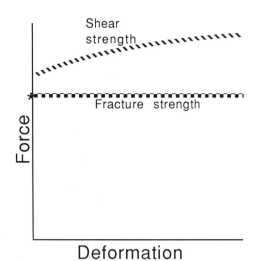

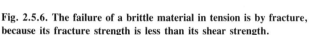

Fig. 2.5.6. The failure of a brittle material in tension is by fracture, because its fracture strength is less than its shear strength.

the same in tension and compression because the type of failure is approximately the same. The strength of a brittle material in compression, however, is much higher than it is in tension. For concrete, brick, and stone of normal strength, the ratio is approximately 10 to 1.

2.6 STRESS AND STRAIN

Stress is defined as *force per unit area,* and *strain* as *elongation or contraction per unit length.* It is convenient to use these concepts, because the same material will always deform plastically, or fracture, at approximately the same stress. The force needed to produce plastic deformation or fracture depends on the size of the material; the larger the piece, the more force that is needed.

When a material deforms elastically, the amount of deformation likewise depends on the size of the material, but the strain for a given stress is always the same, and the two are related by Hooke's Law. Observed by Robert Hooke, scientist and architect, in the seventeenth century, this law may be stated as follows:

Stress (f)/Strain (e) = Modulus of Elasticity (E)

Since strain is a ratio of two lengths, and therefore nondimensional, the *modulus of elasticity* reflects a stress and is measured in megapascals (MPa) or kilopounds per square inch (ksi).

We noted that alloying can increase the strength of metals appreciably by blocking dislocations. In elastic deformation, the dislocations are not moved, and therefore a small amount of alloying material does not affect the modulus of elasticity, E. Even high-carbon

steel contains only about 1 percent of carbon, and the E of steel is therefore almost constant at 200,000 MPa (30,000 ksi).

It is possible to increase the maximum stress at which steel ceases to behave in an entirely elastic fashion and starts to deform permanently from 230 MPa (35 ksi) to 1800 MPa (270ksi) by increasing the carbon content by a small amount and by subsequent cold working (Sec. 10.6). Doing so, however, does not alter the value of E.

A high-strength steel provides the same amount of force with less material, and because there is less of it, the material bends more under the same force. Consequently, deflection must be watched more carefully when high-strength metals are used.

Some structural metals have a low E. For example, aluminum has an E only one-third of that of steel, and deflection is therefore a far greater problem in aluminum structures than in steel structures.

Buckling is a phenomenon that occurs in structural members in compression if they are too thin or too slender. It depends on the value of E, not on the strength of the material. Consequently, it is a greater problem when high-strength steel or aluminum is used (Ref. 2.3).

It is convenient to show the relation between stress and strain on a *stress–strain diagram* (Fig. 2.6.1). This can be derived theoretically, but it can also be measured on a test specimen with a strain gauge while the specimen is being loaded in a testing machine (see Sec. 2.8). From a comparison of the experimental and the theoretical stress–strain diagrams, we can evaluate the mechanical behavior of a material.

The stress–strain diagrams of most metals and plastics show a gradual transition from elastic to plastic deformation [Fig. 2.6.1 (e)] so that a *proof stress* must be defined for the effective beginning of plastic deformation. Structural steel, however, shows a marked yield stress (see Sec. 10.2). Opinions differ on the reason why low-carbon steel behaves in this way. It makes it much easier to determine the yield stress of structural steel, however, than that of most other metals.

In textbooks on rheology, the science of deformation (for example, see Ref. 2.4), models are used to illustrate the relation between stress and strain in different types of materials. Figure 2.6.2 shows the model for elastoplastic deformation. The stress-strain diagrams of concrete and timber will be discussed in the next chapter.

2.7 FRACTURE

Since fracture and boiling both involve the rupture of atomic bonds, one would theoretically expect that the energy needed to fracture a material would be ap-

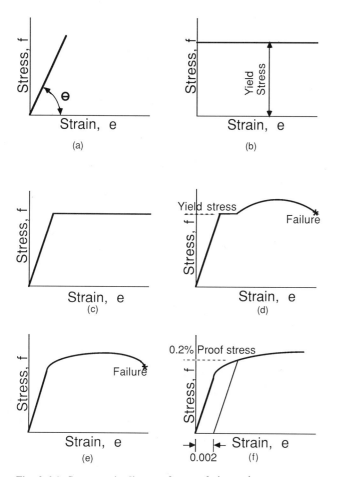

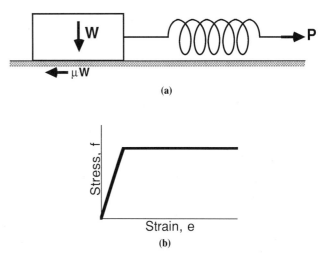

Fig. 2.6.2. Rheological model for elastic and plastic deformation.
One of the features of rheology is the use of models to illustrate deformation. *Elasticity* is represented in (a) by a spring. It deforms elastically as soon as a load P is applied, and the deformation is proportional to the load. If the load is doubled, the extension is doubled. When the load is removed, the spring recovers its original shape. *Plasticity* is represented by a brick of weight W lying on a rough surface. The limiting frictional force between the brick and its supporting surface is μW, where μ is the coefficient of friction. The brick does not move so long as P is less than μW. As soon as P reaches μW, the brick starts to move and continues moving indefinitely. Its movement thus imitates the plastic part of the strain e in the elastic-plastic strain diagram (b).

Fig. 2.6.1. Stress-strain diagram for metals in tension.
(a) *Elastic deformation:* If the material deforms purely elastically, the stress, f, is proportional to the strain, e; the angle θ is a measure of the modulus of elasticity, E. When the test piece is unloaded, the stress-strain curve is identical, and the test specimen finishes with zero stress and zero strain.
(b) *Plastic or ductile deformation:* Plastic deformation occurs at a certain yield stress, which is a characteristic of the particular material.
(c) *Combined stress–strain diagram for elastic and plastic deformation:* The test piece deforms elastically until the yield stress is reached and then deforms plastically at the constant yield stress. In theory, the plastic deformation continues indefinitely, but as the plastic diameter of the test piece is reduced, fracture must eventually occur (see Fig. 2.5.4).
(d) *Practical stress-strain diagram for structural steel:* Structural steel shows a marked yield stress, but yielding at a constant stress does not continue indefinitely. With increasing strain, the stress in the steel increases again because of *strain-hardening* (see Chap. 10). Eventually, failure occurs as the diameter of the test piece is reduced.
(e) *Stress-strain diagram for high-strength steel and for nonferrous metals:* Few metals show a marked yield stress. Plastic deformation occurs gradually while elastic deformation continues. Strain-hardening occurs in most metals.
(f) *0.2-percent proof stress:* If a metal does not have a marked yield stress, it is common practice to take as a criterion for yielding the stress at which a plastic deformation of 0.2 percent (that is, a plastic strain of 0.002) occurs in addition to the (recoverable) elastic strain. This is called the *proof stress.*

proximately the same as the (latent) heat required for its vaporization. In practice, however, the energy needed for fracture is only a small part of that. The discrepancy is due to the presence of minute flaws, or microcracks. If the flaw is large enough and the stress is sufficiently high, fracture will occur.

Cracks are distributed in a random manner, but the probability of encountering a large flaw is higher in a large piece of material than in a small piece. When conducting standard tests, particularly on ceramic materials, it is essential to specify the size of the test piece. The average result from testing several 100-mm (4-in.) cubes and 150-mm (6-in.) cubes of the same concrete differs significantly; the 100-mm cubes give a higher average result, although the concrete actually has the same strength (see Sec. 14.4).

We have already noted that fracture is more likely to occur in metals at low temperatures than at higher temperatures. This is so because the free electrons are less mobile at lower temperatures.

In steel, addition of carbon increases the strength (because it blocks some of the dislocations) but reduces the ductility. High-carbon steels are brittle; that is, they fail by fracture with only a small amount of plastic deformation, and their compressive strength is higher than their tensile strength. This effect is even more pronounced in cast iron (see Sec. 10.2), which contains even more carbon (about 2 percent) than high-carbon steel.

In concrete, about one-third of all flaws develop at the interface of the coarse aggregate and the hardened cement mortar. Another common cause of cracks is local stress concentrations—for instance, at re-entrant corners, which should therefore be avoided.

Tension failure in unreinforced ceramic materials is usually caused by the first microcrack that propagates. The local stress concentration at the end of a crack is high, and once it propagates, it does not stop unless it enters a compressive zone. In compression, however, failure is preceded by progressive cracking; since this absorbs energy, failure is delayed. This is one reason why the compressive strength of such materials is much higher than the tensile strength.

The strength of brittle materials such as concrete and some plastics can be greatly increased by reinforcement with reinforcing bars or fibers or by prestressing that induces a compressive stress before the member is loaded. Both increase the strength by inhibiting the propagation of tensile cracks.

2.8 TESTING OF MATERIALS

The most common test of building materials is the strength test to destruction. This is partly because strength is a very important property of a building material, even a material in a "nonloadbearing" part of the building (Sec. 2.1); partly because strength tests are comparatively simple to carry out; and partly because they offer a guide to other properties, such as durability (see Chap. 8).

The strength of a ductile material such as steel, aluminum, or plastics is usually determined by applying a tensile load. A compression test is used for brittle materials such as concrete, stone, and brick because their tensile strength is low and thus harder to measure accurately.

The method of testing and the dimensions of the test pieces are laid down in the appropriate standards published by the American Society for Testing Materials (ASTM), the British Standards Institution (BSI), the Standards Association of Australia (SAA), etc. (Ref. 2.5).

The *size* and *shape* of the test specimen are particularly important for brittle materials because they influence the number of flaws that are likely to occur in the test specimen. For concrete tests, the standard American and Australian test specimen—a cylinder 150 mm (6 in.) in diameter and 300 mm (12 in.) long—gives a lower result than the standard British test specimen—a 150-mm cube (see Sec. 2.7)—because the former contains more concrete.

The *speed of testing* is also specified. A passage of time is required for both plastic deformation and the formation of cracks, and a faster rate of testing thus gives a higher result.

For tests on concrete and timber, it is necessary to specify *moisture content* because this affects the strength.

A test on a single specimen is unreliable because we do not know whether it is an average test specimen or whether it has fewer or more than the average number of minute flaws (Secs. 2.4 and 2.7). Standard specifications lay down how many specimens shall be tested and how they are to be selected.

Tests of factory-made materials carried out by the manufacturer are usually accepted by the user of the building material unless he has reason to doubt their veracity. Since concrete is made on the building site or brought from a ready-mix concrete plant, its testing becomes the responsibility of the building contractor. This is therefore a more frequent testing activity than that for other materials. Concrete cylinders or cubes are normally tested in a hydraulic press, which may be used exclusively for this purpose. A universal machine for tension, compression, and bending is a more expensive machine based on the same principle (Fig. 2.8.1).

Timber differs from other building materials in that it is produced from growing trees and is thus more variable. Cut timber from virgin forests may consist of a variety of different species. Even timber cut from a planted forest containing trees of the same species all planted at the same time may show appreciable variation between pieces because of knots, bark pockets, gum pockets, or other flaws.

A substantial proportion of timber is used in domestic construction where it is not highly stressed; in such cases, "visual grading" (that is, *merely* looking at it) may be sufficient. Because of the imperfections in individual pieces, "stress grading" is usually more reliable than even accurate testing of selected test pieces. A stress grading machine tests *every* individual piece of timber by a method that is very fast and relatively cheap (Fig. 2.8.2). The machine is based on an empirical relation between the strength and the deflection of timber. Each piece of timber is deflected (but not stressed to its limit) at several points along its length, and the deflection category marked by means of a spot of dye. The timber is then classified visually by its color markings.

The strength of metals is reduced if they are repeatedly loaded alternately in tension and in compression. This is called *repeated loading* if it is applied several hundred or thousands of times, and *fatigue loading* if it is applied millions of times. Fatigue loading is a major problem in machines but rarely in buildings. Wind loads, however, can cause repeated loading in roof structures. There are special machines for testing the strength of materials under repeated loading.

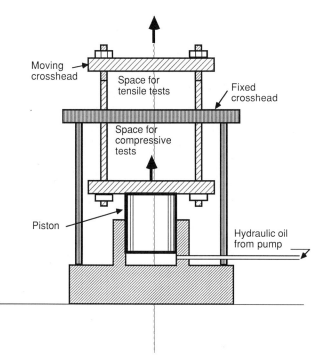

Fig. 2.8.1. Universal Testing machine.
Most of these machines are hydraulically operated and consist of a hydraulic jack, a pump, and a pressure gauge that indicates the load in kilonewtons, pounds, or tons. If the machine is used for one kind of test only (for example, concrete cylinders), it may indicate the average stress directly in megapascals or ksi. A compression testing machine consists merely of a movable plate fixed to the hydraulic press, and a fixed plate that restrains the other end of the test specimen. In a universal machine, the piston is also connected to a movable cross head above the fixed plate; tension specimens are tested in the upper zone. Beams can be tested in the compression loading zone.

Other special tests are for ductility and for hardness. *Ductility* is tested by bending a bar around a pin over a wide angle. *Hardness* is tested by indentation with a diamond or a hardened steel ball. The hardness test is carried out only if an accurate result is required because there is a good correlation between the tensile strength test and the various hardness tests for metals (Ref. 2.6). If the tensile strength has been tested, then

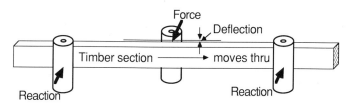

Fig. 2.8.2. Stress grading machine for timber.
Timber is passed along this machine and deflected at various points along its length by the movable cross head. A spot of dye is then squirted on the timber, its color depending on the amount of deflection of the cross head. An empirical relation exists between the strength of the timber and its deflection.

the hardness of the metal can be deduced from that with reasonable tolerance.

The *toughness* of a metal can also be deduced from the tension test. Toughness is defined as the energy required to break a material. Energy is force multiplied by distance, that is, the integral of force in relation to length, or the area contained under a force-deformation curve. Stress is force per unit area, and strain is deformation per unit length, so that the area contained under the stress–strain diagram represents the energy per unit volume (Fig. 2.8.3). The greater the area contained under a stress–strain curve up to failure, the greater the toughness of the material. Consequently, ductile materials that deform plastically are much tougher than brittle materials that show little plastic deformation.

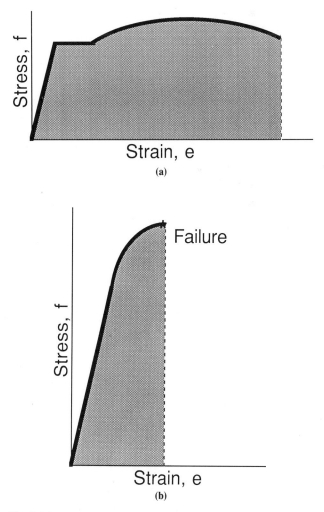

Fig. 2.8.3. Toughness.
The area under the stress–strain diagram of structural steel (a) is greater than the area under the stress-strain diagram of high-tensile steel (b), even though the latter is more than twice as strong. The reason is that structural steel has a much higher plastic deformation. Toughness is defined as the energy stored in a material before it fails and is represented by the area under the stress-strain curve.

REFERENCES

2.1. L. H. van Vlack: *Elements of Materials Science*. Addison-Wesley, Reading, MA, 1964. 445 pp.
2.2. H. J. Cowan and F. Wilson: *Structural Systems*. Van Nostrand Reinhold, New York, 1981, Chapter 10, pp. 181–230.
2.3. H. J. Cowan and F. Wilson: *loc. cit.*, pp. 75–76.
2.4. M. Reiner: *Deformation and Flow*. Lewis, London, 1960, pp. 87–93.
2.5. Handbooks and Standards of the American Society for Testing Materials, Philadelphia PA, U.S.A.; British Standards Institution, London, England; Standards Association of Australia, North Sydney NSW, Australia.
2.6. J. Marin: *Mechanical Behavior of Engineering Materials*. Prentice-Hall, Englewood Cliffs, NJ, 1962, pp. 446–453.

SUGGESTIONS FOR FURTHER READING

N. F. Mott: *Atomic Structure and the Strength of Metals*. Pergamon, London, 1956. 64 pp.
D. Rosenthal: *Introduction to Properties of Materials*. Van Nostrand, Princeton, NJ, 1964. 359 pp.
J. P. Frankel: *Principles of the Properties of Materials*. McGraw-Hill, New York, 1957. 228 pp.

3

Dimensional Stability and Joints

The components of a building move relative to one another as a result of elastic deformation, creep, temperature movement, moisture movement, and shrinkage or expansion of the materials. Unless suitable joints are provided to allow this movement to take place, cracking is liable to occur in brittle materials.

While metals creep only at elevated temperatures, wood and concrete creep at normal temperatures and under quite small loads. This property increases their bending deflection but relieves stress concentrations; in the case of concrete, it reduces its tendency to crack. Fine cracks are unavoidable in reinforced concrete, and cracks up to 0.4 mm (0.016 in.) wide may be considered acceptable in reinforced concrete that is protected from the weather.

3.1 ELASTIC DEFORMATION

Elastic deformation is the type of movement that can be predicted with the greatest accuracy. The elastic deformation caused by tensile and compressive forces is relatively small; the really damaging elastic deformation is caused by bending.

The elastic deflection, δ, of a beam or slab is given by

$$\delta = aWL^3/EI \qquad (3.1)$$

where:

W = the total load carried by the beam or slab
L = the span of the beam or slab
E = the modulus of elasticity (see Sec. 2.6)
I = the second moment of area, also called the moment of inertia
a = a constant

Some values of this constant are given in Table 3.1; others may be found in Ref. 3.1.

The modulus of elasticity, E, for steel is the same for all types of steel: 200,000 MPa (30,000 ksi) (see Sec. 2.6). The value of I for structural-steel sections is listed in standard specifications as well as in the steel-section tables provided by steel manufacturers.

Example 3.1.A: *A universal steel beam, 460 mm deep, weighing 75 kg/m, spans 7.5 m and carries a uniformly distributed load of 12 kN, and also two loads at third points induced by two secondary beams, each transmitting 170 kN. Determine the deflection at the center of the simply supported beam.*

The modulus of elasticity E = 200,000 MPa. From section tables, the second moment of area I = 334×10^6 mm^4 = 334×10^{-6} m^4. From Table 3.1, the deflection at the center of the beam is

$$\delta = \frac{0.0130 \times 12 \times 10^{-3}\,\text{MN} \times 7.5^3\,\text{m}^3}{200,000\,\text{MPa} \times 334 \times 10^{-6}\,\text{m}^4}$$

$$+ \frac{0.0178 \times 2 \times 170 \times 10^{-3}\,\text{MN} \times 7.5^3\,\text{m}^3}{200,000\,\text{MPa} \times 334 \times 10^{-6}\,\text{m}^4}$$

$$= 0.000985 + 0.038221\,\text{m}$$

$$= 39.2\,\text{mm}$$

Example 3.1.B: *A wide-flange steel beam, 18 in. deep, weighing 50 lb/ft, spans 24 ft and carries a uniformly distributed load of 2.4 kips and also two loads at third points induced by two joists, each transmitting 40 kips. Determine the deflection at the center of the simply supported beam.*

The modulus of elasticity E = 30,000 ksi. From section tables, the second moment of area I = 800 in.^{4} The span is 24 ft = 288 in. From Table 3.1, the deflection at the

Table 3.1. Deflection Coefficients for Some Beams.

Type of beam and load		a
SIMPLY SUPPORTED BEAMS		
Uniformly distributed load		5/384 = 0.0130
Central load		1/48 = 0.0208
Two equal loads at third points		23/1296 = 0.0178
FIXED-ENDED BEAMS		
Uniformly distributed load		1/384 = 0.00260
Central load		1/192 = 0.00521
Two equal loads at third points		5/1296 = 0.00386

center of the beam is

$$\delta = \frac{0.0130 \times 2.4 \text{ kips} \times 288^3 \text{ in.}^3}{30,000 \text{ ksi} \times 800 \text{ in.}^4}$$
$$+ \frac{0.0178 \times 2 \times 40 \text{ kips} \times 288^3 \text{ in.}^3}{30,000 \text{ ksi} \times 800 \text{ in.}^4}$$
$$= 0.03105 + 1.41734 = 1.45 \text{ in.}$$

If the deflection of a steel beam is considered undesirably large, it is possible to counteract it by giving the beam an upward camber. Assuming that the deflection is 40 mm (1.5 in.), and that 18 mm (0.7 in.) of that is due to the permanently acting load (dead load) and 22 mm (0.8 in.) is due to the intermittently acting load (live load), the appropriate camber would be 18 + (½ × 22) = 29 mm [0.7 + (½ × 0.8) = 1.1 in.]. If there is no live load acting on the beam, it has an upward deflection of 11 mm (0.4 in.); when it carries half the live load, the net deflection is zero; and when it is carrying the full live load, it has a downward deflection of 11 mm (0.4 in.).

3.2 CREEP DEFLECTION

If a slab of bitumen or asphalt is placed on an impervious surface on a warm day, the bitumen will slowly flow outwards, its height being reduced accordingly. If a heavy weight is placed on the slab of bitumen, the rate of flow is accelerated. This is called viscous flow, or *creep*. Creep increases with temperature because the particles of material move more freely as temperature increases. Creep also increases with stress, because of the forces applied to the particles (Fig. 3.2.1).

Water contained in wood and concrete can be squeezed out of their pores by sustained pressure, thus causing deformation very similar to viscous deformation; this is also called *creep*.

Of the common metals, only lead shows creep at normal temperature and low stress. When lead is used as a covering on a sloping roof, its thickness gradually decreases over a period of a century at the higher levels and increases near the eaves. Steel used for prestressing is subjected to very high stresses over long periods, and there is consequently some loss of prestress as a result of the creep of the steel. Neither phenomenon presents a serious problem. Creep of metals is therefore not a significant phenomenon for building construction, although it is a problem in the design of engines that operate at high temperatures and imposes restraints on the use of certain plastics (see Sec. 18.6).

Creep becomes a significant phenomenon whenever timber or concrete is the material of choice. The stress–strain diagram (see Fig. 2.6.1) of both is curved even at low stresses. The slower the rate of loading, the greater the departure from the elastic straight line for instantaneous loading (Fig. 3.2.2). The effect of creep is thus to reduce the effective modulus of elasticity of wood and concrete (Fig. 3.2.3).

In timber structures, it is customary to allow a 50-percent increase in the elastic deflection for creep in glued laminated members and sawn members installed seasoned, and a 100-percent increase for creep in sawn members installed unseasoned. Nevertheless, creep is not a major problem in timber structures because the resulting deflection is not normally transferred to brittle finishes. In concrete structures, however, creep can result in cracks in brittle finishes, and in brick partitions

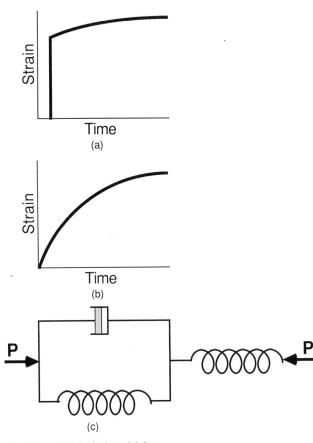

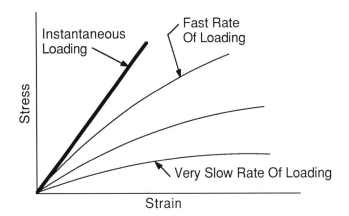

Fig. 3.2.2. Elastic and creep deformation of wood and concrete.
The creep deformation depends on the rate of loading. Instantaneous loading would produce elastic deformation, in which, as for metals (Fig. 2.6.1), the stress is proportional to the strain. In practice, instantaneous loading is unattainable, because the application of the load takes at least a few seconds. In buildings, the load is often applied very slowly as the building is being completed. The dead load is then sustained throughout the life of the building.

Fig. 3.2.1. Rheological model for creep.
(a) If a load is applied to a material liable to creep and then kept constant, instant elastic deformation, indicated by the straight vertical line, takes place, followed by creep deformation; the latter continues for some time, but at a decreasing rate.
(b) If the load is applied gradually, the deformation is partly the result of elasticity, and partly the result of creep.
(c) The rheological model (see Sec. 2.6) for creep consists of a spring and a dashpot in parallel (a device used as a shock absorber in automobiles and motorcycles; it may be seen under the handlebars of most of the latter), with another spring in series. The spring on the right of the model deforms instantly under load. The spring at the bottom is restrained by the dashpot (a piston plunging into a container filled with oil) so that the movement can occur only gradually, and at a reducing rate.

of the concrete. In most design codes, it is taken as proportional to the square root of the compressive strength (Ref. 3.3)—that is, the ultimate stress in the compression test specimens (see Sec. 2.8). For a compressive strength of 25 MPa, E is 25,000 MPa (for a compressive strength of 3,500 psi, it is 3,400 ksi).

Prior to the Second World War, allowances for the creep deflection of concrete were similar to those for timber. Since then they have increased as we have come to realize that concrete creep is greater than we had previously thought. Current concrete design codes specify creep deflections that are double the elastic deflection, that is, the total elastic and creep deflection

that are constructed below concrete slabs and in contact with them.

The calculation of the deflection of reinforced-concrete sections is complicated by the cracking of the concrete in the tension zone as well as the presence of the steel reinforcement, which has a higher modulus of elasticity than the concrete. The calculation of the second moment of area (moment of inertia), I, thus needs quite a lengthy calculation—one that is beyond the scope of this book. The reader is referred to any textbook on reinforced-concrete design (for example, Ref. 3.2). Once the value of I is calculated, the elastic deflection is easily obtained from Eq. 3.1. The value of the modulus of elasticity, E, for elastic deformation in concrete varies; it is mainly dependent on the strength

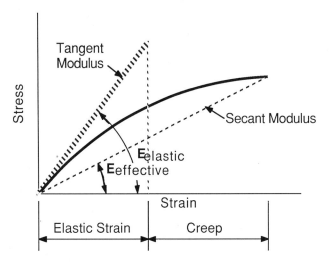

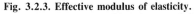

Fig. 3.2.3. Effective modulus of elasticity.
Assuming that the additional creep deformation is equal to the elastic deformation, the effective modulus of elasticity is the secant of the stress–strain curve. The tangent of the curve is the true elastic modulus, corresponding to the unattainable "instantaneous loading".

is taken as three times the elastic deflection. This multiplier applies only to the permanently acting dead and live load; transient live loads produce mainly elastic deflections. Because of their heavy weight, however, the dead load in most concrete structures is higher than the live load. The creep deflection is reduced by compression steel, which is a material not subject to creep, because it replaces concrete, a material that is subject to creep.

If the deflection exceeds the limits specified in the concrete building code (Ref. 3.4), the design must be modified to keep the deflection within permissible limits. It is possible to counteract the elastic deflection by cambering the concrete beam or slab, but this cannot be done for the creep deflection that occurs over a period of several months, and then, at a decreasing rate, continues for several years (Fig. 3.2.4). Any upward camber provided to counter creep would remain for quite a long time until it is eventually cancelled out by creep deflection.

Creep problems are most significant in flat-plate structures, that is, concrete slabs supported directly on columns without supporting beams or enlarged column heads. A great advantage of flat-plate structures is their small depth, but this is also the reason for the relatively low value of I in Eq. 3.1 and *the consequent high* deflection. The latter can be countered by limiting the span, L, of flat-plate structures or by prestressing them. Using the load-balancing method of prestressing (Ref. 3.5), the elastic deflection under the action of the permanently acting loads can be entirely eliminated (leaving only an elastic compression of the slab due to the prestress). Since creep deflection, from the experimental evidence (Ref. 3.6), is directly proportional to the elastic deflection, the creep deflection is also eliminated ($3 \times 0 = 0$), or at least greatly reduced.

Creep deflection directly under reinforced-concrete beams is usually low, but the deflection under a flat

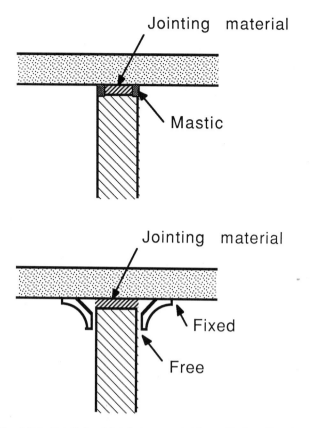

Fig. 3.2.5. Detail for joint between a brick or block wall and a reinforced concrete slab.
Since creep deflection occurs gradually, it cannot be compensated for during construction by a camber. The wall cracks if the slab presses on it as it deflects, and the joint between the top layer of the bricks and the concrete slab should therefore be sealed with mastic or a flexible sealant (see Sec. 19.8), not with cement mortar. The joint also makes allowance for the horizontal movement of the wall (see Sec. 3.6). If a cornice is used, it should be fixed only to the slab, not to the wall, to allow the necessary movement for the joint.

plate along the column lines is substantial. Brick or block partitions built between columns (and any such partitions built elsewhere under a slab) must be detailed to allow for the deflection (Fig. 3.2.5).

3.3 TEMPERATURE MOVEMENT

We have already noted that crystals are formed by atoms in a regular array (see Fig. 2.4.1). The atoms oscillate about an equilibrium position, and their kinetic energy increases as the temperature increases. (Fig. 3.3.1). As the amplitude of the vibrations increases, the material expands.

Most materials expand with increasing temperature and contract with decreasing temperature. Water, however, expands as it cools from 4°C to 0°C and expands further on freezing so that ice floats on water instead of sinking to the bottom. This is one of the few exceptions to the general rule.

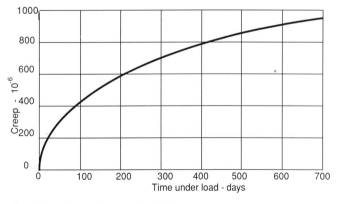

Fig. 3.2.4. Creep of concrete with time.
The rate of creep is most rapid during the first six months, but it continues for several years. (See Ref. 3.6, p. 56.)

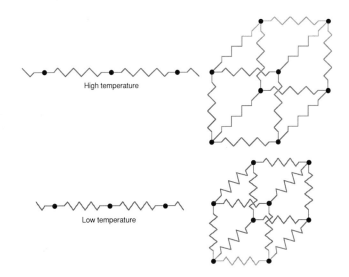

Fig. 3.3.1. Thermal expansion.
The electrical bonds between the atoms of a metal crystal are represented in this model by vibrating springs. As the amplitude of the vibrations increases with temperature, the material expands.

Table 3.2 shows the coefficients of thermal expansion for some of the materials used in buildings. The two columns differ only in the temperature scale used so that the figures in the first column are 1.8 times larger than those in the second.

Most plastics have high thermal expansion, as do some metals. Timber has low thermal expansion along the grain but high expansion across the grain. For this reason, floor boards are laid so that expansion can occur without restraint by the nails (Fig. 3.3.2)

Although the thermal expansion of brick and concrete is comparatively low, it can, if restrained, cause appreciable damage through cracking because of the brittle nature of the materials. Hence, expansion and/or contraction joints must be provided (see Sec. 3.6).

The total change in temperature to be considered in a design is that between the hottest day and the coldest night experienced over a number of years. For interior locations, that means the difference in the indoor temperature. Externally, much higher temperatures can occur, particularly in materials on a roof surface or on outdoor platforms, such as balconies or sundecks. The temperature normally recorded is the shade temperature; the surface temperature of a material in the sun can be 20°C (36°F) higher. At night, surface temperatures can also be much lower than those recorded by a sheltered thermometer because of radiation cooling and chilling by wind, if any. The design temperature differential is therefore much higher than the difference between the highest and the lowest temperatures recorded by the thermometer. It varies with the region in question, being much higher in the interior of a continent in the temperate zone than on a small island near the equator.

Table 3.2. Coefficient of Thermal Expansion.

Material	$m/m\ °C \times 10^{-6}$	$ft/ft\ °F \times 10^{-6}$
Cast iron	10	6
Structural steel, wrought iron	12	6.5
Alloy steels, incl. stainless steel	9–16	5–9
Invar (a low-expansion nickel steel)	0.4	0.2
Aluminum and its alloys	24	13
Copper, bronze, brass	18	10
Dense hardwood:		
with grain	3	1.7
across grain	45	25
Softwood such as Douglas fir, spruce, redwood:		
with grain	4.5	2.5
across grain	80	45
Granite	6–10	3.5–6
Slate	6–10	3.5–6
Marble	2–12	1–6.5
Limestone	3–10	1.5–6
Sandstone	3–16	1.5–9
Concrete	7–12	4–7
Clay brick	5–8	3–4.5
Calcium-silicate brick	10	5.5
Glass	7–10	4–5.5
Nylon	80–150	45–80
Acrylics	50–90	30–50
Epoxy resins	50–90	30–50
Polyethylene	110–180	60–100
Rigid polyvinyl chloride (PVC)	50–60	30–35

The change in the temperature of the external surface of a wall or roof is greatly affected by the absorptivity of the surface (see Sec. 5.5) and by the thickness of the material that forms the surface. A light-colored reflective surface absorbs less heat than a dark surface. A thin metal surface backed by insulation heats up quicker than a thick wall of concrete or masonry because the insulation prevents the transmission of the heat to the interior; conversely, it also cools quicker because the wall stores less heat.

The temperature movement most likely to cause damage is the in-line movement in walls and roofs that produces tensile or compressive stresses if resisted.

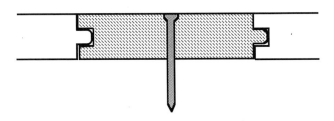

Fig. 3.3.2. Tongue and groove joint for timber floor boards.
Because of high thermal expansion *across* the grain, floor boards must be nailed so that expansion and contraction can take place without restraint by the nails.

Example 3.2: *Determine the extension of a steel railing 10 m (30 ft) long if the temperature changes from −15° to +35°C (+5° to +95°F). Furthermore, determine the stresses caused by this extension if it is resisted.*

The coefficient of thermal expansion for steel (from Table 3.2) is 12×10^{-6} in °C, or 6.5×10^{-6} in °F.

The increase in length of the steel rail is therefore

$$12 \times 10^{-6} (35 + 15) \times 10 \text{ m} = 6 \text{ mm}$$

or

$$6.5 \times 10^{-6} (95 - 5) \times 30 \text{ ft} = 0.21 \text{ in.}$$

The strain in the steel caused by the change in temperature is

$$12 \times 10^{-6} (35 + 15) = 600 \times 10^{-6}$$

or

$$6.5 \times 10^{-6} (95 - 5) = 585 \times 10^{-6}$$

The difference in the two examples is due to slight differences between the lengths and coefficients.

The corresponding tensile stress in the steel is obtained by multiplying the strain by the modulus of elasticity, E, which for steel is 200,000 MPa (30,000 ksi). Consequently, the steel stress is 120 MPa (17.55 ksi) if the railing is fully restrained. This value is within the range of the permissible stress for structural steel, but it is quite a high stress. In practice, however, the railing is likely to be supported, say, on a concrete or brick wall, which will expand by a similar amount.

A brick or concrete wall supporting the railing would be in tension; if it is partially restrained, the tensile stresses in it could be sufficient to produce cracks. However, temperature movement must be considered in conjunction with moisture movement, discussed in the next section.

3.4 SHRINKAGE AND MOISTURE MOVEMENT

Temperature movement is reversible. Materials contract through the same temperature range as much when they are cooled as they expand when they are heated. A great deal of moisture movement is equally reversible.

Moisture movement does not occur in metals and most plastics. Timber, concrete, and bricks expand when they absorb moisture in humid weather or by exposure to rain, and they contract again when the moisture evaporates. In addition, there is an irreversible moisture movement in all three materials. The green timber cut from a tree may be used as it is, but more commonly it is *seasoned,* that is, dried in a kiln or by prolonged storage in air. Some of this moisture is not absorbed again; if the timber becomes wet in rain,

it will reabsorb some moisture, but its moisture content will remain much lower it was than before seasoning.

Concrete, plaster, and calcium-silicate bricks all shrink after manufacture because of chemical changes and evaporation of water, and most of this shrinkage is not recovered.

Clay bricks are molded and then fired in a kiln. The composition of brick clay varies appreciably from one part of the world to another, and the behavior of the bricks varies accordingly. Some shrink after firing, but most expand due to the absorption of moisture.

Moisture movement is a dimensionless ratio (mm per mm or in. per in.). Shrinkage values of wood are given in handbooks (e.g., see Ref. 3.7). They vary appreciably, depending on the species of the timber and the moisture content to which it is dried; at the extreme, they can exceed 10 percent (or 100×10^{-3}).

The shrinkage of concrete cast on site is of the order of $0.2 - 0.5 \times 10^{-3}$, and the shrinkage of concrete bricks ranges from 0.6 to 0.8×10^{-3}. The shrinkage of calcium silicate brick is of the order of 0.3×10^{-3}.

The expansion of clay bricks varies greatly, a phenomenon that has been particularly troublesome in Australia (figures are available in Ref. 3.8). The expansion varies from 0.01 to 2.17×10^{-3} so that it is necessary to obtain data on the characteristics of the actual bricks used to make an accurate allowance for their movement.

Since the reversible moisture movement occurs with changes in the weather, it cannot be avoided, but the effect of the irreversible shrinkage and expansion can be greatly reduced by allocating sufficient time for the seasoning of timber and by allowing the shrinkage or expansion of precast concrete units and of brick to take place before they are used. These precautions inevitably increase the cost.

Temperature and moisture movement occur at the same time and must be considered in conjunction. The greatest increase in length occurs in warm, humid weather, and the greatest decrease in cool, dry weather. It should be noted that as the temperature drops in the evening and during the night, there is an increase in relative humidity because the falling temperature also lowers the dew point. Consequently, if there is no change in the weather pattern, the temperature and moisture movements to some extent compensate for one another during the daily cycle of day and night.

Creep has only a slight effect on the daily variation of temperature and moisture movement because that is insufficient time for significant creep deformation (see Fig. 3.2.4). Creep reduces the effect of the much larger *annual* variation in temperature, however, and thus has a beneficial effect on temperature and moisture movement. Concrete is normally reinforced, even if it does not carry a superimposed load. The steel reinforcement restrains the creep, shrinkage, and moisture movement of the concrete, and to some extent the temperature movement as well, because the change of temperature inside the concrete is, for rapid variations, less than the variation on its surface. As a result, the shrinkage and the moisture movement of the concrete are shared by the steel and the concrete (Fig. 3.4.1), as is the difference in their temperature movement.

3.5 CRACKS

In reinforced concrete, fine cracks are unavoidable but not harmful. The reinforcing steel in common use at the present time has a yield stress (see Fig. 2.6.1) of 400 MPa (60 ksi). The safety margin provided by the combined effect of the load factor and the strength reduction factor (see any textbook on reinforced concrete design, for example, Ref. 3.9) is approximately 1.75 so that the maximum steel stress under the actual service loads is about 230 MPa (35 ksi). Dividing this by the modulus of elasticity, E, the maximum steel strain is about 1.15×10^{-3}.

Concrete cracks at a strain of about 0.3×10^{-3} so that the concrete surrounding fully stressed steel bars is, of necessity, cracked. To avoid cracks would mean that the reinforcement was being stressed only at one quarter of its strength, which would be very wasteful.

Since fine cracks are acceptable, the detail design of the reinforcement of concrete must ensure that a large number of fine cracks are formed rather than a small number of wider cracks. Furthermore, the cover over the reinforcement should be sufficient to prevent water from penetrating to it. Prevention is achieved partly by capillary action (see Sec. 4.2) and partly by chemical action. Any water that penetrates some distance into a crack should combine with the cement before it reaches the reinforcement.

A crack width of 0.4 mm (0.016 in.) may be considered acceptable in reinforced concrete protected from the weather. Reinforced concrete exposed to driving rain or to salt-water spray should not have cracks wider than 0.15 mm (0.006 in.).

Rust, which is iron hydroxide, is water soluble and therefore causes brown streaks on concrete surfaces; these are very unsightly and hard to remove. Moreover, rust has a larger volume than steel, so that its formation accentuates cracking. Eventually, spalling may occur (see Fig. 8.2.4), the repair of which is very costly. Unfortunately, rust streaking and spalling are not uncommon. They have been caused partly by the less severe requirements of earlier concrete codes and partly by lax site supervision. They do not immediately endanger structural safety, but they ruin the appearance of a building.

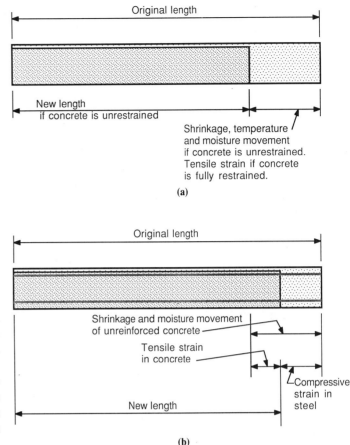

Fig. 3.4.1. Effect of restraint on temperature and moisture movement. (a) No stresses are set up if the movement is not restrained. The original length is changed by the amount of the movement. If the concrete is fully restrained, the length is not altered; in consequence, the concrete is strained (and stressed).

(b) If the concrete is reinforced, the original length is changed by a lesser amount. The new length is intermediate between the original length and the length to which unreinforced concrete would change. As a result, the concrete is put in tension and the steel in compression if the net movement is a contraction. Shrinkage by itself is a contraction.

3.6 EXPANSION AND CONTRACTION JOINTS (CONTROL JOINTS)

Opinions on the need for control joints for reinforced concrete vary appreciably. Since joints are a source of weakness, some designers consider that none should be used and that concrete should be reinforced with small-diameter bars spaced sufficiently close to ensure that no cracking occurs. Others recommend joints at 30-m (100-ft) centers for roofs and 60-m (200-ft) centers for external walls. Various figures between these two extremes have been suggested (Refs. 3.10 and 3.11). It is essential that joints be designed to prevent the entry of water, particularly on roofs (Fig. 3.6.1). Control joints are also needed between concrete slabs and brick or block walls (see Fig. 3.2.5).

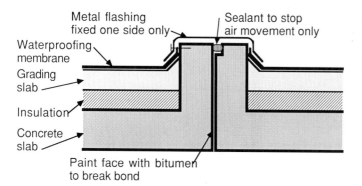

Fig. 3.6.1. Vertical roof joint.
A vertical joint in a roof needs careful design to ensure that wind-driven rain and water accumulating on the roof during a heavy downpour do not penetrate into the building.

Control joints are unquestionably needed for brick and block walls except for small buildings with only short walls. Until the nineteenth century, mortar was mixed from lime and sand, and this material was much weaker than the bricks. As a result, cracks normally formed in the joints (see Fig. 8.2.1), but these could be scraped and repointed. Modern cement mortar being much stronger, cracks are liable to pass right through the bricks, thus making repair much harder.

The spacing required for vertical joints with mastic or sealant (see Sec. 19.8) depends partly on the expansion or shrinkage of the bricks or blocks and partly on the local climate; it is of the order of 24 m (80 ft) for walls of clay brick and 12 m (40 ft) for walls of calcium-silicate brick or concrete brick. The need for horizontal joints between a wall and a floor or roof slab has already been mentioned (Fig. 3.2.5).

Details of control joints may be found in textbooks and handbooks on building construction (for example, see Ref. 3.12).

Slabs of natural stone or precast concrete used for floors or wall cladding are normally mounted individually on a structural frame or concrete backing with stainless steel or brass fittings (see Fig. 12.6.2). The joints may be left open or sealed with a mastic or flexible sealant.

REFERENCES

3.1. *Steel Designers' Manual.* Crosby Lockwood, London, 1966, pp. 29–38 and 43–49.

3.2. P. M. Ferguson: *Reinforced Concrete Fundamentals.* 4th edn., SI version. Wiley, New York, 1981, pp. 210–218.

3.3. H. J. Cowan: *Design of Reinforced Concrete Structures.* Prentice-Hall, Englewood Cliffs, NJ, 1982. p. 76.

3.4. *Building Code Requirements for Reinforced Concrete ACI 318-83.* American Concrete Institute. Detroit, 1983. The British and Australian concrete codes have similar provisions.

3.5. H. J. Cowan and F. Wilson: *Structural Systems.* Van Nostrand Reinhold, New York, 1981, pp. 83–85.

3.6. A. M. Neville: *Creep of Concrete: Plain, Reinforced, and Prestressed.* North-Holland, Amsterdam, 1970. 622 pp.

3.7. American Institute of Timber Construction: *Timber Construction Manual.* Wiley, New York, 1966, pp. 2–8—2–11.

3.8. J. S. Hosking *et al.*: Long-term expansion and contraction of clay products. *Nature*, Vol. 206 (29 May 1965), pp. 888–890.

3.9. P. M. Ferguson: *loc cit.*, pp. 27–29.

3.10. W. C. Huntington and R. E. Mickadeit: *Building Construction.* 5th edn. Wiley, New York, 1981, p. 155.

3.11. F. K. Kong *et al.* (Ed.): *Handbook of Structural Concrete.* Pitman, London, 1983, pp. 32–20.

3.12. C. G. Ramsey and H. R. Sleeper: *Architectural Graphic Standards.* 6th edn. Wiley, New York, 1970, pp. 156, 164, and 313–316.

SUGGESTIONS FOR FURTHER READING

Building Research Station: *Principles of Modern Building.* 3rd Edn., Volume 1. H. M. Stationery Office, London, 1959. 302 pp.

H. J. Cowan and F. Wilson: *Structural Systems.* Van Nostrand Reinhold, New York, 1981. 256 pp.

M. Reiner: *Deformation, Strain, and Flow.* 2nd Edn. H. K. Lewis, London, 1960. 347 pp.

A. M. Neville: Creep of Concrete: *Plain, Reinforced, and Prestressed.* North-Holland, Amsterdam, 1970. 622 pp.

4
Exclusion of Water and Water Vapor

Water penetration can cause damage to a building and its contents, as well as discomfort to the occcupants. The choice of materials and the constructional details of their use play a major role in keeping a building waterproof. A knowledge of local climatic conditions is necessary to allow for the expected precipitation as well as those combinations of temperature and humidity that can lead to condensation.

Porous materials can be used in some locations, particularly in thick sections where moisture penetrates only slowly. Highly impermeable materials are needed for flashings, roof membranes, and damp-proof courses. Vapor barriers are usually needed to limit the migration of water vapor from the interior of a building into insulated walls and roofs.

Roofs and walls can be designed to be completely sealed, or to shed water by gravity. Where wind pressures are high, gravity alone might not be sufficient, and joints may have to be designed with separate rain- and pressure-barriers.

No material can be expected to last forever. Ideally, most materials should last for the expected life of the building in which they are used, but it is common for some metal elements to have a limited life because of corrosion, for flexible elements such as sealants and membranes to become brittle with time, and for painted surfaces to require repainting. The choice of materials involves planning for their maintenance or replacement as well.

4.1 CLIMATIC DATA FOR RAINFALL AND WIND

Water is a major cause of damage to both building materials and the contents of a building, not to mention a source of annoyance to the occupants. The main sources of water are rain and snow, condensation of water vapor from the air, and moisture from the ground.

Building designers need to know the expected climatic conditions so that they may allow for the effects of rain, snow, hail, and condensation. Meteorological offices can usually provide information on precipitation in millimeters per hour or inches per hour, but for building design the intensity over a shorter period—five minutes, say—is more useful.

The combination of wind and rain is important for the design of vertical surfaces such as windows and walls. The *driving rain index* (Ref. 4.1, p. 285) is the product of the annual rainfall and the annual average windspeed. Wind-driven rain can reach surfaces that are protected from vertically falling rain and can even force its way uphill. Since wind speed near the ground is greatly reduced by friction and obstructions, and since the pressure of wind is proportional to the square of its speed, tall and exposed structures are subjected to much higher pressures than low, sheltered ones.

A wind registering 6 on the Beaufort Scale and described as "a very strong wind, leaves torn off, walking difficult" (Ref. 4.1, p. 398) can occur around a single-story building. The velocity of this wind is given as 12.4 m/s (28 mph), and its pressure can lift a column of water 10 mm (0.4 in.). The design wind velocity for a tall building, on the other hand, is about 40 m/s (90 mph), and its pressure can lift a column of water 100 mm (4 in). Therefore, small buildings often make use of joints and flashings that keep water out by gravity; tall buildings, and buildings in exposed locations, need positively sealed joints or drained joints (see Sec. 4.7).

4.2 WATER ABSORPTION OF BUILDING MATERIALS

Capillary action is the effect of surface tension that causes water to rise up a *narrow* tube, against the effect of gravity. In building construction, capillary action can occur between two surfaces placed together, or within porous materials.

Metals, plastics, and glass are impervious to moisture. Timber and masonry contain interconnected pores into which water can be drawn by capillarity. Saturated bricks can hold water equivalent to 10 to 25 percent of their mass. Foamed plastic insulation contains large numbers of *closed* pores; if this material lacks inter-connecting passages, it will not absorb much moisture.

The amount of water present at any time in a material is the result of the dynamic balance between the rate at which it is absorbed and the rate at which it is lost by evaporation.

Capillary moisture is controlled by the following factors:

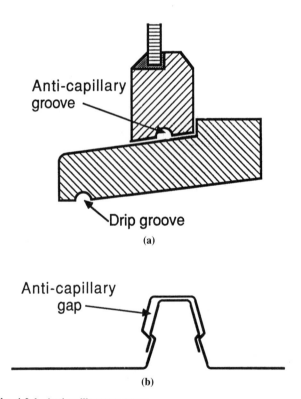

Anti-capillary groove

Drip groove

(a)

Anti-capillary gap

(b)

Fig. 4.2.1. Anticapillary measures.
Water penetrates narrow gaps because of capillary action even against the effect of gravity. To prevent this, the gap can be de-liberately widened locally to stop the capillary action, e.g., (a) in the bottom rail of a sash, or (b) at the edge of a sheet of corrugated roofing where the upper sheet is made with a slightly different profile.

1. Protection of porous materials from sources of moisture
2. Sealing of capillary gaps and cracks with waterproof sealants
3. Gaps sufficiently wide not to form capillaries (See Fig. 4.2.1)
4. Exposure of one or both sides of the material to free-flowing air if the latter is dry enough to draw out water vapor

Concrete is a special case. In high-strength concrete, the pores are discontinuous so that the material itself is reasonably waterproof. Structural concrete normally contains small cracks on the tension face, however, and because of shrinkage small cracks usually form where concrete abuts other materials. Care must be taken to prevent moisture from reaching the steel rein-forcing (see Sec. 3.5), and control joints must be waterproofed if they are to be exposed to the weather (see Sec. 3.6).

4.3 SLOPING ROOFS

There are two traditional approaches to roof construc-tion. Because water runs downhill, the most common is the sloping roof with overlapping pieces of shingle, tile, corrugated metal sheet, thatch, or whatever is available. These roofs are capable of shedding large amounts of water and, if steep enough, snow. Flat roofs are discussed in Sec. 4.5.

Disadvantages of the sloping roof are the extra height of the building and the limitations it places on the plan shape unless internal gutters are introduced. A sloping roof with external gutters is fail-safe; any overflow tends to occur outside the building. Internal gutters have no such margin of safety (Fig. 4.3.1).

Roofing materials may be chosen for their contri-bution to the insulation or the heat-reflecting properties of the roof–ceiling combination or simply as a water-proof layer, the insulation being provided by a separate layer.

Shingles (split from straight-grained, durable wood) and slates (split natural stone) are flat and therefore require considerable overlapping to prevent the water that slips between the side laps from penetrating further. Consequently, the surface area of the material required is about two and a half times that of the roof [Fig. 4.3.2(a)]. Clay tiles, and more recently concrete tiles, are formed with specially made end and side laps, and the amount of overlap required is much less. The laps also incorporate anticapillary grooves [Fig. 4.3.2(b)].

Shingles can also be made from bituminous felt (see Sec. 19.10) or fiber-reinforced cement. As these are not strong enough to support the weight of a worker,

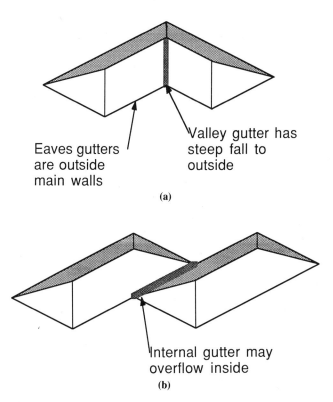

Fig. 4.3.1. Gutters.
When a sloping roof is used over a plan with a re-entrant angle, the roof geometry can be formed with (a) sloping valley gutters that, in the event of overflow, spill the water outside the building, or (b) an internal box gutter with the potential of overflowing into the building.

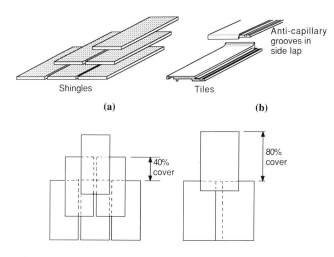

Fig. 4.3.2. Shingles and tiles.
(a) Shingles, made out of flat pieces of material, require large end-laps to keep water out.
(b) Manufactured tiles can be made with molded side and end laps so that smaller overlaps are adequate and the area covered is a much greater percentage of the area of the tile.

they are laid over a continuous layer of boards or plywood. The stronger shingles or tiles can be laid over battens spaced about 150 to 300 mm (6 to 12 in.) apart. This approach saves timber and allows ventilation around the underside of the material.

Wood shingles must be of a very durable species or else treated against dry rot (see Secs. 8.3 and 16.7). In hot, dry climates where rot is less likely to occur, they present a fire hazard.

Metal has many advantages as a roofing material if corrosion can be controlled (see Secs. 10.3 and 11.1). Roofs consisting of sheet lead or copper laid on continuous boarding with hand-made joints at the side laps are now rarely used. Modern roof sheets of galvanized steel or aluminum are corrugated or otherwise profiled to make them self-supporting in one direction. The profile also forms the side lap joint. The material is often factory-painted. Sheets can span 1 to 2 m (3 to 7 ft) so that there is no need for closely spaced battens or continuous boarding.

The first corrugated sheets were made by a process that limited their length to that of the press, about 3.6 m (12 ft). The end laps of the sheets were a major source of corrosion, and a slope of at least 5, and more commonly 15 to 20, degrees, was needed to prevent water from entering through the laps. Sheets are now usually made by the continuous process of roll-forming so that their length is limited only by handling and transport. Roofs of 12- to 15-m (35- to 50-ft) rafter length can be covered with single sheets from ridge to eaves, and slopes can be lower.

Very long sheets are subject to considerable thermal expansion and contraction (see Sec. 3.2), and most methods of fixing through the sheet are not suitable. Profiles have been developed that allow clip-fixing so that the sheet can slide lengthways but cannot lift off (Fig. 4.3.3).

Transparent roof sheets can be made from plastics (acrylics, polycarbonate, or glass-reinforced polyester) if light penetration is needed, but they also admit solar heat unless shaded. The material must be chosen carefully since most plastics suffer some degradation as a result of ultraviolet radiation (Secs. 5.1, 18.4, and 18.5).

4.4 THE NEED FOR SARKING

We saw in Sec. 4.1 that wind pressure can push water upward against gravity and in Sec. 4.2 that capillary action can also cause water to rise in a very narrow cavity. Any roof or wall with overlapping sheets or tiles can suffer from one or both of these problems. If the elements fit closely, they are likely to form good capillary passages, and, in the case of a looser fit, the wind can cause water to rise in a space that appears

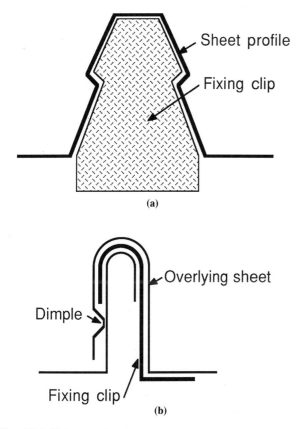

Fig. 4.3.3. Fixing metal roof sheets to allow for expansion.
To allow for thermal expansion in sheet metal roofing, the ribs can be formed (a) to clip over special fixing brackets, or (b) to be positively held down by brackets.

to drain to the outside and can also carry airborne spray through to the interior.

Sarking is an impervious layer under the roof covering that drains into the gutter (Fig. 4.4.1). It can also be used as an impervious layer inside wall cladding. In either case, it performs two functions. First, it becomes

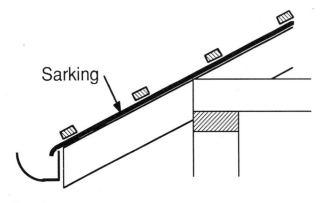

Fig. 4.4.1. Sarking.
Sarking laid under a tile or shingle roof should extend into the gutter. Any water penetrating the outer covering is caught by the sarking and fails to cause damage.

the principal barrier to air pressure so that joints in the outer cladding can behave like *drained joints* (see Sec. 4.7). Second, any water that does penetrate is carried safely away by the sarking instead of penetrating to the interior. If the sarking consists of reflective aluminum foil, it performs a third function of providing reflective insulation (see Sec. 6.3).

The steeper the slope, the more likely it is that gravity will win out over capillarity and wind pressure and keep the water out. Sarking is more essential for roofs of low slope. It is also needed behind walls with vertical boarding; horizontal, overlapping weatherboards do not need sarking except in very exposed locations.

Sarking also constitutes a vapor barrier (see Sec. 4.8).

4.5 WHAT MAKES A FLAT ROOF WATERPROOF?

Unlike a sloping roof, a flat roof can be made to follow any plan shape without creating awkward roof forms or internal gutters. It can also be made available for ready access or planted with a garden. "Flat" roofs usually have a small slope of 1:50 or 1:100 for drainage purposes. With a perfectly flat roof, the deflection of the structure would result in ponding.

Alternatively, roofs without a slope can be designed to hold a permanent pool of water about 150 mm (6 in.) deep that will assist in insulating them against downward heat flow and reduce their thermal movement. This water must be "maintained," however, by replenishment, algae control, and removal of accumulated dust and debris. Such pools are practical only in locations where freezing does not occur.

The simplest flat roof consists of waterproof reinforced concrete without a separate waterproofing membrane. It must be built with a high-strength concrete of low water–cement ratio so that the concrete itself is waterproof. To reduce the size of cracks, a quite substantial reinforcement ratio is necessary in both directions. Minimum steel ratios of about 0.0025 (0.25 percent) are commonly specified in codes, but ratios up to 0.006 (0.6 percent) for distribution steel and a minimum of 0.0035 for flexural reinforcement have been recommended. Curing must be carried out carefully, adequate control joints must be used, and reentrant corners avoided. Slopes are integrally formed either by increasing the thickness of the slab or by sloping both the soffit and the top of the slab rather than by adding a separate screed.

A waterproof concrete slab is particularly useful if a roof is to be used for car parking since any applied membrane is likely to be damaged by traffic. Insulation cannot be placed on top of the slab, however, and if it cracks or leaks, repairs are difficult.

The more common method of waterproofing a roof is to place a membrane over the top. Unlike the tiles on a sloping roof, the membrane must be sealed at all joints. A membrane can be laid over a concrete or timber deck, which does not itself need to be waterproof (see Secs. 11.6, 11.7, and 19.20). Falls can be provided by using tapered joists in a timber deck (to give a level ceiling and a sloping roof) or by adding a screed of lightweight concrete over a structural concrete slab.

The traditional waterproofing membranes are of three kinds: asphalt, laid and rolled to about 20 mm (3/4 in.) thick; built-up roofing of bitumen-impregnated felt, usually in three layers stuck together with bitumen; and single-layer asphaltic sheets, welded at the edges with a blowtorch. More recently, these have been improved by using glass or plastic fibers instead of asbestos or paper felt as the reinforcement and by using highly durable plastics and synthetic rubbers instead of bitumen. Plastics membranes can also be installed by applying the material in liquid form with a spray or roller and then allowing it to polymerize in place as a monolithic membrane.

All these materials are likely to be degraded by exposure to sunlight, which causes embrittlement or breakdown of organic chemicals; by high temperatures, which cause some chemical components to evaporate; by a wide range of temperatures, which may cause a membrane to crack; and by water vapor, which condenses under a membrane at night and vaporizes again during the day. Unless the membrane is ventilated, this vapor pressure causes localized "bubbles," which, if broken, cause leaks. These problems can be partly solved by covering the surface with mineral chips or gravel if it is not required to be walked on, or with precast concrete slabs or a cast-in-place concrete topping if it is.

Insulation should preferably be placed on top of the waterproof membrane (see Sec. 6.3) to insulate both membrane and deck from the extremes of temperature. "High-density," rigid plastic foams can be used if they are covered by a protective layer such as gravel or concrete slabs. These materials are a little denser than the very light insulating foams used for protected locations.

4.6 BRICK AND STONE WALLS

Although stones such as granite and marble are highly resistant to water absorption, the sedimentary stones and bricks and concrete blocks are all porous materials. Furthermore, the mortar joints in masonry walls are also quite porous. Masonry walls are thus neither waterproof nor vaporproof.

Masonry can be used successfully for exterior walls because such walls are relatively thick. Any rain that falls on the wall is slowly absorbed, and when the rain stops, the water is slowly released. The performance of the wall is improved by details that reduce the amount of water entering it, such as:

1. Covering the top of the wall with the roof and overhanging eaves
2. If parapet walls are used, providing flashing through the parapet and using a coping to throw water clear of the wall
3. Using a damp-proof course to prevent groundwater from rising up into the wall
4. Using tooled or weather-struck joints, to discourage water penetration at the joints
5. Painting the outside face
6. In climates where freezing is not a severe problem, using cavity walls so that water penetration is limited to the outer skin

A *damp-proof course* is essential to prevent "rising damp" in any wall that extends to the ground. Unlike the wall, which usually dries out quickly after a rain ceases, the ground may remain moist most of the time, and some of this water will travel up into the wall by capillary action. Damp-proof courses are formed by laying a strip of waterproof material in a mortar joint below the lowest floor level but high enough not to be covered if a garden is built that abuts the wall.

Sheet lead had been used for this purpose, but more recently sheet polyethylene, or a sandwich of polyethylene or bitumen on both sides of a thin core of copper, aluminum, or lead foil, have been used. The course material must be unaffected by the mortar and ductile enough to accommodate movements and small cracks that might occur in the masonry without tearing. It must also be able to resist the compressive stresses in the wall without being squeezed out as a result of creep (see Sec. 2.4). This can be a problem with lead in highly stressed walls.

Where the ground level slopes, the damp-proof course must be taken up or down in the vertical joints to form a continuous barrier. Where windows and doorways penetrate a wall, or where a lower roof abuts a wall, the junction forms a potential source of leakage. This problem will be considered in the next section.

4.7 JOINTS AND FLASHINGS

Joints between different materials, or different components of the same material, are a potential source of water penetration. Small components such as tiles, shingles, and bricks must be designed and installed so that all joints are self-sealing, since it would be impractical to undertake the individual treatment of so many joints. Joints between larger components usually have to accommodate movements that result from shrinkage, expansion, or thermal movement of the materials or of the whole building.

In locations sheltered from extreme winds, horizontal joints can be made with a vertical overlap that will exclude water by gravity. Flashing at horizontal or sloping junctions serves this function. In any other position, water can be excluded either by maintaining an impermeable outer surface—a sealed joint—or by establishing a network of drained channels within the thickness of the wall—a drained joint (Fig. 4.7.1). With thin, impervious materials such as glass, sealed joints must be used; drained joints are more common with thicker components, such as precast concrete.

Flashing at a vertical junction behaves like a drained joint.

The flashing between a brick wall and an abutting roof should be in two pieces. The *cover flashing,* which is built into the wall, is subject to severe conditions because the exposed part changes temperature much more rapidly than the built-in part. It must be chemically unaffected by contact with the wall, and water running from it must not corrode the roof. The *apron flashing* must be flexible enough to make good contact with the roof and yet stiff enough to stay in position and maintain its turn-up behind the cover flashing.

Sheet lead is the traditional flashing material since it is compatible with most building materials and easily dressed to shape. The thermal expansion may easily exceed the low yield stress of the material, however,

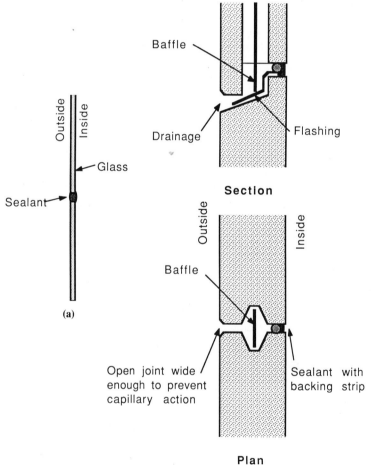

Fig. 4.7.1 Sealed joints.
(a) A joint in a thin external material, such as frameless glass, must withstand exposure and remain waterproof and airtight.
(b) In a thicker wall, it is possible to separate the functions of the joint. The external seal must resist weathering and break the force of driving rain, but if a small amount of rainwater penetrates, it can be drained away from the drainage channel, which is at outside air pressure. The inner seal should be airtight, but it is not subject to severe weathering or solar radiation. A small leak may not cause damage, and it is usually easier to repair because it is accessible from inside.

and in long lengths there is a tendency to buckle or form fatigue cracks. Sheet zinc or aluminum can be used if there is no copper to cause electrolytic corrosion; or copper can be used if none of the other metals present are low in the electrochemical series (see Table 10.1) and in a position to react with it. Galvanized steel is often used, with or without a coating of colored paint, in conjunction with roofs of the same material. It is stiff and has to be machine-bent to profile, whereas the previously mentioned metals can all be obtained in an annealed condition suitable for bending on site. Stainless steel (see Sec. 10.7) is a stiff and expensive but very durable material that is compatible with many other building materials and suitable for flashing in positions of severe exposure or in prestige buildings.

Sealants for nonmoving joints can be based on any adhesive, gap-filling material that is compatible with both the materials being joined (Sec. 19.8). Glass is sealed into timber sashes in small-scale construction with a putty made from linseed oil and whiting (Sec. 19.8). The oil oxidizes on contact with the air, and the putty sets hard and waterproof in a few days, after which it is painted for protection. The panes are not large enough, nor the timber sashes stiff enough, to produce problems of differential thermal expansion.

Larger glass panes and those made with heat-absorbing glass (which heat up more than plain glass), as well as those in heavy metal frames, such as a curtain wall, require a more flexible sealant to allow for relative movement between the glass and the frame. The sealant may be *neoprene,* formed to a profile and held in place by pressure of a glazing bead rather than by adhesion (see Sec. 19.9), or it may be an elastomer such as silicone that adheres to the glass and the frame (see Sec. 19.8). Glass sheets in *frameless* walls are stuck together with clear synthetic adhesives that have high strength but enough flexibility to avoid stress concentrations at the glass junctions.

Panels of precast concrete or brickwork are thick enough to permit the use of drained joints. These are formed with a *rainscreen* on the outer side of the joint that prevents entry of most of the rainwater but is not airtight. The inner face is sealed to be airtight, but this sealant is not exposed to the sunlight nor to appreciable amounts of water. Between them is a network of cavities that drain to the outside, and are much too large to allow capillary action. Because the air in the cavity is at the same pressure as the air outside, there is nothing to prevent the water from draining out by gravity.

A flexible sealant, whether in a sealed joint or in the inner face of a drained joint, must be capable of maintaining not only its adhesion to the faces it joins but also its cohesion within itself over the range of expansion and contraction movements expected of the joint. The properties of the sealant should be determined

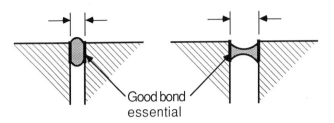

Fig. 4.7.2. Width of sealed joint.
The sealant in a control joint must be able to expand and contract without being squeezed out or losing its adhesion to the two sides of the joint. If a backing material is used behind the sealant, the sealant should not bond to it.

not only under laboratory conditions, but under the actual conditions of exposure, with allowances made for the degree of quality control that can be exercised at a site application.

If a particular sealant is capable of 80-percent elongation and the joint may open up by 8 mm (5/16 in.), then the joint must initially be at least 10 mm (3/8 in.) wide (Fig. 4.7.2). In a thick wall it is neither practical nor affordable to fill the whole thickness with an expensive elastomer. Therefore, the gap is either filled with a compressible strip set back from the face (the usual method for brickwork or cast-in-place concrete) or with a cylindrical foam backing strip pushed in after erection (for precast units), leaving a gap at the face suitable for filling with the sealant; as shown in Fig. 4.7.3 (see Sec. 18.9).

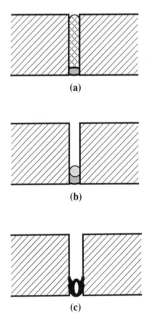

Fig. 4.7.3. Location of joint sealer.
A control joint in a masonry wall can be sealed by (a) building in a compressible joint filler, set back from the face, the front of the joint being filled with a sealant; (b) inserting a pliable backing strip, leaving a space for the sealant; and (c) inserting a ribbed rubber sealing tube that is compressed on insertion and remains flexible to seal the joint as it expands and contracts.

4.8 VAPOR BARRIERS

The air always contains water vapor. The amount it *can* hold without becoming saturated increases rapidly with temperature, whereas the amount it *does* hold depends on climatic conditions. Indoors, it also depends on the rate at which moisture is being produced and the rate of ventilation. Since many activities inside a building produce water vapor, the vapor pressure inside is always higher than it is outside, except when air conditioning or dehumidification is in use.

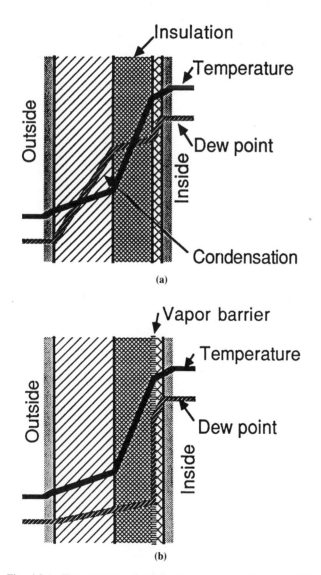

Fig. 4.8.1. The variation of temperature and of moisture content (measured by dew point) through an insulated wall.

(a) *Without a vapor barrier:* Insulation has great resistance to heat flow but not to vapor flow. In the area where the temperature is below the dew point, condensation will occur, with resulting damage to the wall.

(b) *With a vapor barrier:* A barrier placed on the warm side of the insulation has great resistance to vapor flow but not to heat. The moisture content is therefore reduced before the temperature, and no condensation occurs.

Water vapor will readily flow through porous insulating materials. If we analyze the gradients of temperature and vapor pressure across the sections of a wall, we will find the steepest change in temperature across the insulation and the steepest change in vapor pressure across the least permeable layer (Fig. 4.8.1 illustrates the winter condition). Beginning at the inside surface, so long as the vapor pressure reduces faster than the temperature, no part of the wall will be below the *dew point* (see Sec. 6.4), and no harm is done. In insulated construction, therefore, it is sufficient to locate the barrier on the inside of the insulation.

Materials used as vapor barriers include aluminum foil and thin plastic sheeting, either alone or stuck to the surface of insulating boards or to the back of plasterboard. Some paint films are relatively impermeable. Since sarking (see Sec. 4.4) is located on the outside of the insulation, it is not in the right place for a vapor barrier. One solution to this problem is to use *builder's paper* for the sarking. Although relatively waterproof, it is more permeable than most vapor barriers. To reduce its moisture content, the space between the sarking and the insulation can be slightly ventilated to the outside.

Permeability is the mass of water vapor transmitted in unit time, under unit pressure difference, through a unit area of material of unit thickness. *Permeance* is similar except that it refers to a *given* thickness of material. The units of permeance are either nanograms per second, per square meter, per pascal, or, in the customary U.S. units, grains per hour, per square foot, per inch of mercury pressure.

Table 4.1 shows some typical values of permeance. Because the properties of most materials vary between manufacturers and some of the descriptions vary from one locality to another, these values should be taken only as an approximate guide. Actual values of all material properties should always be sought from the manufacturers.

In uninsulated construction, it may be necessary to make a detailed study of the temperature and vapor-

Table 4.1. Permeance of Some Materials.

Material	Permeance	
	ng/sm²Pa	*gr/h·ft²·in.Hg*
Aluminum foil	0.1 to 6*	0 to 0.1*
Polyethylene film, 0.06 mm (0.002 in.)	4	0.1
PVA latex paint, three coats	300	6
Oil paint, three coats	20 to 60	0.4 to 1.2
Waterproof kraft paper	6000	100
Bitumen coated paper	10 to 30	0.2 to 0.6
Plasterboard	3000	50
Plywood, 6-mm (1/4-in.) [interior]	110	2
Plywood, 6-mm (1/4-in.) [exterior]	40	1

* Depends on pin-holes as a result of handling.

pressure gradients across the construction to determine where, if at all, a barrier can safely be placed. A single glazed window is a special case because the glass forms a vapor barrier that is close to outside temperature. Condensation often forms on the inside of the glass, especially in bathrooms, and provision may have to be made to drain it away.

4.9 WATERPROOFING BASEMENTS AND EARTH-INTEGRATED STRUCTURES

Damp-proof courses (see Sec. 4.6) are necessary at the base of masonry walls to prevent moisture rising by capillary action, but when a basement is built below ground, moisture can be present in the ground surrounding all faces of the room.

It is best not to build below the highest expected *water table,* for to do so is to have water under pressure trying to enter through any crack or weakness in the construction. For this purpose, porous granular filling material around and under the building and connected to drainage lines can be used to lower the water table. A fine filter cloth must be used to keep silt out of the drainage system.

Nevertheless, the soil will usually be damp and sometimes may contain water running toward the drainage system. Therefore, the underside of the floor and outside of the walls should be sealed with a waterproof membrane. A heavy polyethylene film, sealed at all joints, will be sufficient. The difficulty is in sealing the joints and preventing damage during the pouring of concrete and backfilling against the walls. For this reason, a bituminous felt is often used to waterproof basement walls, and it can be protected with fibrous cement sheets against damage during backfilling.

Bentonite clay, formed into sheets and laid against the outside of basement walls, is also sometimes used for waterproofing. The clay expands and forms a waterproof and gap-filling layer when wet.

4.10 WHAT MAKES A BUILDING WATERPROOF?

A person walking in the rain can make use of an umbrella, a waterproof coat, and waterproof boots. There is some similarity with a building. The umbrella, or sloping roof, provides excellent protection against vertical rain, but a well-sealed coat is needed when wind drives the rain. The ground remains wet even after the rain stops so that boots are necessary to stop rising damp. And when the waterproof garment is well sealed, condensation will occur from the moisture produced on the inside. The building, however, cannot change its clothes to suit the weather or buy new ones every season. The materials must suit all seasons and last for the life of the building without excessive maintenance.

It is seldom possible to consider building materials in isolation from each other. The exterior envelope must satisfy multiple requirements—resistance to sunlight, abrasion, and water penetration; thermal insulation and vapor resistance; structural strength, transparency or opacity; appearance inside and outside; joints between similar and dissimilar elements—and multiple materials must be used to satisfy them. The complete system consists of the juxtaposition of materials and the plan of preventive maintenance or periodic replacement needed to keep them functioning.

REFERENCES

4.1. S. V. Szokolay: *Environmental Science Handbook.* Construction Press, London, 1980. 532 pp.

SUGGESTIONS FOR FURTHER READING

C. W. Griffin: *Manual of Built-up Roof Systems.* McGraw-Hill, New York, 1970. 241 pp.

Bre Digests: *Building Construction.* The Construction Press, Lancaster, 1977. 271 pp.

GLC Good Practice Details. Architectural Press, London, 1979. 148 pp.

5

Transmission, Reflection, and Absorption of Visible Light and Radiant Heat

Radiation received from the sun includes light and heat. The heat reradiated by a building has a longer wavelength than that of solar thermal radiation. Glass that is transparent to solar radiation may be opaque to that long-wave radiation.

The transparency and absorption of light and radiant heat are determined by the structure of a material, but its reflectance depends on the surface properties.

5.1 RADIANT ENERGY

The sun and other stars emit energy in the form of electromagnetic waves (or radiation). These waves—unlike sound waves (see Sec. 9.1)—require no medium for their transmission. Their velocity—approximately 300,000 km/s (186,000 miles/s)—is the highest velocity attainable for the transfer of energy, expressed as follows:

$$\text{Wave velocity} = \text{Wavelength} \times \text{Frequency} \quad (5.1)$$

where the wavelength is the distance between successive crests of a wave and the frequency is the number of wave crests that occur in any particular place in one second, the latter being measured in hertz (Hz), which is the same as cycles per second.

The longer waves are used for telecommunications under the names of long-wave, short-wave, microwave, and ultra-high-frequency radiation. The shorter waves produce gamma rays (the radiation of radioactive material) and X-rays, such as those used in medical diagnosis. Near the center of the spectrum is visible light, infrared radiation (which transmits heat), and ultraviolet radiation (which produces a suntan on human skin). The three ranges overlap.

Visible light is simply the range of electromagnetic waves that can be seen with the human eye. Its wavelength ranges from red (760 nm) through orange, yellow, green, and blue to violet (390 nm). When all these colors are mixed together, the light is perceived as white.

The wavelength of radiant heat emitted by the sun ranges from approximately 200 to 3000 nm (0.2 to 3 μm). Radiant heat is also emitted by other bodies, such as electric radiators and even human bodies. The wavelength of their peak thermal radiation is longer than that of the sun because, according to Wien's Law (Ref. 5.1), the peak energy occurs at a wavelength that is inversely proportional to the absolute temperature (in degrees Kelvin) of the body emitting the heat. The wavelengths emitted by the human body are in the range of 4 to 50 μm.

5.2 MEASUREMENT OF LIGHT

The unit of *luminous intensity, I,* is the *candela.* This is an absolute unit, defined as a *standard radiator,* which replaces the nineteenth-century *standard candle.*

Luminous flux, F, measured in *lumen,* is the flow of light power (equivalent to the watt). *Illuminance, E,* measured in *lux,* is the luminous flux per unit area. *Luminance, L,* measured in candela per square meter (cd/m^2), is the measure of luminous intensity per unit area.

Illuminance is what a light source produces on a surface reached by it. Luminance is what the eye sees reflected from that surface, or what it sees looking directly at the light source. Both illuminance and luminance are measured with photovoltaic cells adapted for the purpose.

Lighting units and measurements are discussed in specialist books on the subject and also in books on physics and environmental design (for example, Ref. 5.2).

5.3 TRANSPARENCY AND TRANSLUCENCY

Radiant energy is transmitted in discrete units, called *photons.* Materials with free electrons (see Sec. 2.2) absorb photons of radiant energy by raising an electron to a higher energy level and are consequently opaque. Transparency requires the absence of free electrons, and the absence of internal reflecting surfaces. Thus, all metals are opaque except as very, very thin films, and amorphous substances that are free from crystalline interfaces are often transparent. Some crystalline polymers (see Secs. 18.4 and 18.5) are also transparent, however, because their crystalline structure is smaller than the wavelength of light.

Translucent materials are usually transparent materials with surface or interior defects, which may give the material a cloudy, hazy, or milky appearance. Medieval glass was usually only translucent, but it often had a brilliant appearance that glassmakers of the nineteenth century, during the neo-Gothic era, were able to match only after extensive experimentation. It was due to the inclusion of tiny air bubbles, which the medieval glass makers would probably have preferred to do without. Modern translucency is produced by deliberate "defects" (see Chap. 17).

The glass commonly used for windows is of the soda–lime–silica type (Sec. 17.1). It is transparent in the range of visible light—390 to 760 nm—but inevitably admits an appreciable amount of thermal solar radiation as well since the two forms of radiation overlap. The latter heats up the floor, walls, and objects in a room, and these in turn radiate heat at a longer wavelength— 4 to 50 μm (see Sec. 5.1)—because their temperature is much lower than that of the sun. Soda–lime–silica glass is largely opaque at these wavelengths, so that the radiation admitted is not reradiated through the glass. This is known as the *greenhouse effect.*

5.4 REFRACTION, REFLECTION, AND ABSORPTION OF LIGHT

The velocity of light is highest in a vacuum and decreases the denser the medium through which it travels. Thus, the velocity of light in air on either side is higher than that in glass or transparent plastic. The ratio of these two velocities is called the *refractive index, n.* As a result of this change of velocity, the ray of light is bent through an angle, or *refracted,* so that

$$n = \sin i/\sin r \qquad (5.2)$$

where i is the angle of incidence of the light ray with the normal and $r,$ its angle of refraction in the same plane (Fig. 5.4.1). This is known as *Snell's Law* (Ref. 5.3).

Light is also *reflected* at the surface of the glass. If the angle of incidence is high, only a small amount is reflected, but this quantity increases as the angle is reduced (Fig. 5.4.2). The amount can be calculated from Fresnel's reflection formula (Ref. 5.4).

Reflectance may be defined as the ratio of reflected light to incident light, and *transmittance* as the ratio of transmitted light to incident light. If the two do not add up to unity, some of the light is also absorbed by the glass or transparent plastic as heat; that is its *absorptance.*

Normal window glass absorbs only a small amount of light and thermal radiation (Fig. 5.4.2), but this can be increased by altering the composition of the glass to produce a *heat-absorbing glass.* A good heat-absorbing glass may absorb 40 to 80 percent of the infrared radiation, but, if it does so, it will also absorb 30 to 75 percent of the visible light and alter its color. Furthermore, the heat absorbed is reradiated.

An alternative method for excluding heat while admitting light is to increase the reflection of the surface of the glass with a thin mirror coating that transmits

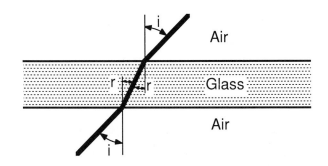

Fig. 5.4.1. Passage of ray of light through a sheet of glass. The ratio of the velocity of light in air to that of light in glass is their refractive index, *n*.

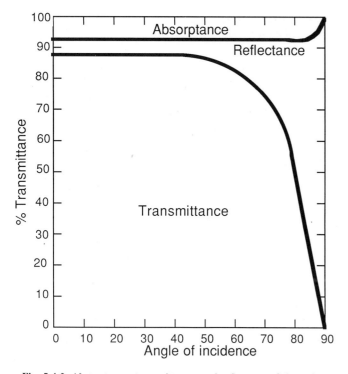

Fig. 5.4.2. Absorptance, transmittance, and reflectance of sheet glass 3 mm thick.
Quoted from a Swedish Report by G. B. Pleijel by R. Persson (Ref. 5.5) and reproduced by courtesy of Statens Råd för Byggnadsforskning.

a substantial portion of the visible light but reflects as much as possible of the longer-wave infrared radiation. Heat-absorbing and heat-reflecting glass are discussed in Sec. 17.5.

5.5 ABSORPTION AND EMISSION OF RADIANT HEAT

For the same wavelength, the absorptivity and emissivity of thermal radiation by a surface are equal, but their values vary greatly with wavelength. The surface of a building absorbs solar radiation of 0.2- to 3-μm wavelength, but the heat radiated by the building has a longer wavelength within the range of 4 to 50 μm (see Sec. 5.1). Thus, a bare concrete surface, a surface painted white, and a surface painted black all have the same emissivity, that is, they are cooled equally at night by radiation to the sky. The proportion of solar radiation that they absorb during the day, however, is quite different. A surface painted black becomes much hotter on a sunny day than one painted white; bare concrete is intermediate between the two.

This effect is also utilized in solar collectors. A temperature adequate for a hot-water service can be achieved with an ordinary black surface. For industrial processes, however, where temperatures above 100°C (212°F) are required, the collectors are coated with selective surfaces whose solar absorptance is much higher than their emittance of long-wave infrared radiation.

REFERENCES

5.1. D. A. McIntyre: *Indoor Climate*. Applied Science, London, 1980, p. 8.
5.2. H. J. Cowan and P. R. Smith: *Environmental Systems*. Van Nostrand Reinhold, New York, 1983, pp. 132–134.
5.3. A. Beiser: *Modern Technical Physics*. Addison-Wesley, Reading, MA, 1966, pp. 519–523.
5.4. C. F. Tweney and L. E. C. Hughes (Eds.): *Technical Dictionary*. W. and R. Chambers, Edinburgh, 1958, p. 355.
5.5. R. Persson: *Flat Glass Technology*. Butterworths, London, 1969, p. 40.

SUGGESTIONS FOR FURTHER READING

L. H. van Vlack: *Elements of Materials Science*. Addison-Wesley, Reading, MA, 1964. 445 pp.
H. J. Cowan and P. R. Smith: *Environmental Systems*. Van Nostrand Reinhold, New York, 1983. 240 pp.

6

Thermal Insulation and Thermal Inertia

The *thermal transmittance* and its reciprocal, the *thermal resistance,* of a wall, floor, or roof are determined by their respective dimensions and by the constants of thermal conduction and convection, which are listed in handbooks. Examples are worked out to show the greatly improved performance brought about by the use of special insulating materials. Good insulation, however, may result in condensation in cold weather.

The choice of building material and type of construction determines the thermal inertia as well as the time it takes for heat to flow through a wall or roof.

6.1 MEASUREMENT OF HEAT

Heat is a form of energy, measured, like all energy in the SI metric system, in joules. The American unit is the British thermal unit, which is approximately 1000 times as much (1 Btu = 1.055 kJ). Heat flow is measured in watt (1 W = 1 J/s) or in Btu/h. Temperature is measured in degrees Celsius or Fahrenheit (1°C = 1.8°F). There are also different freezing temperatures for the two scales (32°F = 0°C).

It is customary in thermal calculations using SI units to employ the Kelvin scale, which is the same as the Celsius scale except that its zero is *absolute zero—*the lowest temperature that can be reached (0 K = −273.1°C). (The degree sign is omitted when the K scale is used.)

6.2 THERMAL CONDUCTION AND CONVECTION

Heat can be transmitted through the emptiness of space only by radiation; however, heat transfer on earth is commonly effected by conduction or convection.

Thermal conduction is the transfer of heat from one part of a body to another or from one body to another with which it is in contact. The energy is transferred because the excess vibrations at the hot end set the neighbouring atoms into vibration so that the heat travels through the solid. Nonmetals have a low *coefficient of thermal conductivity*. Metals have a much higher one (see Table 6.1) because their free electrons (see Sec. 2.3) transfer the vibrations much more rapidly. Thus, metals that are good conductors of electricity are also good conductors of heat.

The quantity of heat transferred by conduction is defined as follows:

$$Q = \frac{k(T_1 - T_2)}{d} \qquad (6.1)$$

where:

Q = quantity of heat passing through a unit area of a body (for example, a wall or a floor) in unit time, measured in W/m^2 or in $Btu/ft^2 \cdot h$

k = the coefficient of thermal conductivity of the material, measured in W/mK or in $Btu/ft \cdot h \cdot °F$

T = temperature on warmer side of body (T_1) and that on the colder side (T_2); the temperature difference is measured in K or °F

d = distance between the two sides of the body, in meters or feet

Thermal convection takes place as a result of the change in density of most liquids and gases as they change their temperature. Usually, they get lighter as

Table 6.1. Thermal Conductivity of Selected Building Materials.

Material	Thermal conductivity, k	
	W/mK	$Btu/ft \cdot h \cdot {}^\circ F$
Copper	386	223
Steel	43	25
Granite	2.80	1.62
Limestone	1.50	0.87
Concrete	1.20	0.69
Glass	1.00	0.60
Brick	0.80	0.46
Sand	0.40	0.23
Gypsum plaster	0.10	0.058
Timber (pine)	0.14	0.080
Water	0.60	0.35
Air	0.023	0.013
Fiber insulating board	0.048	0.028
Glass or mineral wool	0.039	0.023

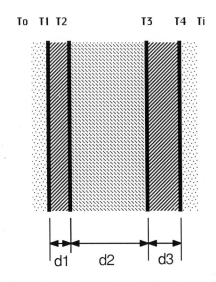

Fig. 6.3.1. Thermal transmittance and thermal resistance of a composite wall or roof.

The wall consists of three materials whose thicknesses are d_1, d_2, and d_3, respectively, and thermal conductivities, k_1, k_2, and k_3. The temperature to the left (the outside) is T_o and the temperature to the right (the inside) is T_i. The temperatures between the boundary layer of air and the first solid layer is T_1, that between the first and second solid layers is T_2, that between the second and the third layers is T_3, and that between the third solid layer and the interior boundary layer of air is T_4. The boundary-layer heat-transfer coefficients for the outside and the interior are h_o and h_i, respectively; the numerical values of these heat transfer coefficients are obtainable from the ASRAE Handbook (Ref. 6.1), as are the thermal conductivities.

they get hotter so that a thorough mixing results which transfers the heat.

In buildings, convection is of particular importance because it increases the transfer of heat by air flowing over the surfaces of walls, floors, roofs, and pipes used for heating and cooling. The quantity of heat transferred, Q, is defined as follows:

$$Q = h(T_1 - T_2) \tag{6.2}$$

where h is the boundary-layer heat-transfer coefficient, measured in W/m^2K or in $Btu/ft^2 \cdot h \cdot {}^\circ F$.

Air, in common with most gases, has very low thermal conductivity. If its convection can be prevented by confining it within a small volume, it makes an excellent insulating material. Most good insulating materials (see Sec. 6.3) are based on this principle.

6.3 THERMAL TRANSMITTANCE, THERMAL RESISTANCE, AND INSULATION

If Q is the quantity of heat passing through a unit area of a wall, roof, or floor and if the temperatures on the two faces, say the outside and the interior, are T_o and T_i, then the *thermal transmittance, U,* is

$$U = Q/(T_o - T_i) \tag{6.3}$$

and the *thermal resistance, R,* is

$$R = 1/U \tag{6.4}$$

As an example, we will consider the composite wall shown in Fig. 6.3.1. Under conditions of steady heat flow, the quantity of heat passing through the boundary layer of air on either side (stated in Eq. 6.2) and through each layer of material (stated in Eq. 6.1) is the same, as indicated by the following:

$$Q = h_0(T_0 - T_1)$$
$$= \frac{k_1}{d_1}(T_1 - T_2)$$
$$= \frac{k_2}{d_2}(T_2 - T_3)$$
$$= \frac{k_3}{d_3}(T_3 - T_4)$$
$$= h_i(T_4 - T_i)$$

From this we obtain the thermal resistance and the thermal transmittance as follows:

$$R = \frac{1}{U} = \frac{1}{h_0} + \frac{d_1}{k_1} + \frac{d_2}{k_2} + \frac{d_3}{k_3} + \frac{1}{h_i} \tag{6.5}$$

Let us examine the significance of this equation through a few simple examples.

Example 6.1.A: *Determine the thermal resistance (R value) and thermal transmittance (U value) of a concrete wall 150 mm thick.*

The thermal conductivity of concrete, k, is 1.20 W/mK (Table 6.1). The heat-transfer coefficients for the inside and outside of the wall are found from Ref. 6.1 to be: $h_o = 20$ W/m^{2}K and $h_i = 8$ W/m^{2}K. Therefore, from Eq. 6.5 the thermal resistance is

$$R = \frac{1}{U} = \frac{1}{20} + \frac{0.15}{1.20} + \frac{1}{8} = 0.30 \text{ m}^2\text{K/W}$$

and the thermal transmittance, U, is 3.3 W/m^{2}K.

Example 6.1.B: *Determine the thermal resistance (R value) and thermal transmittance (U value) of a concrete wall 6 in. thick.*

The thermal conductivity of concrete is 0.69 Btu/ft·h·°F (Table 6.1). The heat transfer coefficients for the inside and the outside of the wall are found from Ref. 6.1 to be $h_o = 4.0$ and $h_i = 1.46$ Btu/ft^2·h·°F. Furthermore, of course, 6 in. = 0.50 ft. Therefore, from Eq. 6.5. the thermal resistance is

$$R = \frac{1}{U} = \frac{1}{4.0} + \frac{0.50}{0.69} + \frac{1}{1.46} = 1.66 \text{ ft}^2\cdot\text{h}\cdot\text{°F/Btu}$$

and the thermal transmittance, U, is 0.60 Btu/ft^2·h·°F.

We will now examine how the thermal performance of this wall could be improved.

Example 6.2: *Determine the thermal resistance and transmittance of a 200-mm (8-in.) thick concrete wall.*

$$R = \frac{1}{U} = \frac{1}{20} + \frac{0.20}{1.20} + \frac{1}{8} = 0.34 \text{ m}^2\text{K/W}$$
$$U = 2.9 \text{ W/m}^2\text{K}$$

or

$$R = \frac{1}{U} = \frac{1}{4.0} + \frac{0.67}{0.69} + \frac{1}{1.46} = 1.90 \text{ ft}^2\cdot\text{h}\cdot\text{°F/Btu}$$
$$U = 0.53 \text{ Btu/ft}^2\cdot\text{h}\cdot\text{°F}$$

This is a very small improvement for a 33-percent increase in the thickness of the wall.

Example 6.3: *Determine the thermal resistance and transmittance of a wall consisting of 150 mm (6 in.) of concrete and 50 mm (2 in.) of mineral wool.*

From Table 6.1, the thermal conductivity of mineral wool is 0.039 W/mK (0.023 Btu/ft^2·h·°F). Then,

$$R = \frac{1}{U} = \frac{1}{20} + \frac{0.15}{1.20} + \frac{0.050}{0.039} + \frac{1}{8} = 1.58 \text{ m}^2\text{K/W}$$
$$U = 0.63 \text{ W/m}^2\text{K}$$

or

$$R = \frac{1}{U} = \frac{1}{4.0} + \frac{0.50}{0.69} + \frac{0.17}{0.023} + \frac{1}{1.46} = 9.07 \text{ ft}^2\cdot\text{h}\cdot\text{°F/Btu}$$
$$U = 0.110 \text{ Btu/ft}^2\cdot\text{h}\cdot\text{°F}$$

This is a very substantial improvement. The thin layer of quite cheap insulating material makes a far greater contribution than the thicker layer of concrete.

Example 6.4: *Determine the thermal resistance and transmittance of a cavity wall consisting of two walls of concrete, each 75 mm (3 in.) thick and separated by an air cavity 50 mm (2 in.) thick.*

The thermal resistance of air spaces varies with their mean temperature, the temperature difference, and the emittance of the surfaces. From the *ASHRAE Handbook* (Ref. 6.2), we chose an R of 0.20 m^{2}K/W (1.36 ft^2·h·°F/Btu). The thermal resistance and the thermal transmittance of the wall are then as follows:

$$R = \frac{1}{20} + \frac{0.075}{1.20} + 0.20 + \frac{0.075}{1.20} + \frac{1}{8} = 0.50 \text{ m}^2\text{K/W}$$
$$U = 2.0 \text{ W/m}^2\text{K}$$

or

$$R = \frac{1}{4.0} + \frac{0.25}{0.69} + 1.36 + \frac{0.25}{0.69} + \frac{1}{1.46} = 3.01 \text{ ft}^2\cdot\text{h}\cdot\text{°F/Btu}$$
$$U = 0.33 \text{ Btu/ft}^2\cdot\text{h}\cdot\text{°F}$$

This 200-mm (8-in.) cavity wall has a thermal performance superior to that of the 200-mm (8-in.) solid concrete wall, but not as good as that of the wall with 50 mm (2 in.) of insulating material. From the thermal point of view, it is better to fill the cavity with insulating material.

Insulating materials have acquired great economic importance since the energy crisis of the 1970s because their use in buildings results in large energy savings, particularly in regions with cold winters, such as the Northeast and Midwest of the U.S.A., most of Canada, Northern Europe, and Northern Asia.

Cooling by air conditioning actually uses more energy per degree cooled, but the temperature differential for cooling in "hot" climates is less than that for heating in "cold" climates. The temperature differential between the desired indoor temperature and the extreme outdoor temperature is less than 10°C (18°F) on a hot day, but more than 20°C (36°F) on a cold night in a temperate climate. In an extreme climate, it is about 15°C (27°F) on a hot day, and 50°C (90°F) on a cold night.

The temperature is moderated by the fabric of a building, and this is greatly enhanced by air gaps or insulating materials, as the above examples show. The most effective thermal insulating materials are, in fact, materials that entrap air, or sometimes another gas with a very low thermal conductivity and whose heat loss by convection is prevented by the entrapment. The materials must also be cheap and durable.

Successful thermal insulating materials in current use are cork, lightweight fiber boards, mineral wool (which may be made by blowing air or steam through molten glass, molten rock, or molten blast-furnace slag), various expanded plastics (such as polystyrene), and various plastics applied as foam that subsequently set hard (such as rigid polyurethane foam).

Some of these materials, notably sprayed rigid foam, prevent the passage of moisture. Their use can produce problems, for example, in cavity walls that are intended to drain any moisture that penetrates into the cavity. If the cavity is filled with foam, drainage is prevented, and this may result in corrosion of metals or dry rot of timber adjacent to the filled cavity. This is an aspect to be considered when insulation is "retrofitted," that is, installed after a building has been completed to improve its thermal performance.

The increased cost of fuel in relation to other commodities, and the higher standard of heating and cooling to which an affluent society has become accustomed, have greatly encouraged the use of special insulating materials where none might have been used previously. Some governments have further promoted their use through tax concessions given for a number of years to reduce dependence on imported oil or to save foreign currency. Their effect is to make the use of insulation economical to the home-owner or occupier when it might not otherwise be so. This political decision is one of considerable importance, since the energy used for heating buildings represents in many countries the largest single use of energy.

It should be noted that thermal insulating materials do not generally make good acoustic insulating materials (see Sec. 9.2) and vice versa.

The term *thermal insulation* is also applied to *reflective insulation,* which is a bright metal foil (usually aluminum) that reflects radiant heat, particularly solar radiation transmitted through a roof covering before it enters a building. It may be used by itself under the roof sheets or tiles, or it may be used as a surface for the batts of insulating material that stop heat loss or gain by conduction and convection (see Fig. 11.5.4). The metal foil then serves also as a vapor barrier to prevent absorption of condensation by the porous insulating material (see Secs. 4.4 and 4.8).

6.4 CONDENSATION

The *absolute humidity* is the mass of water vapor suspended in air per unit mass of dry air. As the temperature decreases, the ability of the air to absorb water vapor also decreases. At 30°C, air can absorb 27 grams of water per kilogram of dry air; at 0°C, it can absorb only 4 grams. The temperature at which air is fully saturated with water vapor is called the *dewpoint.* The *relative humidity* is the ratio of water vapor contained in the air to that contained in saturated air; the relative humidity is 100 percent at the dew point.

The relation between temperature and humidity is shown graphically on a diagram called a *psychrometric chart;* this is frequently reproduced in books on air conditioning, heating, and environmental design (for example, see Ref. 6.3).

Although people tend to complain about "high humidity" in hot weather, relative humidities actually tend to be much higher when it is cool. As warm air—for example, from the inside of a heated building—is cooled, its absolute humidity remains the same until the dew point is reached; thus, air at a temperature of 25°C (77°F) and 60-percent relative humidity reaches its dew point at 17°C (63°F). If it is cooled further, the saturation level of the air is exceeded, and some of the moisture condenses on a nearby surface. This is the reason why condensation forms on the inside of windows (which are poor insulators) during a cold night (see Sec. 17.5). Its appearance is harmless, but condensation formed regularly on timber or metal surfaces is liable to produce decay or corrosion. This is another possibility that must be considered, particularly when insulation is "retrofitted".

The risk of condensation in wall spaces is greatly reduced if insulation is fitted to the *outside* of the wall (see Sec. 4.8). In most buildings, the variation in the interior temperature is kept as low as possible, whereas the outside temperature varies between day and night. If the insulation is on the outside of the wall, then the temperature variation within the wall is greatly reduced; condensation thus becomes unlikely, and heat transfer within the wall is reduced.

This arrangement presents some problems because of the mechanical weakness of most insulating materials. They need to be given a protective covering with a thin sheet that protects them from mechanical damage and water absorption without introducing a thermal inertia. For this reason, thermal insulation is more often placed *inside* the wall, particularly in traditional timber structures.

6.5 VARIABLE HEAT FLOW AND STORAGE OF HEAT IN BUILDING MATERIALS

We have assumed so far that the heat flow is steady, that is, that the temperature at any point does not change with time. Apart from the annual changes of temperature, there are diurnal changes (see Sec. 3.3) that are quite large in a continental climate (see Glossary) but even on a small island near the equator are not negligible.

The theory of variable heat flow may be found in specialist texts on heat transfer (for example, Refs. 6.4 and 6.5). It is beyond the scope of this book, but it is appropriate to draw attention to the variables it introduces.

The outside temperature usually reaches its lowest point at dawn and its highest in the early afternoon, between 2 and 4 P.M. The interior temperature is kept constant in buildings whose heating or air conditioning is automatically controlled, but it fluctuates in most other buildings. Buildings such as schools and offices that are used only part of the time are often allowed to cool during the night, or at least over the weekend. Residential units, whose occupants all go out to work or school, may cool in winter during the day.

To understand the problems of variable heat flow and the storage of heat, we need to be acquainted with two properties of building materials, their heat capacity per unit volume and their thermal inertia.

The *heat capacity per unit volume* of a material is the product of its density and its specific heat per unit volume; it is measured in MJ/m^3K (or $Btu/ft^3 \cdot °F$).

The *thermal inertia* is partly determined by the heat capacity per unit volume and partly by the thickness of the walls or roof in question. In materials such as brick or concrete, it is much greater than it is for timber or for metal.

When a building is first heated in cold weather after a cooling period, a considerable part of the heat is needed to heat walls with a high thermal inertia. When heating is discontinued, this heat is released gradually. Thus, the thermal inertia reduces the fluctuations in the internal temperature, but it also slows the response of a cold room to heating.

The time taken for heat to flow through a wall can be calculated from its physical properties (see Ref. 6.6). For a wall of galvanized steel sheets, uninsulated, on a steel frame, it takes a fraction of a second. For a wall of timber planks 25 mm (1 in.) thick, it takes about 20 minutes. For a concrete wall 200 mm (8 in.) thick, it takes about 3 hours. For a wall of limestone or marble 1 m (3 ft) thick, it takes about three days.

Where the cost of heating and/or cooling is a major item in the running cost of a building, the choice of material and construction should therefore be made to suit the climatic conditions and the system of heating or cooling control to be used.

REFERENCES

6.1. *ASHRAE Handbook—1981, Fundamentals.* American Society of Heating, Refrigerating, and Air Conditioning Engineers. Atlanta, 1981. Table 1, p. 23.12.
6.2. *Ibid.*, Table 2, pp. 23.12–23.13.
6.3. H. J. Cowan and P. R. Smith: *Environmental Systems.* Van Nostrand Reinhold, New York, 1983, p. 59.
6.4. N. S. Billington: *Thermal Properties of Buildings.* Cleaver-Hume Press, London, 1952, pp. 51–83.
6.5. R. W. R. Muncey: *Heat Transfer Calculations in Buildings.* Applied Science, London, 1979. 110 pp.
6.6. H. J. Cowan and P. R. Smith: *loc. cit.*, pp. 74–75.

SUGGESTIONS FOR FURTHER READING

H. J. Cowan and P. R. Smith: *Environmental Systems.* Van Nostrand Reinhold, New York, 1983. Chapters 3–6.
J. F. van Straaten: *Thermal Performance of Buildings.* Elsevier, London, 1967. 311 pp.
R. M. E. Diamant: *Thermal and Acoustic Insulation of Buildings.* Iliffe, London, 1965. 255 pp.

7

Effect of Fire on Building Materials

Fires can cause great material damage and loss of life. Their avoidance depends to a significant extent on the correct use of building materials.

No material is entirely "fireproof," but some are more fire-resistant than others. It is not possible to avoid the use of materials that are combustible and that generate smoke (which is the major cause of loss of life) without producing buildings that are sterile in appearance. The risk of fire can be greatly reduced, however, by not using combustible materials where they are liable to be ignited by heat sources, by giving fire-retardant treatments to these materials, and by installing fire detectors and/or sprinklers.

Before new materials or methods of construction can be used, their fire endurance must be assessed, usually by a fire test. Special attention must be given to the frame of a multistory building to ensure that it cannot collapse as a result of fire.

7.1 HOW FIRES START IN BUILDINGS

Although automobiles kill more than ten times as many people as do building accidents, the loss of life in the latter is a matter for grave concern, and fires are the largest single cause. More than half the people who die in fires are either children under 6 or elderly people over 65. Most deaths result from suffocation due to lack of oxygen (which has been consumed by the fire).

Fires are predominantly caused by people. The majority start between 10 A.M. and 11 P.M. when most people are awake. About half start in private dwellings. These are not subject to the same rigorous fire prevention legislation as commercial and industrial buildings, or to continuous managerial supervision. More fires break out in old than in new buildings, moreover,

partly because legislation in the past may have been less rigorous, but more particularly because the buildings have been allowed to deteriorate. It is also appropriate to note that more than three-quarters of all deaths occur in people's own homes.

Fires are related to the use of energy. There is an almost linear relationship between the number of fires and the energy use per person. Thus, the highest rate is in the U.S.A., followed by Canada (see Refs. 7.1 and 7.11).

Fires are also related to weather. In hot and windy weather, fires that might otherwise have been confined to one house are likely to spread to other buildings. In very cold weather, there is an increase in the number of fires since occupants tend to use heating systems beyond their normal capacity.

Most fires are small when they start. A person who caused a fire may not necessarily be aware that he did so; he could have dropped a cigarette when falling asleep or knocked over an electric radiator on leaving a room. Some fires go out without any further action; for example, a cigarette may burn a large hole in a carpet without setting the house alight. Other fires may smolder for several hours before becoming dangerous, and during that time they can usually be extinguished with ease. On the other hand, a fire in a room may quickly reach the stage where the occupants cannot control it because they lack either the competence or the equipment.

The process of ignition is repeated several times during the early stages of a fire. Combustible objects, such as furniture or papers, may be set alight by radiation or by the convection of hot gases (Fig. 7.1.1). Many combustible materials—for example, wood— are poor conductors of heat. When a wood surface

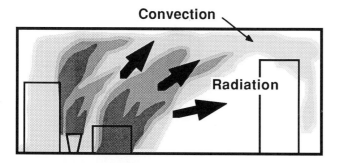

Fig. 7.1.1. Fires can spread to walls and ceilings through radiant heat and through convection currents produced by the heat.

absorbs heat by radiation or convection, the heat transfer by conduction within the wood is slow (see Sec. 6.3) so that the temperature of the heated surface increases quickly.

Furthermore, wood emits flammable vapors at a temperature of about 300°C (about 570°F). A "pilot flame" from a nearby burning object will set these vapors alight and ignite the timber. If the flame is too remote, the gases may ignite spontaneously when their temperature reaches about 500°C (about 930°F). Other combustible materials behave similarly.

7.2 HOW FIRES SPREAD IN BUILDINGS

A fire can spread much faster if it burns on a surface lined with a combustible material. A small fire spreads relatively slowly on a carpet or a wooden *floor,* but when it reaches a *wall* lined with combustible material, it spreads upwards rapidly because the convected heat

above the flame is in contact with the material (Fig. 7.2.1). When it reaches the ceiling, the flames are deflected sideways, and their rate of spread may be increased four or five times (Ref. 7.2).

Many materials generate combustible gases when subjected to great heat; they need not necessarily burn while they do so. These gases are usually lighter than air and collect under the ceiling. If sufficient combustible gases have accumulated, they are ignited when the flames reach the ceiling. The entire room is then likely to be filled with flames so that it becomes impossible to enter it to put the fire out. One of the problems is then to confine the fire to that room.

Larger fires spread more rapidly because they set the walls and the ceiling alight through convection and radiation without having to spread along the floor to reach a wall.

A fire can spread to neighboring rooms either by conduction through the floor to a room above or by conduction through the wall to an adjacent room (Fig. 7.2.2). Most building codes require a minimum insulation for floors, and some codes for walls as well, to prevent this from happening in multistory buildings.

Since fires can spread by convection through staircases (Fig. 7.2.3), fire doors should be installed that close automatically to prevent that. Fire can also spread through elevator shafts (lift wells) to the higher floors of a building, and elevator shaft doors should therefore be fire-resistant and kept closed when not in use.

Windows usually shatter in a severe fire. Since the combustion of flammable gases inside a fiercely burning room may have been restrained by a lack of oxygen and since plenty of oxygen exists outside windows that have been broken, large flames will leap out from them and set the floor above alight unless they are deflected by a spandrel or horizontal projection (Fig. 7.2.4).

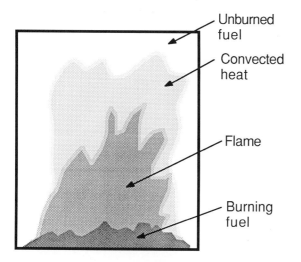

Fig. 7.2.1. When a small fire spreading slowly along the floor reaches a wall lined with combustible material, it will spread upwards on the vertical surface rapidly in the form of flame and convected heat.

Fig. 7.2.2. Transmission of heat by conduction through a floor to the story above and through a wall to an adjacent room.
This can be prevented by providing adequate insulation (Sec. 6.3), or by specifying minimum structural thicknesses, which serve the same purpose.

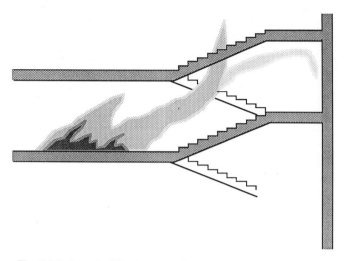

Fig. 7.2.3. Spread of fire by convection through an open staircase. This can be prevented by fire doors leading to the staircase that close automatically at all times, or, alternatively, by doors held back by fusible links that are melted by the heat of a fire.

Fire can also spread by radiation from windows or from a burning roof to other parts of the same building or to nearby buildings (Fig. 7.2.5).

Finally, fire can spread by flying embers of burning wood, which may come from burning roof timber or from burning trees. This is a particular problem in bush or forest fires. The remedy is to avoid platforms and gutters where leaves and other combustible material can lodge and where embers might come to rest and also to make the roof and any wall surfaces noncombustible or, failing that, to protect them by drenching them with water.

7.3 SMOKE

Most of the material damage done by a fire is due to combustion, although the damage done by the water used to extinguish a small fire may exceed that caused by the fire itself. Any loss of life that occurs is more the result of the effects of the smoke produced, however, than of the heat or flames generated by the fire. (Precisely how people are killed by smoke is still a matter for conjecture.)

Fig. 7.2.4. Spread of fire through windows.
In a multistory building, the spread of fire to the story above can be delayed, and perhaps prevented, either (a) by having a spandrel (an upstand fire-resistant wall) under the window, or (b) by a horizontal projection of fire-resistant material, which can also serve as a balcony or as a sunscreen. If there is neither a fire-resistant spandrel nor a fire-resistant horizontal projection of adequate size, the flames emerging from the broken windows of the lower story will shatter the windows of the story above (c) so that the fire spreads to that story.

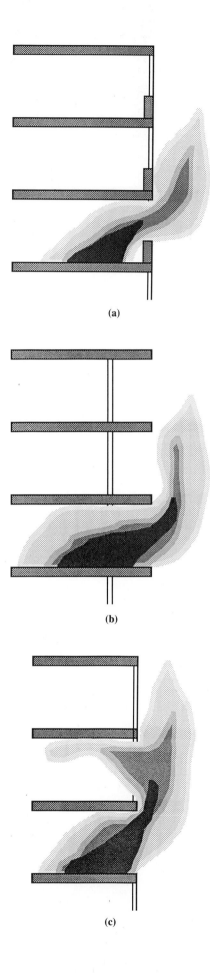

(a)

(b)

(c)

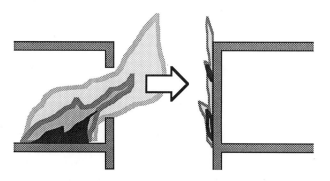

Fig. 7.2.5. Spread of fire by radiation from one part of a building through the outside air to an adjacent part or to a building opposite.

Some materials used in buildings are capable of producing highly poisonous gases under laboratory conditions. Wool and silk can produce hydrogen cyanide when burned; rigid polyurethane foam can produce both hydrogen cyanide and tolylene diisocyanate. It is also possible to produce phosgene ($COCl_2$)—one of the poison gases used during the First World War—from plastics containing chlorine. There is, however, no definite evidence that any of these gases are produced in significant quantities in building fires (see Ref. 7.11). Firefighters have other preoccupations while a fire is active, and the gases are too fleeting to be detected afterwards.

There is no doubt, however, that a fire burning in a confined space depletes the oxygen supply to a dangerously low level. Carbon is present in wood, wallpaper, and plastics. Its normal combustion product is carbon dioxide, but carbon monoxide, which is poisonous, forms if there is insufficient oxygen.

Wood and paper burn with very little smoke when there is plenty of oxygen. Thick smoke and soot (which is carbon that has not been burned) are produced especially when the supply of oxygen is limited. Smoke traps people by making it impossible for them to see where they are going. Various constituents of smoke irritate nose, eyes, and throat, and, with increasing combustion, the lack of oxygen and the formation of carbon monoxide can bring about death.

It is vital to facilitate escape by providing emergency exit signs at frequent intervals that are lit by a power supply connected to an emergency electric system, and to provide fire doors that close automatically when a fire is detected by smoke detectors (see Sec. 7.4). In multistory buildings, fire stairs and refuge areas should be protected from smoke by excess air pressure, generated by putting the airconditioning system in a "smoke-exhaust" mode, and using power, if need be, from an emergency electric generator. The excess air pressure prevents the entry of smoke and thus keeps the escape routes and refuge areas free for escape.

In the present state of our knowledge, there appears to be no reason for prohibiting the use of materials merely because they can, under certain conditions, produce poisonous gases during combustion. The combustible and flammable nature of certain materials should be borne in mind, however, and appropriate safety measures taken, for example, by treating them with fire retardants (see Sec. 7.6).

Smoke vents are installed in the *roofs* of single-story factories (Ref. 7.3), but it is not practicable to install them in the *walls* of multistory buildings since they would admit a fresh supply of oxygen and thus promote combustion.

7.4 FIRE DETECTORS AND SPRINKLERS

Since most fires start small and can easily be extinguished in their early stages, advantages accrue from installing devices that can detect them swiftly and/or others that can extinguish them. Obviously, the cost of these devices must be balanced against the correspondingly reduced risk of fire.

Fire detectors may be activated by a rise in temperature, by the appearance of a flame, by the appearance of flammable vapors, or by the production of smoke. Heat detectors may utilize fusible links, bimetallic strips that deflect when the temperature increases, thermocouples, or thermistors. Flame detectors measure reflected radiation. Detectors of flammable vapors operate on a catalytic principle. The older type of smoke detectors employ a beam of light that shines on a photovoltaic cell and is interrupted by smoke. The more sensitive smoke detectors contain a small quantity of radioactive substance that ionizes the air; combustion products reduce the current flowing through the ionized air, thereby setting off the alarm. Smoke detectors are now the most commonly used fire alarms because smoke can be detected before flame and heat.

In most multistory buildings, stores, and factory buildings, sprinkler systems are installed in addition to fire detectors. These consist of water pipes closed by sprinkler heads (Ref. 7.4) at intervals of 3 to 5 m (10 to 16 ft), which spray the floor once opened. The sprinkler head is opened automatically by a fusible link or by a glass bulb filled with a liquid with high thermal expansion when the temperature rises above a specified level, usually 65°C (150°F). Only a few sprinklers are opened if the area of the fire is limited, and this restriction minimizes the water damage. The operation of a sprinkler head also operates an alarm that alerts the fire department.

Fire fighting is beyond the scope of this book. Reference should be made to a specialized text (see, for example Ref. 7.5).

7.5 SOFTENING, DISINTEGRATION, AND COMBUSTION OF MATERIALS

Clay brick, limestone, and *marble* are the most stable materials in a fire; they do not burn, soften, or disintegrate at the highest temperatures likely to be encountered in a building fire (see Sec. 7.7).

Concrete is also an excellent material for fire resistance provided the aggregate does not contain silica (which is silicon dioxide). At about 300°C (about 575°F), concrete turns pink or red with some loss of strength; at about 600°C (about 1100°F), its strength is seriously impaired. However, as concrete is normally used in thick sections (by comparison with metal or plaster) and has a low thermal conductivity (see Table 3.1), the damage to it during a normal fire is likely to be superficial, although subsequent repair may be costly.

Silica undergoes a change from its alpha to its beta phase at about 600°C (about 1100°F), and if this temperature is reached on the *surface* of the concrete, siliceous aggregates are liable to cause spalling. This may lead to exposure of the steel in reinforced concrete, and consequently to its structural failure (see below). Limestones and basic igneous rocks (such as dolerite) do not contain free silica, but acid igneous rocks (such as granite) do, and many gravels consist almost entirely of silica.

Wood becomes overdry, discolors, and distorts if the temperature rises above 100°C (212°F). At a temperature of about 300°C (about 570°F), it may ignite spontaneously.

Softwood burns more readily than hardwood. Both generate an appreciable amount of smoke and some (poisonous) carbon monoxide, particularly if burnt in a restricted supply of air (Sec. 7.3). Burning wood forms a layer of charcoal on the burnt surface that insulates the unburnt wood and slows down and eventually brings its combustion to a halt. Although small timber sections will burn up completely, large beams and columns may survive a fire still capable of bearing their full load; indeed, they may have a greater fire endurance than unprotected steel sections.

Fiber boards—such as insulating boards, particle boards, and hardboards—are derived from wood fibers and are thus combustible; the rate of flame spread, however, varies according to their density. Their fire resistance can be greatly improved by impregnating them with a fire retardant (Sec. 7.6) or by coating them with an incombustible material, such as plaster or a fire-retardant paint.

The term *plastics* (Chapter 18) covers a wide range of products with very different resistances to fire. They behave differently from traditional building materials in many respects, as two disastrous fires one—at the Cinq-Sept dance hall in the small French town of St. Laurent-du-Pont in November 1970 and another at the Summerland Leisure Complex in Douglas on the Isle of Man, off the west coast of England, in August 1973—showed (Ref. 7.6).

Some plastics produce combustible vapors in quantities greater than are necessary to sustain combustion so that a fire of this sort, once started, continues to burn until the available fuel is exhausted. Some burning thermoplastics melt and throw off drops that can spread the fire.

Some plastics produce a great deal of smoke. Others are virtually incombustible. Some of the latter, referred to as *intumescent,* are converted into a swollen carbonaceous mass as they burn; this mass acts as an insulator and inhibits further combustion to the point of making these materials self-extinguishing.

Silicones, rigid polyvinyl chloride (PVC), polytetrafluorethylene (PTFE), and the melamine laminates have substantial fire resistance. Cellulosic plastics, polyethylenes, polypropylenes, polystyrenes, and acryclics, on the other hand, pose a fire risk unless treated with fire retardants (Sec. 7.6).

The same duality applies to *fabrics.* Untreated natural fabrics, such as cotton and wool, will burn, and some synthetics are liable to melt as they burn. It is possible, however, to improve their resistance with fire-retardant treatments.

Metals present no problem in a fire unless they serve a structural purpose. Their high thermal conductivity (see Table 3.1) ensures adequate heat transfer from any surfaces heated by the fire. Both their melting points and ignition temperatures are higher than those likely to be encountered in most fires (Sec. 7.7). The only exception is lead (still occasionally used for roofs and gutters), which may melt in a severe fire.

Single-story structures have less rigorous requirements for structural fire protection, because the occupants of the building can make their escape on the same level. (see Sec. 7.7). Consequently, bare structural steel and bare structural aluminum can be used for single-story structures and that gives them an economic advantage.

Structural fire protection is needed for multistory structures. The economic advantages of aluminum structures (see Chap. 11) are lost if the metal needs to be covered for fire protection. Structural steel, on the other hand, is still economical, and there are several methods for protecting it.

Steel does not melt until its temperature exceeds 1500°C (2700°F)—a temperature most unlikely to be reached in a building fire—but a structural-steel or a reinforced-concrete frame can *collapse* at a much lower temperature because of the loss of strength of the former or of the reinforcing steel in the latter. The critical temperature is usually taken as that which halves the strength of steel; because the factor of safety used in the design of steel and reinforced-concrete structures is approximately 2, the structure is liable to collapse under the action of the loads it is actually supporting when its strength is halved. For structural steel, this critical temperature is about 500°C (about 930°F); for high-tensile steel, it is the same or a little lower.

Structural steel and the steel in reinforced and pre-stressed concrete needs sufficient thermal insulation, therefore, to ensure that, during the time a fire burns (see Sec. 7.7), the temperature of the steel remains below the critical temperature. In reinforced and pre-stressed concrete, this goal is accomplished by providing an adequate concrete cover, one that ranges from 20 mm (3/4 in.) for concrete slabs reinforced with small-diameter bars to 50 mm (2 in.) for columns.

Ordinary concrete that is 50 mm (2 in.) thick can also be used as fire protection for steel sections, but it adds considerably to their weight. Alternatively, lightweight concrete made with gas bubbles (aerated concrete) or with lightweight aggregate can be used; suitable lightweight aggregates are perlite (a siliceous volcanic rock whose original volume has been expanded about 20 times by heating) and exfoliated vermiculite (a mixture of hydrous silicates of aluminum, magnesium, and iron in the form of thin plates that expand to many times their original volume on being heated).

It is now more common to provide fire protection to steel structures with a sprayed coating, a method that avoids the use of formwork. The coating consists of mineral insulating fibers, or of perlite or vermiculite in gypsum plaster. The thickness is of the order of 50 mm (2 in.) but depends on the composition of the sprayed coat and the degree of fire resistance required.

7.6 FIRE RETARDANTS

Fire retardants have been used since ancient times. The Romans treated the timber of their assault batteries with alum to protect them from incendiary missiles. Since the eighteenth century, two kinds of fire retardants have been in common use for protecting wood. Timber was either given an incombustible covering, such as gypsum plaster or sheet metal, or it was soaked in a proprietary compound. A favorite composition was Wood's Liquid, which contained alum, borax, and ferrous sulfate.

During the last few decades, the technology of fire retardants has greatly improved, and many fabrics and plastics are now routinely treated to make them more fire-resistant. Modern fire retardants are based on halogens (mainly chlorine), phosphorus, nitrogen, and antimony. The chemistry of the compounds and their action in fire is complex; reference should be made to a specialist text (for example, see Refs. 7.7 and 7.8).

Fire-retardant paints (see Sec. 19.3) are used in buildings particularly to protect wood. They are usually applied in several coats, the first of which is often intumescent, that is, it swells on heating to form a thick viscous foam that acts as an insulant. Since this does not weather well, it is covered with more weather-resistant paints containing soluble compounds of chlorine and antimony. The time required for the ignition of wood can be increased up to three times that for wood painted with untreated paints (Ref. 7.9).

7.7 FIRE LOADS AND FIRE TESTS

The design of buildings in relation to fire aims to prevent loss of life as far as is possible and to prevent the spread of fire to other buildings. It has to be accepted that fires will occur in any case and that some material loss will result.

Different rules apply to single-story and multistory buildings because people can walk out of a single-story building in case of fire but must use a staircase to evacuate a multistory building. An exception is usually made for single-family dwellings that have no more than one story above and/or below ground. These buildings do not require structural fire protection. On the other hand, a two-story motel requires such protection (see Sec. 7.5), as do all multistory buildings. This means that the steel used in any structural steel-work must have adequate insulation and that the steel used in any reinforced or prestressed concrete must have adequate cover to prevent loss of strength for the duration of the fire. It has to be assumed that it may not be possible to extinguish the fire and that it will continue to burn until the combustible materials are exhausted.

Buildings above 50 m (150 ft) in height present a special problem, because they are taller than the tallest turntable ladder used by fire departments, making it impossible to rescue people through windows. At the present time, elevators (lifts) are not used for evacuating people from buildings during a fire, and it is not practicable to walk down 60 or more flights of stairs under such circumstances. High-rise buildings therefore rely on refuge areas to which the occupants of the building can be directed. These are protected from fire by well-insulated floors, walls, and ceilings, and from smoke by an excess air pressure produced, if need be, by an emergency electric generator.

The concept of *fire load* was developed by S. H. Ingberg in the U.S.A. in 1928 (Ref. 7.10). This is not a load in the conventional sense, but the heat that would be generated if all the contents of a room were burned. In the 1920s, most combustible materials consisted of timber or timber derivatives, such as paper, and the fire load was expressed as the mass of combustible material per unit floor area in kg/m² or in lb/ft². The range of combustible materials is now more varied, and fire loads are usually quoted in terms of the heat produced in MJ/m² or in Btu/ft².

Surveys have been made from time to time to estimate the amount of combustible material for various occupancies, such as offices, libraries, and department stores, and these form the basis of building codes. Fire tests were then made of model rooms to determine how long it took to burn the contents of a room and how fast the temperature rose in the process. The standard temperature–time curves (Fig. 7.7.1) are based on these tests. If the contents of a room burn, say, for two hours, then its structure requires a two-hour

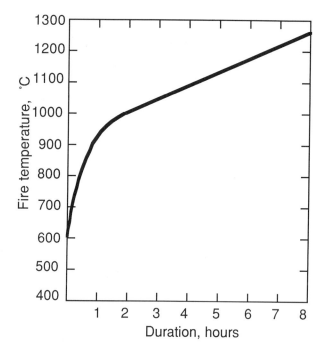

Fig. 7.7.1. Standard temperature–time curve used in the U.S.A. and Canada for testing building materials.
The curve was determined from measurements during a fire produced in a model test room containing the furniture and other contents normally expected in an office building. The standard temperature–time curves used for fire tests in other countries are similar, but not identical.

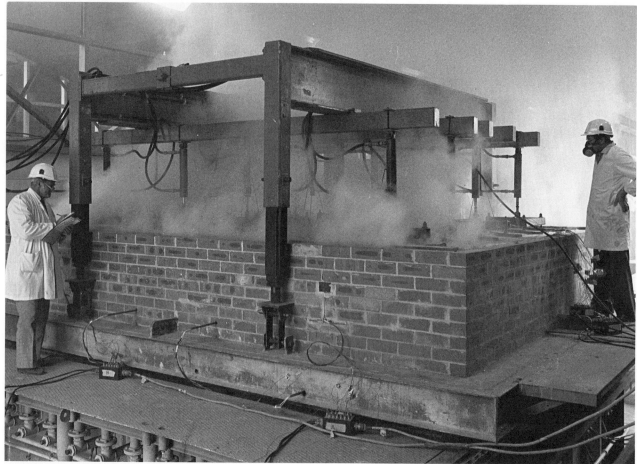

Fig. 7.7.2. Fire resistance test.
Timber floor structure under simulated load during fire resistance test on a horizontal furnace (*courtesy of the National Building Technology Centre, Sydney, Australia.*)

fire resistance, or *rating*. Generally, one and one-half hours of fire resistance are required for apartment buildings, two hours for office buildings, three hours for department stores, and four hours or more for warehouses.

Fire test furnaces have been constructed in fire-testing laboratories (Fig. 7.7.2) that develop temperatures at the rate of the standard temperature–time curve; here, building components are tested to check whether they survive for the specified time (say, two hours).

Fire-resistance ratings for simple assemblies of materials can be predicted from theoretical calculations, but most new materials and forms of construction must be evaluated by tests to determine a reliable rating.

REFERENCES

7.1. E. W. Marchant (Ed.): *A Complete Guide to Fire in Buildings.* Medical and Technical Publishing Co., Lancaster (England), 1973. *Chapter 1:* The Fire Hazard. pp. 1–17.

7.2. G. L. Langdon-Thomas: *Fire Safety in Buildings.* A. and C. Black, London, 1972, p. 34.

7.3. H. J. Cowan and P. R. Smith: *Environmental Systems.* Van Nostrand Reinhold, New York, 1983, p. 126.

7.4. *Ibid.,* p. 124.

7.5. E. W. Marchant: *loc. cit.* Chapters 4–7, pp. 59–109.

7.6. H. J. Cowan and P. R. Smith: *loc. cit.* p. 120.

7.7. P. Thiery: *Fireproofing.* Elsevier, Amsterdam, 1970. 156 pp.

7.8. M. Lewin, S. M. Atlas, and E. M. Pearce (Eds.): *Flame-Retardant Polymeric Materials.* Plenum Press, New York, 1978. 333 pp.

7.9. A. W. Marchant: *loc. cit.* pp. 33–34.

7.10. S. H. Ingberg: Tests on the severity of building fires. *National Fire Protection Association Quarterly,* Vol. 22, No. 1 (1928), pp. 43–61.

7.11. Margaret Law (Ed.): *Fire.* Chapter 4 in *Tall Buildings—Criteria and Loading.* American Society of Civil Engineers, New York, 1980. pp. 219–290.

SUGGESTIONS FOR FURTHER READING

G. L. Langdon-Thomas: *Fire Safety in Buildings.* A. and C. Black, London, 1972. 296 pp.

T. T. Lie: *Fire and Buildings.* Applied Science, London, 1972. 276 pp.

Building Research Station: *Fire Control.* Construction Press, London 1978. 255 pp.

8

Durability

Some building materials are likely to last as long as their building does whereas others will require periodic replacement. In life-cycle costing, the cost of such replacement is taken into account, but it is a matter of opinion whether the choice of a material should be based on its initial cost or its life-cycle cost.

Durability is affected by *changes* in the weather, such as cycles of wetting and drying, or freezing and thawing. Ultraviolet radiation damages many plastics, and corrosion (rusting) is a particular problem with steel. Timber must be protected from dry rot and from termites. Concrete requires careful detailing to prevent the formation of dark streaks. Abrasion resistance must be considered when choosing materials for floors.

Prediction of durability can be aided by tests with weatherometers and wear-testing machines, but more reliable results are obtained by exposure tests in which the time scale is not foreshortened.

8.1 PRESENT COST OR LIFE-CYCLE COST?

Some materials—for example, glazed tile and stainless steel sheet—are extremely durable; once installed in a new building, they may not require renewal during its entire life. Other materials, such as paint and galvanized steel sheet, will need renewal several times during its life. Is it then cheaper to use galvanized steel or stainless steel for the rain gutters? Is it cheaper to use glazed tiles or painted plaster?

In estimating a building on present cost, the maintenance is ignored, or at least not formally considered. In life-cycle costing, the capitalized cost of the maintenance during the entire life of the building is estimated to obtain the total cost. Many materials that require frequent renewal or maintenance have a far higher life-cycle cost than others that cost much more initially,

but require no maintenance. Thus, it is likely that stainless-steel gutters and glazed tiles will have a lower life-cycle cost but galvanized-steel gutters and painted plaster the lower initial cost.

For an owner who is likely to retain a building for its entire estimated useful life—say 80 years—it would be sensible to make the decision of the choice of material on the basis of the lowest life-cycle cost. He may deliberately choose to do otherwise, however, because money is in short supply or because the manager who will reap the benefit of a wise initial investment will be somebody else.

For the owner of a private house, it may actually be unwise to use life-cycle costing. The average period of occupancy in America, Western Europe, and Australia is about seven years. It is unlikely that the sale price of a house will be significantly higher because it has stainless-steel gutters, although glazed tiles might raise the price. If the owner expects to remain in the house for the rest of his life, on the other hand, he would benefit from the use of durable materials provided he can find the money for the higher initial cost.

8.2 EFFECT OF CHANGES IN THE WEATHER

High or low *temperatures* and high or low *humidities* in themselves do not cause significant damage to building materials, but *changes* in temperature and humidity do. Thermal expansion and contraction can cause cracks in brittle materials and so can moisture movement, as shown in Fig. 8.2.1 (see also Secs. 3.3 and 3.4). The alternate wetting and drying that takes place during and after rain can also cause appreciable damage, particularly to materials that absorb some of the water.

Some bricks and natural stones contain soluble salts that rain water can bring to the surface, where they

Fig. 8.2.1. Cracks in brick wall due to temperature and moisture movement.
Failure occurs under the window where the wall has been weakened by the window opening which is shown at the top of the figure.

form *efflorescence*. This can usually be removed with a brush. Efflorescence may also occur on concrete containing unsuitable aggregates.

Limestone, calcareous sandstone, and gypsum plaster are very slowly *dissolved by rainwater*. This process is speeded up if the water contains a little acid; for example, sulfur dioxide produced by coal-burning heat engines and discharged into the air turns into sulfuric acid, which turns the rain into "acid rain." The solubility of limestone is also a problem in a dirt-laden atmosphere if some of the stone is protected from the rain; this part will then accumulate the dirt and turn black, whereas the rest of the limestone will be washed clean by the rain and remain white.

Most climatic zones experience a substantial number of days when the temperature at night drops below the freezing point (0°C or 32°F) and rises above it during daytime. Since ice has a greater volume than water, these cycles of *freezing and thawing* can be very damaging to materials that are both porous and brittle.

The spectrum of solar radiation includes both infrared (heat) radiation with a longer wavelength and ultraviolet radiation with a shorter wavelength; both overlap with visible light (Sec. 5.1). *Heat radiation* can produce overheating of some materials. Thus, bituminous flat roofs are usually covered either with a thin layer of light-colored paint or white stone chips to reflect some of the radiation or with a thicker layer of gravel. *Ultraviolet radiation* is a major cause of deterioration of certain plastics, and some of these cannot be used if they are to be exposed to sunlight.

Sunlight fades certain pigments, mostly those of organic origin, and these should not be used externally either in paints or for coloring anodized aluminum. Sunlight is also a major cause of the breakdown of paint film, which is further accelerated by the thermal movement that occurs (Fig. 8.2.2).

Iron and steel corrode in the presence of moisture by forming *rust,* the common term for hydrated iron oxide ($2Fe_2O_3 \cdot 3H_2O$), unless the climate is extremely dry. Rusting is prevented by galvanizing, sherardizing, or terne-coating (see Sec. 10.3) or by painting the metal with a rust-inhibiting paint (Fig. 8.2.3).

The reinforcement in concrete must be protected by an adequate cover of concrete; if this is insufficient, spalling may occur (Fig. 8.2.4).

The weathering problems of the individual materials mentioned here are discussed in more detail in the appropriate chapters of Part II.

Fig. 8.2.2. Breakdown of paint on a timber post exposed to the sun.

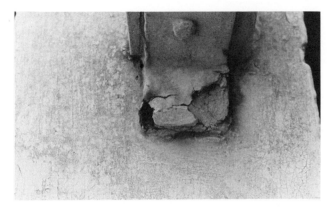

Fig. 8.2.3. Rusting of metal angle due to failure to use a rust-inhibiting paint in the undercoat.

Fig. 8.2.4. Spalling of concrete caused by rusting of the reinforcement, in turn caused by inadequate concrete cover.

8.3 DAMAGE BY BIOLOGICAL AND CHEMICAL ACTION

Timber is susceptible to attack by fungi and insects. The most serious form of fungal decay is *dry rot;* this is caused by a group of fungi, among them *merulius lacrymans.* It is likely that some timber in a building will be infected with the fungus, which will grow when it has sufficient air, warmth, water, and food. Timber not in contact with moisture from the ground can therefore be protected by keeping its moisture content low through a suitable damp-proof course and, if exposed externally, by a suitable paint. Timber dug into the ground, in the form of wooden piles or fence posts, say, is protected by treating it with a preservative that renders it toxic and thus deprives the fungi of food. Wooden shingles are also subject to frequent wetting but are not normally treated with preservative because of the possible staining of the timber below. The shingles are thin enough to dry quickly, and the wood normally used, such as cedar, is relatively resistant to fungal attack.

Timber is also subject to attack by certain *wood-boring beetles,* and timber so infected must be treated with appropriate chemicals. A more serious problem occurs in the tropics and subtropics where wood is liable to be attacked by *termites,* or white ants. Termites live below ground, or sometimes in huge mounds of earth above ground. They shun light, and if they must come to the surface, build "tunnels" of earth held together by a secretion. Since these are clearly visible, the termite colony can be poisoned by arsenic. Termites can usually find cracks in brickwork and concrete in which to build their tunnels without being seen, but a termite shield (see Fig. 16.7.1) of galvanized iron above the brick or stone foundation, but below the lowest timber, discourages them (if they go over the shield, they leave a visible track). Certain timbers are naturally resistant to termites because they are not found palatable; such timbers are particularly suitable for floor structures in single-story houses.

Birds in large numbers can damage buildings with their droppings. This is a particular problem in old buildings with cornices and other projecting ledges on which birds can spend the night. The pigeons of the Piazza San Marco in Venice and of Trafalgar Square in London may be charming to tourists but prove a serious nuisance to the maintenance staffs of surrounding buildings.

The *mosses* and *lichen* that grow on natural stone and brick may do slight surface damage but are generally considered as a sign of graceful aging rather than as an attack on the material. There is, however, some doubt about the extent to which *ivy* ought to be permitted to grow on buildings. It is regarded with some affection in Britain and in America, where it covers the old buildings of some of the most prestigious universities. In a warm, humid climate it can grow too luxuriously, however, and harbor vermin. The suction pods can also be quite destructive to the joints in masonry.

The dark stains and streaks that occur on many concrete surfaces (Fig. 8.3.1) are partly biological and partly chemical. A variety of algae can grow on concrete; these derive their energy from solar radiation, but need rain water for survival. Mildew and moulds, on the other hand, are small fungi that live on decaying organic matter.

Chemical discoloration occurs at joints in the formwork that allow moisture to escape from wet concrete. This flow brings the darker tetracalcium aluminoferrite component of the cement (see Sec. 13.3) to the surface, causing a dark stain. Discoloration is also encouraged by smooth formwork because this results in the formation of a cement-rich laitance (see Sec. 14.11) that crazes easily and collects dirt in its cracks.

Fig. 8.3.1. Dark irregular streaks on concrete caused by rainwater.

The main cause of the discoloration to be observed on a regrettably large number of concrete surfaces is wind-blown soot and dirt, which, when unevenly washed by rainwater, produces irregular streaks. The remedy is, first, to use a more suitable surface finish for the concrete (Sec. 14.11), and, second, to prevent uneven streaking of water over the surface. This can be done either by including projecting copings or sills in the design or by including channels in the surface that keep the rainwater running along defined and invariably repeated paths.

8.4 EROSION, ABRASION, AND WEAR

Erosion of external walls is caused by wind-driven particles of sand. It occurs comparatively rarely since it requires high wind velocities or the formation of eddies, a supply of sand or dust, and soft material in the wall. The main damage is to old buildings that contain deteriorating stone or brick. *Abrasion* is the damage caused by fine solid particles to floor surfaces. *Wear* is a more complex phenomenon that is caused partly by abrasion, but also by compression and by impact. Carpeting, for example, is frequently damaged more by the permanent impression made by heavy pieces of furniture than by abrasion. It is relatively simple to test abrasion resistance, however, and many machines for testing accelerated wear are simply abrasion-testing machines.

Concrete is one of the best floor surfaces for industrial use, and it can be further improved by using a hard aggregate at least for the surface layer. Cast iron tiles may be appropriate for conditions of extreme wear.

Quarry tiles, which are hard-burned, unglazed clay tiles, provide one of the hardest wearing surfaces for commercial and domestic buildings. Tile and stone floors provide heat storage for passive solar design (see Sec. 6.5).

Many kinds of timber, including softwoods, have good wear resistance. When used as a wearing surface, timber is usually polished, and it is the polish that receives the wear, rather then the timber itself.

Linoleum, which is made from oxidized linseed oil and a filler, is being replaced more and more by synthetics, such as polyvinyl chloride (PVC).

Carpeting is used increasingly, both for offices and for homes, because its relative cost has been greatly reduced by modern manufacturing processes that enable the entire floor to be covered wall to wall (see Sec. 18.7). Carpet provides a comfortable walking surface; it is easier to clean than a hard surface; and it is a good thermal insulator and an excellent absorber of impact sound (see Chap. 9).

Wear resistance is also required for table surfaces, notably writing desks and kitchen work surfaces. The development of laminates based on melamine formaldehyde that are extremely resistant to heat and wear has virtually replaced a variety of materials used previously but either more expensive or less satisfactory.

8.5 PREDICTING THE PERFORMANCE OF BUILDING MATERIALS

The only really reliable durability test is one in which the material is exposed to the weather for a reasonable period of time. This was already recognized in Ancient Rome. Vitruvius, who wrote in the first century B.C., recommended the following test for natural stone (Ref. 8.1):

> There are several quarries called Anician in the territory of the Tarquinii. . . . This stone has innumerable good qualities. . . . But since, on account of the proximity of the stone-quarries of Grotta Rossa, Palla, and others, that are nearest to the city, necessity drives us to make use of their products, we must proceed as follows, if we wish our work to be finished without flaws.
>
> Let the stone be taken from the quarry two years before building is to begin, and not in winter, but in summer. Then let it lie exposed in an open place. Such stone as has been damaged by the two years of exposure should be used in the foundations. The rest, which remains unhurt, has passed the test of nature and will endure in those parts of the building which are above ground.

This type of test was still used in the nineteenth century. Today, when materials are manufactured rather than quarried, we are generally content with testing representative samples. The problem arises, however, when a new material is introduced. In the case of natural stone, it is reasonable to argue that if it survives the freezing and thawing of two winters, it will endure for centuries. In the case of a new plastic, the problem may be exposure to ultraviolet radiation, and, if the material is to last for 20 years, then it may have to be given the equivalent exposure.

The only reliable method is to place the material samples on a rack in the open air, together with a set of weather recording instruments, leave them there for an appropriate number of years, and observe the deterioration, if any, at intervals. This method, however, does not help if one wishes to make a quick decision on the suitability of the material.

Weatherometers have been designed for the purpose of speeding up the weather. There are many different types, of which the one shown in Fig. 8.5.1 may serve as an example. Weatherometers can subject the material to various weather cycles, alone or in combination. These include alternate thawing and freezing; alternate

heating and cooling; alternation of sprayed water (rain) and drying; light plus infrared plus ultraviolet radiation alternating with darkness; air pressure or air suction representing wind; and the effect of air pollution by mixing some sulfuric acid with water spray to imitate acid rain. It is possible to reproduce the weather cycles of a year in a few days.

Weatherometer tests are not sufficiently accurate to produce a reliable prediction of weathering properties directly, but they are useful for predicting performance by comparing the test result of a known material with that of a new material. For example, if data are available of a test in a particular weatherometer of a transparent fiberglass roof sheet that has performed satisfactorily over a number of years, we can test a new sheet of a similar plastic in the same weatherometer and assume that it will also perform well if its test result is no worse. We cannot compare a test on a transparent corrugated fiberglass sheet with one on a corrugated galvanized steel sheet, however, because the two materials are too different.

Similar problems arise in testing for wear. The most reliable method is to put a number of materials on the floor of a corridor without side doors so that everybody who enters the corridor must pass along its entire length. The test should include a couple of materials of known performance to provide a comparison: one with a high and one with only a moderate wear resistance. The number of people walking over the materials can be counted by the interruptions of a light shining on a photovoltaic cell. If the corridor carries heavy traffic, a useful result will be available after a few years.

Wear testing machines speed up the process. Most machines for testing wear are straight abrasion machines, which blow or rub corundum or carborundum over the test specimen. Some also apply pressure and/or impact. The loss of weight of the test specimen is then measured. These machines are much simpler than weatherometers, and they certainly measure abrasion resistance. To that extent they are reliable in comparing the wear resistance of two specimens of softwood or of two specimens of concrete. They would be far less reliable, however, in comparing the wear resistance of a specimen of wood and one of concrete.

Tests of compressive or tensile strength (see Sec. 2.8) offer a good guide to durability. If the strength of a material declines from its norm, its durability is also likely to be affected adversely. Since strength tests are easily performed and give reliable results, they are used as control tests for material quality even when strength is not a primary requirement.

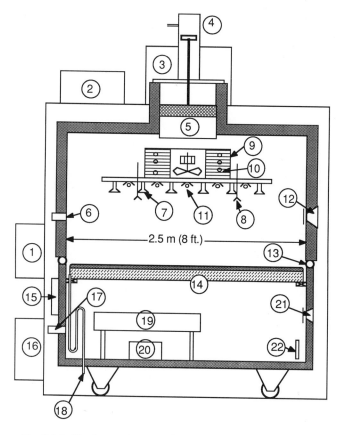

Fig. 8.5.1. Weatherometer.
Different weatherometers are constructed for different materials and environments, this particular machine being used for testing roofing materials in Norway. UPPER BOX: 1. Temperature controller and sequence timer; 2. Cooling apparatus; 3. Instrument panel; 4. Pneumatic cylinder; 5. Air-pressure pulsator; 6. Air suction; 7. Infrared lamps; 8. Waterspray; 9. Air cooler; 10. Heating elements; 11. Ultraviolet tubes; 12. Inspection window; 13. Inflatable rubber hose. LOWER BOX: 14. Roof section undergoing test; 15. Instrument panel; 16. Cooling apparatus; 17. Air-pressure inlet; 18. Water outlet; 19. Air cooler with heating elements; 20. Humidifier; 21. Inspection window; 22. Hygrostat. (*Reproduced from Ref. 8.2. by courtesy of the Norwegian Building Research Institute.*)

REFERENCES

8.1. Marcus Vitruvius Pollio. (Transl. by M. Morgan): *The Ten Books of Architecture.* Dover, New York, 1960, p. 50.

8.2. T. Gjelsk: Large Scale Test Facilities for Durability Studies in Scandinavia. *Rapport 97*. Norges Byggforskningsinstitutt, Trondheim, 1985, p. 16.

SUGGESTIONS FOR FURTHER READING

J. W. Simpson and P. J. Horrobin (Eds.): *The Weathering and Performance of Building Materials*. Medical and Technical Publishing Co., Aylesbury (England), 1970. 286 pp.

R. M. E. Diamant: *The Prevention of Corrosion*. Business Books, London, 1971. 199 pp.

A. J. M. Siemens, A. C. W. M. Vrouwenwelder and A. van den Beukel: Durability of buildings: a reliability analysis. *Heron*, Vol. 30 (1985), No. 3, pp. 1–48.

International Journal: *Durability of Building Materials*, published by Elsevier, Amsterdam, since 1981.

9

Acoustic Properties of Building Materials

Noise control is becoming an increasingly important part of the design of buildings. Air-borne noise can be reduced near its source by sound-absorbing materials, and it can be further attenuated by sound-insulating walls, floors, and roofs. Impact noise can be reduced only by interrupting the transmission path—for example, by floating a floor on a blanket or resilient material.

Materials for auditoria must be chosen to provide sound reflection and sound absorption where each is required.

9.1 NOISE AND ITS MEASUREMENT

Noise is made mostly by people or by machines that people use. The population explosion and the consequent growth of large cities have accentuated the noise problem. The term "noise pollution" is an emotive term that came into use only recently. It indicates the strong feelings that avoidable noise arouses today among many people who consider noise control to be a necessary part of a civilized life. Hence, acoustic properties have become a more important criterion in the choice of building materials than they have ever been.

It is better to use sound absorbing and sound-insulating materials as part of the original construction than to add them subsequently to improve noise attenuation (that is, reduction of noise).

Sound is caused by vibrations or waves in any elastic substance. It travels at a velocity of 343 m/s (1125 ft/s) in air at sea level. Although this is the relevant velocity for air-borne noise, sound travels much faster in solids. For example, the velocity of sound in structural steel is about 5000 m/s, which is relevant for

structure-borne impact noise (see Sec. 9.3). This is still much slower, however, than the velocity of the electromagnetic waves that transmit light and thermal radiation, which is 300,000,000 m/s (see Sec. 5.1). The velocity of both electromagnetic waves and sound waves is defined as follows:

$$\text{Wave velocity} = \text{Wave length} \times \text{Frequency} \quad (9.1)$$

Although light waves are usually identified by their wavelength, it is customary to identify sound waves by their frequency.

The human ear responds to frequencies from about 20 to about 20,000 Hz, corresponding to wavelengths from 17 m to 17 mm. Frequencies above 20,000 Hz are called *ultrasonic*, although some animals can hear within that range. The notes of a modern piano range in frequency from 28 to 4,186 Hz. Sounds above 10,000 Hz are of no significance for the design of buildings.

The vibrations that cause sound produce a change of air pressure. Our hearing is the response of the ear to that change in pressure. The threshold of audibility for most people between the ages of 3 and 40 is about 20×10^{-6} Pa, and the ear begins to hurt at a sound pressure of about 20 Pa (0.4 lb/ft^2). This is still a very small pressure; for comparison, standard atmospheric pressure is 101,325 Pa (2,116 lb/ft^2).

Sound pressure can be measured in pascals (Pa) or pounds per square foot, but because the range of audible sound pressures is about one million to one, it is more convenient to use a logarithmic scale with units called *decibels* (dB).

The decibel scale compares two sounds and therefore, by itself is not an absolute scale. To turn it into an absolute scale, it is related to an internationally standardized *threshold of hearing,* which is called zero decibels (0 dB). Approximate noise levels in decibels are given in Table 9.1.

Sound pressures are measured with a sound level meter. This instrument contains a microphone whose output is amplified and measured with a voltmeter calibrated in decibels. It can be set to a "fast" response, to measure the maximum value of a fluctuating noise, or to a "slow" response, to measure the average noise level.

Because the response of the ear varies with the frequency of sound, the better sound-level meters have built-in weighting networks, that is, electrical circuits to attenuate different frequencies by different amounts. The internationally standardized networks are called A, B, and C. The A-scale has given the best correlation with *loudness,* that is, the sound as perceived by the human ear. Thus, loudness measurements are made with the A-scale of the sound-level meter and expressed in dbA.

Several other criteria have been developed for measuring specific noises:

1. The Noise Criterion (NC) curves, which give a closer specification of sound pressure limits at different frequencies (these were developed by L. L. Beranek and are used particularly in the U.S.A.)
2. The Preferred Noise Criterion (PNC) curves, an improved version of the NC curves
3. The Noise Rating (NR) curves, a European alternative to the NC curves
4. The L_{10} dbA and L_{90} dbA rating, which states the dbA level that is exceeded, respectively, 10 percent and 90 percent of the time
5. The L_{eq} dbA rating, which is the energy equivalent dbA level and now the most common measure of noise
6. The Speech Interference Level (SIL), which gives the arithmetic mean of the sound pressure levels

in the octave bands of sound centered on 500, 1000, and 2000 Hz
7. The Articulation Index (AI), which estimates the proportion of syllables that are intelligible in speech
8. The Perceived Noise Level in dB (PNdB), which is used mainly to measure aircraft noise
9. The Noise and Number Index (NNI), which is a measure of both aircraft noise and the number of aircraft flying over

Some of these indices have a rough correlation with one another. For example, the sound level in PNdB is approximately equal to the sound level in dBA, plus 14.

9.2 ABSORPTION AND INSULATION OF AIRBORNE NOISE

The most effective method of noise reduction is to absorb the sound at its source. Hard, rigid materials reflect sound. Soft, porous materials, whose particles can vibrate easily, absorb sound and convert it into heat. Because sound power is small (Sec. 9.1) the rise in temperature is negligible.

Sound absorption is more effective than heat absorption. Heat-absorbing glass is only partly effective because the heat is not dissipated, merely absorbed and then reradiated in both directions. Absorbed sound, on the other hand, is dissipated by being turned into heat.

The proportion of sound absorbed is called the *sound-absorption coefficient.* A material with a coefficient of 0.80 absorbs 80 percent of the sound, and a material with a coefficient of 0.03 absorbs only 3 percent of the sound; the latter thus provides a sound-reflecting surface.

The sound-absorption coefficients for a few typical building materials are given in Table 9.2. A wider range of coefficients is given in many textbooks (for example, see Refs. 9.1 and 9.2) and in the trade literature supplied by manufacturers.

The sound-absorption coefficients used in calculations for the sound absorption of buildings (and given in tables) are for sound arriving at all angles of incidence. They are determined by measurements with a loudspeaker and a microphone in a reverberant test room.

Some materials absorb more high-frequency sound (which has a wavelength of the order of a centimeter) than low-frequency sound (whose wavelength exceeds a meter), but some do the reverse. Sound absorption coefficients are therefore tested separately over a range of frequencies. Acoustic plaster is most effective in the middle range.

It is not necessary to cover all surfaces of a room with sound-absorbing materials. Panels above, below, or adjacent to a source of noise, such as an office

Table 9.1. Approximate Sound Pressure Levels, in Decibels.

Threshold of hearing, by international standardization	0
Rustle of leaves	10
Background noise in a TV studio	20
Rustle of paper	30
Background noise in a public library	40
Background noise in a quiet office	50
Normal conversation, heard at a distance of 1 m (3 ft)	60
Telephone	70
Road traffic	80
Circular saw at a distance of 3 m (10 ft)	90
Discotheque	100
Pneumatic hammer at a distance of 1 m (3 ft)	110
Threshold of pain; jet takeoff at a distance of 100 m (300 ft)	120

Table 9.2. Sound Absorption Coefficients of a Few Typical Building Materials.

Material	Sound-absorption coefficient at a frequency of					
	125 Hz	250 Hz	500 Hz	1000 Hz	2000 Hz	4000 Hz
Glazed tiles	0.01	0.01	0.01	0.01	0.02	0.02
Concrete with roughened surface	0.01	0.02	0.02	0.03	0.04	0.04
Timber floor on timber joists	0.15	0.15	0.15	0.10	0.10	0.08
Cork tiles, 22 mm (⅞ in.) thick, on solid backing	0.05	0.10	0.20	0.55	0.60	0.55
Draped curtains over solid backing	0.05	0.25	0.40	0.50	0.60	0.50
Carpet, 9-mm (⅜ in.) pile, on felt underlay	0.08	0.08	0.30	0.60	0.75	0.80
Expanded polystyrene, 25 mm (1 in.) thick, spaced 50 mm (2 in.) from solid backing	0.10	0.25	0.55	0.20	0.10	0.15
Acoustic spray plaster, 12 mm (½ in.) thick, sprayed on solid backing	0.03	0.15	0.50	0.80	0.85	0.60
Metal tiles with 25-percent perforations, suspended from ceiling with porous absorbent material laid on top	0.40	0.60	0.80	0.80	0.90	0.80

machine, are particularly effective. They can also be used for speech privacy; for example, near a telephone.

Fixing sound-absorbing material in patches, intermingled with reflecting material, is slightly more effective than fixing the same amount of sound-absorbing material all in one area. Sound waves arriving at the junction of the absorbing and the reflecting material are bent by diffraction towards the absorbing material. The edges of an absorbing material are therefore more effective than the middle.

The sound absorption of a room can be greatly improved by a thick carpet, heavy curtains, soft furnishings, and a sound-absorbing ceiling. Perforated tiles are particularly effective because of the "Helmholtz" effect. In 1862, Hermann von Helmholtz proposed a resonator consisting of a narrow neck connected to a large volume of vibrating air. This sound energy can be fed back into the room, when it is a resonator, or absorbed within the resonator, which then becomes an absorber. The principle still works, although not quite as effectively as with individual absorbers, if a perforated panel is placed over a sheet of sound-absorbing material, or, indeed, over an air space.

Evidently, many *thermal-insulating* materials make good *sound-absorbing* materials for the same reason, namely, that they contain pores of air (see Sec. 6.3). *Sound-insulating* materials, on the other hand, are mostly poor thermal insulators. Sound insulation against *airborne noise,* whether it comes from the outside or from another room in the same building, is almost proportional to the mass of the wall, floor, or roof through which it has to pass. This is known as the *mass law.* The proportionality is not exact (Fig. 9.2.1); for the heavier materials, which are most useful for sound insulation, a doubling in thickness produces a sound attenuation (that is, reduction) of approximately 5 dB (the decibel scale is logarithmic, and halving the

sound pressure would correspond to an attenuation of 6.02 dB).

Sound insulation is not quite as effective as sound absorption for reducing the noise level. Some of the sound is absorbed by the insulator and transformed into heat (producing a negligible increase in temperature), but some is transformed into elastic energy since the insulator is usually a heavy elastic material. This energy is reradiated on both sides since the wall, floor, or ceiling vibrates (Fig. 9.2.2).

The thick masonry walls of many old buildings provide excellent sound insulation, as do solid reinforced-concrete walls, roofs, and floors. It may be worthwhile to use 25 mm (1 in.) more concrete for the concrete floor than the structural design requires in order to improve the sound insulation. The lightweight curtain walls of many modern buildings are usually designed for their thermal insulation and do not provide good

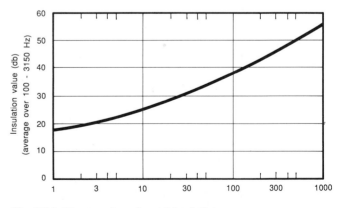

Fig. 9.2.1. The mass law of sound insulation.
The experimental relation between the attenuation (or reduction) of sound and the mass per unit area of an insulating wall, roof, or floor is almost a straight line.

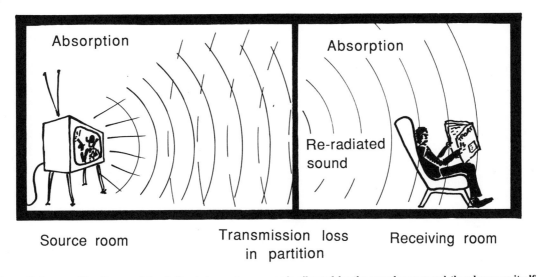

Absorption

Absorption

Re-radiated sound

Source room

Transmission loss in partition

Receiving room

Fig. 9.2.2. The wall that provides the sound insulation between two rooms is vibrated by the sound waves and thus becomes itself a source of sound. The insulation of the wall reduces the noise transmitted, but, as a radiator, the wall also makes a small addition to the (reduced) noise level.

sound insulation. However, if the building is air-conditioned, it may still perform better than one without air conditioning but with more massive walls.

The weak link in the sound insulation of many buildings are their windows and doors. If windows are left open, the sound insulation of the rest of the wall is irrelevant. One is not tempted to leave windows open under conditions that call for good thermal insulation (cold, or dry and hot weather), but one is liable to open windows on a warm and humid day and accept the noise as the lesser evil. The only answer to the problem is air-conditioning, but this is too expensive for many buildings near airports or major highways.

Open or badly fitting doors are also weak links, but doors and windows that have been made weathertight to reduce winter heating or summer cooling provide good sound insulation (see Secs. 19.8 and 19.9). A similar treatment may be needed for internal doors.

9.3 IMPACT NOISE

Impact noise is transmitted directly to the structure or the fabric of a building. Elastic materials, and particularly a steel frame if there is one, can transmit its vibrations throughout the building. The most common impact noises are footsteps and slamming doors, but machinery fixed to the floor, water hammer in pipes, and flushing toilets can be even more disturbing.

Impact noise is not attenuated by additional mass, as is airborne sound. Since it is transmitted by the *continuous* solid parts of the structure and fabric, it can be reduced by interrupting the sound path, for example, by floating a floor on a blanket or resilient material such as rubber or mineral wool (Fig. 9.3.1). This is the equivalent of "insulation."

The impact sound of footsteps can also be suppressed at source by using a thick carpet with a resilient underlay, or reduced by cork, rubber, or plastic tiles. This is the equivalent of "absorption."

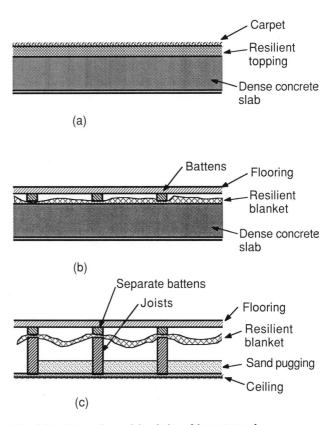

Carpet

Resilient topping

Dense concrete slab

(a)

Battens

Flooring

Resilient blanket

Dense concrete slab

(b)

Separate battens

Joists

Flooring

Resilient blanket

Sand pugging

Ceiling

(c)

Fig. 9.3.1. Absorption and insulation of impact sound.
(a) Thick-pile carpet with resilient underlay on reinforced concrete slab; (b) timber floor supported on reinforced concrete slab through a resilient blanket; (c) timber floor with resilient blanket and sand for impact sound insulation.

9.4 MATERIALS FOR AUDITORIA

Auditoria used for lectures and conferences present a simpler problem, since speech intelligibility is the only acoustic concern. Achieving it presents no difficulty in small rooms. In large rooms, microphones and loudspeakers are unavoidable, unless the lecturer has been trained to project his voice about 9 dB louder than the average person.

In rooms of intermediate size, electro-acoustic aids are now often provided, but they tend to limit discussion from the floor. The acoustics of an auditorium can be greatly improved, and the need for microphones and loudspeakers avoided, by selecting suitable materials.

If an auditorium is filled with people (who are sound absorbers), the floor is not available for reflecting the sound to the rear of an auditorium. If the ceiling is not too high, it provides a suitable sound mirror, which should accordingly be covered with reflecting surfaces such as plywood or hard plaster. It is helpful to place a sound reflector above the area the principal speaker is likely to use, suspended from the ceiling if necessary. Since the wavelength of sound is much longer than that of light, a sound mirror can be formed by any correctly shaped surface with a low coefficient of sound absorption. A polished surface is not necessary.

In large auditoria, speech intelligibility may be impaired by reflection from the rear of the auditorium. The brain tends to perceive speech reflected by a sound mirror and received 35 milliseconds or more after the original sound as a separate sound; this phenomenon impairs speech intelligibility. If the interval is much longer than 35 milliseconds, the sound is perceived as a distinct echo. If the auditorium is sufficiently large, the rear wall and the rear of the ceiling should be covered with sound-absorbing materials.

The design of auditoria for music is much more difficult because the clarity acceptable in lecture rooms is not sufficient. A good concert hall or opera house also requires liveness, warmth, and fullness of tone. The exact nature of these qualities is a matter of opinion. Beranek (Ref. 9.3) considers that fullness of tone depends on the ratio of the loudness of the reflected and the directly received sound, and that liveness and warmth depend on the reverberation of particular frequencies. These, in turn, depend on the use of appropriate materials. The subject is complex, and to some extent controversial, and reference should be made to specialist books (Refs. 9.3, 9.4, and 9.5).

REFERENCES

9.1. P. H. Parkin, H. R. Humphreys, and J. R. Cowell: *Acoustics, Noise, and Buildings.* 4th ed. Faber, London, 1979. pp. 279–283.
9.2. L. L. Beranek (Ed.): *Noise Reduction.* McGraw-Hill, New York, 1960, pp. 349–395.
9.3. L. L. Beranek: *Music, Acoustics, and Architecture.* Wiley, New York, 1962. 586 pp.
9.4. Vilhelm Lassen Jordan: *Acoustic Design of Concert Halls and Theatres.* Applied Science, London, 1975. 231 pp.
9.5. R. Mackenzie (Ed.): *Auditorium Acoustics.* Applied Science, London, 1975. 231 pp.

SUGGESTIONS FOR FURTHER READING

Clifford R. Bragson: *Noise Pollution—The Unquiet Crisis.* University of Pennsylvania Press, Philadelphia, 1970. 280 pp.
L. H. Schaudinischky: *Sound, Man and Building.* Applied Science, London, 1976. 413 pp.
Anita B. Lawrence: *Architectural Acoustics.* Elsevier, London, 1970. 219 pp.
P. H. Parkin, H. J. Purkis, and W. E. Scholes: *Field Measurements of Sound Insulation between Dwellings.* H. M. Stationery Office, London, 1960. 571 pp.

Part II

The Properties of Building Materials

10

Iron and Steel

The invention in the nineteenth century of a process for the mass production of steel resulted in a large increase in its use in buildings, as well as in major changes in the technology of other building materials.

The production of wrought iron, cast iron, and steel will be reviewed here, as well as their phase diagram. From this information the properties of steel can be deduced, as well as technologies for their improvement. Strength and toughness can be improved by heat treatment, by cold working, and by alloying elements. Not merely do these improved steels have superior properties, they also save money because they reduce the amount of material needed.

The corrosion problem of steel can be solved by protective coatings or alloying. Two comparatively recent developments are coating steel with porcelain enamel and the use of cold-formed steel.

The last two sections of this chapter will deal with both ferrous and nonferrous metals. They will examine the manufacture of tubes and the various methods of forming connections between metals.

10.1 THE SIGNIFICANCE OF STEEL TO THE BUILDING MATERIALS INDUSTRY

Gold is the only metal that exists in any quantity in its unoxidized, metallic form in nature. The Stone Age civilizations discovered it in this state much as people found it in the early days of the California Gold Rush. It is neither a plentiful nor a strong material, so it was only when people succeeded, about 4000 B.C., to smelt copper ores to produce metallic copper that metals acquired economic significance. The reduction of iron ore proved to be much harder, and iron was not produced in significant quantities until about 1400 B.C.

There is a reason for copper preceding iron. The former has a melting point of 1083°C (1981°F), but that of iron is 1536°C (2797°F), and the fuel technology to produce temperatures high enough to melt pure iron did not exist until modern times. Heating iron ore on a charcoal fire reduced it to a soft iron sponge but did not actually melt it. This spongy iron could be worked (or wrought) into the desired shape at white heat. It then became possible to make steel from this traditional form of *wrought iron* by heating it for a prolonged period in a charcoal fire, from which it absorbed some carbon. The nature of steel as an alloy was not understood, however. Aristotle knew that bronze was an alloy of copper and tin but thought that steel was merely iron purified by fire. Steel—which had toughness, strength, *and* hardness, and could thus be given a sharp cutting edge—was difficult to produce until modern times and consequently very expensive.

The other traditional form of iron is *cast iron*. Whereas wrought iron is almost pure iron, cast iron contains 1.8 to 4.5 percent of carbon, and it is thus an alloy of iron and iron carbide. Consequently, its melting point is about 250°C (450°F) lower than that of wrought iron (see Sec. 10.5), and this is a temperature that can be produced with no more than a charcoal fire and bellows. The Chinese discovered this process in the sixth century B.C., but it was not developed in Europe until the twelfth century A.D., and the metal did not become a serious competitor to wrought iron until the early eighteenth century.

Iron was an expensive material. Although the principal raw material for tools, in buildings its use was confined to door hinges (and occasionally, complete doors), locks, tie bars for arches, chains, and clamps for masonry.

In the eighteenth century, new and cheaper processes were invented in England for the production both of cast iron and wrought iron. It is a matter of opinion whether these advances in metallurgy created the industrial revolution, or vice versa. By the end of that century, however, a number of textile factories had been built in Britain that had iron engines to drive the machines. The engineers who designed the engines also designed the buildings, and in 1811 William Strutt used cast iron beams in place of timber beams to make the floor structure of a Derbyshire factory incombustible. Nevertheless, the advantages of using iron for beams and columns to make them fire resistant were recognized only slowly.

In 1885, William Jenney used a complete iron frame for a building so that the walls, which had previously carried a large part of the load, became mere "curtains" to keep out the weather (Refs. 10.1 and 10.2). After that, major buildings were increasingly erected with structural frames, floors, and roofs of steel or reinforced concrete (in which steel reinforcement became an essential structural ingredient). Walls became nonload-bearing, and various new materials were introduced for these new walls and partitions.

The other effect of the industrial revolution was a great increase in the cost of labor relative to the cost of most raw materials. The two World Wars of 1914–18 and 1939–45 greatly accelerated this process. Natural stone as a structural material became a luxury, and elaborate bricklaying techniques, such as linear window arches, jack arches for floors, and vaults for ceilings became obsolete, because it was cheaper to use structural steel.

Thus the last few decades have seen great innovations in the use of building materials, brought about by the development of structural steel, after several centuries when changes occurred only slowly; small buildings, such as single-family houses, however, have not been affected to the same extent.

The other major innovation during the present century has been the development of plastics (see Chap. 18). These have provided durable materials for a number of applications where constant renewal had previously been necessary, and they have also replaced existing materials, including metals, for a number of purposes.

10.2 WROUGHT IRON, CAST IRON, AND CARBON STEEL

A small amount of wrought iron is still made by the traditional method whereby the iron is "puddled" in a pasty condition. In the process it absorbs some slag, which gives it not only a fibrous structure but a better rust resistance than that of steel. Wrought iron can easily be formed, for example, into decorative gates and fences, but most of the material used today by that name is a steel with a very low carbon content that has similar properties.

Cast iron, however, still has substantial uses. It is easily cast, provides a hard wearing surface, and rusts less easily than steel. On the other hand, it is a brittle material with low tensile strength. There are two main kinds of cast iron. *Grey cast iron* contains some of its carbon in the form of graphite distributed through the metal as flakes; these weaken the material but also make it easier to machine. In *white cast iron,* all the carbon is in the form of iron carbide, which has a silvery color and is very hard; hence the material itself is hard but also brittle.

Before Henry Bessemer invented in 1856 the process named after him, steel was produced only laboriously and in small quantities. The Bessemer Converter blew hot air through liquid pig iron (that is, unrefined cast iron) until most of the carbon was burned, and the resulting steel was then cast into molds. This resulted in a great reduction in the price of steel, which replaced both wrought and cast iron for most purposes. Modern steel-making processes still employ the same principle.

Most iron ores consist of one of the oxides or hydrated oxides of iron, but some are iron carbonates or silicates. In addition, the ores contain numerous impurities, notably silicon, sulfur, phosphorus, and manganese. In the process of steel making, most of the substances other than iron are either burned or converted into materials that float to the surface of the molten steel as *slag.* A *flux,* usually limestone, is added to promote the formation of the slag. Slag can be used as an admixture to cement or as a lightweight concrete aggregate (see Secs. 13.4 and 14.7).

The only practicable material for a steel furnace is steel although this would itself melt, or at least soften, in contact with molten steel. The furnace and the molds are therefore lined with *refractory materials,* which melt only at a higher temperature (but do not have the strength of steel). There are two main kinds: acid refractories (usually bricks of silicon oxide) and basic refractories (bricks of magnesium oxide or of magnesium and calcium oxide derived from dolomite rock). The choice between acid and basic lining materials depends on the ores used and the desired composition of the steel. The basic refractories are the more common because they remove most of the sulfur and phosphorus, which some iron ores contain in excessive quantities.

The liquid steel is cast into molds. The squat blocks of steel removed from the molds are called *ingots* and weigh several tons. After being reheated to a white heat, they are passed through a *blooming mill,* which turns them into thinner and much longer shapes called *blooms.* Another mill than further reduces the cross section and increases the length to produce *billets.* Billets can be further hot-rolled into structural steel sections (Figs. 10.2.1 to 10.2.5); into bars for reinforced concrete (Fig. 10.2.6) or for other purposes; or into plates.

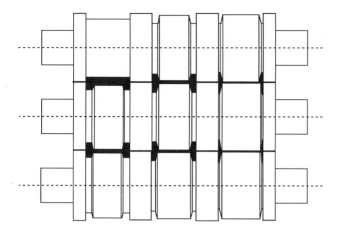

Fig. 10.2.1. The hot-rolling of a rectangular billet into an I-section in six successive stages.

Fig. 10.2.2. A separate set of rollers is required for each width and depth of steel section. The sections are consequently standardized, but from each standard section several thicknesses can be rolled by increasing or decreasing the space between the rollers. The dark cross section shows the thinnest section for a particular set of rollers. The dotted line shows the thicker section that results if one roller is raised. The thicker sections are stronger, but, for the same amount of material, a deeper section would be more economical in resisting bending.

Fig. 10.2.4. Red-hot hot-rolled structural sections of I-shape emerging from a rolling mill at Whyalla, South Australia. (*Courtesy of the BHP International Group, Melbourne.*)

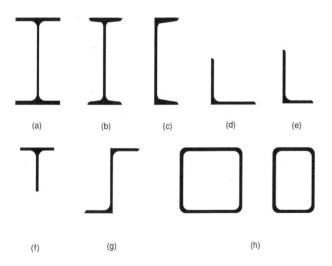

Fig. 10.2.3. U.S. standard steel sections.
(a) Wide-flange beams and stanchions; (b) American standard beams; (c) American standard channels; (d) equal angles; (e) unequal angles; (f) tees; (g) zees; and (h) hot-rolled structural tubing.

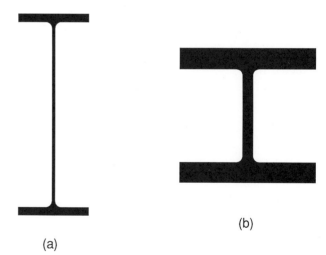

Fig. 10.2.5. Samples of hot-rolled steel I-sections.
(a) Thin deep sections, which are particularly economical for floor beams, and (b) thick sections, which are particularly suitable for heavily loaded columns carrying a mainly vertical load.

Hot-rolled steel plates can be used to strengthen standard steel sections (Fig. 10.2.7). or to form complete new I-sections or box sections.

Hot-rolled steel has a rough, brown surface caused by the oxide skin formed when the steel cools. This is not necessarily a disadvantage since it improves the bond between the steel and concrete in reinforced concrete or in structural steelwork encased in concrete for fire protection; it also improves the bond between

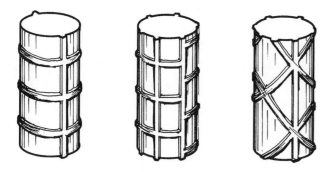

Fig. 10.2.6. Hot-rolled bars used for concrete reinforcement.
To improve the bond between concrete and steel reinforcement, most bars are now hot-rolled with a deformed surface whose projections prevent sliding of the bars within the concrete.

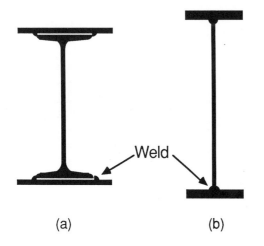

Fig. 10.2.7. Plate girders.
Hot-rolled steel plates can be used to increase the strength of rolled-steel sections, either as beams or as columns (a), or they can be formed by welding into I-sections, which can be bigger than the standard sections available (b).

structural steel and sprayed lightweight fire protection (see Sec. 7.5).

For many purposes, however, a smoother surface is desirable, and this can be produced by cold-rolling so that the steel does not oxidize after the rolling process is complete. Cold steel offers much more resistance to rolling than hot steel, and therefore only thin steel sections can be cold rolled (Sec. 10.9).

Perhaps the most widely seen application of sheet steel is the corrugated sheets used for roofs and also for the walls of factory buildings. The corrugations (Fig. 10.2.8) are needed to give the sheet—which could not be handled if it were flat—bending strength in one direction; strength in the other direction must be provided by supporting steel or timber sections. The corrugations also prove very useful for channeling any rain water that falls on a roof. Modern advances involving the production of longer sheets by a continuous process are discussed in Sec. 4.3.

Fig. 10.2.8. Corrugated steel sheet.

Cold-rolled steel sheets rust easily and must therefore be painted (see Sec. 19.3) or coated with a corrosion-resistant metal.

10.3 CORROSION-PROTECTIVE COATINGS

Corrosion is a conversion of a metal to a metallic compound by which the desirable metallic properties of strength, elasticity, and ductility are lost and substances that lack these very qualities are produced instead.

Energy is required to reduce a metal from its ores. Because metallic oxides contain less free energy than their respective metals, the chemical transformation of metals into oxides is self-perpetuating if there is an adequate supply of oxygen because energy is given off in the process. One method of corrosion protection is therefore to produce a coating that cuts off the supply of oxygen.

Iron combines with oxygen in dry air to form a mixture of *ferrous oxide,* FeO, and *ferric oxide,* Fe_2O_3. These oxides forming on the surface of the iron constitute a barrier to further oxidation, and the oxidation rate is slowed down. In the presence of moisture, the ferrous oxide is oxidized to ferric oxide, and *hydrated ferric oxide,* $2Fe_2O_3 \cdot 3H_2O$, is formed. This is a red, porous substance, known as *rust,* and it is quite loose. In consequence, the reaction continues.

The most useful protection is a coating of zinc. In fact, almost half the zinc produced in the world is now used for protecting steel from corrosion. Zinc is nearer to the anodic end of the electrochemical series than iron (see Table 10.1). Thus, if a zinc coating is scratched and the steel is exposed, the zinc serves as the anode (or positive pole), and the steel as the cathode (or negative pole). Since an electric current flows from the anode to the cathode, the exposed iron does not corrode, and the corrosion occurs in the zinc coating instead. This is called *sacrificial protection* (Fig. 10.3.1).

There are two methods for zinc-coating, or *galvanizing.* One is by electrodeposition either in an acidic bath, using hydrated zinc sulfate, or in an alkaline bath, using zinc cyanide (the latter, however, is poisonous). The other is by hot dipping the steel in a bath of molten zinc at a temperature of 450°C after pickling it in an acid bath.

Galvanizing of concrete reinforcement slightly reduces the bond between it and the concrete, and it also increases the cost of the steel. Galvanized reinforcement should be used, however, where cracks are

Table 10.1. The Electrochemical Series of Metals and Alloys.

When a piece of metal is in contact with an electrolyte, the metal tends to dissolve and send positive ions into solution, leaving the metal negatively charged. This reaction produces an electric potential between the metal and the solution. Different metals have different electric potentials, and they can be arranged in a series of increasing potentials; this is known as the *electrochemical series*, as shown below.

Cathodic End	Gold
	Silver
	Stainless steel (made passive by a chromium-rich oxide film; see Sec. 10.7)
	Bronze
	Copper
	Brass
Reference	Hydrogen
	Nickel
	Tin
	Lead
	Iron and steel
	Cadmium
	Aluminum
	Zinc
Anodic End	Magnesium

Notes: (1) An electrolyte is any liquid that conducts electricity, for example, water.
(2) There are two exactly opposite definitions of anode and cathode. It was originally assumed that a direct current passed from the anode to the cathode. Later, it was discovered that the "cathode," as originally defined, supplied the electrons, and that the electrons traveled in the electrolyte from the cathode to the anode. An exactly opposite terminology is now used in physical chemistry and in materials science, and also in this book: *The anode is the pole that supplies the electrons, and the cathode the pole that receives them.*

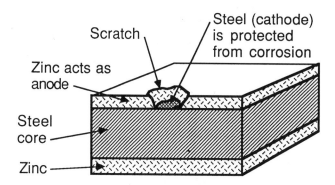

Fig. 10.3.1. Sacrificial protection of zinc coating on steel. Since zinc is nearer to the anodic end of the electrochemical series (see Table 10.1) than steel, a zinc coating acts as the anode, and the underlying steel as the cathode, if the zinc surface is scratched. Hence the steel is protected from corrosion so long as any zinc remains adjacent to the exposed iron.

liable to form, for example, where structural hinges are likely to occur.

Another method, patented by Sherard Cowper-Coles in 1900, is called *sherardizing*. The objects to be coated are packed in a drum together with zinc dust and alumina, and the drum is rotated while the temperature inside is kept at about 360°C. This produces a coating with a number of iron/zinc compounds.

Zinc coatings cannot be used for steel cans containing food, because zinc is attacked by acids and alkalis, and toxic zinc salts might be formed. Tin plate is therefore the common material for food containers, but it is rarely used as a building material.

Terne plate, however, is frequently used for roofs. "Terne" is an alloy of 80-percent lead and 20-percent tin. Both are nearer to the cathodic end of the electrochemical series (Table 10.1) so that this coating, unlike zinc, does not offer sacrificial protection. Lead, however, is a very flexible metal, and terne plate can be bent or otherwise deformed without breaking the coating. It thus relies for its corrosion protection on

the unbroken continuity of the coating. Since it is the only reasonably cheap material that resists sulfur dioxide and sulfuric acid fumes, it is useful in polluted industrial atmospheres. It also forms a good base for the application of paints.

10.4 PHASE DIAGRAMS

For reasons discussed in Sec. 2.4, pure metals are very soft and have a low strength. Even the gold and silver used in jewelry are alloys; for example, the 18-carat gold used for most "solid gold" jewelry is 18/24 or 75-percent gold, the rest being silver and copper.

In actual fact, however, carbon steels contain only a very small amount of alloying material. Even a high-carbon steel contains only about 1 percent of carbon. It may contain another 1 percent of various elements not entirely removed during the steel-making process, but the other 98 percent is iron.

The discovery that such a small amount of carbon would so dramatically change the properties of iron was made thousands of years ago, the carbon being introduced accidentally from the fuel used for smelting. The iron–carbon alloy is unlike most other alloys that consist of two or more metals, since carbon is in the transition range from metal to nonmetal (see Fig. 2.2.1), but it is normally considered to be a nonmetal.

The properties of the various alloys and their improvement by heat treatment are best understood with the aid of diagrams that show their composition on the horizontal axis and the temperature of the vertical axis. These are known as *phase diagrams* or *equilibrium diagrams*. The phase diagram of iron and carbon is quite complex, and it will be easier to follow if we first examine a couple of simple hypothetical phase diagrams.

Figure 10.4.1 shows the phase diagram of alloys of two hypothetical metals, Primum (Pr) and Secundum

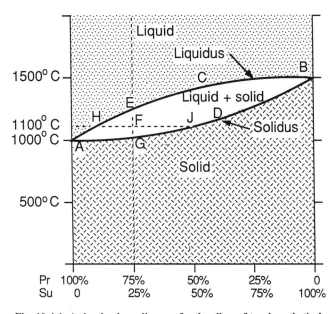

Fig. 10.4.1. A simple phase diagram for the alloys of two hypothetical metals—primum (Pr) and secundum (Su)—which do not form a eutectic.

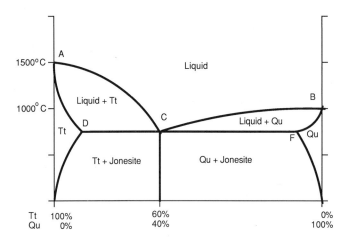

Fig. 10.4.2. A phase diagram for the alloys of two hypothetical metals—tertium (Tt) and quartum (Qu)—which form a hypothetical eutectic, jonesite.

(Su). Primum melts at 1000°C and Secundum at 1500°C. These temperature are joined by two lines, the *liquidus* and the *solidus,* which are experimentally determined. Above the liquidus, ACB, all alloys of primum and secundum are entirely liquid. Below the solidus, ADB, all alloys of primum and secundum are entirely solid.

Between the liquidus and the solidus, ACBDA, the alloy is partly liquid and partly solid. An alloy of 75-percent Pr and 25-percent Su at a temperature of 1100°C is represented on the phase diagram by point F. It starts solidifying when the temperature reaches E and is entirely solid at a temperature G. At the temperature F (1100°C), the composition of its liquid phase is H (about 90-percent Pr and 10-percent Su), and the composition of its solid phase is given by J.

Let us next consider a slightly more complicated alloy formed by two hypothetical metals, Tertium (Tt) and Quartum (Qu), as shown in Fig. 10.4.2. Tertium melts at 1500°C; Qu, at 1000°C. The liquidus ACB is not a smooth curve connecting A and B, however, but dips instead at C, which is at a temperature of 700°C. This is known as a *critical point,* and the alloy with that composition, namely 60-percent Tt and 40-percent Qu, is known as a *eutectic.* Eutectic alloys have a lower melting point than alloys containing more or less of either metal; there could, however, be more than one eutectic alloy in a phase diagram, each having the lowest melting point in that part of the phase diagram.

The eutectic alloy may have a structure quite different from either Tt or Qu. Since eutectics are often named after their discoverers, let us assume that this one was discovered by Dr. Jones and that it is called jonesite.

Let us further assume that the experimentally determined solidus, DCE, is a straight line, which is often the case. At room temperature, we therefore have alloys consisting of tertium and jonesite for tertium contents of more than 60 percent, and alloys consisting of quartum and jonesite for tertium contents of less than 60 percent.

An important alloy not shown on this phase diagram is one called a *eutectoid alloy.* This is formed on cooling from a *solid solution,* that is, from a dip in the solidus line.

10.5 THE PHASE DIAGRAM OF WROUGHT IRON, CAST IRON, AND STEEL

Iron occcurs in four different forms, called alpha, beta, gamma, and delta iron. Of these only, *alpha iron,* also called *ferrite,* and *gamma iron,* also called *austenite,* are of practical significance. Ferrite, a ductile and comparatively soft metal, crystallizes with a body-centered, cubic space lattice (see Sec. 2.4). Austentite, named after Sir W. C. Roberts-Austen, a nineteenth-century British metallurgist, has a face-centered cubic lattice; in carbon steel, it exists only above a temperature of 730°C. In some alloy steels, however, it can exist at room temperature (Sec. 10.7).

The reason why so many materials have two names lies in the empirical nature of practical metallurgy. Many were observed and named before anybody knew about their composition.

The phase diagram in Fig. 10.5.1 is not a phase diagram of iron and carbon, but rather of iron and iron-carbide, a hard and brittle white compound, Fe_3C, that is also called *cementite.* This phase diagram has a eutectic, called *ledeburite,* at a temperature of 1130°C and a carbon content of 4.3 percent. The diagram also has a eutectoid, called *pearlite,* at a temperature of 730°C and carbon content of 0.8 percent. This is a

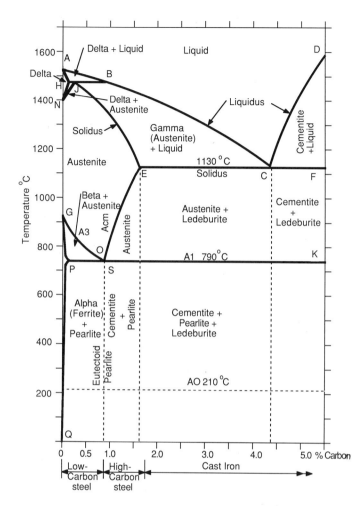

Fig. 10.5.1. The phase diagram of iron and iron carbide for the range covering wrought iron, steel, and cast iron.
The liquidus and solidus lines, the transformation temperatures, the forms of iron, and the eutectic and eutectoid existing at various temperatures are described in the text.

plication as a building material—for paving floors where exceptionally hard wear is expected, for example, and for castings. The iron/iron-carbide alloys with a carbon content above 4.5 percent have little practical use.

The extreme left of Fig. 10.5.1 is the range of traditional wrought iron. Some wrought iron is still made in the traditional manner, but most of the material sold under that name is in fact steel with a very low carbon content; it is called "wrought iron" because of the craftsmanship associated with that term in the eighteenth and nineteenth centuries. This range also includes nails and other connectors that are permitted to deform under an overload but must not fail by shear or rupture.

In the late nineteenth and early twentieth century, the high-carbon steels—those with a carbon content of 0.8 to 1.8 percent—were used extensively, because that was the only way to produce the very hard and very strong steels needed for steel-cutting tools with a lesser carbon content, for springs, and for special structural applications. These high-carbon steels are very brittle, however—that is, they lack ductility—and they have been replaced by high-tensile, low-alloy steels (see Sec. 10.7).

The low-carbon steels, particularly those with less than 0.25-percent carbon, are used extensively for roof sheets, for structural steel, and for concrete reinforcement. Their performance can be improved by heat treatment and by cold working.

The structural use of steels is described in various structural textbooks (for example, see Refs. 10.3 and 10.4).

10.6 HEAT TREATMENT AND COLD WORKING OF STEEL

Three of the principal qualities desired in steel for certain purposes are high *strength, ductility,* and *toughness.* These qualities are defined in Fig. 10.6.1. The fourth quality, which is not shown by the stress-strain diagram, is *hardness.* It is measured by an indentation test (see Sec. 2.8). For many steels, hardness is proportional to strength.

The same steel can be made strong and hard, on the one hand, or ductile, on the other, by a simple heat treatment. Some increase in toughness is also possible by heat treatment, but a more substantial improvement requires a change in the basic composition of the steel. The most common heat treatments go back at least to the Middle Ages (they are mentioned in a number of manuscripts). They can also be easily performed by any reader on pieces of medium-carbon steel, such as steel (not aluminum) knitting needles. If such needles are not available, steel bodkins or long sewing needles will do.

Needles contain about 0.8 percent of carbon, and,

lamellar conglomerate of ferrite and cementite. If etched and viewed under a metallurgical microscope, it looks like mother-of-pearl because of the fine and regular alternation of the two constituents, ferrite and cementite, one soft and the other hard.

The liquidus in Fig. 10.5.1 is the line ABCD; the solidus is the line AHJECF. In addition, there are several transformation temperatures at which changes occur in solid solution. The A1 line—at 730°C—is the line PSK at which austenite begins to form during heating. The A3 line—from 908°C to 730°C—is the line GO, at which ferrite begins to form on cooling. The ACM line, OE—from 730°C to 1130°C—denotes the start of the formation of cementite. The line A0 is the bottom of the *tempering* range (discussed in Sec. 10.6), above which the *martensite,* formed by quenching, is transformed into a tougher, less brittle material that is sometimes called *troostite.*

Cast iron contains 1.8 to 4.5 percent of carbon. Used extensively for machines, it now has only limited ap-

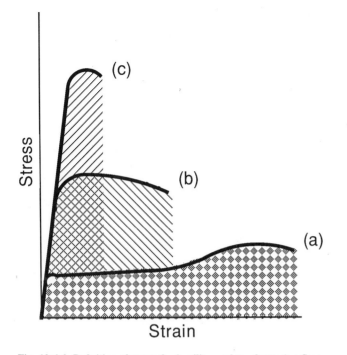

Fig. 10.6.1. Definition of strength, ductility, and toughness (see Secs. 2.6 and 2.8).
Strength is the ability to sustain high stress without yielding or breaking. Ductility is the ability to sustain high strain without breaking. Toughness is the ability to absorb energy without breaking. It is proportional to the area under the stress-strain curve. Thus the steel of curve (c) has the highest strength, the steel of curve (a) has the highest ductility, and the steel of curve (b) has the greatest toughness.

when purchased, are hard, strong, and springy; they also have a certain toughness, so that they do not break too easily if they are bent. Let us now take one of these needles, hold it with pincers or pliers in the flame of a gas stove or a candle until it gives off a bright red glow. Its temperature is then approximately 850°C (1560°F). The needle is held at this temperature for up to half a minute and then allowed to cool in the air for a few minutes. This heat treatment is called *annealing*. The needle is now quite soft, can be easily bent, and does not recover its original shape. We have produced a ductile material from a springy one.

If we now take another needle (or the same needle), again bring it to a bright red heat, and then immediately throw it into a bucket of water, we have performed the heat treatment known as *quenching*. The needle is now hard and has a high tensile strength, but it is brittle and will easily snap if we try to bend it.

We will now take the needle of the first experiment, or a new needle, and quench it, that is, heat it to a bright red heat, and then plunge it rapidly into water. For the next part of the experiment, we need a bright surface, and if the needle has turned dull, we need to polish it with a piece of emery paper. We then hold the needle into the flame until it turns a straw color. Its temperature is then 225°C (435°F). It is important

that it should not turn to a darker color, and it certainly should not become red hot. We then allow the needle to cool slowly in air. We have now performed the heat treatment known as *tempering*. The needle should now be back to its original condition—quite strong and hard, but not brittle; it should also be capable of bending a little and spring back without breaking. We have produced *toughness*.

These heat treatments are quite simple; they require no elaborate equipment and no scientific instruments. They have been used for several centuries at least, although quenching is now generally done in oil, which is less drastic than quenching in water. Why they work, however, was discovered only in the present century.

Heating steel to a bright red heat means that its temperature is about 850°C—well above the A1 line in Fig. 10.5.1. We therefore turn the material into austenite. If the steel is now cooled slowly, the austenite is transformed into ferrite and pearlite, both of them a soft, ductile material. If we plunge the steel rapidly into cold water on the other hand, we produce a different material, called *martensite* (after Adolf Martens, a nineteenth-century German metallurgist). Because of the rapid cooling, the carbon atoms that are in solid solution in the austenite do not have enough time to form cementite, which is one of the constituents of pearlite; instead, they distort the body-centered cubic lattice of the ferrite. Under the microscope, martensite looks like a large number of fine needles scattered at random. It is very hard and strong, but also very brittle.

The material is therefore tempered to restore some ductility without losing too much of the strength and hardness. This means heating it above the A0 line in Fig. 10.5.1, which is at 210°C, but keeping it well below the A1 line (730°C). The exact temperature depends on the use to which the material is to be put. Fortunately, the temperature is indicated with considerable accuracy by the color to which the material turns during tempering (Table 10.2). The color is produced by the formation of an oxide skin.

Two other types of heat-treatment, *normalizing* and *aging* (or age-hardening), are variations on quenching and tempering that are used for machine parts.

Table 10.2 Colors Acquired by Plain Carbon Steel, Heated for a Normal Period During Tempering.

Color	Temperature, °C
Straw	225
Yellow-brown	255
Red-brown	265
Purple	275
Violet	285
Dark blue	295
Light blue	310

Case-hardening is also used mainly for machines, but it has some application to building. When low-carbon steels and certain low-alloy steels are heated to about 925°C (1700°F) in close contact with carbon for several hours, the carbon content of the outer skin of the steel—to a depth of about 1 mm (about 1/32 in.)—is increased to about 0.9 percent, thus producing a very hard skin, but retaining ductility and toughness underneath. This goal can be achieved by packing the steel in a box tightly surrounded by charcoal; a better result is obtained in a bath of sodium cyanide, but the latter is very poisonous. Because of problems of disposing of the cyanide, case-hardening has been largely replaced by *nitriding,* which is done by heating the steel in ammonia (NH_3) at about 500°C (930°F). This treatment forms hard particles of nitride in the skin of the steel.

Work-hardening is the name given to a number of processes that deform the crystal structure of steel by mechanical working and in the process increase its strength, although with some loss of ductility. It is work-hardening that produced the increase in the strength of the steel in Fig. 2.8.3(a) after it had yielded.

Work-hardening is not practicable for the larger structural-steel sections, but it is is employed extensively for the bars and wire mesh used as concrete reinforcement and for the wires used for prestressed concrete and for cable structures. Wires are drawn through a die, which reduces their diameter plastically. Bars are stretched or twisted plastically.

As we noted in Sec. 2.4, plastic deformation occurs by the slipping of one layer of atoms over another. We also noted that dislocations (imperfections in the crystal structure) greatly increase the resistance of crystals to plastic deformation, and hence their strength. Work-hardening produces more and more dislocations, and hence it increases strength, but with an inevitable loss of ductility. The original crystal structure can be restored by annealing. The material then regains its original ductility but loses its increased strength in the process. This fact is of considerable practical importance when two pieces of work-hardened steel are joined by welding. The part that has been heated by welding will lose its high strength if it is allowed to cool slowly.

The most drastic method of work-hardening is *wire-drawing,* that is drawing a bar through a succession of dies to form wire. Each reduces the diameter slightly (Fig. 10.6.2) and increases the strength. After wire-drawing, the coils of wire are *stress-relieved,* which is a form of tempering.

Use of wire hard-drawn through a die in building is mainly for the cables of prestressed concrete. This wire has a carbon content of about 0.8 percent, but, in addition, it has between 0.4 and 1.1 percent of manganese and 0.1 to 0.3 percent of silicon. These additions are necessary to give the steel the necessary

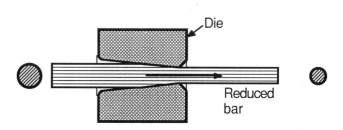

Fig. 10.6.2. Wire drawing.
When a steel bar is drawn through a die of very hard steel, its diameter is reduced, its crystal structure thereby distorted, and its strength consequently increased. The process of wire drawing can be repeated several times; each time, the diameter is reduced and the strength increased. Since work-hardening greatly reduces the ductility, the wire is tempered once the drawing operation is complete, a process known as *stress relieving.*

toughness and make it strictly a low-alloy steel (Sec. 10.7). The wire drawn to a size of 5 to 7 mm (0.196 to 0.276 in.) has an ultimate tensile strength of about 1700 MPa (245 ksi) and a proof stress (see Sec. 2.6) of about 1300 MPa (190 ksi), which is more than five times the strength of high-tensile, low-alloy structural steel (Sec. 10.7).

Wire-drawing is also used to produce the wires from which mats of welded fabric are made for use in reinforced concrete. The proof stress is about 450 MPa (65 ksi).

Larger bars can be cold-worked by stretching or twisting, which increases their strength by more than 50 percent.

10.7 ALLOY STEELS

It is mechanically impracticable to work-harden large structural-steel sections. It is also undesirable to use carbon contents in the same range as in high-carbon steels (that is, above 0.8 percent C; see Fig. 10.5.1), because this seriously reduces the ductility. High-strength structural steels are therefore produced by the addition of small amounts of alloying elements. The composition of these *high-strength, low-alloy steels* varies, but most contain small quantities of manganese and either vanadium or columbium.* Some also contain boron, silicon, nickel, chrome, molybdenum, titanium, and zirconium. Generally speaking, the total amount of alloy is less than 2 percent.

The essential alloying element, however, remains carbon, because it is the iron-carbide that makes hardening and tempering possible; the small quantities of other elements merely modify these treatments. The carbon content in these high-strength, low-alloy steels is usually kept below 0.25 percent so that the steel has the toughness of a structural-grade steel with a

_____
* The metal is called columbium (Cb) in America and niobium (Nb) in Europe.

similar low carbon content, but also the high strength that is provided by the additions of the other alloying elements. All recent specifications include a requirement for weldability (Sec. 10.11).

Although stainless steel was invented half a century earlier, the next topic in logical order is low-alloy *weathering steels,* which are made by several manufacturers under different names, but are best known by the U.S. Steel Company's trade name *Cor-Ten.* These steels contain up to ten alloying elements. They are low-alloy steels, the total additive being less than 2 percent. The carbon content is also low, less than 0.1 percent. Phosphorus is normally regarded as an undesirable impurity, but in this type of steel it contributes to the corrosion resistance. Other beneficial ingredients include chromium, nickel, and silicon. Exactly how these reduce corrosion, however, is not clear at present. All weathering steels are high-tensile, low-alloy steels in spite of their low carbon content.

Weathering steels rust, but the relatively thin, dark, brownish-black rust layer that accumulates over a period of two to three years firmly adheres to the steel and protects it from further corrosion (Fig. 10.7.1). Continuous wetting or immersion in water inhibits the further formation of this protective skin, however, and may reinitiate surface corrosion. Buildings of weathering steel should therefore be designed so that "horizontal" surfaces slope slightly to shed the water.

In some early buildings that employed weathering steels, the steel weathered as predicted, but the rust running off it severely stained concrete and stone below it. Buildings are now designed so that water running off the steel can be drained into a sink. Alternatively, the rust may be allowed to drip on gravel beds or flower beds, which are then periodically renewed, or on asphalt paving that does not show the stains. These expedients obviously impose limitations on the design.

Stainless steel was discovered accidentally in 1913 in Sheffield by Harry Brearley experimenting with alloy steels for gun barrels. He noticed that one of the steel samples, already discarded as unsuitable, did not rust like the other samples, but remained bright. This steel contained 13 percent chromium—the essential ingredient of all stainless steels. The very high resistance to corrosion of these steels comes from their possession of sufficient chromium to form a chromium-rich oxide film. This very thin film is not visible to the naked eye. If damaged—for example, by scratching—the oxide immediately reforms and thus maintains the corrosion protection.

Stainless steels contain 12 to 20 percent of chromium, and most contain other alloying elements—up to 20 percent of nickel, and small quantities of molybdenum, copper, aluminum, and titanium. The carbon content of stainless steels is always low.

We noted in examining the phase diagram of iron

Fig. 10.7.1. The Sydney Tower.
This cable-stayed tubular structure of low-alloy weathering steel (AUSTEN 50) is 6.7 m (22 ft) in diameter and 324.8 (1065 ft) high. (*Courtesy of the Consulting Structural Engineers, Wargon Chapman and Partners, Sydney.*)

and iron carbide that austenite is transformed into other materials when the temperature falls below 730°C (1350°F). In some stainless steels, notably those containing a high percentage of nickel, austenite is retained at room temperature. Such steels are called *austenitic stainless steels* (Fig. 10.7.2). The most common steel in this group contains 18 percent chromium and 8 percent nickel. Although commonly used for sanitary fittings and kitchen sinks, and for curtain walls, it is one of the more expensive stainless steels, and cheaper alloys are substituted if less wear and/or weathering are anticipated.

In spite of the high alloy content, stainless steel has the same high modulus of elasticity as other steels— namely 200,000 MPa (30,000 ksi), and relatively thin stainless-steel parts thus have a comparatively small deflection. In this respect, thin stainless-steel panels, mullions, and covers have an advantage over those of aluminum, copper, or bronze.

The various stainless alloys have differing strengths, ranging from that of structural steel to that of high-tensile steel. The 18%Cr/8%Ni alloy, previously men-

Table 10.3. Inch and Metric Equivalents of U.S. Standard Gauge

Gauge No.	Equivalent in inches	Equivalent in millimeters
10	0.1345	3.42
12	0.1046	2.66
14	0.0747	1.90
16	0.0598	1.52
18	0.0478	1.21
20	0.0359	0.912
22	0.0299	0.759
24	0.0239	0.607
26	0.0179	0.455
28	0.0149	0.378

Fig. 10.7.2. Control tower for shipping movements in the Port of Sydney, clad in austentic stainless steel. (*Courtesy of Mr. C. B. Rolfe.*)

tioned, has an ultimate tensile stress of about 600 MPa (about 90 ksi).

All stainless steels can be welded and cut to take screw threads. They can be glued with epoxy resins and are inert to all mastics and sealers presently in use. Their corrosion resistance is excellent; the stainless-steel sheets used on the Chrysler Building and the Empire State Building in New York more than 50 years ago are still in good condition.

Stainless steel could be used in precisely the same way as structural steel, but solid structural sections would be too expensive. Light-gauge construction (Sec. 10.9) is economically feasible for special purposes. Stainless steel finds its main use, however, in locations that require corrosion resistance (such as sanitary fittings), in railings, in handles and locks where appearance and good wearing properties are important, and in thin facing materials. The austenitic stainless steels are both ductile and tough because of the austenite, and they can be formed into complex shapes. Because of the high strength and high modulus of elasticity of the material, relatively thin sections are feasible. If backed by other material, stainless steel sheet of 22 U.S. standard gauge (0.759 mm or 0.0299 in.) can be used. For column covers used externally—or internally where

bumping (by cars or baggage, say) is not expected— 14 gauge (1.90 mm or 0.0747 in.) is acceptable, but 10 gauge (3.42 mm or 0.1345 in.) is needed where bumping may be expected. (See Table 10.3 for inch and metric equivalents of U.S. Standard Gauge.)

Very thin panels pose a visual problem, however, because it is impossible to produce a perfectly flat surface. The eye instantly detects slight departures from flatness, and this detection is made easier by the reflective nature of stainless steel. Panels should therefore be corrugated to give them extra stiffness, or where this is undesirable for reasons of appearance or drainage, they should be impressed with a decorative pattern that distracts the eye from imperfections in flatness.

Stainless steel used for curtain walls must be backed with an insulating material; this can be poured as a liquid into a form made of the steel.

The main disadvantage of stainless steel is its relatively high cost. Where exceptional corrosion resistance is not required, other materials, such as aluminum (see Sec. 11.2), are usually more economical. The corrosion resistance of stainless steel makes it useful for gutters and downspouts (downpipes). Its main competitor for such applications is copper (see Sec. 11.6), but gutters and downpipes lasting a number of years can be made more cheaply from galvanized iron or plastics (see Sec. 8.1 on life cycle cost).

10.8 PORCELAIN ENAMEL ON STEEL

The craft of enameling metals was already known to the ancient Egyptians, as articles found in their tombs testify. It is today a well-developed art in China and Iran for jewelry, vases, and dishes. The enameling of panels for buildings is based on the same principles; the scale of the operation is much larger, however, and cost a prime consideration. Enameling could be carried out on panels of stainless steel or aluminum, but this would have no particular technical advantage since enameling renders even ordinary steel entirely resistant to corrosion.

Porcelain enamel panels were first used in building construction in the early 1930s. They are made by melting frit, a glass-forming substance, and fusing it to steel sheets at a temperature of 760° to 870°C (1400° to 1600°F). The first coat is applied to both sides, so that the steel is entirely enclosed in an envelope of glass. Further coats are applied only to the visible side.

The thickness of the steel in such panels depends on the size of the panels; however, it must be sufficient to ensure that the panels are flat, since any departure from flatness is easily detected by the eye, and it must be sufficient to prevent any accidental damage to the porcelain enamel as a result of buckling of the panel.

In 1956, the U.S. National Bureau of Standards undertook a seven-year investigation of the durability of porcelain enamel on steel and aluminum panels and concluded that it was excellent—even at very hot and humid sites and at sites subject to appreciable pollution—provided that there are no pinholes in the enamel and that the firing temperature was above 1400°F. Even colors prone to fade in sunlight performed well in porcelain enamel (Ref. 10.5).

Porcelain enamel sheets can be backed with insulating material and used externally like other metal curtain walls. They can also be used as metal sunshades; for this purpose, white is a good color. Internally, they face competition from cheaper plastic materials, except where resistance to heat is needed.

10.9 COLD-FORMED STEEL CONSTRUCTION

We discussed cold-formed stainless steel and cold-formed steel that was subsequently enameled in the last two sections. This section will be concerned with cold-formed steel that needs to be protected from corrosion either by galvanizing or by painting.

Light-gauge cold-formed steel usually ranges from No. 10 U.S. standard gauge to No. 22 gauge (see Table 10.3). Steel of this thickness does not have to be heated to make rolling easier; as a result, the manufacturing plant can be cleaner and smaller than a hot-rolling mill.

Gutters and downpipes made from galvanized steel (see Sec. 10.7) are usually No. 24 gauge.

Air conditioning and ventilating ducts are bent to the calculated rectangular cross-sectional area from flat galvanized sheet of No. 18 to 24 gauge; ducts for high-velocity systems (Ref. 10.6, p. 111) are usually made circular instead to reduce friction losses.

Corrugated sheets have been rolled from wrought iron since the 1820s and from steel since the 1870s. During the late nineteenth century, prefabricated houses of corrugated iron were exported all over the world (Ref. 10.7), and it became one of the most common

roofing materials. Corrugated sheets have already been discussed in Secs. 4.3 and 10.2 (see also Fig. 10.8).

Sheet-steel decking is now commonly used for steel-framed structures, and this can be provided with cells for the electrical services (Fig. 10.9.1).

During the last few decades, light-gauge steel has been used increasingly for steel structures. The steel sheet is bent into angles and channels (Fig. 10.9.2), and used in the same way as hot-rolled angles and channels except that it is limited to carrying smaller loads over smaller spans because of the smaller thicknesses.

For larger sections, buckling (Ref. 10.6, p. 75) becomes a problem (Fig. 10.9.3), and this can be overcome by introducing an extra bend (Fig. 10.9.4). The effec-

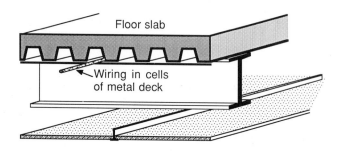

Fig. 10.9.1. Sheet steel decking for a steel structure.
The corrugations needed to make the decking self-supporting during construction can be utilized for ducts for the electrical services.

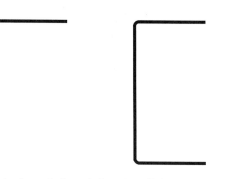

Fig. 10.9.2. Angles and channels bent from light-gauge steel sheet.

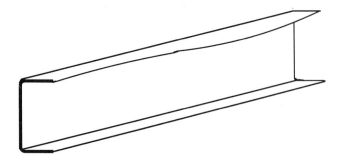

Fig. 10.9.3. For the larger light-gauge steel sections local buckling of the outstanding legs may occur, unless stiffeners are provided (Fig. 10.9.4.).

tiveness of these stiffeners is easily demonstrated by bending a sheet of paper to the shapes in Fig. 10.9.3, and then adding the additional folds of Figs. 10.9.4(a) and (b). A further increase in strength results if an additional stiffener is introduced in the middle of the channel section (Fig. 10.9.5), or if the section is closed by welding a plate to it (Fig. 10.9.6). These closed sections can also be used as cable ducts.

I-sections can be made by welding two channels together and their strength increased by a stiffener at the edge of each channel (Fig. 10.9.7). It is usually sufficient to use spot welds to join light-gauge steel sections and sheets.

Finally, bars bent diagonally up and down can be welded to light-gauge angles to form open-web trusses (Fig. 10.9.8).

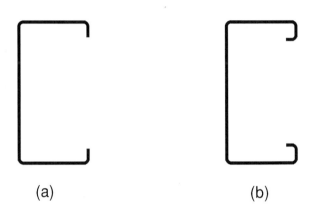

(a)   **(b)**

Fig. 10.9.4. Additional folding at the end of each channel to provide extra stiffness to prevent local buckling (a); if this is not sufficient, an additional fold may be made (b).

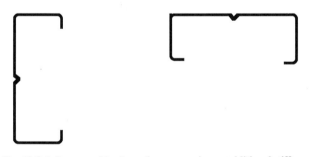

Fig. 10.9.5. Deep or wide channels may require an additional stiffener in the middle of the web to prevent local buckling.

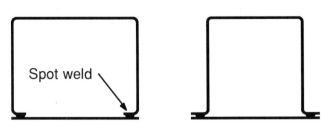

Fig. 10.9.6. Channel section closed by a plate for extra stiffness, and "top-hat" section with outstanding legs and closed by a plate. Both can be utilized as ducts.

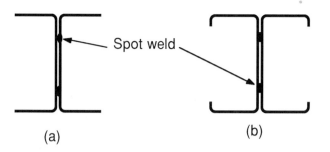

Spot weld

(a)   **(b)**

Fig. 10.9.7. Light-gauge I-section formed from two channels, without stiffeners (a), and with stiffeners (b).

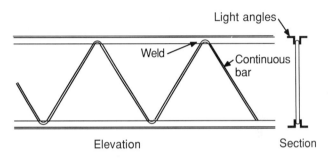

Light angles

Weld

Continuous bar

Elevation   Section

Fig. 10.9.8. Open-web joist formed by light-gauge angles and round bars.
The round bar is bent up and down diagonally to provide the necessary shear resistance and structural depth between the angles.

10.10 TUBES

Tubes can be made by bending metal strip or by punching a hole into a solid bar. The first process is more suited to the larger tubes and harder metals, and the second to the smaller tubes and softer metals.

The Ancient Romans were able to produce lead pipes by the first method; the joint was made by folding and then beating the soft lead. In modern processes, steel, copper, or aluminum strip is fed through a series of forming rolls, which gradually curl the strip to tube shape. The open edges of the tube are then welded by electric induction.

The second process produces seamless tubes. A solid rod of hot metal is rotated between two rollers that pull it forward over a mandril. This punches a hole into the bar, producing a tube with a small hole and thick walls. If a tube with a larger hole is required, the process is repeated.

10.11 CONNECTIONS FOR METALS

The oldest method of connecting two pieces of wrought iron or steel, say a plate and an angle, is by *riveting*. Holes are punched in each piece, a round piece of steel with a head on one end is made red hot and pushed through the pair of holes, and the opposite end is then hammered to produce a second head.

In modern riveting, this job is done with a power tool. As the rivet cools, it shortens, thus pressing the two pieces of metal together. This pressure creates friction between the two surfaces. Since the coefficient of friction of steel on steel is high, this frictional force makes a greater contribution to the strength of the riveted joint than the shear strength of the rivet itself.

Since the handling of red-hot rivets is unpleasant, and since equally effective methods have become available, hot riveting is now rarely used. Riveting is still a common method for joining pieces of aluminum, however, since satisfactory joints can be produced with *cold rivets*. An operator can carry the cold rivets on his person and push them through previously drilled holes. The rivets have a head at one end; the head at the other end is formed with a power tool after the rivets have been inserted in the holes. Rivets of up to 10-mm (3/8-in.) diameter can be driven cold; larger aluminum rivets are unlikely to be needed in buildings.

It is also possible to make riveted aluminum joints where only one side of a material is accessible—for example, in assembling a tube—by using *explosive rivets*. The shaft of these rivets is hollow and filled with a small quantity of explosive that can be set off with a blow from a hammer. The far end of the rivet is blown outwards and forms a secure joint.

Prior to the invention of high-tensile bolting, there were two kinds of steel bolts. *Black bolts* fitted losely into the holes in the two members to be joined. A stronger joint was produced with machined *"bright" bolts,* which fitted perfectly into the two holes and thus had a higher strength. Black-bolted joints are still used for connections of minor importance, but structural joints are now made with *high-tensile bolts*. These are tightened with a calibrated torsion wrench (which must be recalibrated at frequent intervals). As the bolt is tightened with a standard torque, it applies a standard pressure to the two pieces of steel to be joined and thus creates the same friction between the plates as a hot-driven rivet. The calibrated wrench ensures that there is sufficient pressure, but also that the tension in the bolt is not so high that it breaks during tightening.

Bolted joints are rarely used in aluminum structures. If they are needed, steel bolts are often used in preference to aluminum bolts. Since steel and aluminum in contact produce galvanic corrosion, the steel bolts, nuts, and washers must be galvanized or, preferably, cadmium-plated (see Sec. 11.1).

Joints between two metal plates in line may be butted or lapped and then riveted, bolted, or welded (Fig. 10.11.1).

Welding can be done on a building site, but it is better suited to the factory. It generates heat and glare, and the job is well suited to performance by robots if sufficiently repeated.

Most steel structures have factory-welded and site-

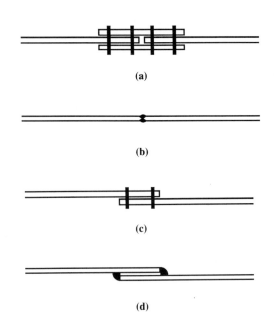

Fig. 10.11.1. Joints for two metal plates in line.
(a) Bolted or riveted butt joint (cover plates required); (b) welded butt joint (cover plates optional; a satisfactory joint can be formed without them); (c) bolted or riveted lap joint; (d) welded lap joint.

bolted joints. Care must be exercised if work-hardened high-tensile steel is used (Sec. 10.6) since it may lose its high strength if heated by welding. Stainless steels can be welded.

Some aluminum alloys can be welded, but others cannot. A large number of aluminum alloys are available (see Sec. 11.3), and there are no simple rules for distinguishing weldable from nonweldable types. However, specifications always state whether welding can be used.

Welding is a fusion proceess. Some of the metal in each of the pieces to be joined is melted, and the two pieces are then fused together by pressure (as in spot welding and tube welding), or, more commonly, by adding additional metal of the same composition (Fig. 10.11.2). The necessary heat can be generated with a gas flame, using either oxygen and acetylene or oxygen and hydrogen from pressure containers. This equipment is entirely mobile.

Most welding is now done electrically, and the steel rod that supplies the weld metal forms one electrode. The other electric terminal is joined to one of the pieces to be welded. It is essential that the fused metal not oxidize during welding since the inclusion of an oxide particle would seriously weaken the weld. The *flux* used for this purpose forms a coating on the electrode that automatically melts as welding proceeds.

Aluminum alloys, which oxidize more rapidly than steel, need extra protection. The welding operation is carried out in an atmosphere of the chemically inert gas *helium,* which is directed into the weld area through a sheath surrounding the electrode, thus preventing oxidation of both the electrode and the weld pool.

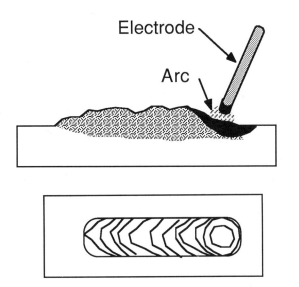

Fig. 10.11.2. Fusion welding.
During welding, some metal in each piece to be joined is melted; additional molten metal of same composition is added to strengthen the joint.

Heliarc welding is also used for stainless steel. Helium is an expensive gas outside North America, and the inert gas *argon* is used instead in Europe and Australia.

The pieces to be joined must be prepared by being cleaned of all dirt and oxide and by cutting them back, if necessary, to make it easier to fuse them with weld metal (Fig. 10.11.3).

In *brazing* and *soldering* (the same process, differing only in the solder used), the metal in the pieces to be joined is not fused, and the strength of the joint depends on the adhesion with, and the strength of, the solder.

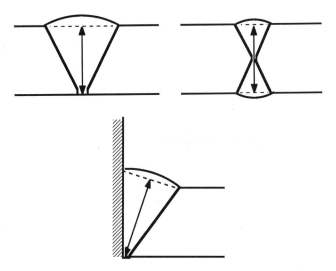

Fig. 10.11.3. Throat of welded joints.
In most welded joints, the parent metal is cut back to make it easier for the weld metal to penetrate into the joint and produce perfect fusion between the two metals. The *strength* of the joint is determined by multiplying the maximum stress of the metal by the cross-sectional area of the "throat," indicated by the arrows.

The solder must have a lower melting point than the pieces to be joined, and this differential needs to be checked in the case of aluminum alloys. For satisfactory jointing, the surfaces must be kept free from oxide films. They must be cleaned beforehand, and oxidation during soldering prevented by a flux that melts at a lower temperature than the solder. The flux is often supplied as a core inside the solder.

A variety of low-melting-point alloys can be used as solders. The essential requirements are that the solder be able to wet the metals to be joined and have a lower melting point. Soft solders consist mainly of lead and tin, from 100-percent lead to 100-percent tin, with small additions of antimony, arsenic, zinc, or silver. Their melting points range from 190°C (375°F) to 325°C (620°F). Low-melting-point aluminum alloys are sometimes used for soldering aluminum.

An alloy of lead and tin in equal parts is a common all-purpose solder; it is also the plumbers' "fine solder." It starts to melt at 183°C (361°F) and is completely molten at 216°C (421°F). Plumbers' "coarse solder," consisting of three parts of lead to one of tin, has a slightly higher melting point (266°C or 511°F).

Lead, copper, brass, tin plate, and galvanized iron are all materials that can easily be joined by soldering. Some aluminum alloys are also suitable.

Siver solders are alloys of silver, copper, and zinc, sometimes with an addition of cadmium or tin; they have a higher melting point. Melting usually does not commence until 600°C (1100°F) and may not be complete below 870°C (1600°F). Silver solders have a higher strength and are used particularly for joining copper and silver alloys. Those with a high silver content have a silvery appearance; those with a high copper content have a brassy appearance.

Brazing solders have a wider range of melting points, from 600°C (1100°F) to over 1000°C (1800°F), but those most used have a higher melting point and higher strength than silver solders. The high-copper alloys are used for brazing steel, copper, and brass, including plumbing fixtures. The high-aluminum alloys are used for brazing aluminum; they can be used for a number of aluminum alloys that are nonweldable.

Metals can also be joined by *adhesives* (see Sec. 19.6), although special care has to be taken if the metals are to be used externally. Glued joints are particularly suitable for light-gauge metals. Adhesives are always used if metals are employed as a facing for plywood.

REFERENCES

10.1. H. J. Cowan: *The Masterbuilders*. Wiley, New York, 1977. Chapter 8, pp. 219–268.

10.2. H. J. Cowan: *Science and Building*. Wiley, New York, 1978. Chapters 2, 3, 4, and 9, pp. 9–118 and 267–300.

10.3. H. J. Cowan and F. Wilson: *Structural Systems*. Van Nostrand Reinhold, New York, 1981, pp. 71–163.

10.4. H. J. Cowan: *Design of Reinforced Concrete Structures.* Prentice-Hall, Englewood Cliffs, NJ, 1982. Chapter 15, Prestressed Concrete, pp. 225–240.

10.5. M. A. Rushmer and M. D. Burdick: *Weather Resistance of Porcelain Enamels.* Building Science Series 4. National Bureau of Standards, Washington, DC, 1966. 16 pp.

10.6. H. J. Cowan and P. R. Smith: *Environmental Systems.* Van Nostrand Reinhold, New York, 1983. 296 pp.

10.7. G. Herbert: *Pioneers of Prefabrication.* Johns Hopkins University Press, Baltimore, MD, 1978. 228 pp.

SUGGESTIONS FOR FURTHER READING

W. Alexander and A. Street: *Metals in the Service of Man.* 8th Edn. Penguin Books, Harmondsworth (England), 1983. 312 pp.

R. W. Cahn and P. Haasen (Eds.): *Physical Metallurgy.* North-Holland, Amsterdam, 1983. 1918 pp.

A. K. Osborne: *An Encyclopaedia of the Iron and Steel Industry.* Technical Press, London, 1967. 558 pp.

R. M. E. Diamant: *The Prevention of Corrosion.* Business Books, London, 1971. 199 pp.

11

Nonferrous Metals

Volume for volume, nonferrous metals are more expensive than iron and steel, but they are also more corrosion-resistant, and that is the main reason for using them. Lead and copper have the best weathering properties, but aluminum can be improved for this purpose by anodizing, and it is lighter and cheaper.

Aluminum is simpler and more versatile than steel to produce and fabricate, but the electrolytic process involved requires a great deal of electric power. Aluminum now has an international coding system that makes it easier to select a suitable material from among the large number available. Anodizing of aluminum has made great strides since the sixties, and it is now possible to color it with perfectly lightfast pigments. Recent decades have seen a great increase in the use of aluminum for windows, curtain walls, reflective insulation, roof sheets, and builders' hardware.

An international coding system also exists now for copper and its alloys. Copper may be less visible today, but we are actually employing more of it than ever before, because it is the best material for electric wiring. The use of lead, tin, and zinc in buildings, however, is on the decline.

11.1 THE CORROSION RESISTANCE ON NONFERROUS METALS

Nonferrous metals are today, volume for volume, more expensive than iron and steel, stainless steel being the exception because it contains a very large amount of nonferrous alloying material. This has not always been so. During most periods, up to the eighteenth century, some nonferrous metals were cheaper than iron. The Romans used lead extensively not merely for water pipes, but also for lining baths. They even used it occasionally as a kind of mortar for heavily loaded masonry; molten lead was poured into the joints to give perfect and strong bearing for blocks of stone.

Copper was also used extravagantly, at least by modern standards. The great bronze doors (which were once gilded) still remain in the Pantheon, built in Rome in 123 A.D., but the bronze tiles covering the roof were removed to Constantinople in A.D. 655 to be turned into guns and coins. Enough bronze, eventually removed in 1626, still remained in the porch to cast the guns of the Castel Sant' Angelo and the huge twisted columns for the baldachino in St. Peter's.

It is likely that today's production cost of these nonferrous metals that were known prior to the nineteenth century is lower that it was in Roman times, the Middle Ages, and the Renaissance. The change is therefore the result of the advances in the technology of ferrous metals, and, more recently, of plastics.

Apart from a few very expensive metals used exclusively in the aircraft and aerospace industries, nonferrous metals are not as strong as steel, and the main reason for using them is their superior corrosion resistance as compared to that of steel (other than of stainless steel). Indeed, stainless steel, although a ferrous metal, may in this connection be classified as a separate material.

We considered corrosion briefly in Secs. 10.3, 10.7, and 10.8. and noted that energy is required to produce a metal from its ore, and, conversely, that energy is generated when a metal changes to a metallic oxide so that the process becomes self-perpetuating unless it is stopped chemically or physically. We noted that the rusting of iron continues because the hydrated ferric oxide formed is a loose and porous substance that flakes off and leaves a less contaminated surface. We also noted that the corrosion resistance of stainless steel is due to the formation of a very thin, chromium-rich oxide film that, if damaged by scratching, immediately reforms and maintains the corrosion protection.

The corrosion protection of aluminum is similar, although it is not quite as effective as that of stainless steel. Aluminum is a silvery metal when it is cut or otherwise exposed to the atmosphere, but an aluminum oxide film forms within a few seconds. This is hard and coherent and protects the metal from further corrosion. The film can be strengthened by anodizing (Sec. 11.4) if the aluminum is to be exposed to weathering or to be used where it is likely to be scratched.

Pure aluminum has better corrosion resistance than most of its alloys, but much lower strength. Hence, aluminum alloys that require weathering resistance are often given a surface coating of pure aluminum—a material known as *alclad*.

The *noble metals* are near the cathodic end of the electrochemical series (see Table 10.1). *Gold* is one of the very few metals that does not tarnish or corrode on exposure to air. The only substance that will attack it is *aqua regia* (the royal liquid), which consists of 25-percent nitric acid and 75-percent hydrochloric acid. It would be an ideal material for metallic building surfaces if it were cheaper. It is, in fact, still used in buildings in small quantities for gilded surfaces, and as a pigment for ruby-red glass. *Copper* is a near-noble metal that can retain its characteristic metallic appearance for many days, even years in a dry climate. It is possible to retain it indefinitely indoors by use of a transparent varnish, which may have to be renewed at intervals. Over a period of time copper surfaces change to a dull brown color as a result of the formation of an oxide coating. This is the color generally to be found on copper pipes, gutters, and downspouts (downpipes). Prolonged exposure on a roof gradually causes a breakdown of this oxide skin to basic copper sulfate and/or basic copper carbonate; this is the green "patina" of copper roofs, caused by the color of the sulfate. Sulfur dioxide and trioxide, as well as carbon dioxide, are absorbed from the air, and the process is faster in an industrially polluted atmosphere. Copper is very resistant to pollution, however, and the formation of the patina may take ten years or more. Copper sheet may be destroyed eventually, but it is an extremely slow process.

Metallic *lead* also has a silvery appearance, but the material oxidizes rapidly. The oxide film absorbs carbon dioxide from the atmosphere to form a dull patina of lead carbonate, which inhibits further corrosion because it is strongly adherent to the metal and insoluble in all inorganic acids. As a result, lead can be used without protection in damp-proof courses, whereas aluminum needs a protective coating—for example, of asphalt.

Lead, however, is attacked by pure water. Most piped water contains some calcium salts that have been dissolved by percolation through rock. If it contains too much, the water is called "hard," it will not lather soap, and it is "softened" by procedures that are beyond the scope of this book. If it contains no carbonates at all, however, which is rare, it is "soft" and dissolves the lead from lead pipes to form soluble lead hydroxide. This compound is poisonous, and soft water in conjunction with lead pipes is a major cause of lead posioning. Lead water supply pipes are rarely installed today, but lead is still used for waste pipes. If lead pipes are used, soft water must be treated with calcium bicarbonate.

Lead is used extensively as a protective coating for steel sheets. *Terne plate* (see Sec. 10.3) is coated with an alloy that is 80-percent lead and 20-percent tin. It does not provide sacrificial protection (Sec. 10.3), because it is on the cathodic side of iron, but, because of its flexibility, it does provide a continuous, unbroken coating that cuts off the supply of oxygen to the steel and thus inhibits corrosion. Lead is also used as a protective coating on sheet copper (Sec. 11.6).

Zinc was at one time used as a sheet metal (Sec. 11.7), but it is now considered too expensive for use on its own as a building material. Its most important use is for the galvanizing and sherardizing of iron and steel (see Sec. 10.3). Because it is on the anodic side of iron (Table 10.1), it offers sacrificial protection, and this makes damage of the zinc coating by scratching less important since the corrosion protection is maintained by the zinc coating around the scratch.

Metallic zinc and zinc coatings oxidize rapidly to form a zinc-oxide coating about one hundredth of a millimeter in thickness. This is changed gradually to zinc carbonate in air or water and to zinc sulfate if buried in soil containing sulfur compounds. Both coatings are highly resistant to corrosion.

The corrosion resistance of the nonferrous metals used in building is therefore greatly superior to that of ordinary steel; it is produced by a ceramic coating of oxide or salt on the metal that inhibits further corrosion.

Nonferrous metals used in contact can produce serious corrosion if they are widely apart in the electrochemical series (Table 10.1). In the early years of this century, when aluminum roof sheets were first introduced, it was not uncommon to consider that such nonferrous sheets ought to be nailed with nonferrous nails, the only nonferrous nails at the time being copper nails. Since copper and aluminum are at the opposite ends of the electrochemical series, however corrosion occurs between them in the presence of rainwater or atmospheric humidity. The copper nails, being cathodic, come to no harm, but they produce holes in the aluminum sheets. Copper and its alloys must obviously not be used in contact with aluminum.

Lead covered with its protective patina is a very

inert material and can thus be used in conjunction with either copper or aluminum or galvanized steel. Lead washers can be used when aluminum sheets are nailed with galvanized steel nails.

Although aluminum nails, clips, and bolts can be produced, the use of steel fasteners is common practice. Some measure of corrosion protection is obtained by galvanizing or sherardizing, but cadmium plating is more effective, even though cadmium is less anodic than zinc. The good results obtained from the use of cadmium-plated fasteners for aluminum is probably due to the fact that its electric potential is very close to that of aluminum in the electrochemical series.

11.2 THE PRODUCTION AND FABRICATION OF ALUMINUM

Aluminum is the only metal discussed in the previous section that was not known to the ancient world. The word is derived from the Latin *alumen,* meaning potash alum, a material used for dying. In 1809, Sir Humphry Davy proved that alum had a metallic base, and, in 1845, Friedrich Wöhler produced a globule of metallic aluminum—the size of a pinhead—from which some of its properties, including its low density, were determined. In 1845, H. Sainte-Claire Deville produced the first ingot of aluminum. The Emperor Napolean III encouraged the production of the new metal and had some aluminum plates made which he used at an official banquet for himself and his most distinguished guests. Lesser mortals were served on silver plate. The *Encyclopedia Britannica,* in describing the physical and chemical properties of aluminum in 1875, explained that the metal was used in jewelry and, because of its light weight, in balance beams.

In 1886, Paul Héroult in France and Charles Martin Hall in the U.S.A. independently invented an electrolytic process in which a solution of aluminum oxide in molten cryolite is electrolyzed between carbon electrodes. (Cryolite is a double fluoride of aluminum and sodium found naturally in Greenland, but now usually made synthetically.) Within a few years, the cost of aluminum dropped to about one-fortieth of its previous price, and production increased about 400 times. The Martin-Héroult process is still used today.

Aluminum is the third most common element in the earth's crust, after oxygen and silicon, but the energy needed to reduce alumina (or aluminum oxide, Al_2O_3) to the metal is very high. There is the additional problem of obtaining the alumina from one of the minerals containing it, the most economical being *bauxite,* a mineral first found at Baux in France. Bauxites, which are found in many parts of the world in thick deposits, differ somewhat in composition, but they all contain 40 to 60 percent of alumina, 5 to 30 percent of ferric oxide, and 10 to 30 percent of water, as well as some

other materials. The process normally used for extracting alumina from bauxite was invented in 1892 by Karl Joseph Bayer and has been named after him. It also requires large amounts of electricity.

At present, the production of alumina from bauxite requires about 30 MJ/kg, and the reduction of alumina to metallic aluminum about 250 MJ/kg, or a total of 280 MJ per kilogram of metallic aluminum (about 120,000 Btu per lb). It is therefore economically expedient to take the bauxite, or at least the alumina produced from it, to a place where electricity can be produced cheaply, even if this means that it has to be transported several thousand kilometers (or miles). The cost of the enormous amount of electric power needed to reduce bauxite to metallic aluminum, even when it is obtained on advantageous terms, makes aluminum more expensive than steel.

Most aluminum is turned into aluminum alloy (Sec. 11.3), and its fabrication depends to some extent on the nature of the alloy, as some are suited to hot-rolling, some to cold-rolling, and some to both. Aluminum ingots can be hot-rolled in a blooming mill, like steel (see Sec. 10.2), or they can be cut with a saw to reduce their size. Aluminum can be hot-rolled into standard sections that look similar to the standard steel sections shown in Fig. 10.2.3, but these are hardly ever used in buildings.

Extrusion is a cheaper and more versatile process for the hot-forming of aluminum sections (Fig. 11.2.1). A new extrusion die costs far less than a set of new rolls for a hot-rolling mill and can cut complex shapes (Fig. 11.2.2) that are beyond the scope of hot rolling.

The melting point of aluminum alloys is between 530° and 650°C, and aluminum can be extruded at temperatures between 400° and 500°C (750° and 930°F), depending on the alloy. The section emerges from the extrusion press with a smooth surface and a protective oxide coating (Sec. 11.1). The coating can be increased in thickness and colored by anodizing, but the section can also be used without any further surface treatment.

Aluminum can be cold-rolled, like steel and stainless steel. As its modulus of elasticity is only one-third that of steel and stainless steel, it is more liable to

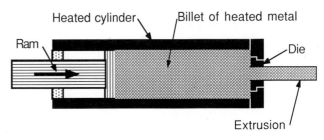

Fig. 11.2.1. Extrusion press.
The aluminum alloy is squeezed through a die at a temperature of about 450°C (850°F) by a hydraulic press, like toothpaste through the opening of a tube.

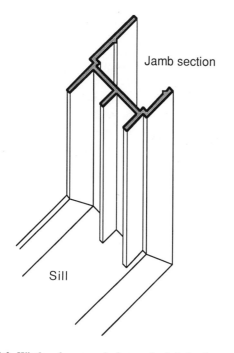

Fig. 11.2.2. Window frame made from extruded aluminum sections. Aluminum alloys can be successfully extruded through dies cut to produce complex shapes. Window and door frames constitute by far the largest single use of aluminum alloys in buildings.

buckle (see Fig. 10.9.3), and it also deflects more. Consequently, the precautions set out in Sec. 10.9 for cold-formed steel construction apply even more strongly to aluminum [see Fig. 10.9.4(a) and (b), 10.9.5, 10.9.6, and 10.9.7(b)]. Because of its higher deflection, it is usually necessary to use aluminum sheet that is thicker than stainless steel sheet would have to be under the same circumstances. On the other hand, aluminum is cheaper and lighter than stainless steel.

A comparison between structural steel, stainless steel, and aluminum is made in Table 11.1. Steel weighs about three times as much as aluminum, and its modulus of elasticity is about three times as high. Its coefficient of thermal expansion is about half.

A comparison of strength is more difficult because of the variety of alloy steels and aluminum alloys. It is frequently stated that aluminum alloys can be produced that are much stronger than structural steel, and this is correct. A fair comparison would be between low-alloy, high-tensile steel and aluminum alloy, however, and on that basis steel is a stronger material.

If a comparison is made with steel on the basis of strength per unit weight, aluminum comes out well, but it is not much better in this respect than laminated timber or plywood, which have very good strength-per-weight ratios.

The main advantages of aluminum over structural and low-alloy steels are its corrosion resistance and good appearance. The lower weight is also a frequent advantage. Its main disadvantages are its higher cost and low fire resistance. If fire-protective coatings are applied, then its main advantages are lost. Because of its low melting point, aluminum is not merely going to soften in a severe fire but is liable to melt (See Fig. 7.7.1).

Aluminum is usually cheaper than stainless steel, and that is the reason it is used in much larger quantities in construction. Since its corrosion resistance is not as good as that of stainless steel, however, one would not, for example, use it for urinals. It has a much lower modulus of elasticity, and thus a higher deflection and a greater tendency to buckle for the same thickness.

11.3 ALUMINUM ALLOYS AND THEIR HEAT TREATMENT

There are many more alloys of aluminum than there are of steel, and each is available in more than one form of hardness or temper. There are thus several hundred materials to chose from, and expert advice is needed.

An international coding system now exists and will be briefly described here. The superseded national

Table 11.1. A Comparison of some of the Properties of Steel, Stainless Steel, Aluminum, and Copper

Property	Steel	Stainless steel	Aluminum	Copper
Specific gravity	7.9	7.9	2.7	9.0
Density				
kg/m^3	7900	7900	2700	8960
lb/ft^3	493	493	169	559
Melting point				
°C	1530	1450	660	1080
°F	2780	2640	1220	1980
Modulus of elasticity				
MPa	200,000	193,000	69,000	117,000
ksi	30,000	28,000	10,000	17,000
Coefficient of thermal expansion				
per °C × 10^6	13	13	24	19
per °F × 10^6	7	7	13	10

coding systems still appear in textbooks, however, and in some trade literature. Both systems distinguish between casting alloys and wrought alloys, the latter being those alloys whose shape is produced by extrusion, stamping, or hot or cold rolling. Since casting alloys find only limited use in buildings, we will consider the coding of wrought alloys only.

The international code consists of four numbers. The first number refers to the principal alloying material:

1 = pure aluminum
2 = copper alloys
3 = manganese alloys
4 = silicon alloys
5 = magnesium alloys
6 = manganese–silicon alloys
7 = zinc alloys

Series 1, 3, 4, and 5 are *nonheat-treatable* alloys, and Series 2, 6, and 7 are *heat-treatable alloys*. There is a secondary coding system for each type.

The nonheat-treatable alloys have a *temper designation*. Their strength is increased by *work-hardening*, most of which occurs while the alloys are being cold-rolled. The increase in strength is accompanied by a reduction in ductility, however, and this may be excessive. If that is the case, the material needs to be *annealed*, either at the conclusion of cold-rolling or during it—that is, the reduction in thickness by cold rolling is interrupted, the material annealed, and the cold rolling then resumed. The annealing operation is essentially the same as the one for steel, that is, the material is heated and allowed to cool slowly.

The temper designations are as follows:

O = annealed and recrystallized
H1 = strain-hardened only
H2 = strain-hardened and then partially annealed
H3 = strain-hardened and then stabilized, that is, stress-relieved

One or two further digits are added to follow these designations and give further information; for example, a second digit 8 means full-hard; 4 means half-hard; and 2 means quarter-hard.

The heat-treatable alloys are given a *thermal treatment designation* instead. These heat-treatment designations are as follows:

T1 = cooled from an elevated-temperature shaping process and naturally aged to a substantially stable condition. (*Natural aging* means precipitation from a solid solution that occurs slowly at room temperature, and results in an improvement in an alloy's properties)

T2 = annealed
T3 = solution-heat-treated and then cold-worked. (*Solution heat treatment* involves heating an alloy at a suitable temperature for a sufficient time to allow soluble constituents to enter into a solid solution, and then *quenching* it so that these constituents are retained in a supersaturated state. Quenching means rapid cooling of the alloy from a high temperature by immersion in a liquid or a gas)

T4 = solution-heat-treated and naturally aged to a substantially stable condition, that is, without cold working

T5 = cooled from an elevated-temperature shaping process and then artificially aged. (*Artificial aging* means that the precipitation from the solid solution occurs more rapidly at a high temperature)

T6 = solution-heat-treated and then artificially aged

T7 = solution-heat-treated and then *stabilized*, that is, stress-relieved

T8 = solution-heat-treated, cold-worked, and then artificially aged

T9 = solution-heat-treated, artificially aged, and then cold-worked

T10 = cooled from an elevated-temperature shaping process, artificially aged, and then cold-worked

Additional digits can be added to these designations to give further information, for example whether stress relieving is by stretching, compressing, or thermal treatment.

These heat-treatment designations therefore involve various combinations of cold-working, quenching, annealing, aging at room temperature, aging at an elevated temperature, and stress-relieving.

Each of the alloy series has its own phase diagram and specific properties.

The *1000 series*—that is, alloys whose code number starts with 1—contain aluminum of 99 percent or higher purity. They have excellent corrosion resistance, excellent workability, and low strength. Their main use in building is as a cladding material. A thin sheet can be placed above and below another aluminum alloy before the cold rolling process so that the alloy sheet emerges from the rolling mill with a protective coating of pure aluminum on each side. The sheet is then called *aluminum clad*, or *alclad*. Cladding is used particularly for alloys in the 2000 series, which have poor corrosion resistance, but it is also used for some other alloys.

The *2000 series* contains the alloys once known as *duralumin*. These were developed in the early years of this century by Alfred Wilm and subsequently revolutionized the design of airplanes and airships. Quite soft in their original condition, their strength can be greatly increased by solution heat treatment. For example, the widely used alloy 2024—which contains 4.4 percent of copper, 0.8 percent of silicon, 0.8 percent of manganese, and 0.5 percent of magnesium—has a range of proof stress from 70 to 410 MPa (10 to 60 ksi) and a range of ultimate tensile stress from 170 to 470 MPa (25 to 68 ksi), depending on its heat treatment. The strength at the top of this range is comparable to that of a high-tensile steel. It should be borne in mind, moreover, that the 2024 alloy has only one-third the weight of the steel.

The principal alloying element in the 3000 series is manganese. Since the maximum permissible amount of manganese is only about 1.5 percent, this is a relatively small series.

The major element in the *4000 series* is silicon, which can be used in large percentages (in excess of 10 percent). The high-silicon alloys become dark grey when the material is anodized, and some excellent architectural finishes can be produced with these alloys.

The *5000 series* contains magnesium as the principal alloying element. Magnesium is considerably more effective as a hardener than manganese and can be added in larger quantities.

The *6000 series* contains both silicon and magnesium in the approximate proportions required to form magnesium silicide. Unlike the series that contain magnesium only or silicon only, it is heat-treatable.

Zinc is the major element in the *7000 series,* which contains some of the highest-strength aluminum alloys.

The alloys with architectural applications are to be found mainly in the 3000, 4000, 5000, and 6000 series.

The specifications for each alloy contain information on its resistance to corrosion, forgability, capacity for cold working, and machinability, and its temper or thermal treatment designation. They also state whether it can be brazed and/or welded. Connections for aluminum have already been considered in Sec. 10.11.

11.4 ANODIZING

Although anodizing was briefly mentioned in Sec. 11.1, it requires more detailed consideration, because it provides not merely weathering protection but also makes it possible to color the metal. The first patents for anodizing were registered in the 1920s, and anodizing on a commercial scale started in the 1930s. Of the variety of processes now available, the sulfuric-acid process is the one used the most widely.

When steel is galvanized or terne-plated, a new layer of metal is deposited on the surface, which covers the original steel plate. Anodizing, on the other hand, converts the surface layer of the aluminum into aluminum oxide and in the process reveals a layer of metallic aluminum that was previously invisible below the surface.

In the sulfuric-acid process, the aluminum to be anodized is immersed in a bath of a 10-percent solution of sulfuric acid and connected to the positive end of a direct-current (dc) electric supply. The cathode is usually lead. The sulfuric acid is decomposed by the passage of the electric current. Oxygen and sulfate ions are attracted to the aluminum anode, and hydrogen ions to the cathode. The oxygen combines with the aluminum in the anode, and an anodic oxide film is built up. In the first minute of anodizing, a thin film is formed that serves as a barrier layer, but later the acid starts to dissolve part of the anodic coating, producing tiny pores in the coating (see Fig. 10.4.1).

There are several other anodizing processes, all electrolytic, but some employing alternating current (ac) and using different electrolytes.

The first attempts to color aluminum as part of the anodizing process were made in the 1930s. Since the anodic oxide coating is able to absorb organic dyes, a variety of colors can be produced. A number of buildings erected in the 1950s had anodized aluminum curtain walls incorporating organic dyes. The colors faded after a few years of exposure to sunlight, leaving the panels with unattractive pastel shades. Organic dyes can be used successfully for interior surfaces that are not exposed to bright sunlight, however, and entire color pictures can be printed on aluminum by offset litho or silk-screen printing during the anodizing process.

The first anodizing processes incorporating inorganic colors also go back to the 1930s, but they did not become commercially successful until the 1960s. There are several processes employed and several coloring elements. The range of colors, however, is at present limited.

Brace and Sheasby (Ref. 1, p. 197) favor a two-stage process in which aluminum panels (to be used, for example, for curtain walls) are first anodized conventionally by the sulfuric-acid process, using dc. The panels are then transferred to a bath containing a metal salt solution, and an alternating current is passed between them and another set of electrodes. The metal-oxide particles are deposited at the bottom of the pores (Fig. 11.4.1).

The most successful inorganic colors are various shades of bronze, produced from electrolytes containing the salts (usually the sulfates) of nickel, cobalt, tin, or copper, or some combination of these metals. A perfect black can also be produced from these electrolytes. Grey colors can be obtained from tin–zinc electrolytes, and blue-grey from bismuth–cobalt electrolytes. These, however, are not as popular as the

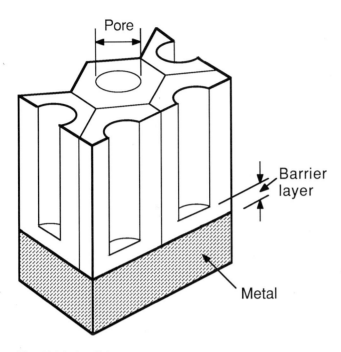

Fig. 11.4.1. Anodizing.
The anodic aluminum-oxide coating produced in the sulfuric-acid process has several million tiny pores per square centimeter (or square inch), according to A. W. Brace and P. G. Sheasby. (*Reproduced by permission from Ref. 11.1, p. 1.*)

bronze colors. Bronze-anodized aluminum looks exactly like oxidized copper or bronze and is much cheaper and lighter. Other light-fast inorganic colors are possible. There are several methods for producing a finish that closely resembles gold, and this is already used widely for costume jewelry. Various shades from pink to maroon can be produced from copper electrolytes, and various shades of blue from molybdenum or tungsten electrolytes.

Finally, the anodized coat must be sealed before it is exposed to the weather. Anodic aluminum-oxide coatings produced by the sulfuric-acid process can be sealed by immersion in water close to its boiling point (98°C or 208°F) for a period that depends on the thickness of the aluminum-oxide film and that ranges from 10 minutes to 2 hours. Sealing can also be accomplished by steam treatment and various nonaqueous sealants that fill the pores rather than close them. One such method is to lacquer the anodized but unsealed panels with a clear, water-based resin and then heating them in an oven to produce a transparent lacquer film about 0.01 mm thick.

Not all aluminum alloys are equally suitable for anodizing. Brace and Sheasby list them together with a scale from 1 (poorest response) to 5 (best response) (see Ref. 11.1, p. 7).

11.5 ARCHITECTURAL USES OF ALUMINUM

Aluminum was a minor building material prior to World War II. Between 1935 and 1944, aluminum production increased approximately 2000 percent, in the early years partly, and in the later years definitely, because of the demand of the military aircraft industry. When the war ended, there was surplus production capacity and a large stock of aluminum metal, and although aluminum usage has increased steadily ever since, it took about 12 years before production again reached its wartime peak.

In the late 1940s, determined attempts were made to find new uses for aluminum in the building industry. Some were successful; some were not. Aluminum has had very limited success, for example, as a structural building material in place of steel. This is only partly the result of its higher cost. Its lower modulus of elasticity (see Table 11.1) is also a disadvantage because it increases the amount of deflection and the tendency to buckle (see Fig. 10.9.3). Aluminum is a useful struc-

Table 11.2. Relative Weights and Melting Points of the Materials Mentioned in Chaps. 10 and 11.

Material and Chemical Symbol	Specific Gravity	Density kg/m³	Density lb/ft³	Melting Point °C	Melting Point °F
Aluminum (Al)	2.70	2700	169	660	1220
Cadmium (Cd)	8.65	8650	540	321	610
Chromium (Cr)	7.14	7140	446	1830	3326
Columbium* (Cb)	8.57	8570	535	2415	4379
Copper (Cu)	8.96	8960	559	1083	1981
Lead (Pb)	11.34	11,340	708	327	621
Magnesium (Mg)	1.74	1740	109	651	1204
Manganese (Mn)	7.39	7390	461	1245	2273
Nickel (Ni)	8.90	8900	556	1455	2651
Silicon (Si)	2.40	2400	150	1420	2588
Stainless steel	7.90	7900	493	1450	2642
Structural steel	7.87	7870	491	1530	2818
Tin (Sn)	7.30	7300	456	232	450
Zinc (Zn)	7.14	7140	446	419	786

*Also called niobium (Nb).

tural material for long spans where the structure carries mostly its own weight and buckling and deflection present no problems—for example, for triangulated or geodesic domes. It also has an advantage if a structure needs to become airborne; it has, for example, been used to replace old church steeples, because the entire steeple can be hoisted into position in one piece (Fig. 11.5.1). It is also a good material for adding an extra story to an existing building without overloading existing columns.

Programs introduced in the 1940s to build prefabricated aluminum houses to solve the post-war housing problem must be deemed a failure. Technically speaking, the aluminum houses were entirely satisfactory. They had good insulation and strength, and the interiors were carefully designed and fitted out. Given mass production, the cost could have been reduced below the level of conventional timber and/or brick construction. One cause of their rejection was a dislike for living in a "tin box"; more important, the houses,

unlike timber and brick houses, were incapable of subsequent alteration because of their all-aluminum construction. Aluminum will continue to play a part in prefabrication, but not as the sole material.

Aluminum has been more successful for curtain walls (Fig. 11.5.2). If backed with insulation, the panels provide good thermal performance. The development of durable bronze-colored anodized finishes in the 1960s (Sec. 11.4) gave aluminum curtain walls a decided advantage over the more expensive bronze panels.

Aluminum has also proved very suitable for partitions, particularly movable partitions because of its light weight and durable surface finish (Fig. 11.5.3). The largest single use of aluminum at present, however, is for windows (Fig. 11.2.2). It has also to a certain extent replaced galvanized steel for use in roof sheets.

Aluminum sheet is increasingly replacing lead for damp-proof courses; unlike lead, however, it needs a protective coating in addition to anodizing, and this is usually asphalt. In competition with lead and copper, aluminum sheet is also used for flashings.

Fig. 11.5.1. Aluminum church steeple.
Because of its light weight, a steeple such as this can be installed in one piece with a crane or helicopter, thus avoiding the costly scaffolding needed had traditional materials been used.

Fig. 11.5.2. Aluminum curtain wall.
The Alcoa building was one of the first (1953) to utilize a complete aluminum curtain wall. The 4.4-mm (1/8-in.) stamped aluminum panels are backed with 100-mm (4-in.) perlite concrete as insulation (see Sec. 14.7).

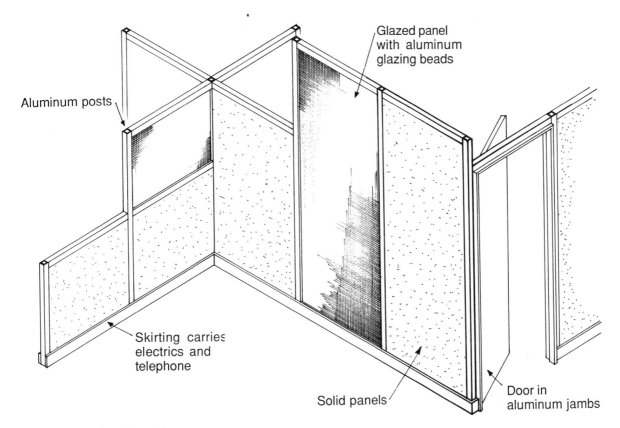

Aluminum posts

Glazed panel
with aluminum
glazing beads

Skirting carries
electrics and
telephone

Solid panels

Door in
aluminum jambs

Fig. 11.5.3. Aluminum-framed partition.

Aluminum foil with a thickness of the order of 0.01 mm (0.0004 in.) is used for reflective insulation in conjunction with thermal insulating materials (Figs. 11.5.4 and 11.5.5). It reflects thermal radiation (Ref. 11.2) and also acts as a vapor barrier (see Sec. 4.8).

Aluminum castings, sometimes anodized to look like brass or bronze, are replacing brass and bronze for door furniture. Aluminum castings have also been used in the restoration of nineteenth-century houses with cast iron balconies (Fig. 11.5.6).

11.6 COPPER AND ITS ALLOYS

We noted in Sec. 10.1 that copper was the first metal to acquire economic significance, about 5000 years ago. The Romans used it extravagantly 2000 years ago (Sec. 11.1), and even at that time it was still a more important building material than iron.

Today, copper is third in importance, after steel and aluminum, and one does not see as much of it in buildings as one did at the beginning of this century. The use of copper in buildings has not, however, decreased in quantity. We use more of it than ever before, because of the growing demand for electric power and lighting and for computer terminals and circuits. Copper has the second-best electrical conductivity of any material (silver is slightly better), and it is therefore the best material for electrical wiring.

The discovery that copper is made harder and stronger by a small addition of tin is very ancient; the fact was well known to the Greeks, who made bronze in the proportion of about nine parts of copper to one part of tin. Today, the term *bronze* is used not merely for copper–tin alloys, but for copper–zinc and copper–silicon alloys that have a bronze color.

Brass, developed in the seventeenth century, is an alloy of copper and zinc, containing up to 40-percent zinc. Both bronze and brass had substantial military uses, which are reflected in their names. Cartridge brass contains about 30-percent zinc, and naval brass about 38-percent. Gunmetal, used at one time for casting muzzle-loading artillery pieces, contains 8-percent tin and 2-percent zinc; the remainder in each case is copper.

There is now an international coding system based on the same principles as that for aluminum alloys (Sec. 11.3). The principal alloys used in building are as follows:

110 Copper: 99.9% copper
122 Copper: 99.9% copper, 0.02% phosphorus (the principal alloy used for copper pipes)
220 Commercial Bronze: 90% copper, 10% zinc (a bronze-colored metal)
230 Red Brass: 85% copper, 15% zinc (the principal alloy used for brass pipes)
260 Cartridge Brass: 70% copper, 30% zinc (a yellow brass)

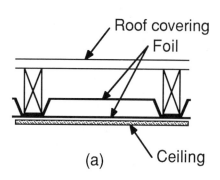

(a)

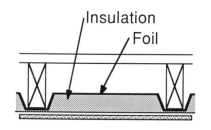

(b)

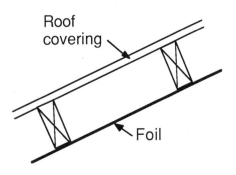

(c)

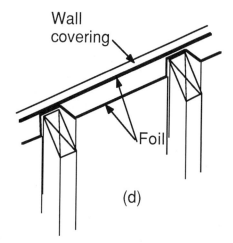

(d)

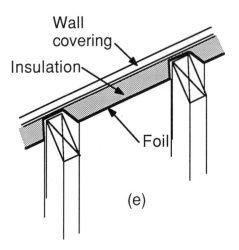

(e)

Fig. 11.5.4. Aluminum foil used as reflective insulation and as vapor barrier

(a) Flat roof with two layers of reflective insulation and air space between to act as thermal insulation.

(b) Flat roof with one layer of reflective insulation backed by lightweight thermal insulation superior to (a) because the foil then also acts as vapor barrier.

(c) Reflective insulation in sloping roof. The thermal insulation is separate and rests on the ceiling (see also Fig. 11.5.5).

(d) Wall with two layers of reflective insulation and air space between. (Roof bearers and wall studs, particularly if they are wooden, should preferably be outside the vapor barrier to avoid deterioration caused by condensed vapor.)

(e) Wall with one layer each of reflective insulation and of thermal insulation.

Fig. 11.5.5. "Silver batts" in sloping roof covered with galvanized steel sheets.

Batts of aluminum reflective insulation backed by thermal insulation are made in easily handled units. For clarity, they are shown installed in part of the roof only. (*Courtesy of Reflective Insulations Pty., Bullen 3105, Australia.*)

Fig. 11.5.6. Aluminum casting replacing a traditional cast-iron railing in the restoration of a nineteenth-century house in Sydney.

280 Muntz Metal: 60% copper, 40% zinc (a reddish-yellow brass)
385 Architectural Bronze: 57% copper, 3% lead, 40% zinc.
655 Silicon Bronze: 97% copper, 3% silicon (a reddish old-gold alloy)
745 Nickel Silver: 65% copper, 25% zinc, 10% nickel. (a silver-colored alloy)
796 Leaded Nickel Silver: 45% copper, 42% zinc, 10% nickel, 2% manganese, 1% lead (a silver-colored alloy)

Cartridge brass is intended for interior use only. The other alloys eventually turn brown and then green if exposed to the weather for a sufficient number of years. The patina can be developed immediately by chemical treatment.

The brown coppery color can be retained externally by oiling or waxing, but this requires periodic treatments. Clear lacquer and baked clear coatings last longer. Indoors, the metallic appearance can be retained by periodic polishing or by lacquer (see Sec. 19.4).

Copper alloys can be fabricated by hot rolling, cold rolling, extrusion, stamping, or casting, but only certain alloys are suitable for each process. Joints can be made with cold-driven rivets, bolts, or screws, or by welding, brazing, or soldering; again, only particular alloys are suitable for each method (see Sec. 10.11).

Apart from its use as electrical wiring, copper and brass pipes and fittings are used for conveying hot and cold water. Galvanized iron pipes are also used for cold water, but need periodic renewal. Plastic pipes are now also used for water supply (see Sec. 18.6). Copper is an excellent material for hot-water tanks and for the solar collectors used in conjunction with hot-water systems. All these uses are largely hidden from view; the visible use of copper has unquestionably declined. Copper is still used as a roofing and facing material where a high-quality finish and/or a completely waterproof surface are required (Fig. 11.6.1). For this

Fig. 11.6.1. Academy of Science, Canberra.
The concrete dome is covered with fully supported copper sheet. (*Courtesy of Dr. Judith Cowan.*)

purpose, pure 110 copper is commonly used, with or without a lead coating; the latter looks like lead.

Since copper is a heavy material (Table 10.1) and expensive, it is normally used in thin sheets that are fully supported by timber or concrete; that is, it does not carry its own weight. The thickness varies from 0.25 to 1 mm (0.01 to 0.04 in.) and is usually specified in terms of weight per unit area of sheet.

Copper is used for gutters and downspouts (downpipes) to avoid the periodic renewal required by galvanized steel or plastics (Fig. 11.6.2). Stainless steel is an alternative material for this purpose. Copper is also used for flashings in place of lead or aluminum. For all these applications, relatively thin copper sheet is suitable.

A greater thickness is needed when copper or bronze are used for curtain walls. Their appearance is widely considered superior to that of aluminum-colored curtain walls, but they are more expensive, and it is now possible to achieve a very similar appearance by the use of bronze-colored anodized aluminum (Sec. 11.4). Anodized aluminum has also largely replaced bronze castings for door furniture. However, the harder bronze and nickel–silver are superior for kick plates.

11.7 OTHER NONFERROUS METALS

The use of *lead* as a building material has definitely declined. Until the early years of this century, it was the major material for plumbing; in fact, the word *plumber* comes from *plumbum,* the Latin word for

Fig. 11.6.2. Copper downspout (downpipe).
The S-bend installed to bypass a projection in the stone wall below is sharp enough to cause water to spill over the outside of the pipe in heavy rain. The resulting corrosion has turned the lower pipe green because of the formation of copper sulfate (see Sec. 11.2), whereas the upper part retains its brown copper-oxide color.

lead. It is still used for waste pipes, but only rarely for water-supply pipes. It was used extensively for fully supported roof covering, and some of the world's most famous domes, such as St. Peter's in Rome (Fig. 11.7.1) and the Aya Sofya in Istanbul, are still covered with lead. However, lead, which was a cheap material in Roman times (Sec. 11.1), has now become comparatively expensive. The principal modern use of lead

Fig. 11.7.1. Lead covering of the brick dome of St. Peter's Basilica, Rome (renewed in 1875).
The horizontal projections protect windows that light the space between the inner and the outer domes.

is for the electric batteries of automobiles. If a lighter battery is ever invented to replace lead batteries, lead will probably become much cheaper.

Lead is one of the most weather-resistant materials; it surpasses even stainless steel and zinc in that respect (however, zinc also offers sacrificial protection to steel; see Sec. 10.3). Lead is, in fact, still used for weather protection in the form of terne-coating (see Sec. 10.3) and as a coating on sheet copper (Sec. 11.6).

Lead is still extensively used for flashings because it is the only weatherproof material that can easily be shaped in position on a building, and it is also still used for roofs, particularly in restorations of old buildings. Lead sheet is now often made from an alloy containing about 6-percent antimony. This increases the strength and stiffness of lead so that thinner sheets can be used. Lead roof sheet must always be fully supported.

Lead is being replaced as a material for damp-proof courses by cheaper aluminum (Sec. 11.1), but there are some applications for which lead has no rival. One of these is for protection from X-rays and gamma rays. Such protection requires either a great thickness of a less dense material (such as concrete) or a much smaller thickness of a very dense material, and lead is the densest material available.

The use of lead for sound insulation depends on both the density and the softness of the lead. A panel of sheet lead placed loosely between two walls, not touching either, acts as a very effective sound insulator, partly because of its mass (see Fig. 9.2.1) and partly because it cannot vibrate since it is not an elastic material. The sound energy is turned into strain energy, causing a slight but permanent deformation of the lead sheet; this deformation is negligibly low because sound energy is so small (see Sec. 9.1)

Lead can also be used to absorb ground vibrations—say from underground railways—by placing a sheet

Fig. 11.7.2. Tiles stamped from solid zinc sheet.
These tiles that form the ceiling of the auditorium of the Sydney Town Hall, built in 1889, are the originals. (*Courtesy of the Sydney City Council.*)

of lead between steel columns and their footings; however, a similar purpose can be accomplished with a pad of rubber or certain plastics.

Zinc was at one time used as a sheet material in its own right (Fig. 11.7.2), because it is durable and easily stamped with patterns. Today, however, its main use in buildings is as a protective coating for steel (Sec. 10.3). Because of the extensive use of galvanized sheet steel, this requires large quantities of zinc, approximately half the world's production. In addition it is used as an alloy for iron, aluminum, and copper.

Although galvanized iron roofs are often called "tin roofs," *tin* has not been used as a protection for steel roof sheets during this century, except as a minor ingredient of terne plate (see Sec. 10.3). Because of its low melting point, tin is a major component of soft solders.

Magnesium is an important structural material in aircraft design and, to a lesser extent, in automobile design. It is produced by electrolysis from sea water. Although this is an inexhaustible source, magnesium is an expensive material because of the large amount of electric power required. It has the advantages and disadvantages of aluminum to an even greater extent. It is very light and can be turned into alloys comparable in strength to those of steel, but its fire resistance is very poor because, apart from its low melting point, it burns when set alight. Unlike aluminum, it requires special corrosion protection with a chromic oxide coat. It could become a useful building material in the future.

Table 11.2 lists some of the properties of the materials mentioned in Chaps. 10 and 11, including those used as alloying materials.

REFERENCES

11.1. A. W. Brace and P. G. Sheasby: *The Technology of Anodizing Aluminum*. Technicopy, Stonehouse (England), 1979. 321 pp.
11.2. H. J. Cowan and P. R. Smith: *Environmental Systems*. Van Nostrand Reinhold, New York, 1983, pp. 76–77.

SUGGESTIONS FOR FURTHER READING

W. Alexander and A. Street: *Metals in the Service of Man*. Penguin Books, Harmondsworth (England), 1983. 312 pp.
E. I. Brimelow: *Aluminum in Building*. Macdonald, London, 1957.
P. C. Varley: *The Technology of Aluminum and its Alloys*. Newnes-Butterworths, London, 1970. 161 pp.
Aluminum: Properties and Physical Metallurgy. The Aluminum Association, Washington, 1984. 417 pp.

12

Natural Stone

Many types of natural stone are so very durable that they still stand in the oldest buildings that survive. The strength and durability of stones, and the ease with they can be worked, depend largely on the material from which they were formed, and on their age and geological history. Although the complete geological classification of rocks is very complex, the industrial classification consists of fewer groups, to which stones with similar properties, if different geological histories, are assigned. The present-day use of stone is mostly in the form of veneers.

Some natural stones deteriorate over a period of time, particularly if they are incorrectly used. Because many old stone buildings are considered an important part of our heritage, much research has been devoted to their preservation and repair.

12.1 THE CHANGING USE OF NATURAL STONE

The first stone buildings were erected in Egypt about 2600 B.C. (Fig. 1.1.1). From that time until the early twentieth century, natural stone has been the principal material for the most important buildings (except in a few Asian countries, notably China and Japan, where timber continued to be favored). This was true even in civilizations that had no metal tools, so that the stone had to be worked with stone tools (see Fig. 1.1.2). Many types of stone are very durable, so durable that some stone buildings are still in a good state of preservation after more than three thousand years.

Most types of stone can be carved; those that can be cut easily are called *freestones*. Stone carving became more elaborate in Egypt after about 2000 B.C., but the most influential classical stone buildings were erected in Greece and the Greek colonies in Asia Minor and in Italy between 600 and 300 B.C. Except for an interlude in the Middle Ages, the Greek classical "Orders" have

influenced Mediterranean and European architecture continuously until the early twentieth century, and, through Europe, the architecture of the Americas, Africa, Asia, and Australia. Even China and Japan have stone buildings with Greek classical columns.

Since we have a great heritage of historically important and beautiful old stone buildings that require repair or restoration from time to time, the skills of the traditional stone carver will continue to be needed in spite of the enormous increase in the cost of labor. By the 1960s, many people considered that most of the stone buildings of the late nineteenth and early twentieth century would eventually be replaced by buildings in the modern style of architecture; many are of high quality (Figs. 12.1.1 and 12.1.2), however, and it seems increasingly likely that a large proportion will be retained and that new uses will be found for buildings that are no longer required for their original purpose.

Although the Ancient Egyptians and Greeks used solid stone, stone (and brick) veneer was already common in Ancient Rome, where concrete was cast with stone or brick as permanent formwork. In medieval cathedrals, thick walls and massive piers usually had an outside layer of cut stone, the core being filled with rough stone and lime mortar—a kind of low-grade concrete.

As the cost of stone increased and brick became cheaper, stone was frequently used as an outer veneer for buildings whose walls consisted predominantly of brick. With the revival of concrete in the eighteenth century, stone came to be used as permanent formwork for concrete walls and columns, and until the 1920s it was widely held that face concrete was not a suitable material for prestige buildings. This view gradually changed between the 1920s and the 1950s, partly because the much higher cost of stone masonry en-

and old stone buildings are often more attractive than new stone buildings. This is rarely true of concrete. Old off-the-form concrete usually looks "dirty" rather than "weathered" if rain water is allowed to run down its surface (see Fig. 8.3.1 and Sec. 14.11). This aspect is rarely mentioned in books on modern architecture; rather, a number of well-known buildings with exposed concrete are shown in their pristine beauty immediately after completion, instead of in their dilapidated present condition.

There is now less insistence on truthfulness in the use of materials, and stone is consequently making a comeback for prestige buildings in the 1980s. The technology in the use of stone veneer has undergone a transformation, however, since the 1920s when the veneer was predominantly used as permanent form-work, that is, the concrete was cast after the masonry had been laid. Stone is now almost invariably fixed to the concrete after the latter has been cast (see Sec. 12.6).

12.2 THE FORMATION OF ROCKS

The earth's crust is an outside layer of rock about 35 kilometers thick. *Sedimentary rocks* are made of frag-

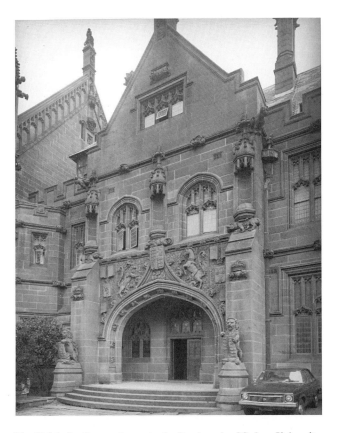

Fig. 12.1.1. Southern entrance to the Quadrangle of Sydney University. Entrance was sculpted in 1917 from Sydney sandstone, a siliceous sandstone of the Triassic Period. (*Courtesy of the Department of Photography, University of Sydney.*)

couraged the use of site-cast or precast concrete finishes (see Sec. 14.11) and partly because of the increasing acceptance of the view that architects should truthfully express the materials they used.

Although the technology of concrete surface finishes has improved greatly since the 1920s, it is still difficult to get a finish that equals that of good stone masonry. Natural stone, if used correctly, weathers gracefully,

Fig. 12.1.2. Sandstone gargoyle with downspout at Sydney University Old Medical School, 1890. (*Courtesy of Mr. Jeremy Steele.*)

Fig. 12.2.1. Sandstone with horizontal bedding planes, as shown by weathering.

ments of pre-existing rocks deposited in layers by water or by air, or of materials produced by plants or small marine animals. Existing *igneous rocks* are usually not part of the original crust of the earth, but rather the result of volcanic action at the surface or of intrusions into sedimentary rocks of molten rock material (*magma*) that solidified before reaching the earth's surface. *Metamorphic rocks* are sedimentary or igneous rocks that have been modified so much by the action of heat and pressure that their structure has been drastically altered.

Most sedimentary rocks were produced by the action of rivers and oceans, and in their original form were deposited largely in parallel horizontal layers (Fig. 12.2.1). These may then be modified by movement of the earth's crust, which can tilt sedimentary layers at an angle to the horizontal, and/or fold them, and/or shear and displace them relative to their original positions (Fig. 12.2.2).

Sedimentary and igneous rocks can be modified chemically and mechanically. For example, water that penetrates into rock may freeze and the expansion displace grains and even large blocks of rock. Roots of plants can split rocks where chemical action has provided them with sufficient food. Variations in tem-

perature can split both sedimentary and igneous rocks. Erosion by water or by glacial ice can remove large masses of rock gradually over long periods of time and form deposits of the eroded products elsewhere.

Carbon dioxide dissolved in rain water reacts slowly with some rock minerals. For example, the feldspars, which are the chief minerals in granite rock, are gradually converted to clay by weathering.

Clay and sand were produced in the first instance by the disintegration of igneous rocks. Clay deposits produced shales and slates. Sand became sandstone. Limestones and marbles resulted from deposits by small marine animals or from chemical precipitations. Coal was produced from plants. All of these are employed for building materials except for coal (although even that has been used by the American architect Bruce Goff).

12.3 THE GEOLOGICAL CLASSIFICATION

Sedimentary Rocks

Sedimentary rocks are geologically classified by their composition and by their age. The oldest of them are three to four thousand million years old. It was not

Fig. 12.2.2. Sandstone with bedding planes that have been folded and sheared by the movement of the earth's crust. (*Courtesy of Dr. Judith Cowan.*)

until about 650 million years ago that the first significant fossils appeared. Thereafter, the relative geological age of rocks can be determined with some accuracy from the fossils in them. In recent years, more precise methods have been used, based on the presence of radioactive substances.

The terminology used to describe the age of sedimentary rocks, together with a rough estimate of their age, is shown in Table 12.1. All primary and most secondary and tertiary deposits are rocks. Quaternary deposits are usually soils that have not yet consolidated into rocks, and the same applies to some tertiary and secondary deposits. The names of geological periods were mostly coined in the nineteenth century, and they are largely based on some geographic region where rocks of that period were first identified. Thus, the Cretaceous Era takes its name from the chalk cliffs near Dover in England. However, Cretaceous rocks are not necessarily limestone; they could also be sandstone, shale, or clay. Generally speaking, the older rocks are denser, stronger, and more durable than the younger rocks, but this is not necessarily so.

The three principal types of sedimentary rock are *sandstone, limestone,* and *shale.* The latter, which is formed by the consolidation of clay, is not a useful building stone, although it provides a raw material for making bricks and portland cement.

Most sands consist of small particles of silica (SiO_2), although they may contain other fragments of rock and fragments of corals or shells. "Black" sands are formed mainly by particles of volcanic rocks, and "white" sands mainly by coral particles.

Grains of sand are cemented into sandstone by the deposition of silica (*siliceous sandstone*—see Fig. 12.1.1), by iron oxide (*ferruginous sandstone*), by lime (*calcareous sandstone*), or by clay (*argillaceous sandstone*). Usually, this cementing is achieved by percolating water. Some argillaceous sandstones are weak and thus not suitable building materials. Calcareous sandstones are easily weathered by rain, particularly acid rain, because of their lime matrix, but many make good building stones, particularly for interior use. Ferruginous sandstones are colored red or brown by the iron oxide. Siliceous sandstones are usually durable, but some are so hard that they are difficult to carve and expensive to cut.

Limestones consist mainly of calcium carbonate, usually with some addition of magnesium carbonate. *Dolomite* (not to be confused with dolerite or diorite; see Table 12.2) contains the double carbonate of calcium and magnesium ($MgCO_3 \cdot CaCO_3$).

Many limestones contain fossil shells that are easily visible with the naked eye. As a rule, these shells are harder than the lime that forms the cement. Since limestone is very slowly dissolved by rainwater, these shells frequently protrude above the general stone surface. *Oolitic limestone* (Fig. 12.3.1) has a texture like the hard roe of a fish; hence its name. It is made up of rounded grains formed by the deposition of successive coats of calcium carbonate on grains of sand or pieces of shell. Oolitic limestone not only weathers evenly, it is easily cut and carved; hence, the stronger varieties make excellent building stones. The best-known is *Portland stone,* quarried in Dorsetshire in southern England and used in many important London buildings, for example, St. Paul's Cathedral. *Chalk* is a soft white limestone from more recent geological formations.

Limestones can be cemented by substances other than lime, and thus there are siliceous, ferruginous, and argillaceous limestones (these terms were previously explained in the discussion on sandstones). Water-

Table 12.1. The Geological Column of Sedimentary Rocks.

Geological Era	Geological Period	Approximate Age of the Beginning of Each Period in Millions of Years
Cenozoic*	Quaternary — Recent	0.01
	Quaternary — Pleistocene	2
	Tertiary — Pliocene	11
	Tertiary — Miocene	25
	Tertiary — Oligocene	40
	Tertiary — Eocene	65
Mesozoic or Secondary	Cretaceous	135
	Jurassic	180
	Triassic	230
Palaeozoic or Primary	Permian	280
	Carboniferous	350
	Devonian	400
	Silurian	440
	Ordovician	500
	Cambrian	600
Pre-Cambrian		

* Quaternary deposits are usually, and tertiary deposits are frequently, soil rather than rock.

Table 12.2. Classification of Igneous Rocks.

	Chemical Composition		
Texture	Acid	Intermediate	Basic
Extrusive (Volcanic) *Glassy or very fine-grained*	Rhyolite	Andesite	Basalt
Minor intrusive (Dykes and sills) *Fine-grained*	Quartz-porphyry*	Porphyrite	Dolerite
Major intrusive (Plutonic) *Coarse-grained*	Granite	Diorite	Gabbro

* The term *porphyry* in common parlance means a fine-grained igneous rock containing large isolated crystals; it could have any chemical composition. The most decorative porphyries, however, are microgranites with some large white or red crystals of plagioclase feldspar (a mixture of $NaAlSi_3O_8$ and $CaAl_2Si_2O_8$).

Fig. 12.3.1. West front of Wells Cathedral in Somerset, England.
Wells was built in the thirteenth century from oolitic limestone of the Jurassic Period and extensively restored at various times, notably in the nineteenth but also in this century.

resistant cement results from the burning together of argillaceous and calcareous material (that is, clay and lime) in the right proportions, and some argillaceous limestones have these very proportions and can thus be used to produce natural cement (see Sec. 13.3).

Limestone can also be produced by chemical deposition from saturated solutions. Stalagmites and stalactites are the columns and pendents, respectively, that form in limestone caves. *Tufa* is formed around calcareous springs. *Travertine* (Fig. 12.3.2) is a variety of tufa into which vegetable matter has been embedded; this subsequently rots, leaving cavities in the rock. Travertine was already highly esteemed in Ancient Rome. Its popularity for floors is partly due to its good and even wearing properties, and partly to its variable texture that is not only attractive in itself but hides dirt marks that would be very obvious on white marble.

Flints are irregularly shaped siliceous nodules found in chalk deposits in some parts of the world. The silica is probably derived from sponges. It is very brittle, and breaks with a sharp fracture. Flint was used ex-

tensively for tools and weapons in the Stone Age. It has also been used as a building stone. The flint nodules are unattractive, but the split or *knapped* flint forms an interesting and smooth surface.

Igneous Rocks

Igneous rocks are classified by their chemical composition and by their texture. The chemical division is into *acid, intermediate,* and *basic* rocks. The textural division is into glassy or very fine-grained *extrusive rocks,* fine-grained *minor intrusive rocks,* and coarse-grained *major intrusive rocks* (Fig. 12.3.3). Extrusive rocks are produced by volcanoes and thus cool rapidly. Intrusive rocks are produced by molten magma from the interior of the earth that cools and solidifies before reaching the surface.

Minor intrusions may be *dykes* (which are cross-cutting fissures filled with igneous rock that have not reached the surface) or *sills* (which are intrusions between beds of sedimentary rock, as shown in Fig. 12.3.4. Major intrusions (or *plutonic rocks*) can absorb

Fig. 12.3.2. Façade of St. Peter's Basilica in Rome.
The facade was built in the seventeenth century with travertine quarried at Tivoli, near Rome.

large masses of sedimentary rock, or they can push the entire sedimentary rock upwards or sideways (Fig. 12.3.5). The sedimentary rock may subsequently be worn away, exposing the igneous rock that has cooled slowly under cover.

Extrusive rocks may be glassy but without a crystal structure, or they may consist wholly or partly of very small crystals, occasionally with a few larger crystals. Dykes and sills are fine-grained; plutonic rocks are coarse-grained (Table 12.2).

Acid rocks contain more silica (SiO_2) and a smaller proportion of metallic oxides than *basic rocks*. Free silica (*quartz*) occurs only in acid rocks; the dark-green *olivine* [$(MgFe)_2 SiO_4$] occurs only in basic rocks. *Feldspars* (alumino-silicates of potassium, sodium, or calcium) and *micas* (hydrous alumino-silicates of iron, magnesium, potassium, etc., which can be split into thin sheets) occur in most types of igneous rock. Basic rocks are darker in color than acid rocks. There are more than 30 minerals that occur in igneous rocks, and reference should be made to a textbook on geology (for example, see Ref. 12.1) for a description of their properties.

Metamorphic Rocks

Metamorphic rocks are sedimentary or igneous rocks whose structure has been modified by the action of heat and/or pressure. This may lead to folding of rocks on a regional scale, or, more locally, rocks near a large igneous intrusion may show the effects of metamorphism.

Marble is metamorphic limestone (Fig. 12.3.6). If the limestone was white, and the recrystallization is complete, the result is a uniform white marble free of any texture—the marble that has been favored for statuary since the time of Ancient Greece. Most marbles contain some materials other than calcium carbonate, however, and these may produce color and texture.

Slate is metamorphized shale (that is, clay sediments turned into rock). The metamorphic action produces cleavage planes, which may not correspond to the original bedding planes of the shale. Because slate can be split into thin slabs, it was at one time widely used as a covering for sloping roofs and for damp-proof courses.

Quartzite is a sandstone in which the original quartz

Fig. 12.3.3. Portico of the Pantheon in Rome.
The Pantheon was built in the second century A.D. using material from an earlier temple of the first century B.C. The columns, each cut from one slab of Egyptian red or grey granite, weigh approximately 60,000 kg (130,000 lb) apiece.

grains and siliceous cement are recrystallized into interlocking quartz crystals, sometimes with partial fusion.

Gneiss, which is produced by the metamorphic transformation of an igneous rock, such as granite, or sedimentary rocks, has a banded texture, with alternating light and dark bands.

12.4 THE INDUSTRIAL CLASSIFICATION OF STONE

The building stone industry uses a simpler classification than the one we have been discussing.

The term *limestone* has a more restricted meaning, since the more decorative limestones capable of taking a polish are classified as "marble."

The term *sandstone* has the same meaning as in the geological classification. Sandstones are divided by grain size, as follows:

Coarse-grained: 1 to 2 mm (0.04 to 0.08 in.)

Medium-grained: 0.5 to 1 mm (0.02 to 0.04 in.)
Fine-grained: 0.05 to 0.5 mm (0.002 to 0.02 in.)

Most of the sandstones used for buildings are fine- to medium-grained.

The term *slate* also has the same meaning as in the geological classification. The terms, *princess, duchess, countess,* etc., used for roofing slates refer not to their quality, but to their size [ranging from 600 × 350 mm to 300 × 200 mm (24 × 14 in. to 12 × 8 in.)]. The best roofing slates are the thinnest, because they weigh less and the roof structure can therefore be lighter. Slates are today rarely used for roofs, however, even in the restoration of old buildings, since a visually similar result can be obtained at a much lower cost with surface-coated slabs of fibrous cement. At present, slate is used more for covering walls and floors, and slates for this purpose are selected for their color and texture; thinness is not necessarily an advantage.

The term *granite* includes all igneous rocks and also

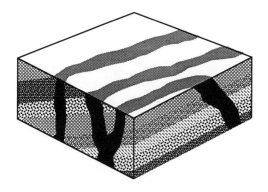

(a)

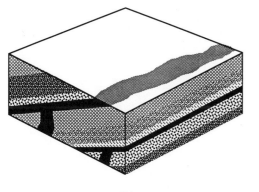

(b)

Fig. 12.3.4. Minor intrusive rocks.
(a) Dykes, and (b) sills on top of dykes.

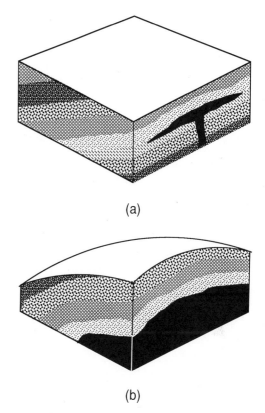

(a)

(b)

Fig. 12.3.5. Intrusions forming plutonic rocks.
(a) Intrusions between the beds of a sedimentary rock (*laccolith*), and (b) intrusion pushing the entire sedimentary rock upwards (*batholith*).

the metamorphic gneiss. Commercial granites thus range in color from pink or red (for acid rocks) through grey (for intermediate rocks) to dark grey or black (for basic rocks), and in grain size from coarse to fine. *Porphyry,* which includes large crystals in a fine-grained matrix, and gneiss, which is banded, are sometimes identified as such, instead of being called granite.

The term *marble* includes not merely the true metamorphic marbles, but also limestones that are decorative in appearance and capable of being given a high polish. Thus, "sedimentary marbles" may have large fossils showing on their polished surface. Marbles are available in a variety of colors, from pure white through pink, red, yellow, green, and blue to black. There are some with bands of different colors. *Serpentine,* which is a green, ultrabasic igneous rock consisting mainly of hydrous magnesium silicate [$Mg_6Si_4O_{10}$ $(OH)_8$], is also classified as a marble.

Travertine (Sec. 12.3) is sometimes described as marble (because it is decorative and takes a high polish) and sometimes as limestone.

Physical Properties

The compressive strength of building stones when dry ranges from 5 MPa (0.7 ksi) for a soft limestone to 200 MPa (30 ksi) for the strongest granites and marbles; the wet strength is two-thirds to one-half of the dry strength. Most granites and marbles are stronger than structural concrete, but many limestones and sandstones are weaker. The density of stone is approximately the same as that of concrete (see Chap. 14), although some of the porous limestones are lighter.

The coefficient of thermal expansion, however, varies greatly from one building stone to another—from about 1 to about 12×10^{-6} per °C (0.5 to 7×10^{-6} per °F). It is essential that stone slabs fixed to a steel frame or to reinforced concrete be able to accommodate differential thermal movement (see Sec. 12.6).

Natural stone is a very variable material. Geologically identical stones quarried in locations only a few kilometers apart may vary greatly from one another. Because of its known reliability, stone of good quality from established quarries is therefore often transported over great distances by sea. The travertine quarries near Rome, which were already worked in the days of the Roman Republic, and the Carrara quarry between Pisa and Genoa, started by the Emperor Augustus, and from which Michelangelo obtained most of his marble, are still in use today.

The selection of stone for concrete aggregate is considered in Sec. 14.2.

Fig. 12.3.6. Parthenon in Athens.
Built in the fifth century B.C. from Pentelic marble, a coarse, white marble containing some mica and quarried at Mount Pentelikon near Athens.

12.5 DETERIORATION OF BUILDING STONES

Many stones form a surface skin when they are exposed to the atmosphere. Some stones are quite soft when they are cut but harden when they dry out. An extreme example is Roman travertine, a porous limestone that can be cut with a spade when it is quarried but subsequently hardens to an extent that makes it a favored flooring material. Thus, as a result of experience, some building stones are allowed to season, like timber, before being dressed (that is, cut to their final shape), whereas others are dressed immediately.

Although a surface skin acts as a protective coat for some stones, it is the cause of failure in others. The sulfur dioxide (SO_2) present in the atmosphere as a result of industrial processes can be carried considerable distances from its source. It combines with water to form sulfurous acid, and with water and the oxygen in the air to form sulfuric acid. These, in turn, combine with the calcium carbonate of limestones or of calcareous sandstones (Sec. 12.3) to form insoluble calcium sulfite and calcium sulfate.

Since calcium carbonate is water-soluble, limestone is normally washed clean by rainwater, but, if sheltered from rain, a skin may form, and, in some limestones and calcareous sandstones, this skin will blister and/or exfoliate (that is, come off in scales) and thus ruin the stone surface (Fig. 12.5.1) Such deterioration can be avoided by designing a building so that walls are washed evenly by rain, or by arranging to have the sheltered parts washed from time to time.

Horizontal projections on which dirt can collect—such as window ledges, copings, and cornices—should be fitted with a throat that collects dirty water and throws it clear off the stone wall (Fig. 12.5.2). Polluted water is particularly damaging to sandstones, which are water-absorbent rather than water-soluble so that they are not washed clean by rain (Fig. 12.5.3).

All sedimentary rocks have *bedding planes* resulting from the gradual deposition of the sediment. At the time of deposition, the bedding planes are horizontal, but subsequent movement of the earth's crust can tilt the planes at an angle, or even to the vertical. The bedding planes may become visible during the quarrying operation, or be known from past experience, but this is not always the case. The tendency of most rocks

Fig. 12.5.1. Skin of calcium sulfide and sulfate on limestone, showing exfoliation over part of the surface.

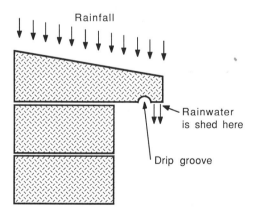

Fig. 12.5.2. Throat cut on the underside of a stone window sill, near its edge, to collect water running off the top of the sill and throw it clear off the wall.
Dirt deposited during a dry period on the top face of a projecting stone is washed off by rain, and this dirty water would produce stains if it fell on a stone surface. Throats are usually cut hemispherical or square.

12.5.3. Staining of sandstone surface by water dripping from a window air conditioner.

to weather more readily along their bedding planes, particularly if they are placed vertically, will eventually spoil the appearance of the stone; indeed, if a bedding plane is placed vertically and parallel to the surface of the wall, a piece of the stone might well fall off because of the preferential weathering of the bedding planes.

Granite, slate, and the harder sandstones are barely affected by wind and rain, but the softer sandstones and limestones gradually show signs of erosion. In fact, many sandstones and limestones weather to a greater extent than a strong mortar. After a time, mortar joints will then project beyond a wall surface, which is unsightly. A mortar should always be used that is weaker than the stone to ensure that this does not happen, and that any cracks that form run through the joints, which can be repaired by repointing, rather than through the stone (Fig. 12.5.4). Limestones should be laid in a mortar that contains more lime than portland cement.

Cracks in stone can give rise to serious deterioration, particularly in climates with frequent cycles of freezing and thawing because the cracks enlarge if water within them freezes. They also provide the points of entry for chemical deterioration. Cracks can result from the excessive use of pneumatic tools and explosives in

Fig. 12.5.4. Cracks in stonework laid with mortar that is weaker than the stone.
The cracks run through the joints without significant damage to the stone, allowing the joints to be repaired by repointing with mortar.

quarries in place of the traditional hammer and chisel, and from careless handling of the stone. All stones are subject to temperature and moisture movement (see Chap. 3). In a wall consisting entirely of one type of stone, this can be accommodated by *expansion joints*. If the stone is used as a veneer, the method of connection must make due allowance for differential movement as well (see Sec. 12.6).

Some stones contain soluble salts that may rise gradually to the surface and form unsightly deposits, called *efflorescence*. These can often be completely removed by washing.

In the past, the normal response to the deterioration of natural stone has been to cut back the damaged stone and replace it with new stone from the same quarry, or with compatible stone of similar chemical composition if the original supply is exhausted (Fig. 12.5.5). For some old buildings, the cost of repeated repairs exceeds the original cost, even when allowance is made for changes in the price of labor and materials. Preservative treatments are therefore of great interest, even though their result is less certain than replacement of the damaged stone.

Vitruvius and Pliny mention the use of beeswax and

linseed oil in antiquity for the preservation of marble sculptures. Beeswax is still used for this purpose on marble sculptures, but a modern silicone wax polish is just as effective and easier to apply.

Waterglass (sodium or potassium silicate) has been employed as a preservative for more porous stones since the sixteenth century. Better results are obtained with silica (SiO_2) dissolved in alcohol. The alcohol evaporates and leaves bars of silica as reinforcement between the grains of stone.

More controversial are treatments with modern synthetics. *Silicones,* developed in the late nineteenth century (see Sec. 18.5), have been used as stone preservatives since the late 1940s. Experiments carried out in England and Wales in the 1960s by the Directorate of Ancient Monuments (Ref. 12.2) showed that the arrest of decay was short-lived, but better results have been reported since then with silicones, acrylic resins, and epoxies both as preservatives and as fillers to repair damage, particularly in Venice (Ref. 12.3).

Silicone was employed to repair Michelangelo's Pietà after it was vandalized in 1972. *Epoxy resins* have been used successfully in the repair of the Roman Aqueduct in Segovia (Spain), in the reconstruction of the Celsus Library in Ephesus (Turkey), and in the re-erection of Rameses II's Abu Simbel Temple after removal from its original site, which has since been flooded by the Assuan High Dam.

12.6 STONE VENEER

Except for small monuments and restorations of old buildings, natural stone is today primarily used as a veneer. Veneers have also become thinner, partly due to the increasing cost of stone relative to other building materials, and partly to improved stone-cutting technology.

For interior use, veneers of strong stone need only be a few millimeters (or a fraction of an inch) thick, and these are fixed with adhesives, such as epoxies (see Sec. 19.6). These thin pieces are usually not much larger than clay tiles.

Floor surfaces require hard stones, such as slates, quartzites, granites, or the harder marbles. Wall surfaces in exposed locations should also be of abrasion-resistant stone, or, alternatively, corners where damage is most likely should be protected with nonferrous metal or stainless steel.

Larger pieces of stone are fixed with metal cramps, and there should be an air space of a few millimeters (a fraction of an inch) between the stone slabs and their supporting structure to allow for differential temperature and moisture movement. Some of the joints between the stones are sealed with a suitable *mastic* (see Fig. 4.7.3 and Sec. 19.8) to allow for differential movement.

(a)   (b)

Fig. 12.5.5. Replacement of decayed stone carving by a new carving made from a block of chemically and geologically similar stone.
In this instance, the quarry from which the original stone had been obtained 90 years earlier was worked out: (a) Original stone carving in the stone-mason's yard after removal; note that the upper part of the pinnacle had been repaired previously. (b) New pinnacle in position; the new carving is very similar to the original, but not identical with it. (*Courtesy of Mr. Robert Marsh, Clerk of Works, University of Sydney.*)

Fig. 12.6.1. Cracks in Greek marble column caused by rusting of iron dowels.
The drums of the column were apparently connected originally by wooden dowels, which were replaced by iron in an ancient restoration.

Iron or steel cramps must not be used, not even if they are galvanized or terne-plated. Although wrought iron has better rust resistance than steel, it will rust eventually and burst the stone (Fig. 12.6.1). The best material for the cramps is stainless steel, but phosphor bronze or gun metal (see Sec. 11.6) can also be used. The cramps must be strong enough to support the weight of the stone (Figs. 12.6.2 and 12.6.3).

The stone slabs must be thick enough to have adequate resistance to local bending. The thickness, therefore, depends partly on the size of the slabs and the spacing of the cramps, on the one hand, and on the strength of the stones, on the other.

Thin slabs of marble (which is calcium carbonate), *alabaster* (which is calcium sulfate dihydrate), and micas (which are hydrous alumino-silicates of various metals) are translucent. Before window glass became readily available, these stones were sometimes employed for windows; some excellent examples survive in a number of churches in Ravenna. In recent years, translucent marble slabs have been used for windowless curtain walls to admit a subdued daylight (Fig. 12.6.4).

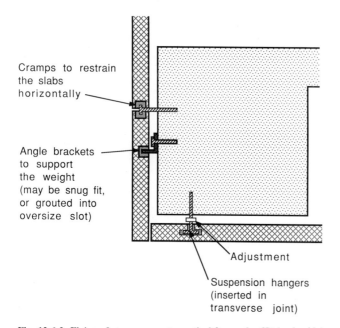

Cramps to restrain the slabs horizontally

Angle brackets to support the weight (may be snug fit, or grouted into oversize slot)

Adjustment

Suspension hangers (inserted in transverse joint)

Fig. 12.6.2. Fixing of stone veneer to vertical face and soffit (underside) of reinforced-concrete structure with cramps, angle brackets, and suspension hangers.

Fig. 12.6.3. Fixing of granite veneer to reinforced-concrete structure of Parliament House, Canberra (due for completion in 1988). (*Courtesy of the Architects, Mitchell, Giurgola and Thorp.*)

Fig. 12.6.4. Translucent marble curtain wall of the Rare Book Library of Yale University, built in 1964 (Architects: Skidmore, Owings and Merrill).

REFERENCES

12.1. F. G. H. Blyth and M. H. Freitas: *A Geology for Engineers.* Arnold, London, 1974. pp. 74–129.

12.2. B. L. Clarke and J. Ashurst: *Stone Preservation Experiments.* Department of the Environment, London, 1972. 78 pp.

12.3. G. G. Amoroso and V. Fassina: *Stone Decay and Preservation.* Elsevier, Amsterdam, 1983. 453 pp.

John Pitts: *A Manual of Geology for Civil Engineers.* Halsted Press, New York, 1985. 228 pp.

R. J. Schaffer: *The Weathering of Building Stones.* Building Research Special Report No. 18. H. M. Stationery Office, London, 1932. 149 pp.

E. M. Winkler: *Stone: Properties and Durability in Man's Environment.* Springer, New York, 1973. 230 pp.

SUGGESTIONS FOR FURTHER READING

Hugh O'Neill: *Stone for Building.* Heinemann, London, 1965. 198 pp.

13

Lime, Gypsum, and Cement

Until the end of the nineteenth century, *lime* was the universal material for masonry mortar. Today, it is employed mainly as an additive. *Gypsum* is still a major building material, but it is used more for drywall construction than for wet plastering.

It is *portland cement,* developed in the nineteenth century, that has become one of the most important building materials. Its chemistry is very complex, but the main cementing compound is calcium silicate hydrate. Ordinary portland cement can be modified for high early strength, for sulfate resistance, for low heat production, or for use in masonry. For architectural use, it can be produced white, black, or in various colors. High-alumina cement and magnesium-oxychloride cement are chemically different from portland cement.

13.1 LIME

Lime is the generic term for calcium oxide (CaO), or *quicklime,* and calcium hydroxide [$Ca(OH)_2$], or *hydrated lime.*

Quicklime is produced by burning limestone, chalk, or seashells [all consisting of calcium carbonate ($CaCO_3$)] in a kiln, a procedure that releases the carbon dioxide (CO_2) as a gas. The resulting lumps of quicklime are then pulverized, and water is added in a hydrator to produce *hydrated lime powder.* This is packaged, like cement, in large paper bags. *Lime putty* is produced by adding water to hydrated lime powder.

Until the early years of this century, hydrated lime was usually produced on the building site by burying quicklime in the ground for some time. This turned into *slaked lime,* a traditional form of lime putty. This method is still used in some countries.

Until the end of the nineteenth century, lime was universally used for *mortar* in masonry of brick and natural stone. Lime mortar consists of sand with sufficient lime putty to fill its voids. The most common mix consists of one part of hydrated lime to three parts of sand, with sufficient water to produce a plastic mix; the mix may range from two to five parts of lime to one of sand. Unlike the action of portland cement, the binding action of lime is physical rather than chemical. On the mortar surface, the hydrated lime combines with the moisture and the carbon dioxide in the air to form a protective crystalline skin of calcium carbonate, but this reaction is confined to the outer layer. The gluing action of the mortar is mainly caused by the stiffening of the paste as water is lost by evaporation and absorbed by the brick or stone. The sand is needed to reduce the shrinkage of the lime.

Pure lime mortar is today used only for restorations of old buildings, because portland cement mortar is much stronger (see Sec. 12.5); however, many authorities consider that some lime putty should be used in cement mortar to improve its workability (that is, make it more plastic) and increase its water retention. The proportion of cement to lime then ranges from 4:1 for the stronger to 1:1 for the weaker mortars. An alternative to the addition of lime is the use of a masonry cement (see Sec. 13.4) that contains an inert filler.

Lime mortar has been used for plastering walls, often mixed with animal hair or vegetable fiber to give it some tensile reinforcement. It is very soft, however, and for plastering today is mixed with portland cement or gypsum in varying proportions, depending on the hardness required.

Limewash or *whitewash* is still in common use as a cheap form of white paint, particularly for external use, and internally in agricultural buildings because of its mildly germicidal qualities. Limewash can be made from quicklime and tallow, from hydrated lime and common salt, or from hydrated lime, alum, and animal glue. A small quantity of blue pigment makes the lime wash appear "whiter." A harder limewash is produced by mixing lime and white portland cement in equal parts.

Sand-lime bricks, also called *calcium-silicate bricks,* are made from sand [SiO_2] and hydrated lime [$Ca(OH)_2$]. These constituents are mixed together, pressed into brick molds, and subjected to high-pressure steam in an autoclave, a treatment that causes the lime and part of the sand to form calcium silicate. The natural color of sand-lime bricks is white, off-white, or yellow. They can be used in exactly the same way as clay bricks (see Sec. 15.2) and are usually made to the same sizes. However, they shrink when they are new, and some shrink appreciably; by contrast, some clay bricks expand (see Sec. 3.4).

Concrete bricks are briefly discussed in Sec. 14.10.

13.2 GYPSUM

Gypsum [calcium sulfate dihydrate ($CaSO_4 \cdot 2H_2O$)] occurs in nature as an off-white, light-grey, or light-pink crystalline mineral. Decorative pieces, which can be used as semiprecious stone, are called *alabaster.*

When heated in the range of 128° to 163°C (262° to 325°F) gypsum gives off three quarters of its water. The resulting *hemihydrate* is called *plaster of Paris.* If gypsum is heated above 200°C (400°F), all the water is driven off, and the resulting material is called *anhydrous gypsum plaster.* The same material, when found in nature, is called *anhydrite.*

When water is added to plaster of Paris, it changes back to the dihydrate, gypsum, and forms an interlocking mass of fine, needle-shaped crystals. It sets in 5 to 20 minutes. This is useful for casting the material into a mold or for repairs of minor damage. If gypsum is used for plastering—that is, applied with a trowel to timber or metal laths—more time is needed, and a retarder, such as *keratin,* is added to produce *retarded hemihydrate gypsum plaster.*

Anhydrite or *hard-burnt plasters* have a much longer setting time than plaster of Paris. A variation of anhydrite called *Keene's cement* is made by heating gypsum first to the 128°–163°C range to form the hemihydrate; the material is then given a bath in alum and heated further to 200°C. This produces a much harder plaster, one with a somewhat faster setting time than anhydrite.

All gypsum plasters expand when they set—a sharp contrast to cement plaster, which shrinks on setting. Gypsum cast into a mold therefore assumes its shape accurately, and there are no shrinkage cracks in gypsum plaster.

Gypsum plasters can be reinforced with animal hair or with vegetable fibers. *Fibrous plaster* consists of precast plaster sheets into which sisal hemp fibers have been rolled as reinforcement while the plaster is wet. By far the largest present use of gypsum, however, is in the form of *gypsum drywall construction,* which utilizes precast gypsum sheet sandwiched between sheets of treated paper (*plasterboard*).

Gypsum plaster has been used for several centuries both in precast units and applied wet to brick or concrete block walls or to lathing. The timber lathing used in the eighteenth, nineteenth, and early twentieth centuries has now been replaced by metal laths. Wet plaster is applied in two or three coats, which may be neat gypsum plaster or gypsum plaster and sand. In three-coat work, the finishing coat is usually neat gypsum plaster to give a hard, smooth finish. Lime putty may be added to the gypsum plaster.

Graffito (or *sgraffito*) work has been used in Italy and some other countries for many centuries for decorative plaster surfaces. The upper coat of the plaster is of a different color from that of the lower coat, or three differently colored coats may be used. The top coat is usually white. While the plaster is still wet, a pattern is scored on it that exposes the lower colors. The technique, which has recently been revived, can also be undertaken with portland cement plaster (Sec. 13.7).

Gypsum plaster can be used in place of concrete for making steel structures fire-resistant. The steel beams or columns are wrapped with metal lathing that is given as undercoat of gypsum plaster with an aggregate of perlite or exfoliated vermiculite (see Sec. 7.5). This is usually finished with a skim coat of hard gypsum plaster (Fig. 13.2.1).

Gypsum plaster can also be used as an *acoustic plaster* for sound absorption (see Sec. 9.2) by giving it a honeycombed structure with an aggregate such as exfoliated vermiculite or porous slag. Alternatively, some aluminum powder can be mixed with the gypsum plaster; this produces bubbles of hydrogen gas that remain in the set plaster.

On the other hand, a solid, hard, smooth surface of gypsum plaster makes an excellent sound reflector. Sound mirrors in auditoria are made either with plywood or with hard plaster.

Gypsum is not suitable for external plastering.

13.3 PORTLAND CEMENT

Lime plaster can be used externally, but it needs periodic repair or renewal. Lime mortar also has limited resistance to weathering. Masonry joints made from lime mortar require repointing from time to time, and lime mortar cannot be used for structures that are permanently or periodically under water, because hydrated lime is slowly soluble in water. There is a lime

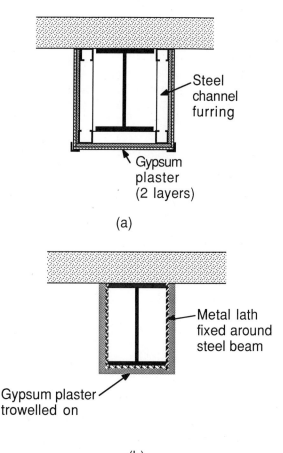

(a)

(b)

Fig. 13.2.1. Fireproofing of structural steel section with gypsum plaster containing vermiculite aggregate.

that can be used for submerged, or hydraulic, structures, however; it is called *hydraulic lime.*

In the second or first century B.C., the Romans discovered that certain materials, when mixed with lime, gave it hydraulic properties. The most important such material was a volcanic ash from Pozzuoli, near Mount Vesuvius, which was named *pozzolana.* Hence, materials that give lime hydraulic properties have since been called pozzolanas (Sec. 13.4). The Ancient Romans thus produced waterproof concrete whose strength and durability equals that of modern concrete. The Romans also made a moderately hydraulic mortar by mixing brickdust with the lime mortar.

The art of making hydraulic mortar was lost after the fall of the Western Roman Empire in the fifth century A.D. Pozzolanic materials continued to be used where locally available, notably volcanic ash deposits found by the Romans near the River Rhine, called *Rhenish trass,* which were used until the early nineteenth century on both sides of the Rhine, and even exported to Southern England.

The immediate cause for the rediscovery of Roman concrete was the construction of a lighthouse on the Eddystone, a rock off the English coast near Plymouth,

which lay on the main shipping route to America (Fig. 13.3.1). Because the rock was awash at high tide, lime mortar could not be used, and the two timber lighthouses that were built in 1699 and in 1706 were destroyed in 1702 and in 1755, respectively. The lighthouse commissioners then turned for advice to the Royal Society, who recommended John Smeaton.

Previous experiments to produce hydraulic lime had been unsuccessful, mainly because the account in Vitruvius' *Ten Books* (Ref. 13.1) that describes the art quite accurately also gives explanations that are incorrect and that misled a number of distinguished engineers to believe up to the eighteenth century that the strongest lime mortar was made from the purest and whitest limestone.

After experimenting with numerous limestones, Smeaton found that grey limestones produced stronger lime mortar than pure white limestones and that they had "hydraulic" properties. The best results were obtained from the bluish-grey Aberthaw limestone. In Smeaton's words:

> On trying Aberthaw lime in this way, it was dissolved in *aqua fortis* [concentrated nitric acid]; but the solution appeared very dark and muddy. . . . . The muddy residuum . . . . being worked into a little ball and dried, in that state it appeared to be a very fine compact clay, weighing nearly one-eighth part of the original mass. One of the balls being burnt became a good compact brick. (Ref. 13.2.)

Smeaton thus concluded that the hydraulic properties of Roman concrete depended on admixture of clay to the lime mortar. Further experiments showed that stronger cements could be obtained from limestones containing actual veins of clay, or clays containing lime nodules. These materials, known as *natural cements,* were first produced in England in 1796, in France in 1797, in America in 1817, and in Australia in 1862.

In 1811, Joseph Aspden made the first artificial cement by burning together lime and clay from different deposits, instead of using the materials naturally "premixed". He claimed that his product was as strong "as the best Portland Stone," which was then the most esteemed building stone in London, and called it *portland cement.* In due course, artificial cement almost entirely replaced natural cement, but it was not until 1902 that the production of portland cement in the United States overtook that of natural cement.

Portland cement is manufactured from limestone (or chalk) and clay (or shale). Limestone, as noted elsewhere, is calcium carbonate [$CaCO_3$]; when heated, it gives off carbon dioxide as a gas, leaving a residue of calcium oxide [CaO]. Clay and shale consist mainly of *kaolinite* [$Al_2O_3 \cdot 2SiO_2 \cdot 2H_2O$]; on heating, this dis-

E D Y S T O N E · L I G H T H O U S E,
The Morning after a Storm at S.W.

Fig. 13.3.1. Frontispiece of Smeaton's *The Narrative of the Building of the Edystone Lighthouse* (Ref. 13.2).

sociates into alumina [Al$_2$O$_3$] and silica [SiO$_2$], and the water evaporates. In addition, some ferric (iron) oxide [Fe$_2$O$_3$] is usually present in the clay, and sometimes also in the limestone.

These materials are first ground and then heated to a temperature of 1450°C (2650°F) in a rotary kiln, along which they travel slowly. In the process, a number of compounds of calcium oxide and silica, and of calcium oxide and alumina are formed. The *cement clinker,* which emerges from the rotary kiln in pieces about the size of children's glass marbles, is mixed with gypsum (see Sec. 13.2) to retard the initial setting of the cement and is then ground to a very fine powder, with a particle size of the order of 5 to 50 μm.

The quantity of portland cement manufactured today is greater than that of any other manufactured material (if one considers treated water as a natural material), and some variation must therefore be expected in the composition of cements from different plants. A number of chemical compounds are present only in small quantities and do not contribute to the cementing process.

In 1897, the Swedish chemist, A. E. Törnebohm, identified four types of crystal—which he named *alite, belite, celite,* and *felite*—and an amorphous substance as the principal components of portland cement. It took another 35 years to establish their chemical composition.

Of these components, alite is the principal cementing compound. It is mainly tricalcium silicate [3CaO·SiO$_2$], and it constitutes about half the total volume of the cement. It is responsible for the early gain in strength of the cement, which is called *hardening.* Belite and felite, which are mainly dicalcium silicate [2CaO·SiO$_2$], constitute about a quarter of the volume of portland cement. Dicalcium silicate "hydrates" (that is, combines with water) more slowly, and it is responsible for the longer-term gain in strength, called *aging*.

The hydration of both the tricalcium and the dicalcium silicates results in the formation of various calcium silicate hydrates in the form of interlocking crystals. The principal reactions are as follows:

$$2(3CaO \cdot SiO_2) + 6H_2O$$
$$= 3 CaO \cdot 2SiO_2 \cdot 3H_2O + 3Ca(OH)_2$$

and

$$2(2CaO \cdot SiO_2) + 4H_2O$$
$$= 3CaO \cdot 2SiO_2 \cdot 3H_2O + Ca(OH)_2$$

Both produce $3CaO \cdot 2SiO_2 \cdot 3H_2O$, a compound that occurs naturally in California, South Africa, and Ireland. It is called *afwillite* and appears to be the material mainly responsible for the strength of concrete.

Törnebohm's celite, which constitutes only about one-twentieth of the volume of the cement, has been identified as tetracalcium alumino-ferrite [$4CaO \cdot Al_2O_3 \cdot Fe_2O_3$]. The amorphous substance in the cement, which accounts for about one-tenth of its volume, is more important, however. This compound is a colloidal gel of tricalcium aluminate [$3CaO \cdot Al_2O_3$] whose hydration is very rapid. It is responsible for the initial setting of the cement, when the material changes from a liquid to a stiff paste. The setting process must allow sufficient time for the concrete (in which the cement is used) to be placed in the formwork and to be worked to fill every corner of it. To provide this time, the setting of portland cement is retarded by the addition of gypsum (Sec. 13.2).

The hydration of gypsum produces calcium sulfo-aluminate [$3CaO \cdot Al_2O_3 \cdot 3CaSO_4 \cdot 30–32H_2O$]. This compound also occurs as a natural mineral, called *ettringite*. The formation of ettringite is an expansive reaction. So long as the concrete is in a plastic (that is, unhardened) condition, it can accommodate the expansion. After it has hardened, the expansion could produce cracks; hence the amount of gypsum must be carefully controlled.

Since the principal hydration products of portland cement—calcium hydroxide and the calcium silicate hydrates—are basic, any reinforcing steel present is not corroded provided that it has an adequate cover of concrete free of large cracks and that the concrete does not absorb corrosive anions, such as chlorides.

13.4 MODIFICATIONS OF ORDINARY PORTLAND CEMENT

Sulfate-resistant portland cement is a cement in which the tricalcium aluminate is kept low enough for only a small amount of gypsum (which is a sulfate) to have to be added; thus, the risk of the formation of an excessive amount of ettringite is reduced.

Low-heat portland cement is a cement in which the amount of tricalcium silicate is reduced and that of dicalcium silicate increased instead, because the more rapidly occurring hydration of the tricalcium silicate produces more heat.

The reverse steps are taken in the production of *high-early-strength cement*—called *rapid-hardening cement* in Britain—in order to increase the rate at which strength is developed. More important, however, is the finer grinding of high-early-strength cement, so as to offer a larger cement surface to the water and thus increase the speed of the hydration process.

We noted in the last section that calcium hydroxide [$Ca(OH)_2$] is produced during the hydration of the calcium silicates. This component does not contribute significantly to the strength of normal portland cement, but it can combine with reactive silica to form more calcium silicate hydrate. Materials that contain reactive silica therefore have "hydraulic," or *pozzolanic,* properties. Economically the most important are *fly ash,* a waste product of coal-fired power stations, and *blast-furnace slag,* a byproduct of steel production. Calcined diatomaceous earth, some volcanic ashes, and some opaline shales and cherts (a type of siliceous rock) also have pozzolanic properties. Portland cement blended with a pozzolana is known as *portland-pozzolan cement;* portland cement blended with blast-furnace slag is known as *portland-blast-furnace cement.* These cements eventually achieve the same strength as ordinary portland cement, but the rate of development of their strength is slower; in consequence, they develop less heat.

Masonry cement is portland cement with a finely ground inert filler, usually limestone, and an air-entraining agent (see Sec. 14.6). It is an alternative, particularly in the U.S.A., to a cement-lime mortar for laying bricks, concrete blocks, or natural stone (Secs. 13.1 and 13.7).

13.5 HIGH-ALUMINA CEMENT

The cement known as *high-alumina cement, calcium aluminate cement,* or *aluminous cement,* is made by burning together limestone (or chalk) and bauxite, which is the principal raw material for the manufacture of aluminum (see Sec. 11.2). The process was developed in France in the late nineteenth century by the French company Ciments Lafarge, but high-alumina cement is now made in many countries. The raw materials are heated to the point of fusion, about 1600°C (2900°F). The ground cement is much darker than portland cement.

High-alumina cement develops its strength much

faster than high-early strength portland cement, and since it generates an appreciable amount of heat in the process, it can only be used in concrete sections that are comparatively thin. Concrete made with high-alumina cement is stronger than concrete made with the same amount of portland cement. The main advantage of the former is that it has excellent resistance to sulfates in soil and to sea water.

The chemistry of high-alumina cement differs from that of portland cement. Its main cementing compound is monocalcium aluminate [$CaO \cdot Al_2O_3$]. When water is added, this hydrates to form mainly $CaO \cdot Al_2O_3 \cdot 10H_2O$ and alumina gel [$Al_2O_3 \cdot aq$]. It has always been known that this hydrate is unstable at high temperatures and that it may convert to another hydrate, as follows:

$$3[CaO \cdot Al_2O_3 \cdot 10H_2O]$$
$$= 3CaO \cdot Al_2O_3 \cdot 6H_2O + 2[Al_2O_3 \cdot 3H_2O] + 18H_2O$$

This *conversion* results in disintegration of the concrete.

Conversion can also occur at ordinary temperatures over a period of years (Ref. 13.3), however, and a number of structures built with high-alumina-cement concrete have failed as a result of the "conversion" of the hydrated cement. For this reason, high-alumina cement is now rarely used for concrete structures merely because of its higher strength and high early strength. Nevertheless, it is still considered a very useful building material where resistance to sulfates or to sea water is required.

13.6 WHITE AND COLORED PORTLAND CEMENT

The color of portland cement is grey, and this is one of the problems to be overcome in achieving a good surface finish on concrete (see Sec. 14.11). The grey color is due to small quantities of iron oxide and manganese oxide, both of which are mainly derived from the clay or shale used in making portland cement. Some iron oxide is also introduced by the limestone, and the iron balls used for grinding the cement are a further source of iron.

A perfectly white cement can be made by eliminating all these sources of iron and manganese. Its raw materials are china clay and a pure white limestone or chalk. Oil is used in the kiln instead of coal. The grinding is done with pebbles, or with balls of a nickel–molybdenum alloy. All these special measures cost money, and pure white cement therefore costs several times as much as ordinary portland cement. Its chemical and physical properties are, however, the same as those of ordinary portland cement.

Off-white cement, on the other hand, costs only a little more than ordinary grey portland cement. It is made from light-colored clay and white limestone, but with normal grinding procedures.

White or off-white cement is needed for the lighter colored surfaces, but grey portland cement is acceptable for the darker shades of red and brown, and for black.

Most *pigments* used to supply color are minerals, although some synthetic pigments have been tried. Yellow, red, brown, and black pigments are obtained from various iron oxides. Brown and black can also be obtained from manganese dioxide, and black from carbon. Chromium oxide is the source of the principal green pigment. One blue mineral pigment is made from cobalt oxide; an ultramarine pigment is now made by calcining china clay, soda, sulfur, and coal (see Sec. 19.2). Pastel shades are produced by using less pigment.

Ultramarine pigment combines with the free calcium hydroxide in concrete, and the color fades slowly in consequence; cobalt blue gives a more permanent blue color, but it is more expensive, and it is a different type of blue. Iron ore and manganese dioxide do not produce perfectly black concrete. Carbon black does, but it reduces the strength of the concrete.

Many commercial mineral pigments are adulterated with *fillers*, such as chalk, barium sulfate, and gypsum. The first two of these fillers are inert in cement and therefore do no harm, but gypsum (calcium sulfate) alters the setting time and causes expansion (Secs. 13.3 and 13.8). Pigments containing it in significant quantities should therefore not be used.

Lead pigments cannot be used, because they seriously impair the setting and the hardening of the cement. Organic pigments have been used, but only rarely with success.

All colored concrete fades over a period of time, not because of any deterioration of the color itself (except for ultramarine), but because of the formation of a surface film of white calcium carbonate. This can be removed by washing the surface with a dilute hydrochloric acid (about 1:10), followed by washing with water.

Concrete paints are considered in Secs. 14.11, 19.1, and 19.3.

13.7 CEMENT MORTAR AND PLASTER

Cement mortar consists of one part of portland cement mixed with three to four parts of sand. The materials can be mixed on the building site, or the dry materials can be delivered premixed in paper bags. Portland cement mortar is stronger than masonry cement mortar or cement-lime mortar. When portland cement is used with additives, however, the resulting mortar is harsh and difficult to work. Furthermore, any cracks that may form are liable to pass through the bricks or blocks instead of following the lines of the mortar joints.

For this reason, portland cement is ordinarily used with an additive to make it more plastic (that is, improve its workability) and to increase its water retention. These goals can be achieved by the addition of an inert filler to the cement in the factory; the resulting cement is called *masonry cement* (Sec. 13.4). Masonry cements are used particularly in the United States.

The alternative is to mix some hydrated lime with the portland cement mortar (Sec. 13.1). The hydrated lime is usually added as a dry powder. Cement-lime mortars are particularly favored in Britain and Australia.

Cement is used for plastering both externally and internally. Gypsum is not suitable for exterior work (Sec. 13.2), and lime is gradually dissolved by rain water and requires periodic renewal. Portland cement mortar is therefore the most common material for exterior plastering. A small amount of lime is sometimes added to produce a "fat," easily workable plaster.

One coat is sufficient for cement plaster, but a second coat containing more cement and less sand than the first coat is sometimes applied. Neat cement cannot be used for plastering, however, and it is therefore not possible to obtain the same smooth finish as with gypsum plaster (Sec. 13.2). Nevertheless, cement plaster is commonly used also for internal work.

Graffito work is briefly discussed in Sec. 13.2.

13.8 THE TESTING OF CEMENT

The test for the setting time of cement, which is still used today, was devised by the French civil engineer, J. L. Vicat, in 1818, and the instrument used for it is called a *Vicat needle*.

The *initial set* is defined as the interval between the time when the water is added to the cement and the time when the cement is no longer sufficiently workable to be placed into all the corners of the mold. The *final set* is the time required for the cement to acquire sufficient firmness. The test is carried out on a circular pad of cement mixed with water to a defined consistency. The pad is 40 mm (1½ in.) thick. The initial set, measured with a weighted needle, is achieved when the needle is no longer able to pierce the cement pad within 5 mm (0.2 in.) from the bottom. The final set is achieved when the needle penetrates less then 0.5 mm (0.02 in.) into the cement pad.

Several tests are in use for checking the *soundness* of cement. It is very important that the hardened cement not undergo a large change of volume; in particular, it must not expand to any appreciable extent, as this could lead to disruption under the conditions of restraint that normally prevail in concrete structures.

The three main causes of unsoundness are an excess of free lime, an excess of crystalline magnesia, and an excessive proportion of sulfates. The first two conditions cannot be detected by chemical analysis, which is unable to distinguish between calcium hydroxide and free calcium oxide, or between crystalline and glassy magnesia. Since unsoundness may not show itself until a considerable amount of time has elapsed, it is necessary to make an accelerated test.

The American standard test (ASTM C 151) is carried out on a bar of hardened cement paste, which is placed in an autoclave (a high-pressure steam boiler) where it is subjected to a temperature of 216°C (420°F) and a pressure of 2 MPa (295 psi) for three hours. The expansion, which must not exceed a specified limit, is measured.

The British standard test (BS 12) consists of boiling a pad of hardened cement paste for an hour and measuring the expansion, which must not exceed a specified limit. This detects unsoundness due to free lime, but not that due to magnesia. However, the raw materials from which British cements are manufactured do not contain large quantities of magnesia.

The *strength* of cement is measured by standard tension and/or compression tests on cement mortar.

The *fineness* of cement was originally measured by passing the cement through a series of sieves and weighing the amount retained on each of them. This is, however, not very accurate for determining the proportion of the finer cement particles, because these tend to clog the very small mesh of the sieves.

In America, fineness is now usually measured with the Wagner turbidimeter. The cement powder is allowed to settle in liquid kerosene (which does not react chemically with the cement). The larger particles settle faster than the smaller particles, so that at any given level at which samples are taken after a certain time, the size of the particles depends on the distance through which they have travelled; the larger particles are nearer the bottom, and the finer particles are nearer the top. The proportion of the particles of any given size is determined by measuring the amount of light that passes through the cement particles suspended in the kerosene at any given level; the measurement is made with a photovoltaic cell.

The British standard test uses the Lea and Nurse Air Permeability Apparatus. It measures the *specific surface* of the cement particles instead of the particle size distribution; one, however, is closely related to the other. The specific surface is the total surface area of all the cement particles in a unit volume of cement; the smaller the particles, the greater their specific surface. The flow of air through a bed of dry cement depends on the size of the cement particles. The specific surface is determined by measuring the drop in air pressure when the air passes through the bed of cement.

13.9 MAGNESIUM OXYCHLORIDE

Magnesium oxychloride is manufactured from magnesite (which is magnesium carbonate) and magnesium chloride. The magnesite is heated until it turns into lightly burnt reactive magnesia (that is, magnesium oxide). This is ground and mixed with a strong solution (about 20 percent) of magnesium chloride. The reaction produces magnesium oxychloride [$3MgO \cdot MgCl_2 \cdot 11H_2O$].

The product of this reaction is strong and hard but not water-resistant. Its most common use is as a flooring material with an inert aggregate, usually colored with a mineral pigment. The surface is ground and then polished with wax dissolved in turpentine to give it protection against water. This is called *magnesite flooring*. Magnesium oxychloride corrodes any iron pipes passing through it.

REFERENCES

13.1. Marcus Vitruvius Pollio. (translated by M. Morgan): *The Ten Books of Architecture*. Dover, New York, 1960. p. 45.

13.2. John Smeaton: *The Narrative of the Building of the Edystone Lighthouse with Stone*. Longmans, Hurst, Rees, Orme and Brown, London, 1813. pp. 107–108.

13.3. A. M. Neville: Study of deterioration of structural concrete made with high-alumina cement. *Proc. Institution of Civil Engineers*, Vol. 25 (1963). pp. 287–324.

SUGGESTIONS FOR FURTHER READING

F. M. Lea: *The Chemistry of Cement and Concrete*. Arnold, London, 1970. 727 pp.

R. H. Bogue: *Chemistry of Portland Cement*. Reinhold, New York, 1955. 793 pp.

14

Concrete

Concrete has become the most important material for large buildings because it is durable, fire-resistant, relatively cheap, and an entire structure can be cast monolithically.

Cement as a constituent of concrete was discussed in the previous chapter. In this chapter, the properties of the aggregates are considered, as well as the design of the concrete mix to produce the specified compressive strength and the required workability. The principal methods of testing are also described. The most important concrete admixtures are air-entraining agents and superplasticizers, but there are several others that are useful.

Lightweight concrete may be structural concrete that weighs slightly less than normal concrete and thus reduces the weight of a structure, or it may be much lighter and used mainly for insulation and sound absorption.

The transportation, placing, curing, reinforcing, and prestressing of concrete are briefly considered, as are the advantages and disadvantages of precasting. The difficult subject of providing a satisfactory surface finish is discussed in detail. Polymer concrete is discussed in Sec. 19.7.

14.1 CONCRETE IN ANCIENT AND MODERN ARCHITECTURE

The Romans discovered the art of making concrete in the second or the first century B.C. and thus completely transformed the architecture of the Ancient World (see Fig. 14.1.1). Concrete is a relatively cheap material, it is durable, it is fire-resistant, and an entire structure can be cast in one piece, which greatly increases its rigidity and strength. These considerations apply both to ancient and to modern concrete. However, ancient concrete differed appreciably from that of today, both in its composition and in the manner of its use.

Modern concrete consists of *coarse aggregate, fine aggregate*, and *cement*. The *mortar,* which is the mixture of fine aggregate and cement, fills the pores in the coarse aggregate. The cement and water fills the pores in the fine aggregate. For concrete used in buildings, the coarse aggregate normally consists of particles smaller than 20 mm (¾ in.); it could be crushed rock, or natural gravel, or crushed gravel. The fine aggregate is normally sand, and the cement is portland cement. The materials are mixed together in a concrete mixer (for very small concreting jobs by hand, with a shovel), water is added to the mixer, and the material is then placed in a mold, whose shape it assumes when it hardens.

The Romans used much larger pieces for their coarse aggregate. For the less important parts of a structure, it consisted of pieces of concrete, brick, or stone obtained from demolished buildings. For roof structures, where weight was important, carefully selected lightweight rocks, such as pumice or tufa, were often used. These rocks were placed in the formwork (which frequently consisted of brick walls serving as permanent forms), and the mortar was then poured in the spaces between the coarse aggregate. The Roman mortar contained natural pozzolana, obtained from deposits of volcanic ash, or artificial pozzolanas made in various ways, depending on locally available materials (see Secs. 13.3 and 13.4).

The Roman art of making hydraulic mortar (see Sec. 13.3) was lost after the fall of the Western Roman Empire, but the technology of using large pieces of aggregate inside a masonry mold continued throughout the Middle Ages and the Renaissance, using a much weaker lime mortar. The interior of their massive ma-

Fig. 14.1.1. The concrete walls of the Baths of Caracalla, built in Rome in the third century A.D. Most of the permanent formwork has fallen off the surface, revealing the concrete, which was hidden from view.

sonry piers and walls usually consisted of rough pieces of stone or demolished work, with the spaces between filled with lime mortar.

This practice is no longer followed today because the modern method of mixing the coarse aggregate with the mortar produces stronger and more reliable concrete. Allowing for the present high cost of labor, it is also ordinarily cheaper.

Concrete has today become the most important material for large buildings, as it was in Imperial Rome, and for the same reasons, already stated: concrete is relatively cheap, it is durable (as the Roman ruins testify), it is fire-resistant, and an entire structure can be cast *monolithically*, that is, cast as one piece as if it were carved from one (*mono*) piece of stone (*lithos*). In natural stone, however, the chemical changes occurred long ago, whereas in concrete (both ancient and modern), chemical changes continue for some years after casting. On the one hand, concrete gains additional strength with age; on the other, shrinkage and creep continue to affect the concrete (see Chap. 3).

Modern concrete differs from Roman concrete (apart from its composition) in two respects. First, the Romans never used metal reinforcement in their concrete; the few metal bars found in their concrete probably had other purposes. Consequently, their long-span structures relied on structural forms, such as arches and domes, that were almost entirely in compression. In modern reinforced concrete (which dates from the 1860s), tensile stresses are resisted by steel reinforcement, so that reinforced concrete can resist tension due to bending and shear and can thus be used for floor slabs (its main use in buildings) that are only 100mm (4 in.) thick. The design of reinforced concrete is beyond the scope of this book. Reference should be made to any textbook on reinforced concrete (for example, see Ref. 14.1).

Second among the differences, the Romans rarely exposed the surface of their concrete, which was usually cast in permanent formwork of brick or natural stone. Only the underside of arches and domes was exposed, because bricks would not have adhered to the concrete in that position. In modern concrete construction, the concrete is usually exposed on the surface, partly to simplify construction and to save money, and partly because some architects and engineers believe that this is required for the sake of structural honesty. Others consider that concrete surfaces should be covered by a veneer of a more attractive material, used either as permanent formwork, or fixed to the cast concrete subsequently. Concrete surface finishes are discussed in Sec. 14.11.

14.2 CONCRETE AGGREGATES

Particle Size

Aggregates for normal concrete used in buildings have the following range of particle sizes: 95 percent (or more) of the *coarse* aggregate passes through a 20-mm (¾-in.) sieve, and 95 percent is retained on a 10-mm (³⁄₁₆-in.) sieve; likewise, 95 percent of the *fine* aggregate passes through a 10-mm (³⁄₁₆-in.) sieve, and 95 percent is retained on a No. 100 sieve. The British (BS) and American (ASTM) sieve sizes differ slightly, but the No. 100 sieve is the same in both series (0.15 mm, or 0.0060 in.).

Mineral Classification

Fine aggregate is usually sand from a pit, a river, or the sea. It may be necessary to wash the sand to remove salt, organic material, or clay particles. Most sand consists predominantly of particles of silica, but white coral sand or black sand of volcanic origin can be used. Fine particles of crushed rock can also be used, if excessively fine particles are removed; however, as such particles are usually more angular than those of sand, the concrete mix may be less workable.

Coarse aggregate may be limestone, sandstone, or granite. Note that in the industrial classification of Sec. 12.4, the term "granite" includes not merely granite, but also other hard igneous rocks, notably diorite, dolerite, and basalt (see Table 12.2). It may be crushed rock or gravel of the right particle size; or large gravel may be crushed to size. Crushed concrete, crushed brick, or crushed artificial materials, such as blast-furnace slag can be used as coarse aggregate, provided they are strong enough and free of deleterious substances.

The strength of concrete can be no higher than the strength of the coarse aggregate (although it may be lower) and the softer sandstones, limestones, and bricks are therefore not suitable. Generally speaking, whole gravel or crushed rock is preferred.

Silica undergoes a change from its alpha to its beta phase at a temperature of about 600°C (about 1100°F) [see Sec. 7.5]. Limestone aggregate is therefore par-ticularly suitable for sustained fire resistance, because sandstone and many granites contain silica.

Lightweight aggregates are considered in Sec. 14.7.

Strength and Abrasion Resistance

The strength of coarse aggregate is determined by a compression test. The aggregate is placed into a standard cylinder, consolidated by tamping, and put under load by means of a piston that fits into the cylinder.

Abrasion resistance is important only for concrete used in floor surfaces. There are several types of abrasion testing machines (see Sec. 8.4). The one most common for aggregates consists of a tumbling barrel into which the aggregate is placed together with steel balls. The dust formed is removed, and the loss of weight of the aggregate is measured.

Specific Gravity and Bulk Density

The specific gravity is the ratio of the weight of the individual aggregate particles to that of an equal volume of water. For most natural stones, it is between 2.5 and 2.8. The corresponding densities of the aggregate material are 2500 to 2800 kg/m³ (156 to 175 lb/ft³).

The bulk density of the aggregate is less, because it includes the voids between the aggregate particles. For example, if a number of spheres of identical size are packed as tightly as possible, as in Fig. 2.4.1(a), the bulk density is 74 percent of the density of the solid material; for the loosest possible packing of the same spheres, it is 52 percent.

There are two bulk densities. One is measured by loosely filling a standard cylinder with the aggregate; the other is measured after the aggregate has been compacted with a tamping rod ("loose" and "compacted" bulk density). The bulk density is measured by weighing the contents of the cylinder and dividing by its volume.

The bulk density depends on the specific gravity of the aggregate material, the shape of the aggregate particles, and the moisture content.

Moisture Content of Aggregate

Most concrete aggregates contain some pores; if they did not, rock would be impervious to water. The porosity is highest in coarse sandstones and in limestones, and lowest in granites. In addition, water is absorbed by the surface of the aggregate particles, and if a pile of aggregate is soaked by rain, water may be held in the spaces between the aggregate particles.

If aggregate is dried in a hot oven, all moisture is removed from the pores [Fig. 14.2.1(a)], but if it is dried in air, some moisture is retained in the inner

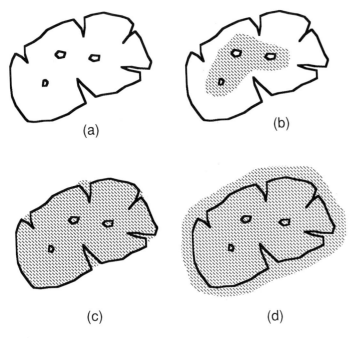

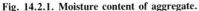

Fig. 14.2.1. Moisture content of aggregate.
(a) *Oven-dry:* Moisture content zero; absorption by aggregate will reduce water/cement ratio. (b) Air-dry: Contains interior moisture; absorption by aggregate will reduce water/cement ratio slightly. (c) *Surface-dry (saturated):* All pores full of moisture; water/cement ratio is not affected by aggregate. (d) *Moist:* Moisture adheres to aggregate surface: Water/cement ratio will be increased by excess moisture on the surface of the aggregate.

pores (b). Moist aggregate (d) is aggregate that has a layer of water on its surface. Surface-dry aggregate (c) is moist aggregate that has been dried with a towel; it represents the neutral state. Oven-dry and air-dry aggregate absorb some of the mixing water, and thus reduce the water/cement ratio of the concrete (Sec. 14.5). Since the surface moisture of moist aggregate constitutes an addition to the mixing water, the water/cement ratio is increased by this *free moisture.*

The moisture content of surface-dry aggregate can be determined by drying it in an oven and measuring the loss of weight. This needs to be done only once for each new source of aggregate, because it is always the same for the same type of aggregate. It varies from ¼ to 4 percent.

The free moisture of moist aggregate is determined most accurately by drying it in an oven and determining the total moisture content from the loss of weight. The free moisture is then the difference between the total moisture and the absorbed moisture content of surface-dry aggregate [Fig. 14.2.1(c)].

There are several faster, if less accurate methods, that can be used to obtain rapid measurements of the free-moisture content of aggregate in different locations within the storage pile. One is to immerse the aggregate in water and measure its apparent loss of weight with

a buoyancy meter; this approach requires a knowledge of the specific gravity of the aggregate material. An even more rapid method for measuring the free moisture content is to use an electric moisture meter, which determines it through the change of electrical resistance in various parts of the aggregate pile.

Bulking of Sand

The volume of sand increases as its free moisture content increases up to a moisture content of 5 to 8 percent, depending on the type of sand. Thereafter, the volume decreases again (Fig. 14.2.2), and the volume of water-saturated sand is the same as that of dry sand. The maximum increase in volume may amount to 35 percent over the dry volume and must therefore be taken into account whenever sand is batched by volume (Sec. 14.3), although this practice is now rare.

The volume of coarse aggregate increases by only a negligible amount as a result of its free moisture content, because the size of the particles is so much greater than the thickness of the film of surface moisture.

Deleterious Substances

Clay and other fine materials coating the surface of aggregate particles prevent adhesion between the aggregate and the cement. Clay or *silt* may be present in gravel or sand that has not been washed. *Crusher dust* clings to crushed rock. The amount of this deleterious material can be determined by a sedimentation test, since fine material remains in suspension much longer than the larger particles.

Organic materials resulting from decayed vegetable matter interfere with the hydration of cement. Their presence is determined by placing the aggregate in a 3-percent solution of sodium hydroxide (NaOH). The bottle is shaken vigorously and then left for a day. Thereafter, the organic content is determined by comparing the color of the solution with a standard chart.

Both fine materials and organic materials must be removed by washing the aggregate.

Opinions differ on the significance of salt contam-

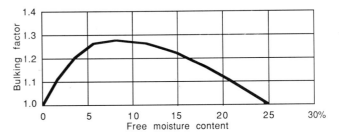

Fig. 14.2.2. Increase in the volume of sand (*bulking factor*) with free moisture content.

ination, which results from the use of sand or pebbles from sea coasts or the shores of river estuaries. Particular care is needed if the sand is excavated near the high-water mark, where the salt content is particularly high. It is better to remove the salt by washing, as it is likely to cause efflorescence (see Sec. 12.5) or may cause slight corrosion of the reinforcement. However, some specifications permit the use of unwashed sea sand.

Even small quantities of sugar can seriously retard the setting of cement, and a 1-percent solution almost completely inhibits setting and hardening (Ref. 14.2, p. 302). Sugar may be introduced accidentally, particularly in sugar-producing regions. Unfortunately, it also provides a simple and potent means of sabotage.

Unsound Aggregate Particles

Many deposits of natural stone have veins of weaker material, such as shale or coal, or layers where igneous rock has decayed to clay. Such veins may produce unsound particles in crushed rock. A more common problem is the presence of soft particles, lumps of clay or particles of coal, in gravel or sand. Most specifications limit the amount of unsound particles. The maximum permissible content is usually on the order of 1 percent by weight.

Alkali-Aggregate Reaction

A number of rocks—notably in the U.S.A., Australia, New Zealand, Scandinavia, and India—contain opaline silica or other reactive forms of silica. These react with any sodium and potassium oxide (Na_2O and K_2O) present in the cement. The reactions can be very damaging, because the resulting expansion often causes the concrete to disintegrate. They occur, however, only when reactive aggregates are used with high-alkali cement. High-alkali cements on their own, or reactive aggregates on their own, cause no damage (Ref. 14.2, pp. 569–576).

Another alkali-aggregate reaction occurs, although less frequently, with certain types of dolomitic limestone found in Canada and the U.S.A. (Ref. 14.2, pp. 575–579).

The best insurance against alkali-aggregate reactions is to use aggregates and cements of known performance. Otherwise, predictions can be made by chemical tests (Ref. 14.2, pp. 573–576) or by casting test bars, storing them in water at 38°C (100°F), and measuring the expansion.

14.3 AGGREGATE GRADING

The 1:2:4 rule for proportioning of the concrete mix goes back to the early years of the nineteenth century,

and it is still a good rule for small jobs where the concrete is mixed by hand or with a small mixer. It means that the concrete consists of one part of cement, two parts of sand, and four parts of coarse aggregate. The unit of cement is usually one bag (94 lb in the U.S.A., and 40 or 50 kg in metric countries); the aggregate is measured by volume in a gauge box.

In the early twentieth century, more scientific methods resulted in the development of optimum aggregate grading curves. Figure 14.3.1 shows the range of particle grading for combined coarse and fine aggregate recommended in Great Britain (Ref. 14.3). The separate grading requirements for coarse and fine aggregate in the American specification for concrete aggregates (Ref. 14.4) are broadly similar.

The No. 1 curve in Fig. 14.3.1 represents the highest proportion of fine material. This is desirable if the particles of coarse aggregate have a sufficiently rough surface texture or are so elongated that more lubrication is needed to place them in the mold. It is also useful if the handling of the wet concrete is likely to result in segregation (see Sec. 14.8) because the larger pro-

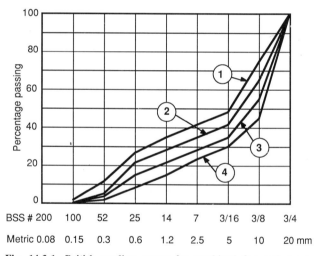

Fig. 14.3.1. British grading curves for combined fine and coarse concrete aggregate of 20-mm (¾-in.) maximum size (*Reproduced by permission from Ref. 14.3, p. 35*).

These grading curves were originally developed by the (British) Road Research Laboratory, and later improved by the (British) Cement and Concrete Association. There are four curves, the highest of which (No. 1) represents the highest proportion of fine particles considered desirable; at each sieve size, Curve No. 1 has a greater proportion of fine particles than any other curve. Similarly, Curve No. 4 contains the lowest proportion of fine particles considered desirable. Curves No. 2 and 3 roughly divide this range into three zones. The vertical axis indicates the percentage passing a particular sieve. The horizontal axis gives the British standard (BS) sieve sizes (which are also the Australian standard sieve sizes) from 20 mm (¾ in.) to No. 200. The American standard (ASTM) sieve sizes are only slightly different. Sieve sizes are plotted on the horizontal axis on a logarithmic scale to produce more compact curves. Similar curves have been produced for combined fine and coarse aggregate with maximum sizes of 40 mm (1½ in.) and 10 mm (⅜ in.) [Ref. 14.3, pp. 34 and 35].

portion of fine particles offers greater cohesion. On the other hand, a large proportion of fine material requires more water to make it workable; this increase in the amount of water either reduces the strength of the concrete or requires the use of more cement (Sec. 14.5). Since cement is the most expensive ingredient, and also the one responsible for shrinkage and creep (see Chap. 3), this is a disadvantage. The opposite considerations apply to the coarser grading represented at its lowest limit by curve No. 4.

Since concrete aggregates vary greatly, the mix required is ultimately determined by making a number of trial mixes and testing for their workability and strength (Sec. 14.4). Concrete mix design was originally developed for dams and other large civil engineering works requiring large quantities of concrete. When concrete was mixed on the building site, the quantities of concrete required were not sufficient to warrant the use of specially graded aggregate.

Today, concrete for most building sites is supplied from a *ready-mix plant* that mixes the aggregates and the cement. The water is added in the mixer truck shortly before arrival at the building site. This arrangement makes it possible to use carefully graded aggregates, the product of blending several different aggregates to obtain the correct overall grading; two coarse aggregates and one fine aggregate are usually sufficient. Because the same mixes are used on many building sites, and therefore in far larger quantities, more care can be devoted to the design of the best grading.

Prior to the introduction of ready-mix concrete, each building site needed a concrete mixer and stores of aggregate and cement. These occupied much space and produced a great deal of dust. The development of ready-mix concrete was consequently a major contributor to increasing the use of reinforced concrete in buildings.

14.4 THE TESTING OF CONCRETE

The removal of concrete mixing from the building site to a central plant has made it much easier to specify concrete by its performance instead of relying on the less accurate specification of the mix proportion. The two main criteria are *strength* and *workability*.

Strength

The strength of concrete is determined by compression tests on concrete cylinders (in America and Australia) or on concrete cubes (in Europe). The cylinders are normally 150 mm (6 in.) in diameter and 300 mm (12 in.) high, and the cubes are normally 150 mm (6 in.) in each direction. They are tested in a hydraulic press, and the maximum load they can support before breaking

is recorded. The strength of concrete in tension and also in diagonal tension due to shear or torsion is normally calculated from the compressive strength instead of being measured directly.

The *specifed compressive strength* of concrete used in structural calculations is the *minimum strength* of the test cylinders or cubes. Since concrete is a variable material, the *average strength* of the cylinders and cubes is higher; the difference between the specified and the average strength depends on the degree of control over the mix design at the mixing plant and on the degree of control at the building site (Fig. 14.4.1).

Workability

Workability is the property of freshly mixed concrete (or mortar) that determines the ease with which it can be mixed, placed in the formwork to fill every part of the form, compacted, and given a satisfactory surface finish. Concrete can be placed in the formwork much more easily if its water content is increased, but this lowers its strength (Sec. 14.5) and leads to the formation of *laitance* (Sec. 14.8). The general aim, therefore, is to produce adequate workability while keeping the water content as low as possible.

The oldest and still the most common test for measuring workability is the *slump test*. This test is carried out by filling a hollow truncated cone of sheet metal (Fig. 14.4.2) with concrete in three layers; each layer is compacted with 25 strokes of a steel rod. The mold is then lifted and the concrete allowed to 'slump' (Fig. 14.4.3).

The slump test is cheap and easy to perform, and it gives good results with concrete mixes containing high proportions of cement and/or fine sand. Harsher mixes, however, have a tendency to produce a shear slump or even complete collapse. Collapse may be due to the concrete's being so very wet that it flows outwards, but it may also occur with a very dry mix, which, had it been a little more cohesive and not collapsed, would have produced zero slump.

Several other tests have been devised to measure workability, and some give better results in a laboratory or a ready-mix plant, but none has replaced the slump test, and workability is usually quoted in terms of "slump." Mass concrete and lightly reinforced concrete require a slump on the order of 25 to 50 mm (1 to 2 in.), whereas normal reinforced concrete requires a slump of 50 to 100 mm (2 to 4 in.).

The alternatives to the slump test measure either the flow of the wet concrete, its compactability, its capacity for remolding, or the penetration of a ball or plunger through the wet concrete.

The *flow test* is standardized by the American ASTM Specifications C109-73 and C 230-74. The concrete is placed in a mold (similar to a slump-test mold) on a

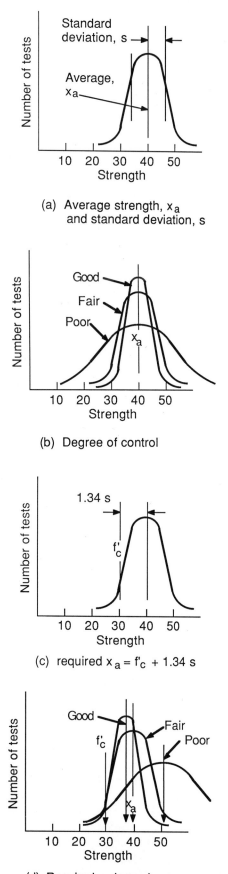

(a) Average strength, x_a
and standard deviation, s

(b) Degree of control

(c) required $x_a = f'_c + 1.34\,s$

(d) Required x_a depends on
degree of control

Fig. 14.4.1. The specified compressive strength, f'_c, of concrete as measured by breaking test cylinders (or cubes) and measuring their maximum strength.
The strength of each cylinder, x, varies slightly from one cylinder to another. A few will give very high results, a few will give very low results (a), but the largest number will be near the average, x_a. The spread of the curve depends on the degree of control; good control results in a steeper curve with less spread than poor control (b). The degree of control is measured by the *standard deviation*, s, a statistical quantity defined in the Glossary and indicated graphically in part (a) of this figure. The specified compressive strength, f'_c, is the *minimum* strength of the concrete, except for a few very low results (c). The location of f'_c on the curve is based on a probability of about 1 in 10,000 that the concrete structure will not suffer any significant damage, and 1 in 1,000,000 that it will not collapse. This strikes a reasonable balance between the social acceptability of failure and the increased cost of stronger concrete. *Complete* certainty that no collapse will ever occur is unattainable. The equation, $f'_c = x_a - 1.34s$, is derived by statistics from these probabilities. Evidently the average strength x_a required for a specified strength f'_c depends on the level of control (d).

flow table. The mold is lifted and the table is raised and allowed to drop several times. The resulting outward flow of the concrete is measured.

The *compacting factor test* is standardized by the British specification BS 1881 (Fig. 14.4.4). The concrete is allowed to drop into a cylinder under standarized conditions and its weight then determined. The ratio of this weight to the weight of an equal volume of fully compaced concrete is the compacting factor.

The *remolding test* is a variation on the flow test, devised by T. C. Powers in the U.S.A. A slump test mold is placed on a flow table (see "Flow Test"), the

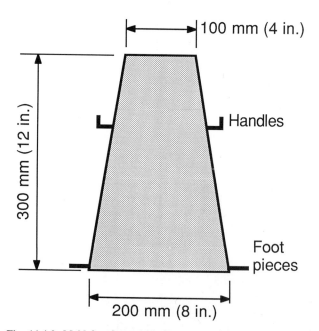

Fig. 14.4.2. Mold for slump test.
The concrete is shoveled in through the 100-mm (4-in.) circular opening at the top.

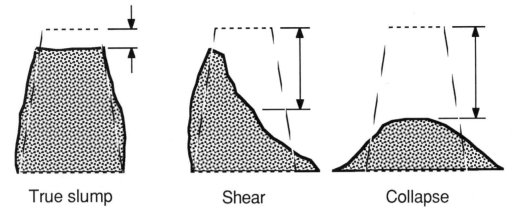

Fig. 14.4.3. Slump test.
The slump can be measured with some accuracy for a true slump (a), which is obtained with mixes containing high proportions of cement and/or fine sand. Harsher mixes produce a shear slump (b) or complete collapse of the wet concrete (c). A shear slump is measured to the middle of slump on each side of the cone, but no satisfactory slump test result can be obtained from a collapse.

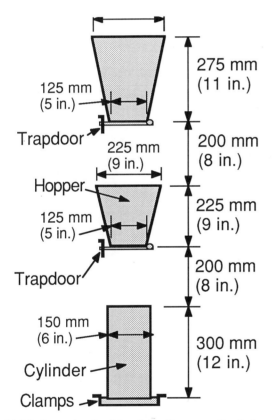

Fig. 14.4.4. Apparatus for determining the compacting factor.
After the concrete is placed in the upper hopper, the trapdoor is opened so that it drops through a standard distance into the middle hopper. The trapdoor of the middle hopper is then opened so that the concrete falls into the cylinder. Any excess concrete above the top edge of the cylinder is removed with a steel float. The cylinder is then weighed, and the weight of the concrete compacted in this standard manner is determined. The cylinder, once emptied and cleaned, is filled with the same concrete mix, but the concrete is fully compacted by vibration. The compacting factor is the ratio of the weight of the concrete compacted by dropping to the fully compacted concrete. A slump of 25 to 50 mm (1 to 2 in.) corresponds to a compacting factor of approximately 0.85, and a slump of 50 to 100 mm (2 to 4 in.) corresponds to a compacting factor of approximately 0.92.

mold is lifted, and the concrete allowed to slump. A cylinder mold is then placed over the slumped concrete, and the flow table is raised and allowed to drop until the concrete fills the cylinder mold that has a larger diameter than the original slump-test mold.

Another remolding test is the *Vebe test,* developed by V. Bährner in Sweden, but widely used throughout the world. It employs a vibrating table, instead of mechanical jolting, and a glass cover over the concrete that makes it easier to determine the time of full compaction.

The most common penetration test in the U.S.A. is the *Kelly ball test,* which is standardized by ASTM specification C360-75. A ball-shaped plunger, weighing 30 lb (13.6 kg) and fixed to a supporting frame, is placed on the concrete surface, and allowed to penetrate into the concrete under its own weight (Fig. 14.4.5). The depth of the penetration is measured.

The Kelly ball test is even simpler than the slump test; unlike the slump test, however, it can be used on harsh mixes that would produce collapse in a slump test (Fig. 14.4.3). The other tests are laboratory tests only.

14.5 CONCRETE MIX DESIGN

Having chosen the best possible aggregate grading, or the best available at a reasonable cost (Sec. 14.3), the concrete mix is designed to give the specified compressive strength, stated in megapascals (MPa) or kilopounds per square inch (ksi), and the required workability, expressed in terms of the slump test or other test chosen. Both properties depend mainly on the content of cement and water and of any admixtures that may be used; the latter will be discussed in Sec. 14.6.

The water/cement ratio, rather than the actual water content, is what is important for strength. D. A. Abrams

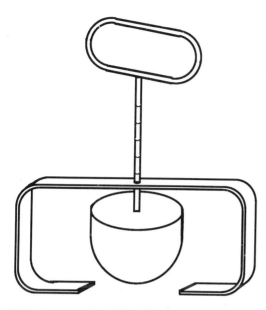

Fig. 14.4.5. Apparatus for Kelly ball test.
The ballshaped plunger is placed on the concrete surface and allowed to penetrate into the concrete under its own weight. The depth of penetration is measured by the gradations on the handle.

in 1919 determined from experiments carried out at the Lewis Institute, Chicago (precursor of the Illinois Institute of Technology) that, with given concrete materials, the compressive strength is inversely proportional to the ratio of water to cement. The curve is thus a hyperbola (Fig. 14.5.1), but this relationship holds true only as long as the concrete is fully compacted. Thus, workability has an important influence on strength.

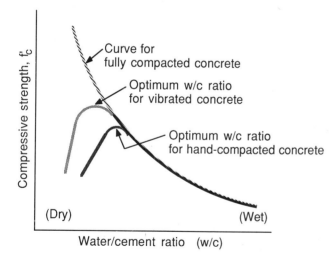

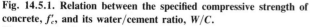

Fig. 14.5.1. Relation between the specified compressive strength of concrete, f'_c, and its water/cement ratio, W/C.
The strength, f'_c, is inversely proportional to W/C, provided that the concrete is fully compacted; thus, the relationship is given by the hyperbolic curve in the figure as long as the water content is sufficient for full compaction. The range of full compaction can be extended by vibration. When the mix is too dry for full compaction, the strength falls below that given by the hyperbolic curve.

Concrete must be sufficiently workable to fill all corners of the formwork and all spaces between the reinforcing bars. For it to do so may require a higher water content than that appropriate for maximum strength, and this reduction in concrete strength must be accepted, because complete compaction of the concrete is a prime requirement.

American and British practice for the design of concrete mixes is based on the same principles, but the procedure is different. The American method uses calculations based on the absolute volume or the estimated unit weights of the materials, whereas the British method uses a series of charts and tables. Reference should be made to the American (Ref. 14.5) and the British (Ref. 14.3) manuals on the subject.

The concrete mix having been chosen, the weights of the materials to be used for a trial mix are calculated. Only a small batch is needed for a trial mix. If the trial mix does not produce the specified compressive strength and workability required, the proportions are modified empirically on the basis of the results obtained. Concrete materials are too variable to make accurate prediction of the mix proportions possible.

Since continuous concrete mixers are now rarely used, the concrete mix is proportioned in distinct batches, the size of the batch depending on the capacity of the mixer. The weights of the individual materials are calculated from the concrete mix proportions.

When concrete is transported from a ready-mix plant to a building site in a mixer truck, the water is usually added just before the truck reaches the building site.

14.6 CONCRETE ADMIXTURES

Admixtures are used to improve certain properties of concrete, or to economize in the use of more expensive ingredients. Some are added to the concrete in the concrete mixer, whereas others are mixed with the cement. Some of the latter were discussed in Chap. 13, namely pozzolanas (including blast-furnace slag and fly ash), inert fillers (in masonry cement), and colors for colored cement.

Air-Entraining Agents

Air-entraining agents are used very widely in the U.S.A. and Canada, and to an increasing extent in other countries. They increase the workability of the concrete, and they improve durability, in particular, resistance to the effects of freezing and thawing. On the other hand, they reduce the strength of the concrete.

About 5 percent of freshly mixed concrete consists of air in cavities; this is called *entrapped air* to distinguish it from *entrained air*. The amount of entrapped air can be reduced by vibration to less than 1 percent. Entrapped air that is in contact with outside air through capillary channels may lead to deterioration of the concrete, particularly during periods of freezing and thawing (Sec. 14.8).

Air-entraining agents, on the other hand, produce minute air bubbles—of the order of 1 to 0.1 mm (0.04 to 0.004 in.) in diameter—that are uniformly distributed throughout the concrete and closed off from outside air so as to act as a kind of additional "fine aggregate" that increases the workability of the concrete mix. Moreover, air-entraining agents capture the entrapped air, which then becomes part of the enclosed bubbles of entrained air. By thus reducing the capillarity of the hardened concrete, this process improves its durability and reduces efflorescence (See Sec. 12.5). On the other hand, the air bubbles reduce strength, usually by about 10 percent.

Air-entraining agents are usually sold as proprietary products. They are made *either* (1) from wood resins, vegetable or animal fats or oils, or the fatty acids or soaps of the latter, *or* (2) from wetting agents or synthetic detergents.

Water-Reducing Admixtures

Water-reducing admixtures reduce the amount of water required for a desired workability, and because they reduce the water/cement ratio, they increase the strength of the concrete. The principal materials are modified lignosulfonates and sulfonated naphtalene or melamine fomaldehyde condensates. These materials have recently been used extensively under the name *superplasticizers* to produce high-strength concrete with normal workability and cement content. This increase in concrete strength has had an important effect in making reinforced concrete more economical for tall buildings.

These are the most widely used admixtures, but there are others of lesser importance.

Accelerators and Retarders

Accelerators and retarders are used to increase the early strength of concrete and to retard the setting of concrete, respectively.

Calcium chloride, the most effective accelerator, is used in cold weather when concreting would ordinarily not be possible, because it speeds up the chemical reaction of cement hydration, which is slowed down by low temperatures, and generates additional heat in the process. Calcium chloride should not be used in prestressed concrete, however, because it may cause corosion, and many specifications forbid its use in reinforced concrete as well. Several other inorganic and organic substances can also be used as concrete accelerators (see Ref. 14.6, p. 81).

As has already been mentioned (see Sec. 13.3), gypsum is a very effective retarder. So are sugar (Sec. 14.2), molasses, and a number of other materials (Ref. 14.6, p. 87). They can be used as coatings on formwork to retard the setting of the cement on the surface layer of concrete, to allow the cement to be removed, and to expose the aggregate (Sec. 14.11).

Integral Waterproofing

The use of *integral waterproofers* is controversial. They consist of pore-filling materials, such as sodium silicate or talc, or of water-repellant materials, such as resins and waxes (Ref. 14.6, p. 91). Many concrete engineers consider that the addition of cement—that is, a richer mix—is more effective than the addition of integral waterproofers. There is general agreement, however, that water-repellant materials are useful in making cement rendering more waterproof.

Shrinkage Compensation

Shrinkage compensation can be produced by blending an *expansive cement* with portland cement. There are several expansive cements, most of which contain calcium sulfoaluminate ($4CaO \cdot 3Al_2O_3 \cdot SO_3$). The expansion results from the production of ettringite (see Sec. 13.3), the mineral formed by sulfate attack on concrete. The expansion caused by the formation of ettringite can be accommodated while the concrete is still in a plastic condition without causing internal strains; once the concrete has hardened, however, the expansion causes internal strains, and these may lead to its disintegration.

Shrinkage-compensating cements are portland cements with a small admixture of expansive cement that is sufficient to produce an expansion of concrete that is equal to its shrinkage (see Chap. 3). This relatively small expansion can be safely achieved (Ref. 14.7), but it compensates for shrinkage only; provision must still be made for temperature and moisture movement.

Much larger expansions have been reported, (Ref. 14.8), including full prestressing by means of expansive cement (without the use of prestressing jacks). These large expansions by chemical means should be used only with the greatest care, however; in particular, it is important to ensure that the expansion stops when it is required to do so.

14.7 LIGHTWEIGHT CONCRETE AND HIGH-DENSITY CONCRETE

The term "lightweight concrete," includes a whole range of materials, from those that are slightly lighter than normal structural concrete but have the same strength, to very light concretes that float on water, have negligible strength, and are used for insulation. A specific gravity as low as 0.15 (corresponding to densities of 150 kg/m^3 or 9 lb/ft^3) can be achieved, as compared to a specific gravity of 2.5 for normal concrete.

Cellular Concrete

The lightest concretes used for insulation are made with air or gas bubbles, cement, and water. For slightly heavier materials, a sand/cement mortar is used with bubbles. Such concretes are known as *cellular concretes* or *aerated concretes,* and they should not be confused with air-entrained concretes (Sec. 14.6). The same additives that are used for producing the air bubbles for air-entrained concrete can also be used for cellular concrete; larger quantities, however, are needed. The lightest materials of all are produced by adding a foam made from a detergent or air-entraining agent to the concrete mix, or by adding a material to the cement that produces gas bubbles. Of the latter, the most common is flaky aluminum powder, which produces hydrogen bubbles. Calcium carbide produces acetylene bubbles, and hydrogen peroxide produces oxygen bubbles. A wetting agent is ordinarily used to control the distribution and uniformity of size of the gas bubbles.

Because of their high cement content, cellular concretes have high shrinkage (Chap. 3). They are normally autoclaved (that is, subjected to high-pressure steam) or at least steam-cured (that is, subjected to steam at normal pressure) to speed up the chemical reactions and ensure that most of the shrinkage occurs during the manufacturing process.

Lime, silica flour, fly ash, ground granulated blast-furnace slag, glass grinding waste, diatomite, pumice dust, or volcanic ash may be added to the cement, partly to reduce cost as well as to reduce shrinkage.

Cellular concrete may be poured into cavities or into the metal trays of curtain walls to act as an insulating material. The heavier varieties can be used for partitions and ceilings where thermal insulation is also the main requirement.

Lightweight Aggregate

Lightweight aggregate varies from very light processed aggregates—such as exfoliated vermiculite—which produce insulating concrete comparable in weight to the slightly heavier, aerated concretes and are sometimes superior in thermal insulation—to the heavier processed aggregates—such as expanded clay—which are lighter than natural aggregates, but just as strong, and thus produce structural concrete that weighs less than normal concrete.

Some very light rocks of volcanic origin, such as pumice and scoria, occur naturally, but most light concrete aggregates are manufactured. The lightest are expanded perlite and exfoliated vermiculite, already mentioned in Sect. 7.5 (dealing with the fire protection of steel). These materials have specific gravities in the range of 0.06 to 0.3, and lightweight concretes made with them have a specific gravity in the range 0.3 to 1.0. The compressive strength of these concretes, however, is only in the range of 0.7 to 6 MPa (0.1 to 0.8 ksi) so that they can be used only for fire protection, thermal insulation, and sound absorption.

Foamed blast-furnace slag, sintered fly ash, clinker, and expanded clay and shale have a wide range of specific gravities, with a corresponding range of concrete strengths. These depend partly on the original state of the materials (most of which are industrial wastes) and partly on the manner in which their weight is reduced by manufacture. Lightweight-aggregate concretes made with these aggregates can be produced with specific gravities in the range of 1.5 to 2—that is, 20 to 40 percent less than ordinary concrete—and with compressive strengths comparable to those of normal concrete. Lightweight aggregates, however, often cost more than normal aggregates.

The main advantage of lightweight-aggregate structural concrete is the reduction in the weight of the structure that allows column sizes to be reduced—an important consideration for tall buildings. Lightweight-aggregate concretes usually have higher shrinkage and a lower modulus of elasticity than normal concrete.

No-Fines Concrete

No-fines concrete is a lightweight concrete made only of coarse aggregate and cement, without fine aggregate. The coarse aggregate usually consists of crushed rock or gravel, but lightweight aggregates can be used. The concrete consists of particles of coarse aggregate, each coated with cement paste, with large pores between. Because of these large pores, the strength of the concrete is low, but there is no capillary moisture movement. The cement content is lower than for normal concrete—about 1:8. No-fines concrete has been used mainly for the walls of low-cost houses. External walls must be rendered with cement mortar.

High-Density Concrete

High-density concrete is used primarily for radiation shielding in atomic reactors. It may occasionally be useful for the same purpose in buildings housing machinery that emits radiation or as a noise barrier. It is ordinarily simpler to use a greater thickness of normal concrete, however, since this achieves the same purpose. The most commonly used aggregates are goethite, haematite, ilmenite, limonite, and magnetite (all iron ores) and barite (barium sulfate). All have specific gravities of about 4, and the resulting concrete has a specific gravity about double that of normal concrete.

14.8 TRANSPORTATION, PLACING, AND CURING OF CONCRETE

When concrete was mixed on the building site and then transported to its final location by wheelbarrow, *segregation* of the concrete mix was not a serious problem. With modern transportation methods, however, which may involve pumping the concrete or sending it by gravity down a chute over long distances, it becomes a problem.

Segregation is a separation of the constituents of concrete so that their distribution ceases to be sufficiently uniform. It may be caused by a differential settlement of the aggregates in which the larger particles, or the heavier particles, travel faster down a pipe or slope, or settle faster in the concrete when they reach their final destination. Another type of segregation, which occurs particularly in wet mixes, results in the separation of the cement grout (that is, the cement and the water) from the aggregate and its formation in a layer on top of the concrete.

Segregation does not occur if the concrete mix is *cohesive*, but a *workable* mix is not necessarily cohesive. The slump test, the compacting factor test, and the Kelly ball test (Sec. 14.4) all measure workability, but not cohesiveness. The flow test, however, does give an indication of cohesiveness. Air-entraining agents (Sec. 14.6) reduce the tendency towards segregation.

Evidently, great economies are achievable by the use of concrete pumps and slides, but these should be manipulated so that the concrete does not have to be moved sideways after it is deposited. The placement of concrete should be designed for it to travel the shortest possible distance to its final destination. Concrete should not be placed in layers thicker than 0.5 m (18 in.) to ensure that the layer below is still soft and that the two layers can be integrated by vibration. The vibration should be limited to the minimum required for consolidation, as excessive amounts produce segregation.

Closely related to segregation is *bleeding,* which is the collection of mixing water on the surface of freshly placed concrete; this water may carry some of the cement with it. Bleeding is a form of subsidence and can be expressed quantitatively as the total settlement per unit depth of concrete. There is an ASTM standard test (C 232-71) for determining experimentally both the capacity for bleeding and the rate of bleeding.

Bleeding is not necessarily harmful if the water that collects on the surface evaporates before the concrete surface is given its final finish with a float. However, if the bleeding water brings cement to the surface, then a layer of set cement is formed on the surface; called *laitance,* this produces a dusty surface and a plane of weakness. If further concrete is to be placed on top, then the laitance must be removed by brushing to ensure proper adhesion of the new concrete. Finishing with a wooden float, instead of a steel float, avoids overworking of the surface and bringing an excess of cement to the top.

Bleeding water may also become trapped under large aggregate particles or under reinforcing bars, where it forms capillary voids on evaporation; these may have an adverse effect on durability, particularly on resistance to frost.

The tendency to bleeding can be reduced by the use of air-entraining agents, by the use of finer cement and a greater proportion of very fine aggregate, by a decrease in the water content, and by a decrease in the water/cement ratio (by reducing water content or increasing cement content).

Both high and low temperatures adversely affect the hydration of the cement. Special precautions are necessary when placing concrete in *hot weather*. The temperature of new concrete should be kept below 32°C (90°F), and preferably below 30°C (85°F). This may be accomplished by mixing crushed ice with the mixing water and by keeping all accessory materials in the shade. The heat of hydration produced by the cement can be reduced by using a low-heat cement (see Sec. 13.4) and by using special care in curing to prevent evaporation of the mixing water.

Special precautions are also necessary in *cold weather*, that is, when the temperature falls below 4°C (40°F). The concrete should be kept above a temperature of 15°C (59°F). This may be accomplished by heating the mixing water and the aggregates; however, the water should not be heated above 65°C (150°F) to avoid a *flash set* of the concrete. A cement with a higher content of calcium aluminate and of tricalcium silicate should be used to generate a higher rate of heat development (see Sec. 13.3). Calcium chloride as an accelerator (Sec. 14.6) increases the rate of hydration and thus generates further heat; in addition, it turns the mixing water into a salt solution and thus lowers its freezing point below that of pure water. The concrete must be further protected against frost during curing.

Curing is the term given to the protection of the concrete during the early stages of hardening, when it requires additional moisture for the continuing hydration of the cement, and to its protection from cold during the night and from heat during the day. The concrete surface can be covered with sand or burlap (a coarse fabric of jute or hemp, called *hessian* in Britain and Australia), which is kept moist by watering or spraying. Precast concrete units and concrete slabs may be covered with water.

Alternatively, the concrete can be covered with a

curing membrane, which provides a physical barrier to the evaporation of its water. This is applied either as a sheet or as a liquid that dries within a few hours to a continuous, adhesive film; a dye is sometimes added to facilitate uniform coverage. Polyvinyl chloride, polyethylene (about 0.2 mm or 0.001 in. thick), or waterproof building paper provide suitable sheet materials. Liquid curing compounds include various wax and oil emulsions as well as various plastics.

Precast concrete units are sometimes steam-cured or autoclaved (cured with high-pressure steam), a treatment that increases their strength and makes it possible to handle and transport them much sooner, thus greatly reducing the amount of storage space required.

14.9 REINFORCEMENT IN CONCRETE

Some of the properties of steel are ideally suited to the requirements of concrete reinforcement. The coefficient of thermal expansion of cement is a little higher than that of steel and that of most aggregates a little lower. As a result, the coefficient of thermal expansion of most concrete is almost the same as that of steel so that no differential stresses are set up between the steel and the concrete as a result of changes in temperature. Steel has the highest modulus of elasticity among the common metals and can thus be effectively utilized even as compression reinforcement (Ref. 14.1, p. 140).

On the other hand, no metal shrinks as a result of chemical action, or changes its length as the humidity changes, nor do any common metals (except lead) creep at normal temperatures. Consequently, differential stresses are set up both in the steel and the concrete by shrinkage and moisture movement, and there is a redistribution of stresses brought about by the creep of the concrete (Ref. 14.1, p. 90). These would occur with any metal reinforcement.

The design of reinforced and prestressed concrete structures is a complex subject requiring a book to itself; an introduction to both structures is given in Ref. 14.1. In this section, we will merely consider the effect of reinforcement on the durability of concrete.

Ancient Roman concrete structures did not have reinforcement. As a result, they were much heavier than modern reinforced concrete structures (although the spans they achieved were much greater than those of the Ancient World preceding them or the Middle Ages afterwards). On the other hand, they were very durable, as the surviving buildings and ruins show.

Most modern reinforced concrete buildings have also proved very durable, but a significant number have deteriorated through the (incorrect) use of reinforcement. Spalling or other deterioration of concrete may occur as a result of chemical action in the concrete—for example, conversion of high-alumina cement (see Sec. 13.5)—or reaction between reactive silica aggregates and alkali oxides in portland cement (Sec. 14.2). The most common chemical action that leads to spalling of concrete, however, is rusting of the steel reinforcement (see Fig. 8.2.4).

The main problem created by the use of steel reinforcement is the fact, already discussed in Sec. 10.3, that hydrated ferric oxide $[2Fe_2O_3 \cdot 3H_2O]$ is water-soluble and occupies a greater volume than the steel from which it is formed. As a result, the rusting of reinforcement, once it starts, continues its corrosion because the rust does not protect the metal underneath (as the corrosion products of aluminum and lead do) and because the expansion of the rust eventually leads to spalling of the concrete (see Sec. 8.2). Even before that occurs, streaks of rust disfigure the concrete, particularly on a façade, and these are very difficult to remove.

The most common cause of rusting of reinforcement is inadequate concrete cover—usually the result of poor workmanship and poor supervision. However, excessive cracking of the concrete may also cause rusting.

Hydrated portland cement usually contains some free calcium hydroxide, and the resulting alkalinity produces a protective oxide skin on the steel. The stability of this film depends on the maintenance of a certain minimum pH value—say 10 or higher—and under these favorable conditions, access of oxygen through minute cracks in the concrete will not cause corrosion. The pH value can be reduced by access of carbon dioxide from the air, however, and access of oxygen and moisture will then produce rusting of the steel. The expansion caused by rusting produces larger cracks that result in a much freer access of air and thus a rapid increase in the rate of rusting.

The increased problems with spalling of concrete reported in the early 1980s are partly due to the appearance of contractors with inadequate standards of performance during the post-World-War II boom period, and partly to the use of higher stresses in the steel and concrete that result in the formation of a larger number of fine cracks. Reinforcing steel is now normally rolled with surface deformations to improve the bond between steel and concrete, and its strength is improved by cold-working or by alloying (see Secs. 10.6 and 10.7); the strength of concrete for normal applications has also increased, largely through the use of super-plasticizers (Sec. 14.6). Since the tensile strength of concrete increases roughly in proportion to the square root of its compressive strength $[f_t \propto \sqrt{f_c}]$, more fine cracks are produced as its strength increases. These considerations point to the importance of ensuring adequate cover for all reinforcement.

Adequate cover is also a primary criterion for the

fire resistance of reinforced concrete, since the principal cause of failure is the loss of strength of the steel reinforcement when its temperature exceeds 500°C (930°F) (see Sec. 7.5).

The cracking of concrete caused by tensile stresses can be prevented by prestressing the concrete (that is, by inducing compressive stresses in the concrete before the load is applied) to a sufficient extent to overcome the tension. Prestressing does not, in principle, require steel, but, in practice, the simplest way of compressing the concrete is through tensioned steel *tendons* (Ref. 14.1, p. 226).

Because prestressed concrete, properly designed, is free from tension cracks under the normal service loads, it is a more durable material than normal reinforced concrete. The prestressing steel requires the same cover as reinforcing steel to protect it against corrosion and fire.

Reinforced and prestressed concrete structures need expansion and contraction joints to allow for drying shrinkage, and temperature and moisture movement (see Sec. 3.6). The spacing of these joints depends on local climatic conditions. Failure to provide control joints leads to severe cracking.

Figure 3.6.1 shows a control joint for a roof slab where weatherproofing is the prime consideration. In floor slabs, a mastic sealant is sufficient, but for a heavily loaded slab, it is necessary to include a shear transfer dowel to transmit the load from one side of the joint to the other.

14.10 CONCRETE BLOCKS AND PRECAST CONCRETE

Concrete bricks, blocks, floor tiles, and roof tiles were originally made as substitutes for clay bricks and tiles in locations where concrete products were cheaper. By now, however, they have acquired a character of their own (Fig. 14.10.1) and offer a wider range of colors.

Concrete blocks can be used to perform the function of a cavity wall (see Sec. 15.6) and can be reinforced, where necessary, with reinforcing bars and site-cast concrete (Fig. 14.10.2). It should be born in mind that concrete products undergo an initial shrinkage, whereas mmany clay products expand initially (see Secs. 3.4 and 15.4). Calcium silicate bricks are considered briefly in Sec. 13.1.

The term *precast concrete* is normally reserved for concrete units that are reinforced or prestressed. Precasting was already used in the nineteenth century, in the early days of reinforced-concrete design.

Precast concrete has several advantages over site-cast concrete and also several disadvantages. If a sufficient number of castings are to be made from the same mold, then it is economical to make this mold

Fig. 14.10.1. Concrete masonry wall in the National Parliament Building of Papua New Guinea, Waigani, completed in 1983. (*Courtesy of the Concrete Masonry Association of Australia.*)

of steel with quick release and re-assembly mechanisms. The mold can be filled, vibrated, and the concrete finished on a mechanized assembly line. The most important advantage of precasting, however, is the better surface finish that can be given to concrete units in a factory. In particular, vertical surfaces can be cast and given their surface finish *horizontally,* which produces much better results (Sec. 14.11).

The main disadvantages are the costs of transportation and the problems of jointing. Floor and roof units can be transported and lifted into position horizontally. Wall panels, however, must either be transported and handled vertically, or else they must be given sufficient reinforcement to enable them to support their own weight in a horizontal position—a requirement that adds to their cost. The expense of transporting large units, particularly through narrow city streets, presents yet another problem.

Since concrete is a heavy material with a high coefficient of friction, precast concrete panel units may be assembled with dry joints that rely on friction. This type of construction, however, could lead to a collapse in the event of a minor explosion (caused by escaping gas, say, or a terrorist attack) and is thus no longer used.

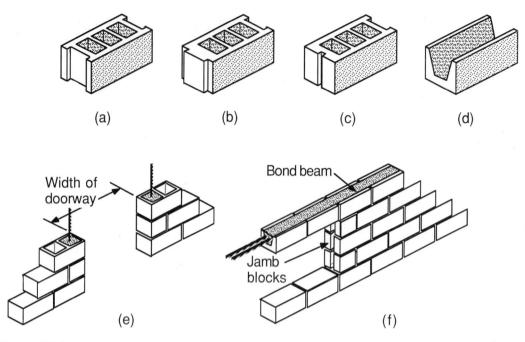

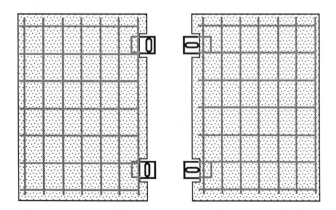

Fig. 14.10.2. Concrete blocks.
(a) Three-core concrete block; (b) special concrete block for use at a control joint; (c) special concrete block for fitting a window sash; (d) concrete channel for use as a bond beam; (e) concrete block with reinforcing bar embedded in site-cast concrete for additional strength adjacent to a door opening; (f) concrete channel with reinforcement and site-cast concrete used as a bond beam over a window opening.

A more positive method of connection, also relying partly on friction, makes use of bolts and lugs cast into the concrete (Fig. 14.10.3). A similar connection can be made by welding together two steel projections. The projecting steel is usually covered with mortar or plaster for rust protection.

Both these connections are less rigid than those of site-cast concrete. Connections comparable to those of site-cast concrete can be made by manufacturing precast units with projecting bars; the actual connection is then made with site-cast concrete (Fig. 14.10.4).

The use of liquid concrete on the site cancels out one of the advantages of precast concrete, however, since construction is no longer entirely dry.

In most countries at most times, the disadvantages outweigh the advantages for precast applications so that casting on the site is the dominant form of structural concrete construction. Under certain conditions, however, precasting has great advantages over site casting. Since the casting operation takes place in a factory that can be heated, concrete construction can continue in very cold weather, and this is helpful in countries

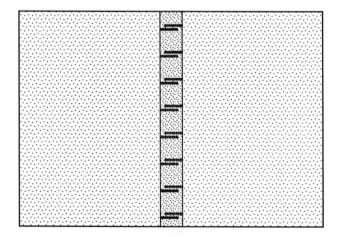

Fig. 14.10.3. Dry connection between precast concrete wall panels.
Both panels have projecting slotted steel plates that are welded to the reinforcement. One slot is vertical and the other horizontal so that a bolted connection can be made without requiring excessive precision in the casting of the panels.

Fig. 14.10.4. Connection between precast concrete panels using site-cast concrete.
Both panels have projecting reinforcing bars; the connection between the units is achieved through bond with the site-cast concrete.

Fig. 14.10.5. Precast concrete units serving as permanent formwork for site-cast reinforced-concrete columns of MLC Building in Sydney, Australia.
The precast formwork becomes an integral part of the columns, and contributes to their strength. (*Courtesy of the Contractor and Structural Engineer, Civil and Civic Pty. Ltd*).

with long, cold winters. Because the factory can be mechanized, the need for skilled labor on the building site is reduced. Precasting is therefore useful when there is a shortage of skilled labor, as for example, in some developing countries and in most countries after a war that has seriously interrupted the training or apprenticeship of skilled labor. Thus precasting was used extensively after both World Wars.

Precasting has decisive advantages, as already men-

tioned, for providing a good surface finish on vertical surfaces. Precast units can thus be used dry as curtain walls, as load-bearing walls, or as permanent formwork for site-cast concrete (Fig. 14.10.5).

14.11 CONCRETE SURFACE FINISHES

Most natural stones and bricks age gracefully, and old stone and brick buildings often look more attractive than when they were new. By contrast, untreated concrete surfaces rarely improve with age. This failure is largely due to the continuing chemical action of the cement, which causes the formation of minute cracks that collect dirt; but, in addition, the unattractive grey color of ordinary portland cement presents a real esthetic problem.

There are, however, a number of ways to improve the appearance of concrete surfaces, as follows:

1. By changing the color of the cement
2. By removing the cement from the concrete surface
3. By masking blemishes on the concrete surface with a stronger pattern
4. By a combination of these methods
5. By covering the cement

As noted in Sec. 13.6, the grey color of cement is due to impurities, and a pure *white cement* can be produced by a careful selection of raw materials and a more expensive manufacturing process. White cement is consequently much more expensive than ordinary cement, but this is not necessarily an important economic consideration if the white cement is used only for the surface layer of concrete. A cheaper *off-white cement* is often as suitable as pure white cement.

White and off-white cement is commonly used in conjunction with exposed aggregate or with a surface pattern (see below). The lighter shades of *colored cement* are made from off-white cement, whereas some of the darker shades can be made from grey cement (see Sec. 13.6). Colored cement is commonly used in conjunction with exposed aggregate or in terrazzo floors.

The finishing course of a *terrazzo floor* is laid on a mortar bed on top of a reinforced-concrete slab. A typical terrazzo mix consists of colored cement, a fine aggregate of crushed marble, and a coarse aggregate of crushed colored marble. Divider strips of brass, copper, or a suitable plastic are cast into the terrazzo as control joints to prevent cracking. After the terrazzo concrete has been cured, it is ground wet and any surface blemishes are filled with mortar. The grinding and filling are repeated several times with successively finer grades of carborundum. After the surface has been cleaned, it is waxed several times and finally treated with a sealer.

Plain concrete surfaces with a rough texture or *exposed aggregate* finishes are used where *floor surfaces* are exposed to the weather. For the latter, the coarse aggregate should be a small, well-rounded gravel for comfortable walking. A maximum aggregate size of 10 mm (⅜ in.) is suitable, and the colors should be carefully chosen; white or off-white cement should be used. For walls, it is possible to use an exposed aggregate that is merely sprinkled on the surface, but for a floor surface the decorative aggregate must be

present in some depth since some of the surface particles will be lost through wear. The "exposed aggregate" on the surface layer is sprinkled over the concrete surface after it has been screeded and is then rolled in.

The simplest procedure for casting high-quality *exposed-aggregate wall surfaces* is to cast them horizontally. This is feasible, of course, only if the wall unit is *precast* and subsequently fixed with the exposed aggregate surface in a vertical position. The panel is usually cast "face up"—that is, the exposed aggregate is sprinkled on the surface after the panel has been screeded and it may or may not be rolled in (Fig. 14.11.1). The exposed aggregate may be gravel or crushed rock. Its size depends to some extent on the distance from which the panel is likely to be seen. The greatest distance from which the texture of an exposed aggregate panel is clearly visible is 25 m (80 ft) for aggregate of 10-mm (⅜-in.) maximum size; 60 m (200 ft) for 20-mm (¾-in.) aggregate; and 150 m (500 ft) for 40-mm (1½-in.) aggregate.

If the aggregate is too small, the various particles will blur into a general background color. Thus, a mixture of white marble aggregate mixed with black basalt aggregate will appear grey if seen from too great a distance. Most exposed aggregate finishes with a mixture of colors will present a single, indifferent, and

Fig. 14.11.1. Precast concrete panel cast "face up."
The exposed aggregate consists of stone chips of varied color, with a maximum size of 10 mm (⅜ in.). These are sprinkled on the horizontal concrete surface and rolled in while the concrete is still wet. The panel is intended for eventual use as a vertical surface. [*Courtesy of the Cement and Concrete Association of Australia (CACA.)*]

usually dirty-looking color. On the other hand, aggregates that are too large in size give a rusticated appearance, which may not be appropriate in a particular location. Exposed aggregate finishes of mixed color are therefore suitable only in places where the viewing distance remains approximately constant and is not too great. This restriction excludes their use on the upper stories of tall buildings. Exposed aggregate of a single color, matched by the color of the cement, can be used in any location. The most suitable combination is white aggregate with white or off-white cement. Marble and limestone chips have a dull-white appearance, whereas quartz chips have a shiny surface.

There are several methods for exposing *aggregate on site-cast concrete*. Decorative aggregate can be rolled into wet concrete on a horizontal surface, as mentioned above, but this is not possible on a vertical surface. However, decorative aggregate can be transferred from the vertical faces of a timber mold by the *aggregate transfer process*. The timber of the mold is coated with a suitable adhesive (such as paraffin wax), and the aggregate is sprinkled on it. After the concrete has hardened, any adhesive still adhering to the aggregate is removed by washing or scrubbing.

A more common method is the *removal of the cement skin* to expose the aggregate although that finish is usually not as decorative as aggregate applied to the surface. The cement skin can be removed while the concrete surface is still green, that is, before the final set of the cement. To ensure that the concrete is hard enough for the removal of the vertical formwork while the concrete surface is still green, a *retarder* is usually applied to the vertical forms that retards the concrete surface but not the interior concrete. Among several suitable retarders (Sec. 14.6), solutions of sugar or molasses serve this purpose well. The cement skin can be removed by scrubbing or washing with water (Fig. 14.11.2) or dilute hydrochloric acid.

Alternatively, the cement skin can be removed mechanically from a hardened concrete surface, that is, without making use of a retarder. This can be done by sand blasting or with a pneumatic tool with a serrated face called a *bush hammer*.

Most concrete is still constructed with the cement showing on its surface. If the cement is trowelled smooth on the surface, or if the concrete is cast against a mold with a hard, flat surface, the resulting finish is smooth, and it looks attractive when the concrete is new. Fine shrinkage cracks inevitably form in concrete, however, and these are particularly noticeable on a plain surface. A *surface pattern* helps to mask these fine cracks and other imperfections in the surface. Boards of sawn timber are not now as common for concrete formwork as they once were, but they are sometimes used specifically for the purpose of imparting a surface texture to concrete. The boards may be

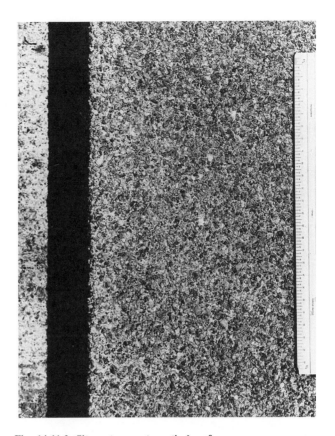

Fig. 14.11.2. Site-cast concrete vertical surface.
The aggregate, with a maximum size of 10 mm (⅜ in.), is exposed by retarding the setting of the cement near the surface and removing the surface cement by washing. Molasses is spread on the vertical formwork to serve as a retarder. (*Courtesy of the CACA.*)

naturally or artificially weathered to emphasize the texture of the timber growth rings (Fig. 14.11.3).

A stronger pattern is produced by deliberate breakage of the concrete surface (Figs. 14.11.4 and 14.11.5). This looks somewhat brutal at close quarters, but it is a surprisingly effective finish when seen from a distance where the lack of "readability" of exposed-aggregate finishes limits their usefulness.

A sculpted surface finish is suitable for surfaces that will be seen at close quarters as well as from a distance. It may consist of a single sculpture or a repetitive pattern (see Fig. 18.4.3). The appearance of board-marked and sculpted surfaces is much improved by the use of white cement.

Finally, the grey color and the fine shrinkage cracks of concrete can be covered. *Painting* concrete is a better solution for interior surfaces, where the paint does not need to be renewed as often as it does externally. Painting is one of the more expensive surface finishes for concrete if the capitalized maintenance cost is taken into account. It is appropriate to note that timber and steel are painted for durability and appearance, whereas concrete is painted only to improve its appearance (except in swimming pools and

Fig. 14.11.3. Board-marked surface finish used in conjunction with off-white cement. (*Courtesy of the CACA*).

Fig. 14.11.4. Rough concrete surface finish intended to be viewed from a distance. (*Courtesy of the CACA*).
Small square timbers are nailed to the interior of the formwork so that the concrete has a ribbed finish. The tops of the ribs are then broken off with blows from a sledge hammer.

fountains, where the paint serves as a waterproof membrane).

The most durable paints for concrete are cement-based, that is, they consist mainly of colored cement. The range of colors available, however, is limited (see Sec. 13.6). Alternatively, conventional paints (see Chap. 19) can be used, provided they are based on an alkali-resistant vehicle; tung oil, PVA, and acrylics meet that requirement.

Natural stone or *tiles* provide a more durable and attractive cover. Prior to 1939, when natural stone was still a normal building material, it was extensively used as permanent formwork for concrete, which was cast directly in contact with the stone. This form of construction ceased when it became fashionable in the 1950s to express concrete construction openly by showing concrete surfaces on the façade. Although the technology of concrete surfaces has significantly improved since that time, it has become evident that concrete surfaces are not suitable for buildings of the highest quality, and natural stone surfaces have come back into favor since the 1970s. The stone is ordinarily used as a thin veneer and fixed to the concrete with stainless-steel cramps (see Sec. 12.6) after the concrete has been cast.

Glazed ceramic tiles (see Sec. 15.1) can also be used for walls and curved roofs (Fig. 14.11.6), but great care must be taken in chosing a method of fixing that is suitable for the climatic conditions. Falling tiles can do appreciable damage and injury, and their replacement may be very expensive.

Quarry tiles provide a good and relatively cheap surface finish for factory floors, corridors, and other surfaces that receive a great deal of wear; they are unglazed, hardburnt clay tiles (see Sec. 15.9). Tile mosaic was the normal concrete floor finish for palatial houses and public buildings in Ancient Rome, usually with elaborate decorations. Today a more mundane form of mosaic is used mainly for bathrooms.

Stone floors are common in the countries surrounding the Mediterranean Sea, applied as veneers or tiles on reinforced-concrete slabs and on stairs. Only hard stones can be used as floor finishes (see Sec. 12.6). In North America, Northern Europe, and Australia, wall-to-wall carpet has become the most common concrete floor finish for multi-story buildings. The thermal properties of terrazzo, tile, and stone floors, on the one hand, and of carpeted floors, on the other, are

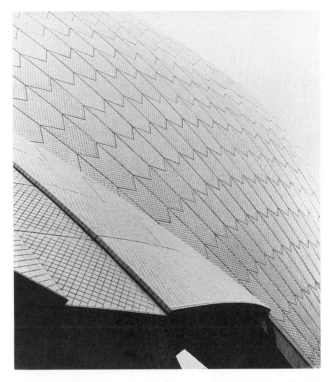

Fig. 14.11.6. White ceramic tiles cast into concrete slabs forming the roof of the Sydney Opera House. (*Architect: Jørn Utzon; courtesy of the New South Wales Department of Public Works*).

Fig. 14.11.5. Rough concrete surface finish intended to be viewed from a distance. (*Courtesy of the CACA*).
Ropes are cast into the concrete near the surface and pulled out after the concrete has hardened, leaving a rough surface between the textured imprint made by the ropes.

entirely different, and this aspect must be considered if passive solar design is to be used (Ref. 14.9).

REFERENCES

14.1. H. J. Cowan: *Design of Reinforced Concrete Structures.* Prentice-Hall, Englewood Cliffs, NJ, 1982. 286 pp.

14.2. F. M. Lea: *The Chemistry of Cement and Concrete.* Arnold, London, 1970. 727 pp.

14.3. J. D. McIntosh: *Concrete Mix Design.* Cement and Concrete Association, London, 1964. 112 pp.

14.4. *Standard Specifications for Concrete Aggregates. ASTM C 33-78.* American Society for Testing Materials, Philadelphia 1978. 7pp.

14.5. *Recommended Practice for Selecting Proportions for Normal Weight Concrete (ACI Committee 211),* in *ACI Manual of Concrete Practice, Part 1,* Section 211.1. American Concrete Institute, Detroit, 1973.

14.6. D. F. Orchard: *Concrete Technology.* Fourth Edition. *Applied Science,* London, 1979. Volume I: *Properties of Materials,* 487 pp.

14.7. *Expansive Cement Concretes: Present State of Knowledge (ACI Committee 223),* in *ACI Manual of Concrete Practice, Part 1.* American Concrete Institute, Detroit, 1976. Section 223, 28 pp.

14.8. V. V. Mikhailov: Selfstressed concrete. *Proc. Sixth Congress, Fédération Internationale de la Précontrainte (FIP),* Prague 1970, pp. 3–15.

14.9. H. J. Cowan and P. R. Smith: *Environmental Systems.* Van Nostrand Reinhold, New York, 1983. pp. 88–95.

SUGGESTIONS FOR FURTHER READING

W. H. Taylor: *Concrete Technology and Practice.* McGraw-Hill, New York, 1977. 846 pp.

A. M. Neville: *Properties of Concrete.* Pitman, London, 1963. 532 pp.

S. Popovics: *Fundamentals of Portland Cement Concrete: A Quantitative Approach.* Volume 1: *Fresh Concrete.* Wiley, New York, 1982. 477 pp.

D. F. Orchard: *Concrete Technology.* Applied Science, London. Volume 2: *Practice,* 1979. 511 pp. Volume 3: *Properties and Testing of Aggregates,* 1976. 281 pp.

15

Clay Products

Earth is an abundant, naturally occurring building material. Clay is a fine-grained, cohesive earth that can be formed to shape while damp and then retain its shape when dried. Its durability and strength are greatly increased, however, by firing it in a furnace until it begins to vitrify.

Glazes are mixtures of earthen material that melt at a lower temperature than the base material does and are used to apply an impervious, decorative surface to clay articles.

15.1 MANUFACTURE OF CLAY PRODUCTS

Clay products are among the artifacts that have been preserved from many ancient civilizations (Fig. 15.1.1). The raw material for them is readily available to be dug from the ground, and the technology of forming

Fig. 15.1.1. Roman brickwork in Trajan's Market in Rome (second century A.D.)
Roman bricks were longer and thinner than modern ones. The walls and vaults were quite thick and often consisted of brick facings with a rubble concrete core.

wet clay into any desired shape is quite simple. The process of firing the clay, to make the product durable, is more advanced, but the temperatures required for making earthenware are in a range—950° to 1150°C (1750° to 2100°F)—that is comparable with the smelting of bronze rather than of iron and thus more available to an earlier age.

Unfired clay products have also been used since ancient times, but they are not particularly durable unless protected and maintained. Unfired bricks will be dealt with in Sec. 15.10.

Pure clay is hydrous aluminum silicate ($Al_2O_3 \cdot 2SiO \cdot 2H_2O$). On heating, the alumina and silica dissociate and the combined water is driven off. Pure clay is very refractory, that is, it resists melting until quite high temperatures. Natural clay usually contains impurities—mainly potash (K_2O), soda (Na_2O), and lime (CaO)—that are formed from the weathering of feldspar and limestone. These act as fluxes and allow the clay to melt at lower temperatures. The process of the melting and subsequent hardening of the clay–flux compounds is called *vitrification,* and the product is a type of glass (see Sec. 17.1). To avoid having the products completely lose their shape in the kiln, they are heated only until partially vitrified.

There is a range of fired-clay products that extends from fine porcelain and chinaware to heavy, inexpensive articles like bricks. Some of the texts on pottery describe the crafts involved in detail (e.g., Ref. 15.1).

Earthenware usually refers to products made from natural clay fired at temperatures below vitrification. It is porous and may be of low strength.

Stoneware refers to products made from natural or prepared clay fired at around 1260°C (2300°F). It is hard, vitreous, and waterproof. Therefore stoneware can be used for drainage pipes without further treatment; earthenware must be *glazed* to render it waterproof.

Fig. 15.1.2. Terra cotta facings on a brick building, c. 1900.
The terra cotta is formed into decorative moldings that might otherwise have been carved in stone. Terra cotta is cheaper, however, and more durable than soft stone.

Glazing first requires firing the clay product to give it strength. It is allowed to cool and its surface then painted with a mixture of clay and glass-forming fluxes. When it is refired at a lower temperature, the body is unaffected, but the glaze melts to form a smooth, glassy surface coating. Different additives produce glazes of different colors; for decorative work, an article may be fired several times with different glazes. For further information on glazing, reference should be made to a specialist text (such as Ref. 15.2).

Salt-glazed ware is made by throwing common salt (NaCl) into the kiln at the end of the firing. The sodium combines with the clay to form a soda glaze on the surface of all the items in the kiln. It is an economical way of glazing and waterproofing bricks and pipes, since only one firing is required.

Terra cotta refers to earthenware or stoneware formed of a mixture of natural clay and finely ground, prefired clay known as *grog*. Since the grog does not shrink or distort during firing, products can be made more accurately to size and shape than if they had been made entirely with fresh clay. Terra cotta was widely used in the nineteenth and early twentieth century for decorative tiles and sculptural work on building facades (Fig. 15.1.2).

15.2 CLAY BRICKS

Bricks are formed into their shape by pressing or extruding moist clay or a mixture of clay and shale (Sec. 12.3). In the *dry-pressed process,* the raw material is ground with very little moisture to a crumbly consistency and mechanically compressed into molds with considerable force. Apart from pressing a depression or "frog" into one surface of the brick, little can be done to form holes or other shapes in the brick. In the *stiff-plastic* and *semidry-pressed processes,* a slightly moister mix is similarly pressed into molds.

In the wire-cut or *extruded process,* the clay is mixed to a plastic consistency and extruded from a die. The strip of extruded material has the dimensions of the length and width of a brick and is cut into brick thicknesses with a taut wire. The extrusion may include holes through the thickness of the bricks for the pur-

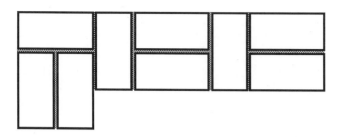

Fig. 15.2.1. The length of a brick is equal to twice the width, plus one joint.
Headers and *stretchers* can be used together either in the same course or in alternate courses.

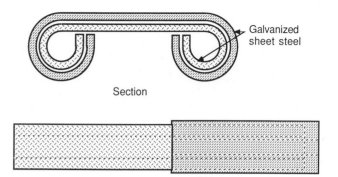

Fig. 15.3.1. Tie for use at control joint.

poses of reducing weight, improving the bond with the mortar, improving the thermal insulation, and speeding the drying and firing processes.

After the moist clay has been formed, it is capable of being handled and stacked. To avoid distortion and damage, it must be dried in warm air and gradually warmed. It is then fired in a kiln for several days and allowed to cool. During the firing, the clay is *partially* vitrified. Too little firing produces a soft brick, with little durability or strength. Too much vitrification causes the brick to melt, lose its shape, deform, and adhere to other bricks in the stack. These over-burnt bricks, known as *clinker bricks,* have at times been fashionable for rustic buildings but are difficult to lay accurately.

The size of a brick varies little from one country to another. It must be convenient to pick up and handle with one hand. The length is "twice the width plus one joint," so that a one-brick thick wall can be built with both *headers* (bricks laid with the length across the thickness of the wall) and *stretchers* (bricks laid with the length along the length of the wall) (Fig. 15.2.1). The proportion of length to height gives the characteristic appearance of a brick wall. Common sizes are 200 to 230 mm (8 to 9 inches) long, 65 to 75 mm (2 ½ to 3 inches) high, and 3 to 4 kg (7 to 9 lb) in weight.

Sand–lime bricks and *concrete bricks,* which are briefly described in Secs. 13.1 and 14.10, are used in a similar way to clay bricks. *Concrete blocks,* which are described in Sec. 14.10, are usually hollow, much larger than clay bricks, and used differently; for example, it is easier to incorporate reinforcement (see Sec. 15.7) into hollow blockwork than into brickwork.

15.3 EXPANSION AND CONTRACTION OF BRICKS

After bricks are removed from the kiln, they expand slightly (Sec. 3.4). This phenomenon, known as *brickwork growth,* decreases over a period of time. Much of the long-term growth will have taken place in the first six months after firing, but for some bricks, ex-

pansion continues for many years at a reducing rate. It does not occur equally in all types of bricks so that local knowledge is essential to enable adequate allowance to be made for it.

In addition to growth, brickwork expands and contracts with temperature changes. The coefficient of thermal expansion is about 6×10^{-6} per °C (3×10^{-6} per °F), which is a little less than that of concrete. When the two materials are used together, the relative movements caused by concrete shrinkage and brickwork growth outweigh any relative thermal movement.

All but hard-burnt bricks absorb considerable amounts of water (Sec. 4.6), and this causes a small amount of expansion. The main disadvantages are the increased weight to be carried by the structure, the risk of dampness being transferred to the interior or to metal fittings bedded in the brickwork, temporary discoloration, and *efflorescence*. Efflorescence occurs if any soluble salts present in the bricks are carried to the surface and precipitated there as the water evaporates. The precipitate shows up as a white outcropping on the surface of the bricks.

Vertical expansion joints (see Sec. 3.6) are needed in any long brick wall. Horizontal expansion joints may be needed at the top of panels of brickwork supported on a framed building, but it is not necessary (or possible) to insert horizontal expansion joints into loadbearing walls. Masonry walls gain most of their stability by virtue of intersecting at corners and being tied together by a roof or floor at their top. Therefore, any expansion joints that must be introduced reduce their strength by making them discontinuous. Various metal ties consisting of one tube sliding inside another have been developed to provide lateral restraint while allowing longitudinal freedom (Fig. 15.3.1).

15.4 MORTAR FOR BRICKS

Brickwork, like *squared masonry,* originally relied on the rectangular shape and *interlocking bond* of the bricks, the mortar merely taking up the irregularities in the mating surfaces and providing some adhesion. Since modern mortar based on cement (see Sec. 13.7)

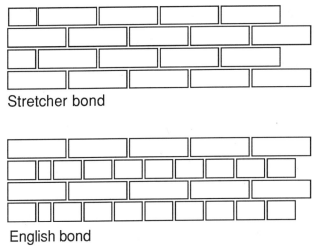

Stretcher bond

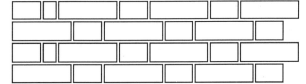

Flemish bond

English bond

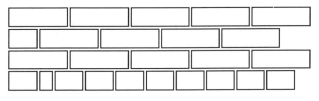

Colonial bond

Fig. 15.4.1. Patterns of brick bonds.

is of similar strength to the bricks themselves, the interlocking bond is of less importance than it was with weaker mortars. Nevertheless, interlocking bonds are still commonly employed. Some bond patterns are used for decorative as well as structural purposes (see Fig. 15.4.1).

A strong mortar obviously has advantages in a heavily loaded wall. Thin layers of mortar are normally in compression and, under high stress, are better able to resist being squeezed out from between the bricks, with consequent damage to the edges of the latter. If there is any tension in the wall caused by wind loads or eccentric vertical loads, then the tensile capacity of a strong mortar is also advantageous.

On the other hand, a soft mortar allows the wall to accommodate small movements without cracking. Lime-rich mortar has the capacity to heal small cracks, since the lime never sets hard (it has practically no tensile strength).

An important property of mortar is the ease with which it can be used by the bricklayer. Lime, or plasticizers, or both are added to control its consistency so that it is soft enough to allow the brick to be pressed into place and so that the overflow squeezed out of the joint is cohesive enough to be removed cleanly with the trowel without marking the face of the wall.

The *initial rate of absorption* is a property of the brick to absorb water out of the mortar. Too much absorption makes the mortar stiffen before the brick is adjusted into position, whereas too little allows the brick to continue to settle after it has been positioned.

15.5 FACE BRICK AND PLASTERED BRICKWORK

Brick is a durable material eminently suitable for exposure to the weather. Plastering does not improve the durability of an external wall in good condition,

although it may improve its water resistance (Sec. 15.6). Brickwork can be exposed internally as well, of course, but then its rough texture and potential for holding dust in the joints must be considered along with its appearance. *Face bricks* are specially made to be attractive to the eye. They are a little more expensive than common bricks, and it costs more to have them laid as *facework* because of the extra care needed. Nevertheless, face brickwork is almost always cheaper than plastered common brickwork, and it does not require painting.

All bricks deform a little during firing, so that they are not accurately square or uniform in size. It is not possible, therefore, to lay a *single-skin* wall that looks equally good on both sides. This is another reason why most internal walls are plastered. Internal plaster needs to be painted or papered (see Chap. 19). This is an additional cost, and it implies periodic repainting or repapering, whereas face brickwork should require no maintenance.

15.6 CAVITY WALLS

Although brickwork is porous (see Sec. 4.6), brick walls are sufficiently resistant to water if they are made thick enough, or built with a cavity. Water penetrating the outer skin runs down the cavity and is allowed to escape through weepholes at ground level or over flashing above the openings (Fig. 15.6.1). The *cavity wall* is ventilated with air bricks.

The ventilated cavity improves the thermal performance of the wall in resisting solar heat loads but reduces its performance in preventing heat losses. In a cool climate, additional insulation is needed, and this is usually applied to the inside face of the wall. In a cold climate, an open cavity cannot be used because water would freeze inside it, but the cavity can be filled with an impermeable insulating material such as

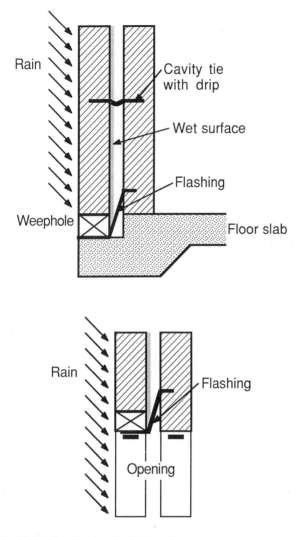

Fig. 15.6.1. Details of cavity brick wall.
When the outer skin becomes damp during rain, some water will run down its face in the cavity. At openings and floor levels, this water is collected by the flashing and escapes through weepholes. Metal cavity ties have a drip formed in them to prevent the water from traveling across to the internal skin.

sheets of rigid polystyrene foam (Sec. 18.4) or foamed-in-place polyurethane (Sec. 18.5).

The bricks in the outer skin are selected for appearance and weather resistance; those in the inner skin can be common bricks but are plastered on the inside face. The inner skin carries most of the loads of roof and floors, but the outer skin adds some stiffness by virtue of metal ties across the cavity (Fig. 15.6.1). The ties are of galvanized steel, or preferably stainless steel, since they become damp and remain concealed for the life of the wall. To prevent water running across the ties to the inner skin, the ties are formed with a bend to make the water drip off in mid-cavity. Care must be taken to clean mortar droppings off the ties and flashings; otherwise, these will form water bridges.

15.7 REINFORCED BRICKWORK

All masonry materials, including concrete, are much weaker in tension than in compression. Furthermore, the fact that all are brittle when subjected to tensile forces presents a serious limitation to their use in anything but thick walls and piers and in arches in which the stresses are compressive throughout. Many building codes do not permit the use of unreinforced masonry in seismic areas because of the danger of sudden collapse in an earthquake. In concrete, the addition of steel reinforcement transforms the nature of the material (Sec. 14.9). Brickwork also benefits from the addition of reinforcement, but this is more difficult to achieve.

Reinforcement can be introduced into normal solid brickwork in several ways: Thin bars or mesh can be laid in the bed joints, or vertical voids can be formed within the thickness of the wall and filled with concrete to encase vertical bars. The latter approach requires the wall to be at least one-and-a-half bricks thick (Fig. 15.7.1). If it is necessary to reinforce a thinner wall, purpose-made bricks with large holes for reinforcing can be used. It is also possible to introduce prestressing rods into a cavity wall, stressing the brickwork between the footing and a capping beam.

Horizontal joint reinforcement is often used at locations of stress concentration—such as above and below openings—to reduce the risk of cracking. The head over an opening can be supported entirely by a built-in reinforcing bar [Fig. 15.7.2(a)]; this must have downward-projecting lugs to hang the course of bricks below it. A reinforced lintel requires much less steel

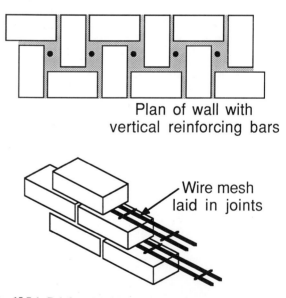

Plan of wall with vertical reinforcing bars

Wire mesh laid in joints

Fig. 15.7.1. Reinforced brickwork.
In a wall one-and-a-half bricks thick, vertical cores can be left in the middle to allow reinforcing bars to be built in; thin bars or wire mesh can be laid in the thickness of the joints.

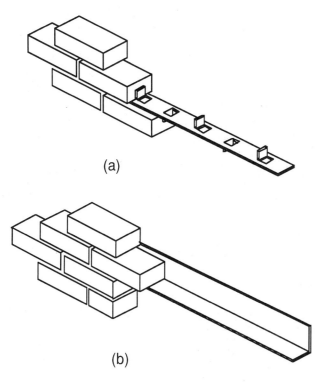

(a)

(b)

Fig. 15.7.2. Lintels over openings.
(a) A lugged bar acting as reinforcement forms a deep reinforced brickwork beam over the opening, and (b) a steel angle (or a flat for a small opening) carries the brickwork by acting as a steel beam.

than a steel bar that supports the weight by itself [Fig. 15.7.2(b)], but it must be temporarily supported while the mortar sets, since the brickwork above the opening is part of the lintel.

15.8 OTHER HOLLOW CLAY PRODUCTS

Hollow terra cotta (Sec. 15.1) products can be extruded with walls about 12 mm (½ in.) thick and then burned at relatively high temperatures to produce very hard and very strong lightweight units. Blocks of this type are often used, particularly in parts of Europe and Latin America, to form voids on the underside of reinforced concrete slabs, or, with a little mortar, as the structure for vaulted roofs. The ancient Romans used clay pots to lighten their concrete vaults in much the same way. Hollow terra cotta is cheaper and lighter

than reinforced concrete but more labor-intensive and therefore mainly used in countries with low labor costs unless the production system can be adapted, for example, to reduce the cost of formwork or provide some other benefit.

A system used mainly in Europe to achieve such benefits is shown in Fig. 15.8.1. Terra cotta tiles about 50 mm (2 in.) thick are made with grooves to accept prestressing wires; these are pretensioned and grouted in place with high-strength mortar so as to form prestressed terra cotta planks. The planks form the bottom face of a ribbed-slab floor, the voids being formed with hollow terra cotta blocks and the top surface with cast-in-place concrete. Formwork is limited to supporting the planks at intervals of about 2 m (7 ft).

The use of clay products as formwork for concrete is also seen in a system of vaulting brought to the USA in the late nineteenth century as *Guastavino vaults* (Ref. 15.3). In this case, solid, rather than hollow, clay tiles are laid over simple curved formwork to form thin, shallow vaults; the vaults are supported on columns and later covered with concrete to form a level, unreinforced concrete floor of great strength and fire-resistance. A similar method has been used to form the domes on a number of public buildings.

Hollow clay tiles are also used instead of bricks for nonloadbearing walls. They have a good fire rating and good thermal insulation. The lighter weight is an advantage to the supporting structure, but reduces the sound attenuation (Sec. 9.2).

There can be considerable distortion during firing, and much care goes into designing a pattern of ribs and hollows that will hold its shape in the kiln. A hollow block wall requires plastering on all exposed faces for the sake of appearance.

15.9 CLAY TILES

Roof tiles and shingles are often made of terra cotta, either vitrified to make it waterproof or glazed. This material is very durable when exposed to the weather. Although it can be molded to form weather-resistant joints (see Sec. 4.3), some distortion occurs during firing that limits their accuracy. The largest sizes are about 400 × 300 mm (16 × 12 in.). Above this size,

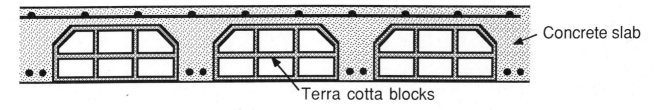

Concrete slab

Terra cotta blocks

Fig. 15.8.1. Hollow terra-cotta blocks used as permanent formwork.
The blocks are strong and lightweight, and add thermal insulation to the construction. They permit a flat ceiling for a ribbed-concrete slab.

it is difficult to handle the pressed clay before firing, and distortion becomes excessive.

Wall and floor tiles are made by glazing over an earthenware, terra cotta, or chinaware base, usually about 6 mm (¼ in.) thick. These tiles must be made to close tolerances, particularly in the case of wall tiles requiring a high gloss glaze since any irregularities will be more noticeable. Floor tiles must have a nonslip finish. Those for domestic use are usually double-glazed, the second application being spattered on to make the surface rougher, although this will wear off with heavy use. For heavier wearing qualities, they can be made of a fine unglazed clay to provide the same texture all the way through.

Quarry tiles are made of stoneware, usually about 25 mm (1 in.) in thickness, of coarse texture, and in natural earth colors. To reduce distortion in the kiln, they are fired in pairs back-to-back and split apart before use. The surface is naturally rough and non-slippery but more difficult to clean than that of the smoother tiles.

15.10 UNBURNED CLAY—ADOBE AND PISÉ

Unburned earthen construction predates the use of baked bricks and must have been used extensively throughout history although relatively few ancient examples remain because of the poor water resistance of the material. In many parts of the world with suitable climates and low labor costs, earth construction is still widely used.

Adobe refers to construction using *mud bricks* that are formed to shape, dried in the sun, and subsequently laid into walls. The bricks are large, requiring two hands for lifting and accounting for the full thickness of the wall. A common length, width, and height is about 400 × 300 × 150 mm (16 × 12 × 6 in.), but as the bricks are made on each site specifically for one building, there is no need for standardization. Although mud bricks are traditionally made by forming the material into a very simple mold by hand, there are also available presses operated by a hand lever that make a denser and more uniform brick.

The main advantage of adobe over burned bricks is the possibility of constructing a solid and comfortable building from materials available on site, and at no cost except a large input of manual labor. There is no apparent reason to use the material unless the labor can be supplied virtually free of cost, for example, by the householder and family members. Nevertheless, adobe has become sufficiently fashionable in some places that it is occasionally specified for a contracted house. There are even examples of *imitation* adobe finishes applied over wood-framed construction, with none of the advantages of the real material.

The earth is available free on site only if the naturally occurring soil is suitable for making bricks. For precise advice about the selection of raw materials, the reader should refer to one of the many specialist books on the subject, such as Ref. 15.4. A certain proportion of clay is essential to make the earth bind together, but too much clay will result in excessive cracking during the drying process. Straw (Ref. 15.5) or grass fiber may be added to the wet earth mix to improve its strength and make the blocks easier to handle without fracture. The mortar used for laying is a similar mixture.

An otherwise unsuitable earth can sometimes be stabilized with the addition of cement or lime. Cement-stabilized bricks are often used for the footings and for walls below the dampcourse.

The finished walls are subject to erosion and destruction by running water. They can prove quite satisfactory, however, if the overhanging eaves protect the walls and if groundwater is kept away from the base of the walls. Maintenance of the roof, flashings, and drainage system is essential, and any storm damage to the walls must be repaired without delay. An occupied and well-maintained adobe building can last a very long time, but if it is neglected, it will fall into disrepair faster than a more conventional building.

Pisé refers to damp earth that is rammed into formwork in place to make a wall. The pisé is placed in layers of about the same height as a course of adobe bricks (about 150 mm, or 6 in.) and allowed to dry partially before the formwork is raised and another layer placed on top. Pisé gives a smoother finished appearance than adobe, in which the shape of the bricks is strongly evident.

Earth walling is popular for passive solar construction, particularly in arid climates where the very mass of the construction is an advantage to the thermal performance of the building (see Sec. 6.5). Additional mass and thickness incur little cost penalty, since the material is not suited to thin walls anyway and the raw material is virtually cost-free.

REFERENCES

15.1. J. B. Kenny: *The Complete Book of Pottery Making*. Pitman, London, 1949. 242 pp.
15.2. D. Green: *A Handbook of Pottery Glazes*. Faber, London, 1978. 277 pp.
15.3. L. M. Roth: *McKim, Mead and White, Architects*. Thames and Hudson, London, 1984. 441 pp.
15.4. P. G. McHenry: *Adobe and Rammed Earth Buildings: Design and Construction*. Wiley, New York, 1984. 217 pp.
15.5. *Exodus*, Chapter 5, verses 7–11.

SUGGESTIONS FOR FURTHER READING

C. C. Handisyde and B. A. Haseltine: *Bricks and Brickwork*, Brick Development Association, London, 1974. 142 pp.
A. B. Searle: *Modern Brickmaking*. Ernest Benn, London. 1956. 734 pp.
C. Beall: *Masonry Design and Detailing for Architects, Engineers and Builders*. Prentice-Hall, Englewood Cliffs, NJ, 1984. 491 pp.
S. Sahlin: *Structural Masonry*. Prentice-Hall, Englewood Cliffs, NJ, 1971. 290 pp.

16

Wood

Wood grows as a natural, organic substance. As a result, its properties and characteristics are unlike those of manufactured building materials. In the use of timber, more than most other materials, the designer is limited by what is available either in the local lumber yard or on special order. Timber cannot be made to order, although it can be considered a renewable resource. Nevertheless, the industry that provides timber products to the building trades is able to process and market them to specification in much the same way as any other material.

Timber can be used as round logs, sawn or dressed sections (lumber), glue-laminated sections, plywood, particle board, or hardboard. Its natural deficiencies are the presence and uneven quality of defects; its significant movements with changes in moisture content; and its vulnerability to attack by insects, fungi and fire.

Although the joints achievable with timber have some limitations, one of its advantages is the ease with which it can be worked and joined with simple tools.

16.1 THE GROWTH AND STRUCTURE OF WOOD

Wood is the material that trees are made of. Once it has been prepared and used for construction work, the North Americans call the material *lumber,* whereas the British call it *timber.* Lumber, in particular, has the connotation of a manufactured or processed product; hence, the Lumber Manufacturers' Associations. Timber has a slightly wider meaning and is used in this chapter for that reason.

Wood is a natural product; some species have been cultivated in reforestation programs, but new species have not been developed as in the case of many horticultural and cereal crops. The supply of raw material is renewable, but its quality and availability are limited by the characteristics of the growth of any particular tree.

A tree grows by adding material at its *cambium layer*, which is the growing layer just under the bark. The wood laid down in the center of the trunk remains there throughout the life of the tree. The annular region of wood inside the cambium layer transports moisture within the tree and is called *sapwood.* The inner part of the trunk eventually ceases to perform this function, although it continues to provide strength to the tree. It is the *heartwood.* The sapwood is usually lighter in color than the heartwood. In the living tree, the sapwood is the more resistant to decay, but in use the heartwood is the more durable.

The structure of wood consists of small, hollow, fibrous, elongated cells, consisting mainly of *cellulose* and *lignin*. The cells that grow in the springtime, when growth is rapid, tend to be larger with thinner walls; in the late summer, growth is slower, and the cells laid down then are smaller, with relatively thicker walls. Therefore, the *summer wood* or *late wood* is denser, stronger, and usually darker in color than the *early wood.* This difference gives rise to the distinctive annual *growth rings* seen in many trees, which allow their age to be determined.

The prominence of the growth rings depends on the climate where the tree is grown and on the growing characteristics of the species. Trees grown in cool to temperate climates have very noticeable rings, whereas species grown in moist tropical conditions show little variation throughout the year. These characteristics are significant for the appearance of the timber, and also for its usefulness for carving or turning, as well as its structural behavior.

The fibers of the wood are arranged mainly in the longitudinal direction, and therefore wood is strong in that direction. This directional effect, in the context of the structural properties, is called the *grain* of the wood. The strength in the other two orthogonal directions is much lower. There is a slight difference between the radial and tangential directions because of the way the rings are laid down, but no distinction is made between the strength properties in these directions. The shrinkage, however, can be significantly greater in the tangential than the radial direction. The other properties are described simply as "parallel to grain" and "perpendicular to grain."

The effect of the growth rings on the appearance of a piece of sawn or dressed timber is commonly described as "grain," although the term *figure* is preferred. Dressing is discussed in Sec. 16.8.

16.2 HARDWOODS AND SOFTWOODS

Trees are classified botanically as *hardwoods* or *softwoods* according to details of the cellular structure of the wood. These terms are also broadly descriptive of the wood obtained from them. Most hardwoods are harder and more durable than most softwoods, but this is not universally so. The best known exception is balsawood, the lightest and softest wood, used both for modelmaking and as a lightweight filler in some fiberglass panels. Balsa is technically a hardwood.

Softwoods can also be identified by their evergreen needle leaves and by the bearing of cones. Hardwoods have broad leaves, and most are deciduous, although large groups such as the eucalypts do not lose their leaves in winter. Many of the softwoods have numerous, regular branches, whereas hardwoods mostly branch randomly and rather sparsely. The commercial softwoods are usually stable and easy to work for both framing and finishing timbers, whereas many of the hardwoods suffer from excessive drying shrinkage and can be hard to work with after drying. The best of the hardwoods are very strong and durable and consequently used for marine structures and bridges, as well as for furniture and flooring where a hard-wearing surface is necessary.

16.3 THE TIMBER INDUSTRY AND COMMONLY USED SPECIES

Thousands of species of trees exist in the world, and hundreds of these are economically significant as building materials. To make the handling and marketing manageable, the number of species commonly on sale in any one locality is much more limited, and many species with similar characteristics are sometimes mixed together under a broad trade name, such as *European Whitewood* or *Hem-Fir*. Alternatively, mixed species can be offered for sale according to their *stress grade*

(Sec. 16.6), a method that simplifies specifying and ordering when the main purpose of the timber is structural.

Historically, builders have used wood from locally growing trees. Regions with little tree growth traditionally used mud, reeds, or other locally available materials rather than wood, and the vernacular architecture developed accordingly. The location of good supplies of desirable species became known, however, in spite of the difficulty of transport. There are records of large pieces of timber being imported for important buildings, such as the cedars and pines brought from Lebanon to Jerusalem at the time of King Solomon (Ref. 16.1). In this case, the logs were floated by the supplier as far as possible by sea; the overland transport then became the responsibility of the users. The floating of logs in rivers (but not the open sea) remains a common means of transport today.

The exploitation of readily available and desirable trees has led to a significant reduction in the world's forests. This is, at best, a serious threat to the long-term viability of the timber industry; at worst, some environmentalists see it as a threat to life on earth. The industry and some of the governments concerned have long been carrying out reforestation programs to replace the trees cut. The new forests are sometimes allowed to regenerate by leaving a few seed trees, but most commonly they are planted with a single species in regular rows so that the trees grow uniformly straight. A forest is a very long-term investment, and some of the trees are harvested at intervals during their growth, both to thin the forest and also to gain some early return on the investment. As a result, small-diameter logs have become available in large numbers, and the building industry is finding new uses for them, mainly for landscaping.

Harvesting trees all of one species and size is advantageous for the supplier. Eventually a few species may become almost universally available, at least for general-purpose framing and lining applications. This supply will simplify the designer's choice.

At present, Douglas Fir and Hemlock from North America, and European Redwood and European Whitewood from Scandinavia, are fairly widely available as general framing timbers. North American redwood (Sequoia) and Western Red Cedar are also exported to many countries for use under severe exposure conditions. These are light, soft, but highly durable timbers that command high prices because of their qualities. Most of the hardwoods come from the tropical zone; although widely used in the countries of origin, their use is relatively uncommon in other countries, except as flooring and decorative veneers. The (British) *Timber Designers Manual* (Ref. 16.2), for example, devotes only one of its 25 chapters to hardwoods, arguing that most timber engineering calls for softwoods. Australia

Fig. 16.3.1. Timber roof of the Great Hall, University of Sydney. The neo-Gothic hammerbeam roof trusses are made of hardwood, faced with cedar boards about 25 mm (1 in.) thick. The hardwood is very strong, while the softer cedar has a more attractive appearance and is easier to carve. (*Courtesy of University of Sydney Photographic Dept*).

uses many locally grown Eucalypt hardwoods but exports only a few especially durable species.

The requirements of strength and availability for large structural sections, on the one hand, and of attractive appearance and easy carving for exposed decorative timber, on the other, are not always compatible. In the Great Hall at the University of Sydney, a neo-Gothic building dating from 1880 (Fig. 16.3.1), this problem was solved by using readily available local hardwood of great strength for the heavy structural sections and facing them with cedar boards about 25 mm (1 in.) thick.

16.4 REDUCTION OF THE TREE, OR MANUFACTURE OF LUMBER

Round logs have limited uses in building construction, although they are widely used in engineering construction for piles, poles, bridges and marine structures. The natural log has the advantage that the grain, no matter if it is straight or twisted, is reasonably continuous along its length. Its main disadvantage is the difficulty of making neat carpentry with irregular ma-

terials. For that reason, most building timbers are rectangular in section.

A log is cut longitudinally in a series of cuts that produce useful square or rectangular sections. The various sizes into which a log is cut have names that vary from one country to another. Sections less than 38 mm (1 ½ in.) thick are called *boards* (or if narrow, *strips* or *lath*); framing members from 50 × 50 mm (2 × 2 in.) upwards to about 75 × 400 mm (3 × 16 in.) are called *dimension lumber* (2 × 4, 4 × 4, etc.), *studs*, or *scantlings;* and larger sections are called *timbers, balks,* or *flitches.*

A common size of framing timber for domestic-scale construction is 100 × 50 mm [formerly known as a 4 × 2 (in.)] in Britain or a 2 × 4 (in.) in North America. The first reduction of a log will often be into various multiples of these dimensions, whereas material intended for use as boards will be cut into thinner sections for easier seasoning (see Sec. 16.5). When a section is recut, there will be some material lost to the sawcut, as well as a shrinkage loss as the piece seasons. The trade allowances for these losses vary betwen countries, and sometimes between species. The local trade rules should always be ascertained, particularly before specifiying structural timber sizes. The actual size of a section may be considerably less than its "nominal" trade description. Its strength and stiffness depend on its actual size. (See also Sec. 16.9 for the effects of dressing.)

When a round log is cut into a series of rectangles (Fig. 16.4.1), the orientation of the grain will differ from one to the other. As a result, both the appearance of the faces and the way the pieces shrink will be different. Structural members are preferably *quarter-sawn* (i.e., with the annual growth rings forming a close, almost uniformly parallel pattern along the length of the broad faces), whereas decorative boards are preferably *backsawn* (with the growth rings only roughly parallel to the length of the broad faces, converging at various points and thus producing a more interesting figure). Quartersawn members shrink with little distortion. Since backsawn members tend to "cup" on drying they are seasoned before being finally dressed flat.

Apart from sawing into rectangular sections, logs can be reduced to *veneers* for manufacture into plywood (Sec. 16.11) or pulped for manufacture into particle board or hardboard (Sec. 16.12).

16.5 SEASONING AND MOISTURE MOVEMENT

The sapwood in a living tree may contain well over 30 percent of moisture, consisting of the moisture absorbed into the fibers as well as the free sap contained in the cells. After felling of a tree, its moisture content decreases until it attains equilibrium with the ambient

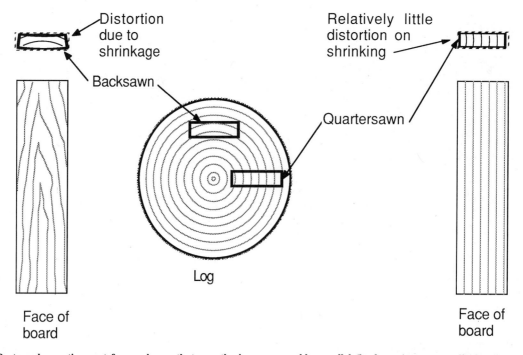

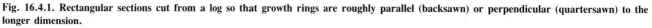

Fig. 16.4.1. Rectangular sections cut from a log so that growth rings are roughly parallel (backsawn) or perpendicular (quartersawn) to the longer dimension.
The shrinkage is more uniform for the *quartersawn* section, whereas the figure is more interesting on the face of the *backsawn* one.

humidity. As mentioned in Chap. 2, timber expands as its moisture content increases and shrinks as it reduces. Shrinkages of 3 to 5 percent are possible from the green condition to the fully seasoned, and these can cause movements of 10 mm (½ in.) or more in a platform frame (Fig. 16.5.1). Moisture movements

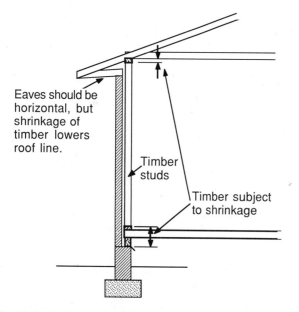

Fig. 16.5.1. Platform house frame.
In platform construction, walls are supported on top of floor timbers; the shrinkage in all horizontal members adds up, therefore, to produce a considerable movement at roof level. If there is masonry veneer or a chimney in the building, this movement may cause problems.

in seasoned timber as it adapts to changes in the weather are much smaller but often cause doors or windows to stick in wet weather or unsightly cracks to open up in wide boards.

Moisture movement occurs across the grain; it is negligible along the grain. Plywood (see Sec. 16.11) overcomes the shrinkage problem by virtue of the plies being at right angles to each other.

The moisture content of a sample of wood is determined in the laboratory by weighing the sample, drying it in an oven overnight, and then weighing it again. This method is accurate, if time-consuming and impractical for routine measurement. A field moisture meter has two sharp blades, about 25 mm (1 in.) apart, with a battery and electrical circuitry. The blades are driven into the surface of the piece, and the moisture content is determined from the electrical resistance through the timber between them. The actual relationship depends on the species, but, if that is known, then the moisture content can be determined within about 1 percent, which is adequate for normal purposes.

Natural seasoning is carried out by stacking timber in the open air, preferably under cover, in a stack that allows free flow of air around each piece. Boards can be naturally seasoned in less than a year; larger sections or whole logs may take a number of years. Since it is costly, inconvenient, space-consuming, and a potential fire risk to keep large quantities of timber stacked for natural seasoning, kiln-drying is ordinarily preferred.

Sawn timber stacked on carts is placed in a kiln through which hot air is passed to remove the moisture.

All pieces in any one kiln should have approximately the same cross section so as to dry equally. Kiln drying is normally limited to sections of 50-mm (2-in.) thickness or less. If a large cross section with a known moisture content is required, it can be made by glue-laminating dried boards (see Sec. 16.11). Kiln-dried timber can be supplied to any required moisture content, whereas naturally seasoned timber depends on the weather.

The equilibrium moisture content (that is, the percentage value a piece of timber will reach if left for a long time in a sheltered place) is usually about 12 to 15 percent; it is lower in a heated building or a dry climate and higher in a warm humid climate. Inside a building, air conditioning keeps the humidity, and therefore the moisture content, of wood fairly constant throughout the year, but in naturally ventilated buildings the seasonal swelling and shrinking of timber continues throughout its life.

When high-quality joinery work is required inside a building, the problems of moisture movement can be minimized by seasoning the timber to the correct moisture content, wrapping it in plastic to avoid changes during transport, and operating the air-conditioning system before the joinery work is commenced. Alternatively, the joinery can be detailed to allow for the movement. Many traditional details, including the *tongue-and-groove joint* and the *shiplap joint* (Fig. 16.5.2), derive from this requirement.

During the seasoning process, timber dries unevenly from the outside in. The resulting shrinkage of the outside layers often gives rise to *seasoning checks,* longitudinal cracks extending from the exposed face inwards for a short distance. Seasoning checks mostly detract from the appearance of the piece, but they may reduce its strength as well. They are likely to be more severe if whole logs are seasoned before being sawn.

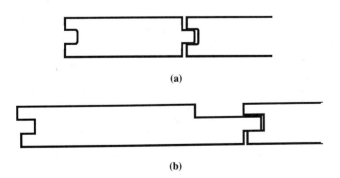

(a)

(b)

Fig. 16.5.2. Joints for moisture movement.
(a) Tongue-and-groove joint, and (b) shiplap joint. Both these joints are designed to allow for shrinkage in each board without complete separation. The tongue-and-groove, which is used for flooring, shows a small gap on the surface when the boards shrink. The shiplap joint is used mainly for wall lining; any change in the width of the recess between boards is not noticeable.

16.6 MECHANICAL PROPERTIES, DEFECTS, AND STRESS GRADING

The strength properties of a small sample of clear (defect-free) wood can easily be determined by testing specimens in the laboratory. The strength of a piece of timber, however, depends not only on the properties of the clear wood, but also on the size and location of defects.

Common structural defects include knots, sloping grain, splits, pockets of resin, and insect damage. It is not economical to discard any piece of timber that contains a defect, but *grading rules* have been developed by the timber industry and the regulating authorities to allow the effect of defects to be taken into account in a systematic manner. Within any species (or trade grouping of species), these rules allow each piece of timber to be allocated one of several grades. When these grades are merely descriptive, such as "select" or "standard," it is necessary for the structural designer to resort to a table that allocates specific working stresses to each grade in each species. To simplify the use of timber in structures, it can be graded directly in terms of the nominal allowable stress that it can support, and then sold by species and stress grade.

Although timber has traditionally been assigned descriptive grades or stress grades by visual examination against a set of grading rules, this method is both labor-intensive and subject to human error. Testing to destruction of random samples remains available as a check on the accuracy of the grading, but this practice is even more costly and its results not necessarily representative of every piece. A good statistical correlation between strength and stiffness has been observed, and on this principle (see Sec. 2.8 and Fig. 2.8.2) a mechanical, nondestructive grading method has been developed.

The *average* modulus of rupture of a small piece of clear wood tested in bending is commonly 50 to 80 MPa (8000 to 12,000 psi) for softwoods and up to 150 MPa (20,000 psi) for hardwoods. The *basic* working stresses in bending for the softwoods used in building work are between 5 and 8 MPa (800 and 1200 psi), whereas those for high-grade hardwoods can be as high as 20 MPa (3000 psi). The apparently high factor of safety implied by these figures takes into account the inevitable presence of defects in any piece of timber of practical size and the variability of the wood from any given species. Most building codes assign a basic working stress that is then modified by a series of factors that take into account some of the peculiarities of the material.

Timber is particularly suitable for resisting loads of short duration, such as wind loads. One of the modifying factors is an allowance for higher stresses under such loads. When conditions are moist or very hot, the allowable stresses are reduced. When several pieces share a load, the allowable stresses are increased, because of the lower probability that all pieces will have a major defect.

Although timber is strong in the longitudinal direction, it is weak across the grain, and this leads to a low resistance to shear. Whereas concrete is weak in tension but *isotropic,* and therefore shear in a concrete beam leads to diagonal tensile cracks (see Ref. 16.4), the *orthotropic* nature of timber leads to horizontal shear cracks (Fig. 16.6.1). The high shear strength of steel makes it economical to use I-shaped sections (see Fig. 10.2.2), but there is little advantage in fabricating I-shaped sections from three pieces of timber because in many cases the web would be overstressed in shear. However, I-beams and box sections are sometimes made using plywood for the webs, because of its much higher shear resistance (Sec. 16.11).

When timber is visually stress-graded, the higher grades usually have fewer visible defects, and therefore the better structural grades are also likely to be more suitable for use when appearance is important. Nevertheless, the specifier may wish to impose additional esthetic requirements. Knots are particularly troublesome. The grain is distorted around them and therefore difficult to plane smooth (Sec. 16.8). Their different grain direction and harder wood absorb paint differently than plain timber does, and sometimes they ooze resin, which either reacts with the paint or penetrates through it to leave a sticky residue on the surface. Therefore, if knots occur in painted timber, they should be adequately sealed before painting (see Sec. 19.3). Some pines are selected specially for their knotty, rustic

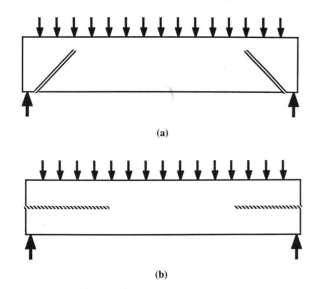

(a)

(b)

Fig. 16.6.1. Cracks caused by shear failure.
(a) In reinforced concrete beam, and (b) in timber beam. Cracks in concrete are caused by *diagonal tension;* those in timber are caused by *horizontal shear.*

appearance and are clear-finished. So long as the knots are firm and their species does not produce much resin, they are quite satisfactory.

16.7 DETERIORATION AND PRESERVATION OF TIMBER

In nature, wood is the food of many insects and fungi, which aid in returning fallen trees to the ecological cycle. In addition to these destructive agencies, sunlight and weather cause gradual discoloration and separation of the fibers of unprotected wood, and wind-blown grit severely abrades its surface. In a building, these processes must be prevented for the life of the building.

Wood-destroying insects fall into two main categories: *termites,* which have a life cycle and social structure similar to ants, with the adults attacking timber for food; and *borers,* which are the larvae of various beetles whose egg, larval, and pupal stages occur in the wood.

Termites are prevalent in the warmer climates, and particularly destructive in the tropics. The most common are *subterranean termites,* which live in nests in the ground and travel through underground galleries to reach food supplies. They reputedly can travel 50 to 100 meters (several hundred feet) underground, but they avoid coming into the open air, building mud galleries over obstacles if necessary, for instance to climb a brick wall to reach timbers above ground. *Dry-wood termites* make a nest in wood above ground, but otherwise behave similarly. Since termites shun light, they maintain a thin layer of sound timber around the surface of a piece while eating out the center. This habit makes detection difficult until major structural damage has taken place.

Many species of insect produce larvae that attack wood, and these are commonly referred to as "woodworm" or "borers." The *anobium,* or *furniture beetle,* attacks mainly the sapwood of softwoods. The larva lives inside the timber for long periods, up to six years. The adult is a small beetle that emerges through an exit hole of 1- to 2-mm (about $\frac{1}{16}$-in.) diameter and does not feed during its short life. It is identified by the gritty *frass* or boredust from its workings and by tunnels that are mainly parallel to the grain. Its long life cycle in the timber makes it difficult to eradicate or to detect until considerable damage has already been done.

The *lyctus,* or *powder post beetle,* lives only in the sapwood of hardwoods with a high starch content. Its larva lives about a year before emerging. It can be identified by a fine, nongritty frass. The interior of the wood is converted to a mass of small tunnels parallel to the grain; after a severe attack, the sapwood is completely destroyed, but the heartwood is left untouched. Lyctus does not attack softwoods.

There are a number of borers such as *ambrosia* and

bostrychid that attack unseasoned wood but do not re-enter seasoned wood. They may cause unsightly holes in exposed timber but usually do not pose a serious structural problem.

The spores of *fungi* are abundant in the atmosphere and can settle on any surface. Several species germinate and develop in wood with a moisture content in excess of 20 percent. The most common is *merulius lacrymans,* which develops *hyphae,* or branches, that spread out over the surface of the wood. It is known as *dry rot,* because the hyphae can extend from a moist piece of wood to a drier one, transporting enough moisture to enable the fungus to consume both. In an advanced stage, the wood is reduced to a spongy mass of no strength, and the fungus produces fruiting bodies that contain more spores.

Mechanical protection is useful in preventing the access of termites from the ground to structural timbers (Fig. 16.7.1). Since adult beetles lay their eggs in cracks in the surface of wood, a coat of paint or varnish will deter them, although it is difficult to be sure there are no unprotected crevices available. Painting, adequate ventilation, and detailing to prevent water remaining next to timber are all useful in preventing fungal attack by keeping the moisture content of the timber low.

In the case of subterranean termites, *soil poisoning* introduces a chemical barrier to prevent access from the ground to the building. In termite-susceptible areas, chemical treatment of the soil can be carried out at any time under suspended timber floors but is possible under on-grade concrete floors, of course, only before construction. The chemicals used are usually the highly persistent organochlorides. The intention is for the chemical to remain undisturbed under the slab almost indefinitely, so that the hazard to humans is limited to the workers applying it.

Preservative treatments can be applied to deter either insects or fungi, or both. Liquid chemicals can be applied to timber by *brushing* or *spraying* (with little

penetration), by *dip diffusion* (dipping the timber into a vat of preservative and allowing it to diffuse into the pores), or a *pressure-impregnation process,* where the timber is placed in a pressure vessel and the preservative forced into the pores under pressure. For even greater penetration, a vacuum can be drawn first so as to expel air from the pores.

Preservatives may be any of the following:

- Tar-oil-based, such as *creosote,* a coal-tar derivative that offers good protection against all forms of decay but interferes with subsequent painting and has a pungent odor
- Organic compounds dissolved in mineral solvents, such as *zinc naphthenate* in white spirit
- Water-based, such as *copper-chrome-arsenate,* a multipurpose preservative that is *fixed* in the wood and does not readily wash out, or simpler nonfixed salts used against specific pests such as lyctus.

16.8 DRESSING OF TIMBER (LUMBER)

Sawn timber is preferred to round logs for carpentry work because of its uniform size and shape, but the rough sawn surface is unsuitable for many purposes. Timber is therefore *dressed* smooth for applications where it comes into contact with people or fabrics; where painting is necessary; where a smooth finish is esthetically required; or where a special molded shape is needed.

Timber for dressing is first sawn to the nominal size and then passed through a rotary planing machine in which rotating knife blades take a thin layer off the surface to remove the uneven saw marks. Timber can be ordered dressed on any or all of its four faces— DAR (dressed all 'round) being the most usual. The planing machine removes about 2 mm (1/16 in.) from each face, so that a piece of dressed timber finishes significantly smaller than its nominal dimensions, particularly if the local trade practice also allows for the deduction of sawing and seasoning tolerances. When a specific finished size is required, it can be so specified.

Specially shaped timber sections are machined out of rectangular sections by using planing knives ground to the appropriate profile. Common sections are shown in Fig. 16.8.1.

Machine-dressed timber is sufficiently smooth for many purposes, but it shows small indentations on the surface that are not acceptable for high-grade joinery work. Better results are obtained by hand-planing, hand-scraping, or hand- or machine-sanding. Large objects such as doors are finished with a belt sander, in which a long continuous belt of abrasive paper passes close to the surface and is pressed against part of it by a movable pressure pad. The finishing paper is about 150 grit (150 grits to the inch, or 6 to the

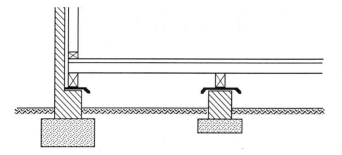

Fig. 16.7.1. Termite shields (made of galvanized steel or aluminum). The shields prevent termites from gaining access to a building from the ground; to be effective, they must be provided across all possible points of access. Parts of the building clearly exposed to view are in less danger, however, since the termites' earthen tunnels would be easily detected there.

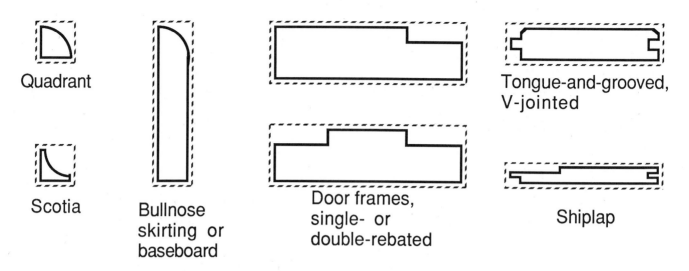

Quadrant

Scotia

Bullnose skirting or baseboard

Door frames, single- or double-rebated

Tongue-and-grooved, V-jointed

Shiplap

Fig. 16.8.1. Common timber moldings made by planing from a rectangular section.

mm). Much finer abrasives are used for polishing metal or paint surfaces, but the fibrous texture of wood will not accept these very fine finishes.

When dressed or sanded timber surfaces are painted (see Sec. 19.3) or varnished (see Sec. 19.4), loose surface fibers damaged during the finishing process are raised and held firm by the coating. If a smooth final coat is required, it is essential to sand back these fibers after the first coat has hardened.

16.9 JOINTING OF TIMBER

A great advantage of timber over other materials is the ease with which it can be worked and joined by hand, but the joints produced are much less efficient than those available with metals. This is because of timber's weakness across the grain and because it offers no equivalent to welding or soldering. In the last few decades, considerable advances have been made in adhesives (see Sec. 19.6), and it is now possible to join wood with very strong waterproof glues. Nevertheless, these alternatives are usually reserved for factory fabrication of laminated materials or components rather than for general site jointing.

Traditional joints were made by removing part of each piece to be joined [Fig. 16.9.1(a)], and therefore the joint was significantly weaker than solid timber. Many *post-and beam structures,* however, carried their main loads by the bearing of one piece on another so that the jointing detail was for positioning rather than loadbearing [Fig. 16.9.1(b)]. *Wooden dowels* or *pins* or *wrought-iron bolts* and *straps* could also be used, but the cost of metalwork and the need to employ a metalworker as well as a carpenter reduced the popularity of the latter. Nails were also available, but they were hand-made from wrought iron or copper and thus quite expensive and not particularly strong.

The invention of the machine-made *steel nail* brought about a major change in timber framing. Steel nails are cheaper and stronger than those of wrought iron. *Nailed joints* are quickly made and require less skill than matched timber joints. Traditional buildings were designed to use large timber sections spaced a considerable distance apart. Nailing, however, is more suitable for smaller sections. These have to be used closer together, and the now-common domestic framing system developed in the U.S.A. in the mid-nineteenth century (Sec. 16.10).

Nailing guns are presently widely used for repetitive applications. The fixing of sheathing, flooring, and siding (weatherboards) is made much easier by mechanical nailing. Much framing is also fixed by gun, but since many of the joints require skew-nailing and most guns are more efficient for straight nailing, the carpenter's hammer is still in use. Nailing guns, which are powered by compressed air, use either a "clip" of T-headed nails lightly stuck together side by side, or a similar clip of staples, or a roll of regular-headed nails spaced a little way apart and held together by thin wires that are broken when each nail is fired. In each case, the nail is driven by a heavy, slow-moving piston so that the nail itself does not have high energy once the piston reaches the end of its travel.

Explosive-powered fastening tools are used for fastening timber to masonry, concrete, or steel; their charges are too expensive (and unnecessary) for fastening timber to timber.

Nailing is adequate for *locating* those joints where the main load is taken directly by bearing of one member on another, and also for those where the nails are only lightly stressed. A stronger method is needed both for highly stressed members, such as the chords of trusses, and also for joining the larger timber sections used in bigger buildings.

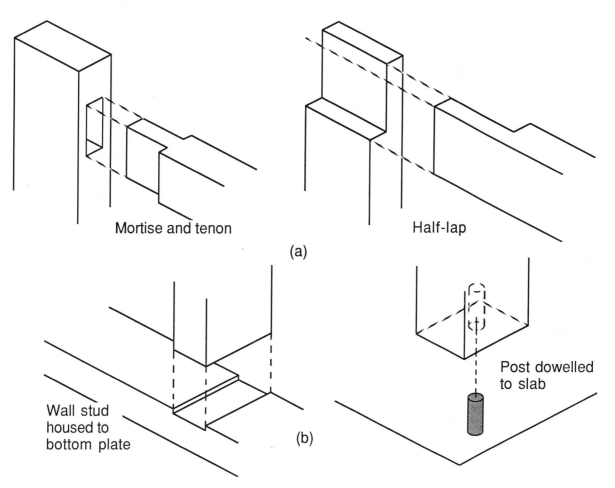

Mortise and tenon   Half-lap

(a)

Wall stud
housed to
bottom plate   (b)

Post dowelled
to slab

Fig. 16.9.1. Traditional timber joints.
(a) Traditional carpentry loadbearing joints, and (b) joints that provide location of the parts only, since the main load is carried by one member bearing on the other.

When *bolting* timber with *steel bolts,* the high shear strength of the bolt is not matched by the bearing strength of the timber, especially if the load is perpendicular to the grain in one of the members. This disparity can be overcome by using *ring connectors,* which consist of a piece of steel strip bent into a circle resembling a short length of tube, about 25 mm (1 in.) long and 3 mm (1/8 in.) in wall thickness. The two most common sizes have diameters of 65 and 100 mm (2 1/2 and 4 in.). A circular groove of the appropriate diameter and depth to take half the length of the tube is cut into each piece of timber to be joined (Fig. 16.9.2). This creates a much larger bearing area on the timber without excessive reduction of its cross-sectional area.

A joint using bolts or a ring connector requires that the two pieces to be joined lie alongside each other rather than in the same plane. This is easily arranged for parallel-chord trusses if each chord is a double member and the web members are single. It does not work for a triangular truss if a perfectly symmetrical cross section is required, since the chords must be connected both to other web members and to each

other. Other methods are needed to join members in-plane, for example, *gusset plates* over the joint areas (Fig. 16.9.3).

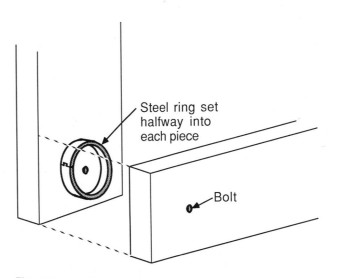

Steel ring set
halfway into
each piece

Bolt

Fig. 16.9.2. A *ring connector* used to connect two pieces of timber lying side-by-side.

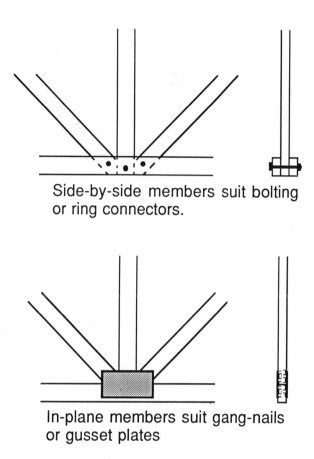

Side-by-side members suit bolting
or ring connectors.

In-plane members suit gang-nails
or gusset plates

Fig. 16.9.3. Joints in timber trusses.
Member of trusses may be side-by-side, or in the same plane.

Gusseted joints can be made using plywood or steel for the gussets. The joint is made by multiple nailing or bolting through the gussets into the members or by adhesives. The gussets are as large as is necessary to accommodate enough nails or glue to carry the load. *Nail plates* are standard pre-punched, galvanized-steel gusset plates suitable for small trusses. Their need of many nails is labor-intensive unless a mechanized method is used.

Toothed-plate connectors consist of a sheet of galvanized steel punched to form many small "nails" that are bent out from the surface. One toothed plate of appropriate size is placed on each face of the joint and pressed into the timber with hydraulic power. The entire roof truss is assembled and clamped into a jig, and all the connectors are pressed home. The method is suitable for factory production of light, strong, and accurate trusses for spans up to about 12 m (40 ft), although longer spans and complete wall frames can be fabricated within the limits of the available transport. Toothed-plate connector joints, like nail-plate joints, can develop close to the full strength of the timber because the load is well distributed over the surface of the timber. The cost of assembly is also much less than for hand-nailing.

16.10 TIMBER IN DOMESTIC CONSTRUCTION

We saw in the previous section that traditional jointing methods favored the use of fewer but larger frames, with some kind of infill, whereas simple nailed joints are more appropriate for smaller members, each carrying only a small load. Domestic-scale buildings are therefore framed with members about 100 × 50 mm spaced on 400- to 600-mm centers (2 × 4 in. spaced on 16- to 24-in. centers), wherever possible, with additional supports or larger members where it is necessary to span more than about 2 m (6 ft.). The exceptions are:

- Floor joists on upper floors or above basements where sections up to 300 mm (12 in.) or more in depth are sometimes necessary, depending on the span
- Lintels over openings
- Roof framing, whose size depends on the span, roofing material, and availability of internal supports
- Studs alongside openings carry higher loads (the easiest way to handle this situation is to use double studs of the same dimensions as common studs)

The *sizes* of timber suitable for domestic framing are usually given in building codes. The cost of structural calculations does not justify the small savings in material that might result from designing specifically for each new building, unless the design can be done by a computer program that is already used to do the ordering and preparing cutting lists. Some codes allow less important members to be as small as 38 × 75 mm (1 ½ × 3 in.). The minimum width is determined as much by the need to nail lining materials to the framing as by structural considerations. (When two boards butt at an end joint on a joist, it is difficult to nail them both into a face less than about 38 mm wide.) Thinner framing members can be used in prefabricated components, where the fixing system can be designed to suit the dimensions of the framing.

Sheathing is commonly used over timber frames in North America and in some other countries. It consists of a layer of rough plywood or boarding fixed to the timber framing before the final strip flooring, exterior wall lining, or roofing is placed. It acts as bracing to the frame and also reduces air infiltration. It contributes significantly to the thermal insulation in an otherwise uninsulated building, but when separte thermal insulation of appropriate thickness (see Sec. 6.3) is used, the additional benefit of the sheathing becomes negligible.

Exposed *timber flooring* can take the form of boards or parquetry. In either case, hardwood is preferred because of its abrasion resistance and hard-wearing qualities. The boards have a tongue-and-groove jointing to allow for moisture movement (see Sec. 3.4) and also to distribute concentrated loads over several boards (Sec. 16.5 and Fig. 16.5.2); they are laid either directly across joists or over sheathing laid as a subfloor. *Parquetry* consists of small pieces of wood, 6 to 12 mm (¼ to ½ in.) thick, laid in a pattern and stuck to a structural floor of either timber or concrete. After laying, the flooring is sanded and sealed with a wax compound or a hard plastic coating.

Polished timber flooring has an attractive appearance, and for some purposes, such as a dance floor, is a necessity. *Carpeting* however, (see Sec. 18.7) provides more comfortable walking and reduces both airborne and impact sound (see Sec. 9.2 and 9.3). The cost of cleaning and maintenance is generally lower for carpeting than for polished timber (at least in countries with high labor costs), a consideration that accounts for the widespread use of carpet in commercial buildings. If a timber floor is to be covered with carpet, then high quality hardwood flooring is not necessary. Softwood boards are satisfactory and cheaper, but plywood (Sec. 16.11) or particle board (Sec. 16.12) in large, tongue-and-groove jointed sheets is more convenient to lay; they also suffer less from shrinkage and have fewer joints that allow air infiltration.

External walls can be lined with *siding* (clapboards or weatherboards) laid horizontally and profiled to shed rainwater (Fig. 16.10.1). The shape of the profile provides only minimal protection against driving rain; it is therefore preferable to fix the boards over plywood sheathing, waterproof builder's paper, or aluminum foil. Vertical boarding is sometimes used, with tongue-and-groove or shiplap jointing. Since its protection against wind-driven rain is even less, a backup waterproofing layer is essential.

Walls and *roofs* can be covered with *wood shingles* (Sec. 4.3). A durable species, such as Western Red Cedar or timber impregnated with preservative, is essential for shingles.

16.11 GLUE-LAMINATED TIMBER AND PLYWOOD

Two of the major limitations inherent in timber are the limited size that can be cut from a tree and the inability to obtain a sheet of it with strength in both directions. Adhesives enable both of these limitations to be eased.

Glue-laminated sections are made by laminating a number of boards together on their broad faces (Fig. 16.11.1) to make a deeper section, either because the required size is not available in a single piece or in order to obtain better quality. The boards, which are usually 20 to 40 mm (¾ to 1½ in.) in thickness, must be dressed to provide a close-fitting surface for the glue. Boards of this thickness can be kiln-dried so that the completed section is supplied seasoned; kiln drying for a solid section would take a long time and run the risk of seasoning checks (see Sec. 16.5). The boards can also be stress-graded, either visually or mechanically, with much more certainty of detecting defects than a large solid section could be. If major defects are found, moreover, it is necessary to discard only a single board instead of the whole piece. Such defects as are permitted have relatively little effect on strength provided they do not occur close to each other in adjacent laminates.

It is not necessary that each board be the full length of the completed section. Laminates can be joined end-to-end by *scarf-jointing* or *finger-jointing* (see Glossary) with little loss of strength. If there are many laminates, even a butt joint has little effect on the strength of the whole section. End joints in the laminates should be distributed along the length of the beam so as to avoid a concentration of weakness.

Since each board is relatively thin, it can be bent to a curve, and hence large *curved sections* can be built up. The laminates must be firmly clamped together until the glue sets. Curved timber arches are used for churches and community halls, where the appearance of timber is desired for its own sake, and for large industrial buildings and hangars, where it is mainly chosen for its economy and corrosion resistance. The fire resistance of large timber cross sections is quite good (see Sec. 7.5).

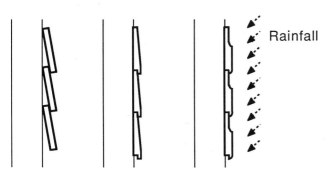

Rainfall

Fig. 16.10.1. Clapboards or weatherboards used horizontally on walls. The boards are shaped to shed normal rainwater, but additional protection is desirable against wind-driven rain.

Part elevation   Section

Fig. 16.11.1. A glue-laminated section made up of many boards. Scarfing, finger-jointing, or even butt jointing of individual laminates is possible so long as joints in adjacent layers are spaced far apart.

Plywood is made by reducing logs to thin layers and then gluing them together with the grain running in alternate directions. Most of the laminates for plywood are made by *rotary peeling*. A log of 2 to 3 m (6 to 10 ft) in length is set up in a lathe, and a sharp knife blade of the same length is fed against the side of the log as it rotates. (The log is soaked in water before peeling in order to make it less brittle.) A layer of timber 2 to 3 mm (1/16 to 1/8 in.) in thickness is peeled off. The thin veneer obtained is quickly dried by being passed through a hot air kiln before gluing, and if any preservative is required, it can be added easily at this stage.

The veneer obtained by rotary peeling does not use the attractive figure in the wood to the best advantage. Expensive and desirable veneers are obtained by *slicing*. A portion of a log is selected and the direction of the most attractive cut determined. It is then sliced by a reciprocating knife taking parallel, flat layers from one face. The resulting veneer strips are less than 1 mm (about 1/32 in.) thick and must be trimmed and laid side-by-side to form a large enough sheet. These *high-quality veneers* are used on the outer faces of plywood that is intended to be clear-finished or polished.

Plywood is glued together in a heated press. Many sheets of plywood are laid up on top of each other and pressed together. Plywood is made in sheets from the size of a standard door up to about 3 × 15 m (10 × 50 ft), and, for building purposes, in thicknesses from 5 to 20 mm (3/16 to 3/4 in.). Thinner and thicker sheets are used for other purposes such as marine craft (very thin for racing craft and very thick for commercial barges).

In both glue-laminated sections and plywood, the *adhesive* is important for the strength and durability of the product (see Sec. 19.6). Early plywood, made with nonwaterproof glues, had a poor reputation for durability. Glues of low water resistance are still used in *interior-grade plywood*, but greater resistance is required for humid tropical climates or in the more humid parts of buildings. *Exterior-grade plywood* requires both a high-quality adhesive and suitably durable timber. Most codes also have a marine grade, in which the specifications for both adhesive and timber are even more stringent. Resorcinol, phenol formaldehyde, and melamine are among the most durable of timber adhesives. Glue-laminated structural sections are always made with high-strength, water-resistant adhesives.

16.12 PARTICLE BOARD AND HARDBOARD

Whereas sawn sections and plywood make use of the tree by reducing it but maintaining the original cellular structure of the wood, particle board and hardboard are made by reducing the wood to a lignocellulose pulp and recombining this pulp.

Particle board is made by pressing together the lignocellulose material (usually wood pulp, although other sources are theoretically possible), with the addition of a binding agent or adhesive. Because the binder is a considerable proportion of the total mass of material (6 to 10 percent), it is essential that it be cheap. Urea formaldehyde (see Sec. 18.5) is generally used. Particle board has reasonable stability for interior use but quickly deteriorates when wet and suffers from creep deflection when used, for example, as shelving carrying heavy loads.

Particle board used for domestic flooring is likely to be exposed to some moisture before the house is completed. A more waterproof binder is thus required. If phenol formaldehyde is used, the resulting material will be darker in color.

Thicknesses of 5, 10, and 20 mm (3/16, 3/8, and 3/4 in.) are common for furniture and building applications, whereas solid-core doors and partition panels may be up to 75 mm (3 in.) thick; the thicker panels often have core holes for lightness. The surface of standard particle board is slightly uneven, but it will take a matt paint finish. A smoother finish and stronger panel can be made by applying a layer of smaller particles with more filler to each face of a panel that uses coarse particles in the interior. High-quality surfaces can be obtained by veneering the particle board with timber veneer or melamine.

Screws can be used in the face of particle board, but their holding power is not good. There is no satisfactory fixing into the end grain, but many special fittings are available for making connections in furniture. In most building applications, either the material is fixed *to* another material, or another material is glued to it.

Hardboard is made from lignocellulose pulp that is pressed together into a dense sheet with little or no additional binder. Its strength derives from the interlocking of the fibers and the natural adhesive effect of the lignin. It is formed under pressure and heat, one side of the sheet finishing smooth and the other with a fine wire-mesh pattern. The smooth surface tends to show irregularities, especially when finished with a gloss paint.

After manufacture, the hardboard sheets have a very low moisture content. If fixed into a building in that condition, they gradually absorb moisture from the environment, expand, and buckle between the fixings. To avoid this, they can be either preconditioned by the manufacturer or else wetted by the user and allowed to stand before fixing. If a slightly over-damp sheet shrinks after fixing, it will tend to pull straight, but allowance must be made at the joints for the shrinkage.

Hardboard is widely used for lining the inside of cupboards and for furniture. Although it can be used for wall and ceiling linings, it is less attractive than plasterboard (see Sec. 13.2) because the joints cannot be disguised. It can be used as an underlay for floor coverings over old or uneven floorboards. *Tempered hardboard* is treated to be more water-resistant than the standard grade and can thus be used in kitchens and similar moist locations, although care is needed to avoid continuous exposure to moisture. *Structural grade* tempered hardboard is available with specified properties suitable for requirements similar to those satisfied by structural plywood.

REFERENCES

16.1. *First Book of Kings*, Chapter 5, verses 8–10.
16.2. J. A. Baird and E. C. Ozelton: *Timber Designers Manual*, Granada, London, 1976. 624 pp.
16.3. K. R. Bootle: *Wood in Australia—Types, Properties and Uses*, McGraw-Hill, Sydney, 1983, 443 pp.
16.4. H. J. Cowan: *Design of Reinforced Concrete Structures*, Prentice-Hall, Englewood Cliffs, NJ, 1982. pp. 150–156.

SUGGESTIONS FOR FURTHER READING

P. B. Cornwell: *Pest Control in Buildings—A Guide to the Meaning of Terms*, Hutchinsons, London, 1973. 189 pp.
L. E. Akers: *Particle Board and Hardboard*, Pergamon, Oxford, 1966. 172 pp.
H. J. Andrews: *An Introduction to Timber Engineering*, Pergamon, Oxford, 1967. 221 pp.
J. D. Wilson: *Practical House Carpentry*, McGraw-Hill, New York, 1973. 424 pp.
F. X. Brochard: *Bois et Charpente en Bois—le Materiau et son Utilization*, Editions Eyrolles, Paris, 1960. 226 pp.
W. A. Chugg: *Glulam—The Manufacture of Glued Laminated Structures*, Ernest Benn, London, 1964, 423 pp.

17

Glass

Glass consists mainly of silica, a readily available raw material. Since silica is a stable oxide, glass is very durable. It can easily be colored or patterned. The structure of glass as a supercooled liquid is responsible both for its transparency and for its brittleness. The brittleness can be countered by the insertion of wire mesh or plastic laminations or by "toughening" the glass through a heat-treatment that prestresses its outer layers.

Glass is not a good thermal or acoustic insulator, mainly because it is a relatively thin material. This deficiency gives rise to many design problems. Glass is transparent to solar radiation but opaque to the long-wave radiation to which solar radiation is converted inside the building. This property can easily result in overheating unless the glass is shaded or solar-control glass is used. The latter alternative reduces the transmission of visible light and changes its color.

17.1 THE PHYSICAL AND CHEMICAL STRUCTURE OF GLASS

A *glass* is a supercooled liquid, a solid in which the atoms are arranged amorphously as in a liquid. A number of glasses of various chemical compositions have been produced by volcanic action; the word "glass," however, is reserved mainly for a group of materials whose main constituent is *silica*. The art of glassmaking was discovered several thousand years ago, as manufactured glass beads found in Ancient Egyptian tombs attest.

There are several types of silica glass. *Window glass* is soda–lime–silica glass: a mixture of silicon oxide (SiO_2) and smaller quantities of calcium oxide (CaO) and sodium oxide (Na_2O). It is made by melting together sand (which is mostly silica), soda ash, limestone, dolomite, and feldspar at a temperature of about 1500°C

(2700°F). It is also called *crown glass,* because this type of glass was used in the traditional crown glass process (Sec. 1.4).

Glass made with *lead oxide* is a much heavier and more expensive material. It is used for *cut crystal* because this material, once cut, has a sparkle lacking in soda–lime glass. In England where it was developed in the seventeenth century, it was made from flints (see Sec. 12.3), which were considered a particularly pure source of silica. Hence it is also called *flint glass.*

Glass made with *boric oxide* has a low thermal expansivity, can thus withstand thermal shock better than other glasses, and is therefore used for glass overware and industrial heat-resisting glasses. The Corning Company's trade name for it is *Pyrex* (see also Sec. 17.4).

Despite these various properties, only soda-lime-silica glasses are used extensively as building materials.

When a liquid cools and reaches the temperature at which it changes to solid crystals, there is a contraction of its volume because solid crystals occupy less space. This contraction does not occur, however, in the normal glass-making process; rather, the material passes through its normal freezing point and gradually turns into a solid supercooled liquid. If the liquid glass is kept at its freezing point for a sufficiently long time, *devitrification* (which is partial or complete crystalization) may occur, particularly if a glass crystal is placed in the melt to serve as a nucleus.

As the glass is cooled past its freezing point, its viscosity increases rapidly, thereby impeding atomic migrations and thus the formation of crystals. The attainment of a glassy state depends on fairly rapid cooling through this critical temperature range.

The *transparency* of glass, which is the main reason for its use as a building material, is a product of this glassy state. Glass, like a single crystal or a liquid, consists of one large molecule. It contains no internal surfaces, holes, or inclusions with dimensions of the same order of magnitude as the range of wavelengths of visible light; hence, it does not provide any obstruction to the passage of light.

On the other hand, glass is not transparent to radiation over the entire electromagnetic spectrum. This transparency varies with its composition. Soda–lime–silica glass is transparent to the thermal radiation emitted by the sun, known as infra-red radiation, but it is opaque to the long-wave thermal radiation produced by the surfaces of a building after absorbing solar radiation. This gives rise to the *greenhouse effect*. The solar radiation can enter through the glass window, but the resulting long-wave radiation cannot escape.

Glass is the most corrosion-resistant of all the common building materials, largely because of its composition. It consists entirely of fully oxidized substances.

Glass is also the most brittle of the common building materials (see Sec. 2.5), and this creates serious structural problems. It is easily broken in an accident, is vulnerable to vandalism and terrorism, and poses a serious hazard in a major fire (see Sec. 7.2). The brittleness is due to the fact that a fracture, once started at a weak point, can travel throughout the material without hindrance. In a metal, each grain boundary is a new obstacle that may stop the propagation of a crack, and the same applies to the polymer chains of the plastics. Because of this characteristic, it is important that glass be cut cleanly so as not to produce any stress concentrations that could start a crack.

17.2 THE MANUFACTURE OF GLASS

In the Ancient Middle East, where glass was first produced, it was used for bottles and drinking glasses and for jewelry, all of which were made by casting. The first blown glass has been discovered near Sidon (present-day Lebanon) and probably dates from the third century B.C. Glass is the only material that can be formed in this way (by blowing); as a supercooled liquid it softens gradually, and there is no marked yield stress or proof stress (see Sec. 2.6) as there is in metals. In consequence, glass does not form a "neck" (see Fig. 2.5.3) like a metal in tension; rather, it extends uniformly. This ability of glass to be drawn uniformly is the basis for most modern processes for making window glass.

The first use of glass as a building material was in Rome, where glass was used for windows, although to a very limited extent, from the first century A.D. onwards. These early window panes were cast; they were 3 to 6 mm (⅛ to ¼ in.) thick and of a green or blue tint. By the fourth century, it had become possible to make glass almost transparent. After the fall of the Western Roman Empire, the glass industry

declined in the West (see Fig. 12.6.4), but it continued to improve in the East, and Eastern techniques were established in Venice during the Crusades. From Venice they spread to other parts of Europe.

Glass was increasingly produced by blowing rather than casting so as to produce a product with a smoother surface. Glass blown as a cylinder (Fig. 17.2.1), however, had to be flattened on some kind of surface, and contact with that surface impaired its surface finish. This problem was solved only when the *crown glass process* was introduced, whereby blown glass was flattened by rotating it in air (Fig. 17.2.2) without making contact with any surface. This process, a medieval Syrian invention perfected in Venice, was introduced into England in the seventeenth century. It was first used for Inigo Jones' Banqueting Hall in Whitehall, London, and later by Christopher Wren at Hampton Court. Balanced sliding sash windows, filled with brilliantly clear, usually slightly curved crown glass, became a characteristic feature of Georgian architecture.

From the early eighteenth century on, *plate glass* was made in France by casting and subsequent polishing. In 1832, Lucas Chance introduced in England an improved process for sheet glass, in which a blown cylinder was flattened on a bed of smooth glass to give a better surface. This produced clear glass that was relatively cheap and provided the material used in the Crystal Palace for the first international exhibition in London in 1851.

In 1905, the American Libbey-Owens Company patented a process for drawing glass directly from the furnace as a continuous ribbon and cooling it as quickly as possible with water coolers. It is then reheated and straightened in an annealing furnace.

In 1955, the British Pilkington Brothers Company developed *float glass* (Fig. 17.2.3). After being drawn

Fig. 17.2.1. Glass originally blown as a cylinder with both ends removed and split longitudinally, ready at this point to be flattened into a sheet by gentle heat in an oven (from D. B. Harden; see Ref. 17.1).

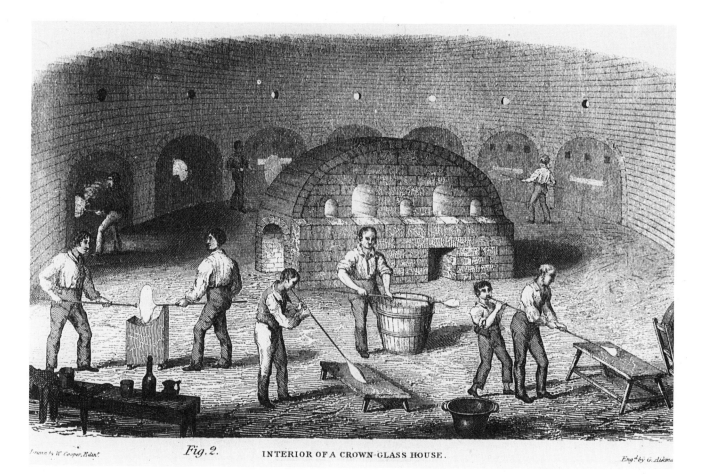

Fig.2.   INTERIOR OF A CROWN-GLASS HOUSE.

Fig. 17.2.2. The various stages of the process of making crown glass (from William Cooper; see Ref. 17.2).

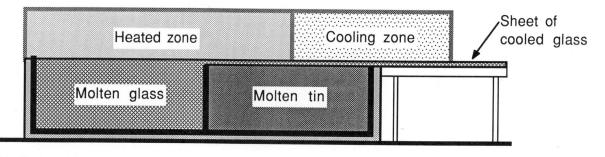

Fig. 17.2.3. The float glass process.

from the furnace, the glass is floated on a bed of molten tin, and heat is applied from above and below to give it the "fire polish" first introduced by the crown glass process. This material is now used for glass in curtain walls.

17.3 COLOR AND TEXTURE

Color classification is discussed in Chap. 19, which deals with pigments (see Figs. 19.2.1 and 19.2.2). Clear glass transmits light from the entire visible spectrum; red glass transmits red only, absorbing all other colors.

Most of the glass produced in antiquity that has been found is colored. It was much more difficult to produce clear glass then because as little as 0.1 percent of a metallic oxide can produce a deep color. Iron presented a particular problem, because it is present in small amounts in most sands (see Sec. 12.3). Ferrous oxide (FeO) produces a blue-green; ferric oxide (Fe$_2$O$_3$), a yellow to green color.

Medieval *stained glass* was a mosaic of colored glass joined with lead cames (H-shaped bars) and painted with an opaque pigment. The glass was entirely colored in the older windows, but in the late Middle

Fig. 17.3.1. Example of the French stained-glass technique called *dalle de verre.*
It places fairly thick blocks of glass, rough on one side, in reinforced cement mortar (*Photograph by courtesy of the Cement and Concrete Association of Australia*).

Ages clear glass coated with molten colored glass, or colored glass coated with another color, was also used. Colors were derived from metals or metallic ores, including manganese for purple, cobalt for blue, copper for green, silver for yellow, and gold for red.

A wide range of colors can in fact be produced, and the same metal can be made to produce quite different colors by altering the composition of the glass; for example, copper can be used for giving colors ranging from blue through green to red. For soda–lime glass, cobalt oxide is still a useful blue pigment, but carbon is now generally used for yellow and selenium or cadmium sulfide for red. Greens are obtained from chromium oxide and iron oxide.

Stained glass windows are still produced in the medieval manner, but an alternative technique is to set fairly thick blocks of glass (about 50 mm or 2 in.) in reinforced cement mortar (Fig. 17.3.1). This technique, called *dalle de verre,* was developed in the 1930s in France by A. Labouret and P. Chaudière.

Glass that is patterned, and sometimes also colored, is used in windows and partitions for privacy. Patterns are produced by engraving the rollers through which the soft glass passes. *Figured glass* has a definite, usually repeated pattern, whereas *cathedral glass* has merely a slightly wavy texture, sufficient to prevent visibility through the glass.

Opal glass can be made with an opacity ranging from faintly milky to fully opaque, characteristics produced by minute crystals in the matrix of clear glass. A matte or "frosted" surface can also be made by sand-blassting or by acid-etching; these processes can be used to produce a pattern or writing on glass (Fig. 17.3.2).

Mirrors are made by giving glass a thin coating of metal. This coating is usually applied on the back of the glass, which then protects the metal film. For instruments requiring accurate reflection without refraction, however, the coating must be applied on the front. The traditional method, invented in Venice in the fourteenth century, was to coat the glass with an amalgam of tin and mercury, but the usual metal coating today is silver. This can be deposited electrolytically or as a spray, using silver nitrate and a reducing agent.

Fig. 17.3.2. Decorated panels of toughened glass used as partitions in the National Westminster Bank, Hong Kong. (*Courtesy of Pilkington ACI, Melbourne.*)

Gold, tin, and aluminum can also be deposited electrolytically. Bluish or pinkish mirrors are produced by a combination of a suitable metal and tinted glass.

Glass can be given an opaque ceramic coating, which is fused to its surface. This is useful for providing continuity of glazing while limiting the area of transparent or translucent glass. The most suitable material for ceramic coatings is *toughened glass* (Sec. 19.4). A wide range of colors is available.

Glass blocks are used in locations where daylight is desired, but windows would not be admissible because of the closeness of a property boundary or unsuitable because of possible invasions of privacy. Glass blocks are made from two pieces of cast glass, usually with a ribbed pattern, which are fused together at a high temperature. A partial vacuum is set up as the inside of the block cools.

The French method of construction known as *béton translucide* is made with solid lenses of toughened glass (Sec. 19.4) that are cast into reinforced-concrete slabs or shell roofs to admit daylight. The glass has about the same strength as the concrete, which it can therefore replace in the reinforced-concrete structure.

17.4 WIRED GLASS, TOUGHENED GLASS, AND LAMINATED GLASS

Wired glass is glass that contains a steel wire mesh. When the glass is broken by a fire or by an accident, the pieces do not fall apart because they continue to be held together by the wires; wired glass is therefore a safer glass. It is not a reinforced glass, however, and its strength is no higher than that of the same glass without a wire mesh. The wires usually form a square mesh that is electrically welded. The mesh can be fed between two separate ribbons of glass that converge to embed it. Alternatively, the mesh can be forced into a single ribbon of glass by means of a roller. Wired glass may be transparent, but it is more often patterned.

Toughened or *tempered glass* (see also Sec. 17.1) is produced by heating glass plate until it is soft, but not soft enough to lose its shape. The outside of the glass on both sides of the sheet is then rapidly cooled by jets of cold air or by immersion in a bath of oil, but this cooling is stopped before it can penetrate into the interior of the glass, which is allowed to cool slowly. The external layers of the glass are thus put in compression, and brittle fracture cannot occur until the compression is reversed.

As the compressed layers must have a reasonable depth, the minimum thickness of toughened glass is 4 mm (3/16 in.). Toughened glass is much stronger than ordinary glass, and its fracture behavior is quite different as well. If a single crack forms, cracking occurs all over the sheet because of its highly stressed condition, and it disintegrates into small fragments that usually lack the sharp cutting edge of ordinary broken glass.

Toughened glass cannot be cut or worked, because any cutting may result in fracture. All cuts and holes must be made before the glass is toughened. Toughened glass panels can be assembled into walls or ballustrades with clamps that are fitted through previously drilled holes. They can also be used for frameless doors.

Laminated glass is produced by placing a layer of vinyl plastic (Sec. 18.4), such as vinyl butyral, between two layers of glass in a room that is entirely free of dust and moisture, and passing the assembly between heated rollers. Such glass can withstand flying debris generated by a cyclone (or hurricane), or a terrorist or bandit attack with a flying brick, a hammer, or an axe. Several layers of laminations are needed to make laminated glass resistant to bullets. Laminated glass may crack, but the laminations hold the pieces together.

17.5 THERMAL PROPERTIES OF GLASS

Windows have a number of conflicting functions. They admit daylight, and this was a matter of great importance prior to the mid-nineteenth century when artificial lighting was an expensive commodity, and when most materials used for lighting, such as tallow and oils, also served as foodstuffs and supplies of food were short. Electric lighting is now a simple matter, however, and the only aspects that need to be considered are its cost and the heat generated by the lamps. Moreover, daylight is useful only within a few meters or yards of a window (Fig. 17.5.1). The utilization of daylight and design for daylight, as well as associated problems

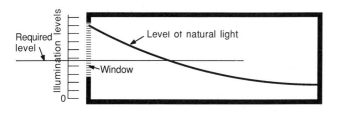

Fig. 17.5.1. Fall in the level of daylight with distance from a window in a room of normal height.

such as glare are discussed in specialized books (for example, see Ref. 17.3, pp. 130–157).

The view of the outside world that windows afford is a separate issue, its importance proved by the high prices that offices, hotel rooms, and private houses with a fine view command. People who shop in department stores are rarely disturbed by the fact that most are structurally windowless, nor do many who work there complain about it. On the other hand, offices and factories without windows often give rise to adverse comments, and hotel rooms and apartments without or with very few windows are hard to let, however well ventilated.

Although there is a clear case *for* windows, the need for large areas of glass is more debatable. They appealed to the pioneers of the Modern Movement, because they demonstrated the lightness of the structural frame, as compared with the dependence of older structures on loadbearing walls. One might argue that the point has now been made and that it is no longer necessary to repeat the demonstration. Large areas of glass and, indeed, complete glass walls still have an appeal because of the crystalline appearance of the material and the generally good durability of glass, which retains its surface finish is it is washed regularly.

The main argument against the use of large areas of glass is poorness of thermal performance, although this can be tempered by the use solar-control glass and by constructional devices. There are two essentially separate problems here. One is the loss of heat through windows when a building is being heated, which either increases the expenditure of energy on heating or reduces the indoor temperature below the comfort level. The other is the gain of heat through windows, which does the opposite if the building is air-conditioned. Most buildings in cold climates have some kind of equipment for heating, but buildings in warm climates do not necessarily have air conditioning, and, for these, window design is particularly critical.

The energy needed for heating in cold climates is usually greater than the energy needed for cooling in warm climates, because the difference between the desired indoor temperature and the maximum exterior temperature is greater for cold nights than for hot days. In a temperate climate, it is less than 10°C (18°F) for a hot day, but more than 20°C (36°F) for a cold

night. In an extreme climate, it is about 15°C (27°F) for a hot day and 50°C (90°F) for a cold night.

The heat input required can be compared by calculating the difference between the mean daily temperature and a reference temperature—usually taken as 18°C (65°F)—and adding the positive numbers for the entire year. This gives a measure of the amount of heating required during the year in *degree days* (see Glossary). The number of degree days for various cities is given in Fig. 17.5.2. This number influences the pattern of energy consumption in industrialized countries. In countries with degree days exceeding 3000 (based on 18°C, or 5400 based on 65°F), space heating uses more energy than any other single source, such as automobiles or industrial processes, and the correct design of windows therefore becomes a matter of considerable importance. This applies to the whole of Canada and the northern part of the U.S.A. as well as to most of northern and central Europe.

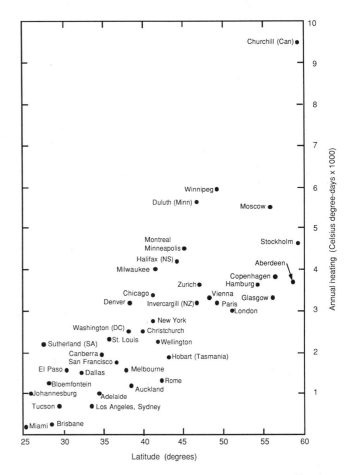

Fig. 17.5.2. Relationship between latitude and the amount of heating required, in Celsius degree days, based on 18°C (to convert to Fahrenheit degree days, based on 65°F, multiply by 1.8).
All points fall within a strip whose center line is proportional to the latitude. Cities near the bottom of the strip—like Brisbane, Los Angeles, Rome and Glasgow—have a maritime climate. Those near the top—like Johannesburg, Denver, and Winnipeg—have a continental climate.

Fig. 17.5.3. The High Court, in Canberra, Australia, a building with a very large, sealed, double-glazed window, completed in 1980. (*Courtesy of the architects, Edwards Madigan Torzillo Briggs International.***)**

The coldest temperatures occur during the hours of darkness when the visibility provided by windows is not required, and indeed is not desired. The insulation of the window (see Sec. 6.3) can therefore be greatly increased by drawing heavy curtains across it on the inside—a general practice. A further great improvement can be achieved by putting window shutters on the outside and closing them at night. The most effective energy conservation measure is, of course, to limit the number and size of the windows.

The poor insulating value of window glass is not due to its thermal conductivity (see Table 6.1), which is about the same as that of concrete and only slightly worse than that of brick, but due to the relatively small thickness of window glass. As Examples 6.1 through 6.4 show, an increase in the thickness of the glass would make only a small improvement, and it is not practicable to place an insulating layer between two sheets of glass without a loss of transparency. A great improvement can be achieved, however, by using two sheets of glass with an air space between. Double windows are traditional in the northern countries of the European continent and some parts of North America. In buildings with curtain walls, double glazing produces a great improvement in thermal performance (Fig. 17.5.3), and even triple glazing may be worthwhile.

To achieve the best possible performance, any thermal path through a metal window frame should be broken by a plastic insert. The double window should be sealed (Secs. 17.8 and 17.9) and all moisture removed from it to avoid condensation (see Sec. 6.4) in the space between the two panes of glass. These precautions also eliminate, or at least greatly reduce, the heat loss caused by the leakage of warm air from the interior, which is a major source of loss in traditional windows. The effectiveness of the selaed double and triple window is therefore only partly the result of the low thermal conductivity of the air space; it owes more to the reduced loss by thermal convection. The loss by thermal radiation depends only on the overall thickness of the

Fig. 17.5.4. Solar house in New Mexico.
"Greenhouse" on groundfloor collects heat for winter heating that can be stored for a few days. Upper windows admit solar radiation in winter but are shaded in the summer. Building also has a solar water heater and photovoltaic cells for generating electricity.

glass; it is not affected by double or triple glazing (see Sec. 5.5 and 6.2).

Another approach to the problem is to utilize the greenhouse effect (Sec. 17.1); this is possible, of course, only in climates where winter days are predominantly sunny. Soda–lime glass is transparent to thermal radiation emitted by the sun but opaque to the long-wave thermal radiation produced by the surfaces of the building after absorbing solar radiation; thus, the heat cannot escape. The entry of this solar radiation through large windows as if through a "greenhouse" (Fig. 17.5.4) is helpful in cold weather to heat buildings in daytime. Such heat can be stored by the thermal inertia of the building (see Sec. 6.5). This approach, called *passive solar design,* is discussed in a number of textbooks (for example, see Ref. 17.1, pp. 88–96).

The hot-weather problem is essentially different. In a building that is not air-conditioned, the difference between indoor temperature and outdoor temperature in the shade is relatively slight in summer, and, even in an air-conditioned building, it is very much less than that encountered on a cold winter's night. On the other hand, the thermal resistance cannot be increased by drawing curtains and closing shutters without a concurrent loss of daylight, although this tactic may sometimes be practiced in hot, arid climates.

The main problem is created by the solar radiation transmitted by the glass, which can cause serious overheating in warm weather and can do so even when the outside shade temperature is *below* the desired indoor temperature because of the accumulation of heat from solar radiation.

There are three principal solutions to this problem. The windows can be shaded to prevent the entry of solar radiation when this is undesirable, but to admit it in winter when the building needs heat (Fig. 17.5.5).

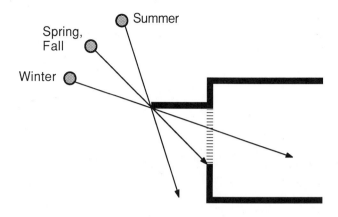

Fig. 17.5.5 Sunshade to admit solar heat during winter months but exclude it completely during summer months.
The design of these sunshades is discussed in specialized textbooks, for example, Ref. 17.1, pp. 41–52.

The windows can be shaded throughout the year; the extra expenditure on winter heating then required may be compensated by the simpler shading devices.

These two solutions are, however, not possible, if the building is to be designed with an unencumbered curtain wall, and particularly if that wall is to be entirely of glass. In the latter case, the entry of solar radiation must be reduced by the use of *solar-control glass*.

Body-tinted glass is manufactured by the addition of color to the glass melt to give a uniform color throughout the thickness of the glass. The first of these glasses to be developed utilized ferrous oxide [FeO], which produces a green tint; the resulting glass absorbs a substantial part of the solar heat radiation but also some of the visible light. For example, glass 6 mm (¼ in.) thick transmits only 49 percent of the solar heat, but it also transmits only 78 percent of the visible light. For the same material 10 mm (⅜ in.) thick, the corresponding figures are 36 and 69 percent, respectively. More recently, grey and bronze glasses have been developed that have similar properties but lend a more agreeable color to the daylight transmitted.

The solar heat the body-tinted glass absorbs is re-radiated partly to the outside and partly to the inside. Some of it therefore enters the building as reradiated heat. Thermal efficiency is greatly improved if the body-tinted glass is used as the outer leaf of a sealed, double-glazed window. The other leaf is made of clear glass, and an airspace of about 12 mm (½ in.) is left between them. The heat reradiated by the body-tinted glass has a longer wavelength than the solar heat does, and the clear glass is opaque to it, although it is transparent to solar radiation.

Whereas body-tinted glass absorbs and reradiates solar heat, *heat-reflecting* glass reflects it to the outside by means of a metallic coating. However, it also reflects a part of the visible light. The glass appears like a mirror when seen from the outside and transmits a bronze-colored light. A sheet of glass 6 mm (¼ in.) thick transmits 43 percent of the solar heat and 33 percent of the visible light.

Heat-absorbing and heat-reflecting glasses significantly alter the interior aesthetics of a building by changing the color of the daylight; whether for the better or for the worse is a matter of opinion. Heat-reflecting glass has an even more pronounced effect on the exterior aesthetics of the building, because the façade becomes a mirror that reflects its surroundings but hides the interior (Fig. 17.5.6).

Both types of glass also have a marked effect on the exterior thermal environment because the heat, whether absorbed or reflected, does not disappear; it is merely redirected.

17.6 OPTICAL AND ACOUSTICAL ASPECTS

A certain amount of light is reflected even by clear glass (Sec. 5.4), and this is a disadvantage for shop windows and other displays. The difficulty can be overcome by using a cylindrically curved sheet of glass with a center of curvature at the point where the eyes of the person viewing the display are likely to be (Fig. 17.6.1). Since this is an expensive technique, a cheaper solution is to use a tilted sheet of glass protected by an overhang to eliminate likely sources of reflection (Fig. 17.6.2).

The opposite problem arises when one wishes to prevent people from viewing the activities in a room while allowing a view from within of the exterior. This aim can be achieved by applying a mirror surface to glass, such as heat-reflecting glass that is thin enough to allow for some transparency. A person in full daylight outside cannot see through the mirror; he only sees his own reflection. The position is liable to be reversed at night, however, when the interior illumination is much more intense than that outside.

A striped mirror consisting of bands of silver coating about 20 mm (¾ in.) wide, with stripes of clear glass about 1½ mm (¹⁄₁₆ in.) wide in between the silver bands, also acts as a one-way mirror. From one side, it gives the appearance of a fully silvered mirror. From the other, it is possible to see through the stripes of clear glass.

The sound insulation of windows presents problems that can be almost as difficult as those of thermal insulation (Fig. 17.6.3). The mere fact that a window is closed, however, produces very appreciable sound attenuation. The worst complaints about noise occur in summer in nonairconditioned buildings whose windows are left open to provide natural ventilation. A single sheet of glass greatly reduces the noise.

Insulation against airborne sound is governed by the mass law (see Sec. 9.2 and Fig. 9.2.1), and although glass is a moderately heavy material, its mass is low

Fig. 17.5.6. World Headquarters of R. J. Reynolds Industries, a building with heat-reflecting glass that acts like a mirror to its surroundings. (*Architects Odell Associates Inc.: courtesy of PPG Industries, Pittsburgh PA.*)

because the sheets are relatively thin. Double glazing does not, of itself, have any effect on sound insulation. The sound attenuation of two sheets of glass separated by an air space in exactly the same as that of a single sheet of double thickness. It is, however, possible to line the surround of the air space between the two

sheets of glass with a sound-absorbing material, such as fiber glass, and this significantly aids the sound attenuation.

Double glazing with efficient sealants (Sec. 19.8 and 19.9) has one great advantage: it seals all air gaps and thus prevents the entry of sound around the window. The sound attenuation of windows in traditionally built houses is much lower because the windows do not fit

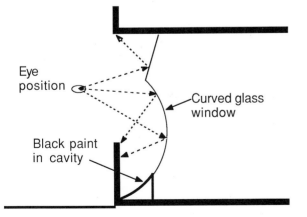

Fig. 17.6.1. Cylindrically curved window to eliminate the reflection of a person viewing its display.
The center of curvature of the glass should be located at the level of the average viewing person's eyes.

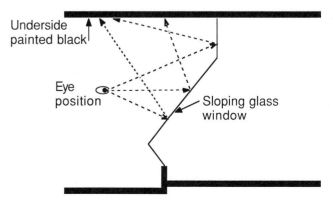

Fig. 17.6.2. Inclined window with roof overhang to eliminate possible sources of light that could produce an inclined reflection.

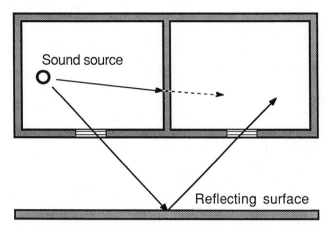

Fig. 17.6.3. Diagram illustrating why windows are often the weak points in the soundproofing of a building.

as well and sound can enter through the narrow, but unobstructed, spaces around them.

Since windows offer much less sound attenuation than the more solidly constructed parts of a building, it is desirable to keep their number and size as small as possible wherever noise levels are high. The only other solution is expensive: to use thicker glass or heavier glass that contains lead oxide.

REFERENCES

17.1. D. B. Harden: *Domestic window glass, Roman, Saxon, and Medieval*. Chapter 3 in *Studies in Building History*, edited by E. M. Jope. Odham's Press, London, 1961. pp. 39–63.

17.2. William Cooper: *Crown Glass Cutter and Glazier's Manual*. Reproduced from the *Encyclopaedia Britannica*, 9th ed., Vol. X, Edinburgh, 1875.

17.3. H. J. Cowan and P. R. Smith: *Environmental Systems*. Van Nostrand Reinhold, New York, 1983. 240 pp.

SUGGESTIONS FOR FURTHER READING

Raymond McGrath and A. C. Frost: *Glass in Architecture and Decoration*. Architectural Press, London, 1961. 712 pp.

R. Persson: *Flat Glass Technology*. Butterworths, London, 1969. 167 pp.

G. O. Jones: *Glass*. Chapman and Hall, London, 1971. 128 pp.

John Peter: *Design with Glass*. Reinhold, New York, 1965. 159 pp.

18

Plastics and Carpets

Plastics may constitute only about 1 percent of the materials used in a building, but they play an important and fast-growing role in architectural design.

Plastics can be categorized either as thermoplastic materials, which soften when heated, or as thermosetting materials. The principal groups of plastics will be described here, and their properties, fabrication, and use in buildings discussed. Their importance to paints, adhesives and sealants will be considered in Chap. 19.

The final section of this chapter will deal with linoleum and carpets.

18.1 THE PHYSICS AND CHEMISTRY OF PLASTICS

During the last 60 years, the plastics industry has grown from a minor one making a few substitute products to a major industrial complex that produces an enormous variety of materials with widely differing properties. Plastics are replacing other materials—particularly nonferrous metals, wood, and glazed clay products—because they are not only cheaper for some particular purpose, they often also perform certain functions better than the materials they replace.

Despite all this, plastics are still used in much smaller quantities than wood, clay products, or concrete. The subject can be covered only superficially here, and reference should be made to specialized books (for example, see Refs. 18.1 and 18.2).

In Sec. 2.4, *plasticity* was defined as the capacity of certain materials (mostly metals) to deform permanently at normal temperature, but at high stress. Failure of these materials occurs only after a great deal of plastic deformation. Some plastics fail in this manner, but others do the exact opposite; they fail by brittle fracture (see Sec. 2.7). Plastics are therefore not necessarily plastic in the sense in which the term is understood in materials science. They are, however, plastic in the sculptural sense, because they can be formed into complex shapes during the manufacturing process. It is rarely necessary to cut or machine them like natural stone or metal. This is one reason why plastic components are so economical.

Plastics can be categorized either as *thermoplastic* or as *thermosetting materials*. Thermoplastic materials deform under heat or pressure, or both, and they can then be formed to the desired shape; they retain that shape at normal temperature and pressure. If the process is repeated, the materials soften again. Thermosetting materials undergo chemical change at high temperatures and do not soften when they are heated again. These materials can be formed only once, but they can also be used at higher temperatures.

All plastics contain carbon. The carbon atom has four vacancies in its outer shell of electrons (see Sec. 2.3), and it has therefore a *valency* of four, that is, it can form four links with other atoms. Unlike any other element, however, carbon atoms can combine with other carbon atoms to form rings or long chains (Figs. 18.1.1, 18.1.2, and 18.1.3). The branch of chemistry that deals with these compounds is called *organic chemistry,* because it was at one time thought that all compounds containing carbon rings or long chains were derived from organic materials. This is not the case, even though some plastics are, in fact, made from agricultural waste products.

The relatively small molecules illustrated in Figs. 18.1.1 to 18.1.3 can be extended into long chains by a process known as *polymerization* (from a Greek adjective that means "having many parts"). The short molecule is called a *monomer,* and the long chain that results from it is called a *polymer*. Thus the monomer, vinyl chloride, is polymerized to become *polyvinyl*

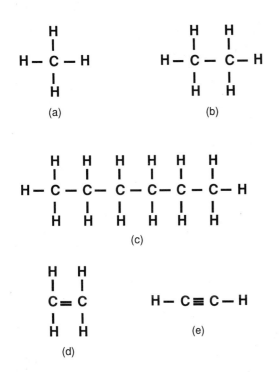

(a)

(b)

(c)

(d)   (e)

Fig. 18.1.1. Some examples of carbon-chain molecules comprised of carbon and hydrogen atoms only.
(a) Methane, CH_4; (b) ethane, C_2H_6; (c) hexane, C_6H_{14}; (d) ethylene, C_2H_4, the simplest compound of the *olefine* series; (e) acetylene, C_2H_2, the simplest compound of the *acetylene* series.

Chain molecules built on the pattern of (a), (b), and (c) are called *paraffins*. Methane and ethane are gases at normal temperature, whereas hexane is a liquid. The longer-chain paraffins are wax-like solid substances.

The two carbon atoms in ethane are joined by a single bond; in ethylene, they are joined by a double bond, and in acetylene, by a triple bond. The result is that there are fewer bonds available for the hydrogen atoms.

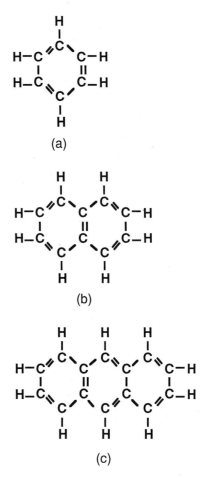

(a)

(b)

(c)

Fig. 18.1.2. Some examples of carbon-ring molecules comprised of carbon and hydrogen atoms only.
(a) Benzene, C_6H_6; (b) naphtalene, $C_{10}H_8$; (c) anthracene, $C_{14}H_{10}$.

chloride, and the monomer, styrene, is polymerized to become *polystyrene* (Figs. 18.1.3 and 18.1.4). The *polymer chain* may be built up from many thousands of monomers, but even so it is too small to be seen under an optical microscope. The manufacturing process whereby materials are polymerized varies from one plastic to another. Some are formed by the *copolymerization* of two different monomers.

In thermoplastic materials, the polymer chains are not interconnected, so that they can slide past one another under pressure or under heat [Fig. 18.1.5(a)]. Thus thermoplastic materials can be shaped with the application of only small force at an elevated temperature and/or under pressure. For the same reason, their coefficient of thermal expansion (see Sec. 3.3) is usually much higher than that of metals or concrete (five times as much, or more).

Thermosetting materials undergo a chemical change that causes cross-linkages between the polymer chains [Fig. 18.1.5(b)] so that the material becomes rigid and is not thereafter softened by heat and/or pressure.

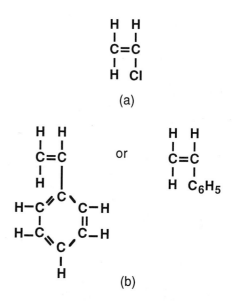

(a)

or

(b)

Fig. 18.1.3. Two examples of a modified ethylene chain molecule.
(a) If one (monovalent) hydrogen atom is replaced by one (monovalent) chlorine atom, the material is called *chloroethylene* or *vinyl chloride* ($C_2H_3 \cdot Cl$ or $CH_2 : CH \cdot Cl$). (b) If a hydrogen atom is replaced by a benzene ring (see Fig. 18.1.2), the resulting material is called *styrene* ($C_2H_3 \cdot C_6H_5$ or $CH_2 : CH \cdot C_6H_5$).

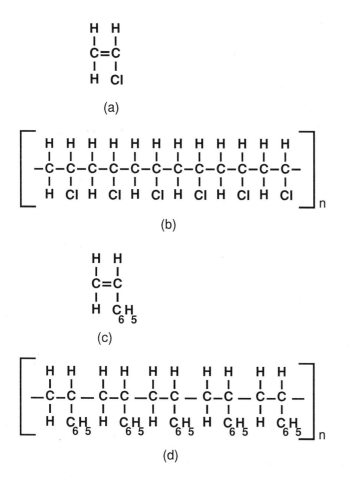

Fig. 18.1.4 Two examples of polymerization.
(a) Monomer: vinyl chloride [CH₂:CH·Cl]; (b) Polymer: polyvinyl
chloride [CH₂:CH·Cl]ₙ; (c) Monomer: styrene [CH₂:CH·C₆H₅]; (d)
Polymer: polystyrene [CH₂:CH·C₆H₅]ₙ.

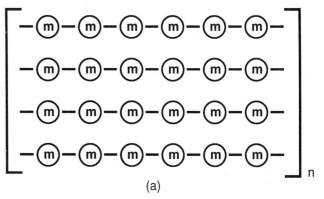

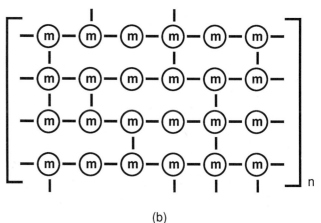

Fig. 18.1.5. Linkages between monomers m (a) in thermoplastic materials, and (b) in thermosetting materials (which have some cross-linkages).

18.2 AN HISTORICAL NOTE

Naturally occuring plastics have been used for many centuries. They include the resins that are exuded by many plants, naturally occurring asphalt, natural rubber, and gutta-percha (obtained from the latex of a tree found in Southeast Asia and used as a waterproof electric insulating material).

In the early nineteenth century, some of these materials were modified chemically. In 1836, Charles Goodyear *vulcanized* rubber, a natural polymer, by treating it with sulfur. This produced cross-linkages between the polymer chains of the material [Fig. 18.1.5(b)], and made it much harder; at the same time, the polymer chains lost their ability to slide spast one another, which gave the natural material its "rubbery" elasticity.

In 1838, vinyl chloride (Fig. 18.1.4) was polymerized for the first time—by exposure to sunlight—but the polyvinyl chloride did not at that time have a useful application.

In 1870, John Wesley Hyatt synthesized *celluloid*

from nitrocellulose, using camphor as a plasticizer. At that time, ivory was considered to be the only suitable material for piano keys and billiard balls. Ivory was very expensive, and the demand for it was threatening elephants with extinction. Celluloid was promoted as the solution to this problem, but it soon found other uses.

By 1900, vulcanized rubber and celluloid were still the only commercially useful manufactured plastics. Phenol-aldehyde resins were developed in the first decade of the twentieth century, and urea formaldehyde, which has a lighter color, in the 1920s. Polystyrene, polyvinyl chloride, and polymethyl methacrylate (Plexiglass, Perspex) all date from the 1930s.

Polyethylene and polyamide (better known under its trade name, Nylon—a compounded abbreviation of New York and London) were discovered in the 1930s but became commercially important only after World War II. In the 1950s, there was a significant improvement in the quality of the existing plastics, a great increase in the quantity produced, and several new materials were introduced.

The world production of plastics was approximately 300,000 tons in 1939. By 1950, it had grown to 2,000,000 tons; by 1960, to 6,000,000; by 1970, to 20,000,000; and by 1980, to 50,000,000 tons (approximate figures).

Throughout the 1960s, several large chemical companies promoted the concept of an all-plastic house, perhaps more as an exercise in publicity than as a serious attempt to revolutionize the housing industry. In less spectacular ways, however, plastics began to transform the building industry, even though they still constitute only about 1 percent of the total materials used. Plastics replaced the more expensive and heavier metals for a variety of fittings; they replaced traditional vehicles in paint (see Sec. 19.1) and traditional adhesives (see Sec. 19.6); and they made it possible to reconstitute woodchips into useful timber planks and boards. They also provided new products for vapor and water barriers, for abrasion- and heat-resistant surfaces, and for thermal insulating materials.

18.3 THE FABRICATION OF PLASTICS

Some of the raw materials for the manufacture of plastics are still of organic origin: cellulose is derived from timber and cotton fibers, and casein from the waste-products of cheese-making are the most important examples. Most plastics, however, are manufactured from the byproducts of the destructive distillation of coal (to produce coke) or of the cracking of crude oil (to produce gasoline and fuel oil).

The resulting momomers (Sec. 18.1) are polymerized or copolymerized, usually by heat and/or pressure. Fabrication of thermoplastic materials (Sec. 18.1) is often facilitated by the use of a *plasticizer*—a small quantity of material added to facilitate the separation of the polymer chains by heat and thus reduce the temperature and the force needed to produce plastic deformation.

Most plastics are delivered to the fabricators as small particles that may result from grinding, cutting, extrusion, or emulsion. These may be irregular or in the form of tiny spheres, cubes, or cylinders. Some plastics come in the form of flakes or powder. An exception is polymethyl methacrylate (Plexiglas, Perspex), which is produced immediately in the form of transparent sheets and rods. Plastics may be fabricated by extrusion, by blow molding, by compression molding, or by injection molding.

The *extrusion* process is used for the production of thermoplastic sheets, films, tubes, and more complex sections. The principle is similar to the aluminum extrusion process (see Fig. 11.2.1) except that the material entering the extruder in granular form is carried forward by a screw conveyor. If the work done on the plastic material in the process is not sufficient to melt it, additional heat can be applied in the extruder to soften it before it is squeezed through the die.

Extrusion is used less commonly for thermosetting

materials. In their case, the extrusion press has a plunger (as in Fig. 11.2.1) instead of a screw conveyor.

Blow-molding is a variation of the extrusion process for thermoplastic materials. The softened material is blown through the extrusion die against a mold, which is not restricted in size as is the case in compression molding; quite large objects can be produced as a consequence.

Compression molding is at present used exclusively for thermosetting materials. The mold consists of a male and a female part, as it does for the molding of sheet metal, but the raw material is granular. A weighed quantity of plastic grains is fed into the mold and liquified by heat and pressure. The molding emerges from the press completely finished, except for a thin flange where the two plates of the press join, and this is subsequently removed by grinding.

In principle, compression molding could be used for thermoplastic materials, but finished articles would have to be allowed to cool before being removed from the mold, and that would make the process uneconomic. Thermosetting materials achieve their strength through chemical action and do not need to cool before being removed from the mold.

The *injection-molding* process was developed from the die-casting of metals. Thermoplastic material is rendered fluid in a chamber outside the mold, transferred by pressure into the mold, and there cooled. When thermosetting plastics are injection-molded, the material is rendered fluid as it is being injected into, and just before it reaches, the mold cavity.

Most thermoplastic materials are easily welded and glued. *Welding* can be done with a welding rod, as it is for metal; this is melted by a jet of hot air, or, better, by an inert gas such as nitrogen or carbon dioxide. The gas is usually heated electrically. Alternatively, the two pieces of material to be joined can be softened by heat and then butted together under pressure. *Gluing* is best accomplished with a glue made from the material to be joined, dissolved in a suitable solvent.

Expanded or *foamed plastics* can be produced from thermoplastic or thermosetting materials by a number of different processes. Air can be entrained mechanically by agitating a thermosetting raw material; the resulting foam is then polymerized and becomes rigid in the process. Another method suitable for thermoplastic materials is to incorporate a volatile solvent, which is vaporized by heat. Small pellets thus become large beads containing bubbles, and these can be fused into slabs to take the shape of a mold.

Woodchip board was originally developed as a means for utilizing and disposing of a waste product. It has become a valuable product in its own right, however, with properties in many respects equal, or even superior, to boards cut from natural timber. To produce

Fig. 18.3.1. Laminate glued to wooden table.
The timber grain is photographed and then printed on the top layer of paper used in the laminate; the high scratch and heat resistance of the top layer is due to its impregnation with melamine formaldehyde.

a high-quality product, the wood chips must be of optimum shape and moisture content, established by tests for that particular species of wood; however, wood offcuts that would otherwise be wasted can be used. Urea formaldehyde resin is the most common adhesive for chipboard, using 5 to 10 percent of the weight of the timber. The sheet is compressed to the required density and thickness at a temperature of about 150°C (300°F).

Plastic *laminates*, which were developed in the early years of this century, can be made from a number of different plastics. Their most important application in the building industry is for high-pressure decorative surfaces for tables and counters. Any decorative pattern capable of being printed on paper, and any color, can be used. The texture of timber used for the natural surfaces of a table can be imitated by photographing the grain of the wood and using a print of that photograph in the laminate (Fig. 18.3.1). The process, developed in the 1930s, utilizes the hardness, scratch-resistance, freedom from discoloration, and heat resistance of melamine-formaldehyde resin to impregnate the decorative sheet of paper and serve as a protective translucent outer sheet. Because of the high cost of this resin, the lower layers are impregnated with less expensive phenolic resins. The assembly is cured under pressure at a temperature of about 150°C (300°F).

High-pressure laminates can be produced with metallic finishes, using anodized aluminum (see Sec. 11.4) in various colors.

18.4 THERMOPLASTIC MATERIALS

Polyethylene is the polymer of ethylene [C_2H_4] [for which see Fig. 18.1.1(d)], and its general formula is [CH_2]$_n$. Its Vicat softening point (defined as the temperature at which a standard needle penetrates into the material by a specified distance under a standard load) occurs at a temperature ranging from 85°C (185°F) to 130°C (265°F), depending on its specific gravity. The specific gravity ranges from 0.91 to 0.97 (slightly less than that of water). The material was first produced by ICI in England under the trade name *Polythene*, and it is still widely called by that name.

The most common use of polyethylene is as a transparent sheet or thin film, but it is also used as an insulating coating for wires, tubes, and pipes. Its main advantages are low cost, easy processing, good flexibility, good resistance to water and to many chemicals, and good electrical insulating properties. Its main disadvantage is its poor durability outdoors as a result of its degradation by ultraviolet radiation.

Polypropylene, the polymer of propylene [C_3H_6], is similar to polyethylene but has greater stiffness, tensile strength, and resistance to heat. It is used as a fiber for carpets. Otherwise, its uses are generally similar to those of polyethylene (Figs. 18.4.1 and 18.4.2), although it finds fewer applications in buildings. Its specific gravity ranges from 0.89 to 0.92.

Polyvinyl-chloride is the polymer of vinyl chloride [CH_2:CH·Cl] (Figs. 18.1.3 and 18.1.4). Generally called *PVC*, it was originally produced in rigid form, and that is still its main mode although it was soon found that a flexible PVC could be produced by blending it with plasticizers, such as a tritotyl phosphate. The specific gravity of PVC ranges from 1.2 to 1.7.

PVC is widely used in building because of its low cost, excellent resistance to tearing, good weathering properties, and good resistance to water and many chemicals (Fig. 18.4.3.). Rigid PVC is self-extinguishing when set on fire, but some of the flexible grades burn slowly, because some of the plasticizers burn. PVC cannot be used at elevated temperatures. For some grades, the upper limit is 60°C (140°F), although others

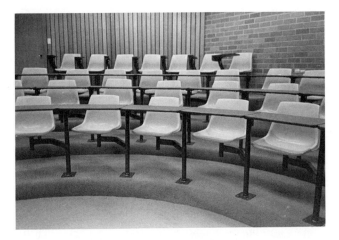

Fig. 18.4.1. Rigid classroom chairs moulded from polypropylene.

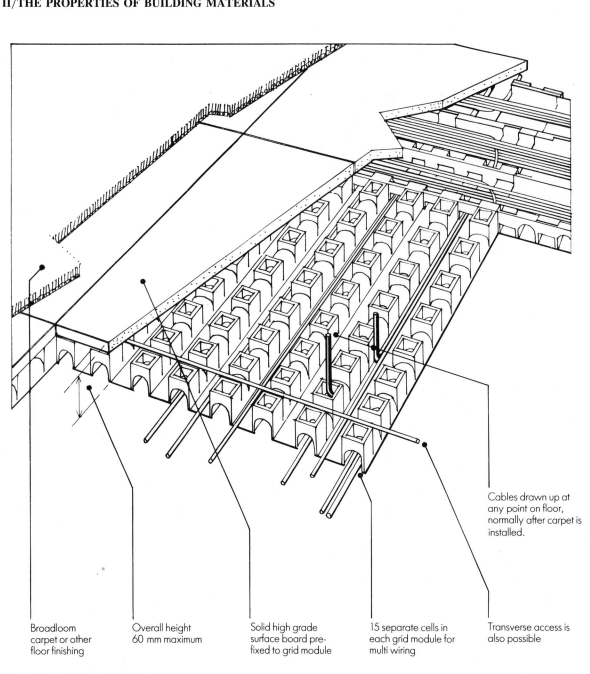

Cables drawn up at any point on floor, normally after carpet is installed.

| Broadloom carpet or other floor finishing | Overall height 60 mm maximum | Solid high grade surface board pre-fixed to grid module | 15 separate cells in each grid module for multi wiring | Transverse access is also possible |

Fig. 18.4.2. Multiduct polypropylene floor system.
A raised-floor system for use in new buildings, or for the renovation of old buildings, which provides separate spaces for different services below floor level. [*Courtesy of the manufacturers, H. H. Robertson (Australia) Pty., Chatswood 2067.*]

can be used up to 100°C (212°F). Flexible PVC remains flexible at temperatures well below the freezing point; for some grades, the limit is as low as −60°C (−75°F). Most types of PVC have good resistance to ultraviolet radiation, but some transparent types may be degraded by it.

Rigid PVC is used for hot and cold water pipes, rain gutters, and downspouts; it is also used for ducts, corrugated sheets, window frames, panels, and tiles. Flexible PVC is used for films and sheets, flexible tubes and hoses, flashings and vapor barriers, flexible floor covering (particularly in the form of tiles), as a

leathercloth, for covering steel, and for covering electrical cables. PVC can also be produced as a rigid or a flexible foam.

Polyvinyl acetate (PVA) is the polymer of vinyl acetate [$CH_2:CH\cdot OOC\cdot CH_3$]. Because of its high rate of flow, it cannot be used for extrusions or moldings, but it is extensively used in emulsion paints (see Sec. 19.1) because of its good adhesion to most materials.

The best known of the *fluorocarbons* is polytetra-fluoroethylene (*PTFE*). Its chemical structure is similar to that of polyethylene, except that fluorine atoms are substituted for hydrogen atoms. PTFE is an expensive

Fig. 18.4.3. Sculptured surface finish in precast concrete slabs made by a flexible former of polyvinyl chloride inside the mold (the same former can be reused many times).

material and a relatively heavy one (specific gravity, 2.0 to 2.2). Best known for its use in nonstick frying pans, it has excellent chemical resistance and a much wider temperature range than most plastics, but because of its high cost it has yet to be used in building construction.

The best known *acrylic plastics* have the trade names *Lucite, Perspex,* and *Plexiglas.* All are polymers of methyl methacrylate (Fig. 18.4.4). Their most important property is their transparency, with about 92 percent overall light transmission. Acrylics are scratched more easily than glass, but their scratch resistance is quite high for a plastic material, being about the same as that of aluminum. The scratches are much more in evidence, however, because the material is transparent.

$$CH_2 = C - CO.OCH_3$$
$$|$$
$$CH_3$$

18.4.4. Chemical structure of methyl methacrylate, the monomer of polymethyl methacrylate.

Acrylics, which have a specific gravity of about 1.2, soften at a temperature between 130° and 150°C (265° and 300°F), at which time they can easily be formed into complex shapes. Acrylics are made as cast sheets or rods, or as granular materials that can be used for injection molding. They can be fabricated to be transparent (clear or colored) or opaque. They have excellent weathering resistance, including exposure to ultraviolet light. Their cost is in the medium range.

Acrylics are made into light fittings, advertising signs, and skylights, and also into sanitary fittings, doorknobs, etc. Their versatility extends from fibers for carpets to vehicles for paints (see Sec. 19.1) and for sealants and adhesives (see Secs. 19.8 and 19.6).

Polystyrene is the polymer of styrene $[CH_2:CH \cdot C_6H_5]$ (Fig. 18.1.4). Its Vicat softening point lies in the range, 78° to 93°C (172° to 200°F). Its specific gravity ranges from 1.04 to 1.08, and it is slow-burning if ignited. It is possible to make it colorless and transparent. Polystyrene is a low-cost plastic that is easy to mold, drill, turn, polish, and glue. It can be decorated by printing, lacquering, and metallizing, the latter by giving it a thin coating of metal (usually copper).

Most solid polystyrene is used for making components for refrigerators, television and radio sets, household goods, and furniture. Its main use in buildings is for decorative wall tiles, because of its high gloss and the wide range of colors available, and for light diffusers, particularly in conjunction with fluorescent tubes, because it is cheaper and lighter than acrylic. Polystyrene is also used for handles and for partitions.

A very important building application of polystyrene is the expanded foam which is made from its beads. For this purpose, a low-boiling-point hydrocarbon, such as pentane, is introduced into the polystyrene beads during the polymerization process. When the beads are heated, the polystyrene softens and the pentane vaporizes, expanding the beads to about fifty times their original volume. The beads are allowed to mature in warm air, so that the air diffuses into the beads. The beads are then reheated and either molded or extruded. Under the influence of heat, the beads expand further until they are fused together into a solid mass of *expanded lightweight polystyrene.* For use as insulation, its specific gravity is normally 0.018.

High-impact polystyrene, abbreviated *HIPS,* is produced by dissolving butadiene rubber $[CH_2:CH \cdot CH:CH_2]$ in the styrene monomer. The material is similar to normal polystyrene, but it has better shock resistance.

Styrene-acrylonitrile copolymer, abbreviated *SAN,* is produced by polymerizing two monomers—styrene $[CH_2:CH \cdot C_6H_5]$ and acrylonitrile $[CH_2:CH \cdot CN]$—together. *Acrylonitrile butadiene styrene,* abbreviated *ABS,* is an alloy of SAN copolymer and of the polymer of butadiene rubber $[CH_2:CH \cdot CH:CH_2]$. Both materials are similar to polystyrene, but stronger, tougher, and more shock-resistant. Their main use in buildings is for sliding-door and window tracks, for weather seals, for concrete forms, and for drain, waste and vent pipes.

Cellulose plastics have been in use for more than a hundred years, celluloid having been first produced in 1870 (see Sec. 18.2). Celluloid is still made, but it is no longer an important material. Cellulose acetate is now the principal plastic in this group, but there are several other thermoplastics based on cellulose. These are relatively expensive materials, their main use in buildings being for fittings, such as handles, light fixtures, and toilet seats. In addition, they are used as lacquers for wood and for metals (Sec. 19.4).

The thermoplastic materials in the *polyamide* group are usually called by the trade name *Nylon* given them by the Du Pont Company in 1939; the Du Pont patents have now expired. Their structure is complex, and reference should be made to specialized texts (for example, see Ref. 18.1, pp. 435–466). Nylons are tough and abrasion-resistant and have a very low coefficient of friction. Their main use in buildings is as a fiber for carpets, for door-latch parts, and for slides and rollers.

Polyacetal—a polymer of formaldehyde [H·CHO]—is relatively expensive but has high strength, stiffness and toughness, and good resistance to wear. It can be used for many applications where metals have been considered necessary in the past. In buildings, it appears primarily in plumbing systems, for example, for faucets (taps), shower heads, and waste-line T-junctions.

Polycarbonate has a complex chemical structure, and reference should be made to a specialized text (for example, see Ref. 18.1, pp. 499–521). Being the strongest and toughest of the transparent plastics, it is therefore used for safety lights and for vandal proof lights. It is an expensive material but retains its strength at temperatures well below the freezing point and above the boiling point of water.

18.5 THERMOSETTING RESINS

Thermosetting materials are commonly called *resins*, because most can be used for the same purposes as natural resins.

The oldest thermosetting material is *phenol-formaldehyde* (or *PF*) resin, which was first produced commercially in 1910 and named *Bakelite* after its inventor, Leo Baekeland. A dark-colored material made from formaldehyde [H·CH·O] and phenol (Fig. 18.5.1), PF resin is used as an adhesive for plywood and as a binder for hardboard and for thermal insulation. With a filler (such as wood flour or glass fiber), it is used as a molding compound for making handles, toilet seats, etc. It is a low-cost material with high heat

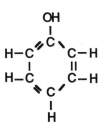

Fig. 18.5.1. The chemical structure of phenol.
A phenol is a benzene ring [see Fig. 18.1.2(a)] in which one hydrogen atom has been replaced by a hydroxyl (–OH).

resistance, dimensional stability, and good resistance to chemicals. Its disadvantage is that it is available only in dark colors.

Urea formaldehyde (or *UF*) resin is polymerized from urea (Fig. 18.5.2) and formaldehyde [H·CH·O]. Unlike PF, it has a light color. It is also a low-cost material, and its uses are similar to PF.

Melamine formaldehyde (or *MF*) resin is polymerized from melamine (Fig. 18.5.3) and formaldehyde. More expensive than UF, MF produces surfaces that are colorless and very hard, with excellent scratch and heat resistance. It is the principal material for decorative laminates (Sec. 18.3).

The *polyester resins* are a diverse group of materials that have in common an ester (–COO–) link, which enhances the flexibility of the polymer chains. They are also known as *alkyd resins*, a name derived from the combination of alcohol and acid.

The material commonly called *fiberglass* or *GRP* (glass-reinforced plastic) is, in fact, polyester sheet reinforced with glass fibers, which may take the form of a woven mat or of random short fibers (Fig. 18.5.4). GRP is a particularly useful material where translucent roof sheet is required for admitting natural light, but the polyester deteriorates slowly on exposure to the weather.

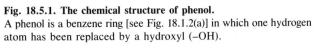

Fig. 18.5.2. Chemical structure of urea.

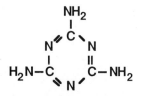

Fig. 18.5.3. Chemical structure of melamine.

Fig. 18.5.4. Sabemo Centre, North Sydney. The walls of the building are of reinforced concrete, site-cast with fiberglass formwork to give a smooth finish to the concrete. The dome, assembled from fiberglass segments, has a polyurethane infill. (*Courtesy of Sabemo Pty, North Sydney.*)

Fig. 18.5.6. Rigid polyurethane cornice, imitating eighteenth-century gypsum-plaster moldings.
The moldings, made in Belgium, are much lighter than those of plaster and easily attached to ceilings and walls. (*Courtesy of Scrimshaw Pty., Adelaide SA.*)

Polyester is also used for fluorescent light fittings (luminaires), for molds, for ducts and pipes, and for partitions. It is used as a surface coating and as a vehicle in paints (Sec. 19.1). The textile fibers *Terylene, Mylar,* and *Dacron* are extruded from polyester.

The materials in the *polyurethane* group contain a urethane link (Fig. 18.5.5 and 18.5.6). About half the world's production of polyurethane is used for flexible foam; another quarter, for rigid foam. The remainder is used for coatings, sealants, and adhesives.

Polyurethane flexible foam is used mainly in the clothing and furnishing industries; the rigid foam, mainly in buildings. It can be fabricated in slabs, formed in place in a wall cavity, or applied with a spray gun in a number of layers, each approximately 6 mm (¼ in.) thick. The methods used for foaming depend on the method used for placing the foam; all, however, introduce a volatile liquid that is vaporized during the chemical process. The rigidity of the foam depends on the number of cross links between the chains [Fig. 18.1.5(b)].

The *epoxy resins* ordinarily contain an epoxy group (Fig. 18.5.7) *at the end* of each polymer chain. They are used as adhesives for a variety of purposes, including the fixing of ceramic and resilient floor tiles, the repair of damaged concrete, and for coatings. The two components of epoxy resin must be mixed together immediately before it is used (Sec. 19.6).

The *silicones* differ from all other plastics because they are built around long chains of silicon and oxygen atoms rather than long chains of carbon atoms. In buildings, silicones are used mainly as sealants (Secs. 19.8 to 19.10) and as water repellents (Sec. 18.7).

18.6 CHOICE OF PLASTICS

Although plastics are *manufactured* in large chemical plants, they can be *fabricated* in small factories. It is therefore possible for the designer of a large building to have its plastic components made to his specification; for a small building, it is necessary to use components from stock. Since there are numerous materials in most of the groups listed, the range of choice is cor-

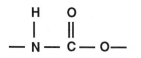

Fig. 18.5.5 Chemical structure of the urethane link.

Fig. 18.5.7. Chemical structure of the epoxy group.

respondingly large. Price constitutes a major consideration, the more expensive materials being used only for special applications.

The specific gravity of plastics varies roughly over the same range as that of the various species of timber; since plastic components are usually thinner than timber ones, however, they are also lighter. When plastics replace metals or clay products, there is a great saving in weight.

Since the strength of plastics varies over a wide range—from 10 to 1000 MPa (1.5 to 150 ksi)—it should be possible to find a material strong enough for any given purpose.

Many plastics have excellent resistance to tearing, which is generally superior to that of timber or metals of the same tensile strength. Most of them have a low modulus of elasticity—as low as 100 MPa (15 ksi) and rarely exceeding 15,000 MPa (2000 ksi). Since plastic components are often thin, excessive elastic deflection can be a problem (see Sec. 3.1). Furthermore, most thermoplastic materials have a high rate of creep, and continuing creep deflection presents a further problem (see Sec. 3.2). These drawbacks limit the use of plastics as load-bearing members where deflection control is a consideration.

Plastics have a wide range of hardness and abrasion resistance, and there should be no difficulty in finding a suitable material. Few plastics deteriorate as a result of contact with water, and some are resistant to various acids and alkalies.

There is also a good range of transparent plastics. Most are scratched more easily than glass, but they have a ductility that is lacking in glass. Indeed, safety glass is glass laminated with a transparent vinyl plastic, such as vinyl butyral (see Sec. 17.4).

Many plastics are degraded by ultraviolet radiation, that is, by exposure to sunlight. It is often possible, however, to choose a material that is not susceptible to such degradation. It is also possible to coat a polymer with an ultraviolet absorber. Several chemicals can be used for this purpose (Ref. 18.1, pp. 134–137).

Some thermoplastic materials have a low softening point, well below the boiling point of water. Such materials obviously cannot be used for hot-water pipes or for waste pipes that may receive hot liquids. Plastics are being increasingly used for plumbing, but some authorities forbid their installation at present because of concerns about deterioration.

The most serious problem encountered in the use of plastics in building, however, is their capacity to burn, and the dense smoke that many of them emit. The problem is discussed in Sec. 7.5 and in Ref. 7.6. Some plastics—the silicones, PTFE, and MF laminates—have substantial fire resistance. Rigid PVC is intumescent, that is, it is converted into a swollen carbonaceous mass, which acts as an insulator and extinguishes the fire. Polyethylene, polypropylene, the acrylics, polystyrene, and the cellulose plastics are slow-burning, but all pose a fire risk if they are present in sufficiently large quantities, and they should be treated with fire retardants (see Sec. 7.6) where appropriate.

18.7 LINOLEUM AND CARPETS

Floor coverings have been discussed previously: natural stone in Sec. 12.6, magnesium oxychloride in Sec. 13.9, concrete and terrazzo in Sec. 14.11, quarry tiles in Sec. 15.9, timber in Sec. 16.10, and PVC sheet and tiles in Sec. 18.4. Although this chapter is concerned with plastics, it seems appropriate to mention here two other floor coverings, namely linoleum and carpet.

Linoleum was developed about 1860. It is made from linseed oil, which is oxidized (that is heated, not boiled), and a natural resin. Cork, wood flour, or whiting are added as fillers, and pigments are used to give the material its color. A "marble" effect is achieved by blends of two or more colors. Linoleum can be used in the form of sheets or tiles.

Carpets have been used since antiquity, and quite large carpets were originally made by hand. Since the 1830s carpets have been woven by machine. Carpets made in long rolls were sewn together to cover an entire room wall to wall. In the early 1900s, the *broadloom* process was introduced whereby carpets could be made to a width of 3.65 m (12 ft); this has since been extended to 5.48 m (18 ft.). The use of wall-to-wall carpets has increased greatly since the 1950s because of the increasing use of concrete floors.

A carpet consists of a *pile* and a backing fabric, whose threads are called the *warp* and the *weft*. The warp are the threads stretched lengthwise in the loom, and the weft, the threads that cross the warp at right angles. In traditional hand-made carpets, the pile was fixed to the warp and the weft and still is in some machine-woven carpets; these are called *tufted carpets*.

Most machine-made carpets are woven in one process. The three types are called *Axminster, Wilton,* and *Brussels* carpets; these do not identify a company or the place of origin, but a particular technique of carpet making. In a Brussels carpet, the loops of the pile are left uncut; in the other two, they are cut so as to form a "velvet" pile. In an Axminster carpet, the pile is made by weaving separate short tufts of pile yarn with the backing threads; the other two types are made by looping the pile yarn over rods, which are then withdrawn.

The traditional carpets were made of wool or other animal hair, and in China also from silk. The best carpet wool is coarse wool, shorn from unimproved breeds of sheep. Since World War II, cotton, nylon, polypropylene, acrylic yarn, viscose rayon, and, to a lesser extent, polyester yarn have also been used. Cotton and rayon produce cheaper carpets of inferior durability. The synthetic materials were considered in Sec. 18.4, except for *viscose rayon*, which is a cellulose fiber made from purified woodpulp.

The natural and synthetic fibers can be used singly, or they can be mixed. The *resilience* of the pile (that is, the recovery of its original thickness after being walked on) is better for wool and other animal hair than for synthetic fibers, and it is better for nylon and acrylics than for polypropylene and rayon. The cost of a carpet and its quality depend largely on the weight of the pile. This is partly determined by the density of the pile—that is, the number of tufts per square meter—and partly by its thickness—that is, the height of the pile above the backing.

Since wool and animal hair scorch and burn slowly, they are more resistant to fire than synthetic fibers (which melt as they burn) and cotton. Acryclics are slightly more flammable, and rayon significantly more flammable, than nylon and polypropylene. Scorch marks on wool are easier to remove than melted material from synthetic carpets.

The durability of nylon and polypropylene under normal wear is superior to that of wool and acrylics, and much superior to that of rayon and cotton.

Carpets can be treated to improve their performance. Wool carpets are usually mothproofed. The spread of fire can be reduced by the use of flame retardants (see Sec. 7.6). Staining and dirt absorption can be reduced by treating the carpet with a water repellent such as silicone.

Static electricity may accumulate in nylon carpets when the humidity falls below 65 percent, and in wool carpets when it falls below 20 percent. This can pose a particular problem in areas where computers or elec-trical instruments are used. The most effective method of static control is the use of a special carpet with a pile containing some stainless-steel threads.

Wall-to-wall carpet is normally laid on an underlay of jute, hair, or foam rubber to improve both the resilience and the insulating qualities of the carpet.

Carpet is a good absorber of airborne sound and one of the best absorbers of impact noise. It is also a good thermal insulator. On the other hand, its properties as a thermal insulator prevent the absorption of solar energy by the material of the floor structure it covers, say concrete, and thus limit its use in buildings designed for the passive exploitation of solar energy.

REFERENCES

18.1. J. A. Brydson: *Plastics Materials*. 4th edn. Butterworths, London, 1982. 800 pp.
18.2. Irving Skeist (Ed.): *Plastics in Building*. Reinhold, New York, 1966. 466 pp.

SUGGESTIONS FOR FURTHER READING

E. G. Couzens and V. E. Yarsley: *Plastics*. Penguin Books, Harmondsworth (England), 1968. 386 pp.

Lionel K. Arnold: *Introduction to Plastics*. Iowa State University Press, Ames, 1968. 212 pp.

R. Reboul and R. G. Bruce Mitchell: *Plastics in the Building Industry*. Newnes, London, 1968. 226 pp.

The Engineering Equipment Users' Association: *The Use of Plastics Materials in Building*. Constable, London, 1973. 163 pp.

L. Holloway (Ed.): *The Use of Plastics for Load Bearing and Infill Walls*. Surrey University Press, Guildford (England), 1975. 218 pp.

S. C. A. Paraskevopoulos (Ed.): *Architectural Research on Structural Potential for Foam Plastics for Housing in Underdeveloped Areas*. University of Michigan, Ann Arbor, 1966. 282 pp.

M. Lewin *et. al.* (Ed.): *Flame Retardant Polymeric Materials*, Vol. 2. Plenum Press, New York, 1978. 333 pp.

J. L. Moilliet (Ed.): *Waterproofing and Water-Repellency*. Elsevier, Amsterdam, 1963. 502 pp.

19

Paints, Adhesives, and Sealants

Paints have been used since antiquity. but there has been a dramatic improvement during the last hundred years in the range and quality of the pigments employed and of the vehicles that bind them as a result of the discovery of new synthetic materials. Paints are used today as much for the protection of materials from deterioration as for appearance or decoration.

Stains, varnishes, lacquers, clear coatings, and *wallpapers* are also briefly discussed in this chapter.

Glues and *adhesives* are used in building not merely for joining two pieces of material, and for fixing sheet materials to their base, but also for the production of completely new materials, such as plywood, particle board, and polymer concrete.

Sealants and *gaskets* have acquired particular importance since the development of dry construction for curtain walls.

Asphalts (bitumens) remain the principal materials for waterproofing basements, but synthetic rubbers are now used to an increasing extent for waterproofing flat roofs.

19.1 THE CLASSIFICATION OF PAINTS AND PAINT VEHICLES

Paintings covering large areas are found in Egyptian tombs from about 2600 B.C. (Fig. 19.1.1). By that time, craftsmen had discovered vehicles for binding their pigments so that they would not rub off. These consisted of plant resins, such as the water-soluble gum from the acacia tree, and animal products, such as raw egg or milk. We now call paintings made with water-soluble vehicles *distemper* or *tempera* paintings, from the Latin word *temperare* (to mix in the right proportions).

About 1700 B.C., a technique of painting was developed by the Minoan civilization in Crete and several other Aegean islands that is now called *fresco* painting.

The wall to be painted is first plastered with lime plaster (see Sec. 13.1), and the desired pigments, mixed with lime water, are then painted directly on the wet plaster. The carbon dioxide in the air reacts with the lime to form calcium carbonate, and the colors are thus fixed, that is, rendered insoluble in water. It is, however, necessary to complete the painting while the lime plaster is wet, and this restriction imposes a severe timetable on the painter.

Fresco painting was practiced by the Etruscans and the ancient Romans, and it was independently discovered in India and in China. Many of the finest European wall paintings between the thirteenth and the seventeenth centuries were done in fresco. The quality of these late Medieval and Renaissance paintings is, however, due to the skill of the painters, not to the fresco technique.

Linseed oil was already in use in ancient Roman times for varnishes. From the fourteenth century on, it began to be employed as a vehicle for painting on walls, and it gradually superseded fresco painting.

By the eighteenth century, the two principal types of vehicle were thus water and water-soluble glues—used in limewashes and distempers—and linseed oil—used in oil paints. The water-based paints were increasingly employed on building exteriors as cheaper plastered brickwork replaced natural stone and was painted to look like it. In interiors, lath-and-plaster began to be used extensively, and paint was needed for its decoration. The range of pigments grew gradually, with a dramatic increase in the nineteenth century when many synthetic pigments were developed (Sec. 19.2).

Since the 1930s, *synthetic polymers* have been used as paint vehicles, both *as an alternative to oil or in conjunction with oil,* in paints classified as *enamel* (very high-gloss) *paints, high-gloss paints, semi-gloss*

Fig. 19.1.1. Wall painting from the Mortuary Temple of Queen Hatshepsut.
The painting in this temple, built near Karnak, Egypt, in the fifteenth century B.C., displays five colors based on water-bound mineral pigments.

paints, and *flat paints.* The difference between the various degrees of gloss is due to the *pigment/volume concentration,* which is 15 to 30 percent for enamel paints, 30 to 45 percent for high-gloss paints, 40 to 55 percent for semi-gloss paints, and 50 to 65 percent for flat paints. The vehicle in any of these paints could be a straight drying oil (*oil paint*), a mixture of oil and a synthetic resin (*oleoresinous paint*), or a synthetic resin only (*resin paint*). The most common drying oil is still linseed oil, but others—such as fish oil, tung oil, and dehydrated castor oil—are also used extensively. The most common synthetic resins in gloss paints are the *alkyd resins,* which belong to the polyester group, and the *phenolic resins* (both discussed in Sec. 18.5).

The oil, synthetic resin, or mixture of both forms a *vehicle* in which the *pigment* particles are dispersed: These give the paint color, opacity, and, for some applications, increased durability. The vehicle must adhere to the *substrate,* that is, the surface of the wood, metal, concrete, etc. To do so, it must be applied as a liquid that wets the substrate. Wetting agents may have to be added to paint to improve its *wetting ability,* but this may still not suffice for all surfaces. The lower the wetting ability, the more thoroughly must the substrate be cleaned and smoothed to ensure adhesion of the paint film.

The paint received from the paint factory should contain an adequate quantity of volatile constituents for it to be sufficiently fluid for application to the substrate. Paint that has been stored for some time may require a *thinner,* usually mineral turpentine or white spirit (a petroleum distillate). The same material can be used to clean the brushes or rollers used to apply the paint.

On drying the liquid oil, oleoresinous or resin paint is converted to a paint film (containing the pigment particles), which should adhere firmly to the substrate. This is a chemical process, initiated by atmospheric oxygen, that results in cross-linkages of the polymer chains and therefore in film formation. Plasticizers are added to some paint vehicles to impart the desired degree of flexibility to the dried paint film.

In 1949, *water-based paints using synthetic polymers* were introduced under the name plastic paints, latex paints, or *emulsion paints.* The most common vehicles for these paints are polyvinyl acetate (PVA) and the acrylics (see Sec. 18.4).

In emulsion paints, the formation of the paint film results from coalescence of the paint particles when they are brought into close contact when the water evaporates. As the last part of the water is vaporized, capillary forces deform the long-chain polymers to fill the voids left by the water so that fusion takes place and a continuous film formed.

Water-based emulsion paints can be thinned with water, and the brushes or rollers can be cleaned with water. They are consequently much easier to use—a particular advantage when the painting is done by a home-owner who is not a skilled painter.

Most emulsion paints give a flat or matte finish, but gloss and semi-gloss finishes are obtainable.

Emulsion paints have largely replaced flat oil paints, as well as the traditional water-based paints. Limewashes and distempers are, however, still useful for gardens, for agricultural buildings, and in developing countries. Cement paints also remain in use for concrete surfaces (Sec. 14.11).

Paints for swimming pools are briefly discussed in Sec. 19.3, and bituminous paints in Sec. 19.10.

19.2 PIGMENTS

We have little information on the pigments used in Ancient Greece, but it seems likely that the white marble that remains of the Greek temples was painted when the buildings were erected and that the paint has disappeared through weathering. The pigments used in Ancient Egypt and Rome were briefly discussed in Sec. 1.3.

The same pigments were still used in the Middle Ages and the Renaissance. Some were cheap—for example, the yellow and brown pigments ochre, sienna, and umber, made from readily available iron and manganese oxide minerals. Others, made from scarce materials, were very expensive. Ultramarine (*azzuro oltremarino*, blue from beyond the sea), a deep blue highly esteemed in the late Middle Ages and the Renaissance, cost more than its weight in gold, because it was made from the semiprecious stone lapis lazuli, which at that time was found only in present-day Afghanistan. In the 1820s ultramarine was analyzed and found to be a complex aluminosilicate $[3Na_2O_3 \cdot 3Al_2O_3 \cdot 6SiO_2 \cdot 2NaS]$. It is now manufactured quite cheaply by heating a mixture of china clay, soda, sulfur and coal. Many pigments that occur naturally are now produced synthetically because a better control over the color can be obtained that way.

The two most common measurement systems for *color* are the Munsell Color Solid (Ref. 19.1) and the CIE Chromaticity Chart (Ref. 19.2), as shown in Figs. 19.2.1 and 19.2.2. Color matching is usually accomplished by comparing two color samples, and this is a sufficiently accurate method for most purposes.

Color as seen by the eye, however, depends on the illuminant; precise color matching must therefore be done with a colorimeter or a spectrophotometer. A *colorimeter* is a photometer equipped with three or four selected color filters. A *spectrophotometer* provides a curve of luminous reflectance of the samples across the complete color spectrum.

When selecting a paint of a particular color, it is important to know its *opacity* or *hiding power*. This is the combined effect of the light-absorbing powers of the pigment and the vehicle of the paint. A thin layer of an opaque paint may have the same hiding

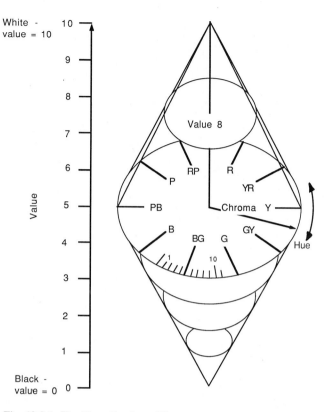

Fig. 19.2.1. The Munsell color solid.
A. H. Munsell arranged colors according to *hue, value,* and *chroma*. The *hue scale* consists of the basic colors red [R], yellow [Y], green [G], blue [B], and purple [P], and five intermediate colors identified by combinations of these letters. The *value scale*, which correlates with the degree of lightness to which the color is perceived to belong, ranges from 0/ for ideal black to 10/ for ideal white. The *chroma scale*, which correlates the saturation of the color, ranges from /1 in arbitrary steps to express the departure from the equivalent grey to the saturation desired. The *power scale* is the composite of Munsell value and chroma; thus 4/14 means a color slightly darker than the middle value between black and white, and 14 steps from the equivalent grey, that is, highly saturated. The interrelations of this classification are illustrated by the Munsell color solid, but it is easier to use the *Munsell Book of Color* (Ref. 19.1), in which each color is illustrated by a color sample.

power as a thick layer of a more transparent paint. The hiding power can therefore be measured in terms of the weight of paint needed to obliterate completely a standard board of alternating black and white squares.

The hiding power of *white pigments* poses a particular problem. The most stable opaque white pigment is titanium dioxide $[TiO_2]$, a modern nontoxic material made from the mineral ilmenite. Other opaque whites are zinc oxide [ZnO] and antimony oxide $[Sb_2O_3]$, the latter of which has fire-retardant properties. White lead $[2PbCO_3 \cdot Pb(OH)_2]$, a traditional opaque pigment, is unfortunately posionous.

Several other traditional white pigments lack the necessary opacity and are today considered as *extenders* rather than as pigments. These are china clay, or kaolin $[Al_2O_3 \cdot 2SiO_2 \cdot 2H_2O]$; whiting, or chalk $[CaCO_3]$; talc,

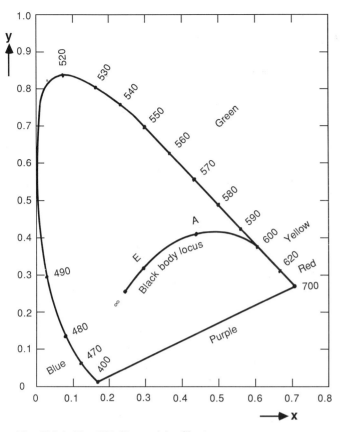

Fig. 19.2.2. The CIE Chromaticity Chart.
The chart produced by the International Commission for Illumination (CIE) uses two chromatic variables, x and y, to specify the color according to its wavelength in nanometers (nm). A third variable is needed to specify its luminous reflectance.

or French chalk [$H_2Mg_3(SiO_3)_4$]; and barytes, or *blanc fixe* [$BaSO_4$].

Bentonite, a very fine clay, is used as a thickener in emulsion paints. Powdered mica (which consists of hydrous alumino-silicates; see Sec. 12.3) forms tiny flat plates that align themselves parallel to the surface. This property, known as *leafing*, improves the moisture resistance and helps to seal porous surfaces in primer coats.

Most *black pigments* are made from carbon black, which is produced by the incomplete combustion of vegetable or animal matter, or of mineral hydrocarbons. In industrialized countries, carbon black is now usually made by burning natural gas or petroleum. Black iron oxide [Fe_3O_4] is another traditional pigment.

Red iron oxide [Fe_2O_3] is a traditional *red pigment*, one that can be made in a range of reddish colors. Another red pigment (cadmium red) is produced by blending cadmium sulfide [CdS] with cadmium selenide [$CdSe$]; the ratio of the two components determines the shade of red.

Red lead [$PbO_2 \cdot 2PbO$] has rarely been used as a pigment, but it is an excellent rust inhibitor in primer coats for structural steel. Because it is poisonous, it

has been largely replaced in building construction by the yellow pigment zinc tetroxychromate [$ZnCrO_4 \cdot 4Zn(OH)_2$], which is now used extensively as a primer for steel and aluminum alloys. It is nontoxic and imparts good adhesion to subsequently applied coats of paint (see Sec. 19.3).

The principal *yellow pigments* are zinc chromate [$ZnCrO_4$], lead chromate [$PbCrO_4$], cadmium yellow (or cadmium sulfide) [CdS], and hydrated yellow iron oxide [$Fe_2O_3 \cdot (H_2O)_n$]. The latter is one of the traditional pigments but is now often made synthetically; the synthetic iron oxides have a wider color range, from bright yellow to dark yellow-brown.

The *blue pigment* ultramarine has already been mentioned earlier in this section; it is now a synthetic pigment. Prussian blue is ferric-ferro-cyanide [$Fe_4(Fe(CN)_6)_3$]. Another widely used blue pigment is copper phthalocyanine blue, a complex organic pigment containing a large number of benzene rings (see Fig. 18.1.2).

Copper phthalocyanine green is similar to the blue pigment, but most of the hydrogen atoms have been replaced by chlorine atoms. The two principal inorganic *green pigments* are chromium oxide [Cr_2O_3] and Brunswick green, which is a blend of lead chromate and Prussian blue, both mentioned above.

There are numerous *organic pigments* with a variety of colors, but many of these fade in sunlight and are thus unsuitable for most building applications.

The two most widely used *metallic pigments* are aluminum powder and zinc powder. Aluminum powder is employed both in decorative finishing coats and in primers for wood. Zinc powder is used mainly in primers for steel because it provides sacrificial protection to the steel (see Secs. 11.1 and 19.3).

Most of the colors produced by paint manufacturers, the ones shown in their standard color charts, are blends of standard pigments.

Paint can be mixed shortly before use from concentrated pigment and a white base. Paint that has been stored for some time usually needs to be remixed to ensure that the pigment, the vehicle, and its solvent are uniformly distributed throughout the container.

19.3 PAINT AS PROTECTION AND PAINT AS DECORATION

Most of the paint used today in buildings is applied initially to protect certain materials from chemical or biological degradation. Steel rusts unless it is painted; even galvanized steel is usually painted to improve its durability (see Sec. 10.3 and 11.1). Most species of wood require a protective coat of paint when used externally, and varnish or paint when used internally (see Sec. 16.7). The paint on the paper surface of gypsum drywall construction (see Sec. 13.2) is needed to give it better abrasion resistance, but it also hides an uninteresting color and surface texture. Cement plaster is painted mainly for decorative purposes, but some paints also serve as waterproofers. Paint provides an essential waterproof membrane in swimming pools. Materials that specifically require paint for protection ordinarily need a *primer,* or base coat of paint that adheres firmly to the material and offers the necessary protection. Some materials require a middle coat, or *undercoat,* to "hide" the color of the primer, adhere firmly to it, and provide a base for the decorative *top coat.* For other materials, two coats of paint are sufficient.

Even where paint is meant to be purely decorative, two coats are usually needed, because coats of paint should be kept as thin as possible to ensure that they dry uniformly and thus provide good adhesion and durability. As a rule, a single coat of paint does not have the necessary hiding power (see Sec. 19.2), unless the material to be painted is of a similar color.

Before a primer is painted on steel, all traces of corrosion must be removed from the metal surface. (The corrosion of *steel* was discussed in Sec. 10.3.) Removal can be accomplished in a factory by pickling the steel in hot dilute acid. It can also be done in the factory or on the building site by "blast cleaning"—with an air jet containing metal shot or nonmetallic grit—or by "flame descaling"—with a very hot flame that loosens the oxide skin, followed by scraping or wire brushing.

The traditional primer, consisting of red lead (Sec. 19.2) in a vehicle of linseed oil, is used mainly where exposure is severe, because red lead is poisonous. Many steel primers are now based on zinc. Zinc-rich primers consist of about 90-percent zinc dust in a vehicle such as chlorinated rubber; or zinc tetroxychromate or zinc chromate in an oleoresinous or synthetic resin-vehicle.

Galvanized steel does not require the same degree of protection from its primer because of the steel's prior protection by galvanizing, but it may need some. Unfortunately, many steel primers have poor adhesion to galvanized surfaces. If the latter are still new and shiny, they must be etched before a primer or undercoat can be applied. If the conditions of exposure are not going to be severe, an undercoat with an oleoresinous or synthetic resin vehicle may be applied directly to the galvanized surface, followed by a topcoat.

Nonferrous metals are painted only rarely in buildings. Zinc chromate and zinc tetroxychromate primers can be used on aluminum surfaces, should painting be required. Copper, brass, and bronze are usually chosen because of their color and metallic appearance but turn dull with the passage of time, particularly in humid climates; they are best protected by a coating of clear varnish (Sec. 19.4).

Wood requires special protection when used externally. Some hardwoods can be used without a protective coating, and these are always chosen for wooden shingles (see Sec. 4.3) and sometimes for wooden siding (weatherboards). Timber window and door frames, however, which are usually made from softwood, require a protective coat of paint when used externally, usually a primer, undercoat, and topcoat. Wood used in interiors is often treated with lacquer, varnish, or stain, but these materials do not weather as well out of doors as paint.

Since it is more easily attacked by dry rot or termites (see Sec. 16.7) when it is damp, and since ultraviolet radiation causes disintegration of the cell structure of some species, timber must be protected from water, rising damp, and radiation. Such protection can be better provided by the topcoat than by the primer. Topcoats for timber used externally, therefore, usually have a high gloss. A favored pigment for white and light-colored timber topcoats is titanium dioxide (Sec. 19.2), which is a stable, nontoxic pigment of high opacity that absorbs ultraviolet radiation.

The primer, rather than protecting the wood, protects the paint from the latter's exudations, such as the resin that continues to form at knots in the timber (Sec. 16.6). The primer also acts as a filler for any irregularities on the wooden surface.

Gypsum plaster, cement plaster or *render, concrete,* and *fiber-reinforced cement panels* do not require protection from corrosion, but these materials frequently contain water, which was added during construction or fabrication and has not completely evaporated, and they all contain free alkaline oxides or salts when they are new. These elements attack several paint vehicles and a few pigments. The alkali attack diminishes as the chemical action becomes neutralized by aging, but this takes several years.

The principal pigments whose color changes in contact with alkalies are Prussian blue, lead chromate, and Brunswick green. The paint vehicles most affected are oils and alkyds. Alkalies turn linseed oil into a kind of soap (toilet soap is made from various vegetable oils and caustic soda), although the alkali-resistant tung oil can be used.

The most suitable vehicles for alkaline surfaces are those that are highly polymerized, such as copolymer emulsions of polyvinyl acetate and acrylics. Cement paints (see Secs. 13.6 and 14.11), can be used for cement surfaces.

The inside of swimming pools is painted partly for decoration, but the paint very significantly contributes to the waterproofing of the concrete. For the latter purpose, a solvent-soluble vehicle is preferable to the water-soluble vehicles used in emulsion paints. Chlorinated rubbers and styrene-butadiene copolymers are suitable vehicles.

No particular problems are encountered in painting *gypsum wallboard* in drywall construction (see Sec. 13.2). An emulsion paint is suitable as a primer-sealer, and the same type of paint or an oil-based or alkyd-based paint can be used as a topcoat.

Fire-retardant paints, which were discussed in Sec. 7.6, must employ vehicles that do not propogate flames, that is, the paints should have an alkyd- or phenol-base instead of an oil-base. Certain pigments, such as white antimony oxide (Sec. 19.2), have fire-retardant properties. Furthermore, fire-retardant compounds can be blended with the paint; for example, brominated phenol is compatible with phenolic resins and renders them fire-retardant.

19.4 STAINS, VARNISHES, LACQUERS, AND CLEAR COATINGS

Stains are water-soluble dyes whose main use in buildings is to decorate—and, to some extent, protect—timber used internally. The dye is more readily absorbed by the soft, porous portion of the timber, particularly in softwood, than by the hard, resinous part; it therefore emphasizes the grain. Stains are available in many colors, but those most used range from light yellow to brown. Stains can be applied with water, spirit, oil, varnish, or wax as a medium.

Stains made from a number of vegetable dyes have been used since antiquity. Today, however, most stains are produced synthetically.

Varnishes have also been used since antiquity, being a product of natural resins; indeed, the original meaning of the word *resin* was the gummy material emitted by a tree or plant. Another traditional raw material for varnish is *shellac,* which is derived from the excretions of certain tropical insects. Varnishes can also be made from various synthetic resins, such as phenolic and alkyd resins. Synthetic resins are now used for varnishes more than natural resins.

Resin can be dissolved in oil or in spirit. An *oil varnish* is made by cooking the drying oil and the resin together until partial polymerization occurs, and then adding a drier and a solvent to the cooled ingredients. If the proportion of oil to resin is high, the varnish dries slowly and the coating has good elasticity; if more resin is used, the varnish dries faster, and the film is not only harder and less elastic, but has poorer exterior durability. Varnishes normally produce a glossy finish, but an eggshell or flat finish can be obtained from a varnish with a high resin content by adding a suitable wax. The formation of the film of an oil varnish is mainly due to the oxidation of the oil.

Resin can also be dissolved in spirit, and the film of *spirit varnish* is formed mainly by the evaporation of the spirit.

Lacquers are synthetic materials that form a solid film by evaporation of volatile solvents. The term was used in the nineteenth century mainly for Chinese and Japanese varnish of superior quality, but it is now employed for quite different materials. The most widely used synthetic lacquers are solutions of nitrocellulose, but there are also vinyl lacquers, acrylic lacquers, polyurethane lacquers, and others. The term "lacquer" usually implies a material that dries rapidly by evaporation. It can easily be applied, usually by spraying, and since the dried film is soluble in the original solvent, it can easily be repaired.

Highly abrasion-resistant *clear coatings* of thermosetting resins, such as *polyurethane* and *epoxy resins,* are used as sealers for wooden floors (see Sec. 18.5).

This section has so far dealt entirely with clear coatings for timber, but they are also useful for *nonferrous metals,* notably copper and its alloys, bronze and brass. Small articles can be kept bright by the use of brass polish, but this can be very laborious, and sometimes impracticable for metal fittings in buildings. A transparent varnish can maintain the bright metallic appearance for many years. Polyurethane or alkyd varnishes are suitable for this purpose.

19.5 WALLPAPER

Wallpaper has been used in Europe since the sixteenth century, but in China it goes back to the third century, and Chinese designs exercised considerable influence on West-European designs in the eighteenth century. Wallpapers were popular in the nineteenth and early twentieth century, but their use has declined as a result of the advances in paint technology, particularly the development of emulsion paints that have made it easy for untrained homeowners to do their own painting. Paperhanging requires the exercise of some skill.

The cheapest wallpapers have a printed pattern on a background that is the natural color of the paper itself. The cost increases progressively if the entire paper is printed, if fine engraving is used, if the surface is varnished, and if the pattern is embossed.

Flock papers have a surface of finely divided cotton, wool, or silk fiber. *Fabric papers* are also made, with various surfaces from grass cloth to silk.

Wallpapers can be printed with photographic reproductions of wood grain, but extremely thin wood veneers mounted on paper are also obtainable at much higher cost.

Wallpaper is glued, or "hung," to walls with a paste made from flour or some other starch. Wallpaper does not adhere well to walls that have been painted with distemper, because this does not itself adhere firmly to a wall; thus, the distemper must be scrubbed before papering. Wallpaper also does not adhere well to walls painted with high-gloss paint; before papering, therefore,

Fig. 19.5.1. Nursery wall paper, screenprinted in 1957 by Wallpaper Manufacturers Ltd. in England. (*Courtesy of the Victoria and Albert Museum; see Ref. 19.3, p. 36.*)

the gloss must be "killed" with a solution of caustic soda or rubbed with abrasive paper to provide a key for the paste.

Wallpapers can provide an elaborate pattern on a wall at a small fraction of the cost of actually painting that pattern. They have been used in recent years particularly for feature walls in living rooms and to tell a story in rooms used by children (Fig. 19.5.1).

19.6 GLUES AND ADHESIVES

Animal glues and *casein,* derived from milk, were already used by the Ancient Egyptians for making the furniture that has been found in their tombs. Similar glues are still used today for making furniture.

Vegetable glues include the starches—used for hanging wallpaper (Sec. 19.5)—and cements made from natural rubber—used for laying linoleum and fixing floor tiles, wall tiles, and acoustical material to ceilings. *Natural asphalts* (bitumens) are used extensively for joining sheets of bituminous roofing felt and for joining the felt to vent stacks and flashings (Sec. 19.10).

Synthetic rubbers and *asphalts* (bitumens) can be used for the same purpose as natural rubbers and asphalts (bitumens).

Until the 1930s, glues and adhesives were almost exclusively produced from natural materials. Since then, a variety of synthetic adhesives have been discovered, and new building materials have been developed in consequence.

Synthetic glues usually have greater strength and better durability than natural glues. For example, plywood was first produced in the late nineteenth century, but it became an important building material only when durable, high-strength synthetic resins became available. The reconstitution of wood chips into particle board (see Secs. 16.12 and 18.3) would not have been possible without synthetic resins. Wood products are today one of the biggest users of adhesives in the building industry.

The cheapest suitable, and now predominant, adhesive for particle board is *urea formaldehyde,* which contains up to 10 percent of adhesive, the remainder being wood particles. Plywood contains less than 4 percent by weight of adhesive, but the strength of the glue is more critical, and the more durable (and more expensive) *phenol formaldehyde* or *resorcinol formaldehyde* is usually preferred. For exterior use, the even more expensive *melamine formaldehyde* may be required. Similar considerations apply to laminated timber beams and to finger joints.

Although most of the plastics considered in Secs. 18.4 and 18.5 can be utilized as adhesives, the most important and versatile high-strength adhesives are the *epoxy resins.* These are usually supplied in two parts—the resin and the catalyst—which are mixed together immediately before use. The resin hardens at room temperature by a chemical action called *curing.* Unlike most other adhesives, it neither depends for its strength on the cooling and solidification of a component, nor on the evaporation of a solvent, both of which produce strains in an adhesive. Nor is it necessary to apply a high contact pressure during curing. Epoxy resins are, however, expensive, and their high strength is needed in buildings for only a few specialized applications.

One of these is the repair of damaged concrete. Epoxy resin adheres well to portland cement concrete and can therefore be used for the repair of small damaged sections. This is preferable to repair with portland cement concrete, because new portland cement concrete does not always adhere to the old and because wet concrete may cause damage to other parts of the building. Epoxy resin can also be used to repair stone or brick masonry. It serves as the adhesive in reconstituted stone or brick, which is made from epoxy resin and stone or brick dust. It is often impossible to distinguish the reconstituted stone from natural stone that has recently been cleaned (see Sec. 12.5).

For all adhesives, the glue line should be as thin as possible, since the strength of a properly bonded joint, both in shear and in tension, is invariably much higher than the strength of the adhesive by itself. In this respect, adhesive joints differ from joints made with portland cement mortar, where a substantial joint thickness is acceptable, and indeed desirable.

The adhesive action of glues is due to physical and chemical processes that vary between different adhesives. In some materials, adhesion results merely from the cooling of the glue or the evaporation of its solvent, whereas in others it is developed by a chemical action that usually involves polymerization.

All adhesives must wet both surfaces to be glued together to perform satisfactorily; this is a prime requirement. It particularly limits the adhesives that can be used for metals. To ensure proper wetting, some surfaces must be cleaned or degreased before the adhesive is applied. Most building materials can be glued with any one of several different adhesives, although manufacturers often prescribe and supply a specific adhesive.

Although this section is limited to materials normally called glues and adhesives (lime, gypsum, and portland cement are considered in Chap. 13; the welding, brazing, and soldering of metals in Sec. 10.11; and the welding of plastics in Sec. 18.3), it must be noted that a number of materials can be joined satisfactorily by quite disparate methods. For example, ceramic tiles and thin stone slabs can be either laid on a relatively thick bed of (grey or white) portland cement mortar or fixed with a thin layer of adhesive. Nonferrous metal sheets can be joined either by soldering or brazing or by adhesives. Several thermoplastic materials can be welded—that is, joined through the application of heat and pressure, but without adhesive—or joined with adhesive, usually at room temperature.

19.7 POLYMER CONCRETE AND POLYMER MODIFIED CONCRETE

Polymer concrete is concrete in which portland cement is replaced by a polymer. It consequently has a lower water absorption, better resistance to cycles of freezing and thawing as well as to various chemicals, and generally higher strength. Polyesters and acrylics are the most commonly used resins, but the more expensive epoxy concrete exhibits the best adhesion to most other building materials.

The plastic material is mixed with the aggregate as a monomer (Sec. 18.1) or as partial polymer, together with a "hardener" (which is a cross-linking agent) and a catalyst to provide full polymerization. *Polymer concrete* is often reinforced with metal fibers, glass fibers, or glass-fiber mats. *Polymer-cement concrete* is a similar material in which the plastic material replaces only part of the portland cement.

Polymer-impregnated concrete is hardened portland-cement concrete that, using pressure or a vacuum, has been impregnated with monomers in the form of a gas or a low-viscosity liquid (which may be mixed with a catalyst). The monomers are polymerized by the catalyst, by heat, or by ultraviolet radiation. As a rule, only a surface layer of the concrete is impregnated, but this forms a continuous layer free from any voids. At present, the acrylics are the most commonly employed monomers, but others can be used.

19.8 SEALANTS

Sealants are used to seal joints, partly to improve appearance, but mainly to exclude rainwater and air currents. The term ordinarily excludes materials, such as portland cement, that are used in "wet" construction (see Chap. 13).

Most of the joints in brick and concrete construction are made "wet" with mortar or concrete, but flexible sealants are needed (Fig. 19.8.1) in the control joints for temperature and moisture movement (see Sec. 3.6 and Fig. 3.6.1). In the interior of the building, soft sealing compounds are needed in the joints between floor slabs and the walls below because of the movement occurring between them (see Sec. 3.2 and Fig. 3.2.5).

The job of sealants in curtain walls of "dry" construction is much more demanding. Not only are they used to make all the joints, (Fig. 19.8.2), but these must prevent the entry of rainwater driven by wind (see Sec. 4.1), which may hit the wall at a large variety of angles, even in an upward direction. Since curtain-wall buildings are heated or air-conditioned, the joints must also prevent leakage of air, which would greatly increase the expenditure of energy for heating and

Fig. 19.8.1. Temporary strip of polyethylene foam used in control joint in concrete structure.
Strip is removed after the concrete has been cured, leaving a space for laying the sealant. (*Courtesy of Selleys Industrial Div., Revesby, NSW 2122, Australia.*)

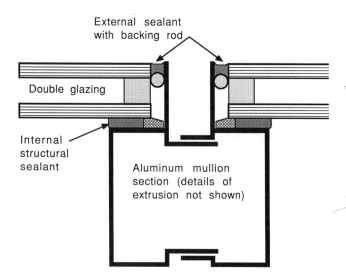

External sealant with backing rod

Double glazing

Internal structural sealant

Aluminum mullion section (details of extrusion not shown)

Fig. 19.8.2. Dry joint in curtain wall, made with a sealant.

cooling. The design of suitable joints is discussed in Sec. 4.7.

Sealants can be divided into caulking compounds, (sometimes called *mastics*)—which are soft, dough-like materials that adhere to the surfaces with which they are in contact—and elastomeric compounds—which are applied to the joint as pastes but turn into rubbery materials. Preformed sealants, such as gaskets and tapes, are discussed in Sec. 19.9.

Prior to 1950, all *caulking compounds* were made with a base of linseed oil. Window putty, for example, consists of approximately 12 percent of linseed oil and 88 percent of whiting (which is powdered chalk, $CaCO_3$). In traditional construction, it is applied with a putty knife and left to harden in contact with air. Its surface must be protected with a coat of paint. Caulking compounds of greater plasticity can be produced by the addition of castor oil or soybean oil. These can be applied with a knife or with a caulking gun under pressure, which requires less labor.

Oil-based caulking materials have been largely replaced by synthetic materials. Most latex caulking compounds have a PVA-base (see Sec. 18.4), which is also used in emulsion paints. Consequently, tools and hands can be cleaned with water, and spills can be removed with a damp cloth. Latex caulks, which are supplied in cartridges for application with a caulking gun, are used mostly for smaller buildings, particularly for window glazing, for door and window perimeters, for sealing around air-conditioners, and for sealing cracks in concrete. The material adheres well to concrete, brick, wood, and aluminum.

The *elastomeric sealants* are used mainly for sealing the curtain walls of large buildings; they can also be used for control joints in concrete, brick, and steel. Their adhesion characteristics vary; some require that adjacent materials be cleaned with a solvent and/or

painted with a primer, whereas others can be applied directly.

Some sealants are used with a filler. *Fillers* reduce the cost of the sealant and usually increase its strength because they act as reinforcement; they may also color the sealant. Suitable fillers are powdered chalk, mineral fibers, and carbon black (or some other pigment).

All polymers used as curtain-wall sealers must have good resistance to ultraviolet radiation.

Acrylic and butyl sealants "cure" (that is, change from a dough-like material to a rubbery one) by evaporation of their solvents. They are normally applied by extrusion from a cartridge with a caulking gun. Acrylic polymer is thermoplastic (see Sec. 18.4); its cartridge must be heated to about 50°C (120°F) before use. Butyl sealant has a base of synthetic rubber. Both materials remain tacky for a day or two after application, and complete curing of the sealant bead takes a few weeks.

Polysulfide, polyurethane, and silicone sealants cure by chemical action, that is, they are converted from a dough-like material to a rubbery one. Polysulfide polymer, for example, is a thick liquid that is converted gradually into a rubbery solid by the addition of lead dioxide. The two materials, supplied separately, are mixed immediately before use (the sealant must be applied within a few hours after mixing). Polysulfide sealant is therefore a two-component sealant, one with a filler and a plasticizer.

Silicone sealant is a one-component sealant. It is soft in an unopened cartridge. If a cartridge is only partly used, a plug of cured sealant forms in the opening and effectively closes it. This plug of cured material must be removed and discarded before the cartridge can be used further. Silicone sealant is used with a filler.

Polyurethane sealant, usually called urethane sealant, is also a one-compound material. It can be used by itself or combined with acrylic or epoxy resin. It may be used with or without a filler and plasticizer.

19.9 GASKETS AND TAPES

Preformed gaskets can be made from neoprene, butyl, styrene-butadiene, vinyl, silicone, or other rubber. The gasket is usually fixed without an adhesive, and the seal is produced by the compression of the gasket. To achieve a perfect seal, solid gaskets are compressed by as much as 50 percent during installation. One method of producing this compression is the use of a zip-in strip (Fig. 19.9.1). An alternative method is the use of an inflatable tubular gasket. This is particularly suitable for windows in curtain walls that are designed to be opened for cleaning only.

There are two types of *sealing tapes*. One consists of ribbons of sealing compound, supplied as rolls with

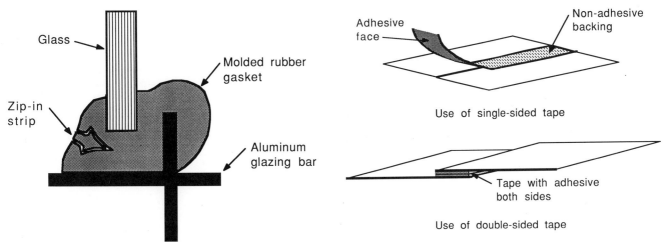

Use of single-sided tape

Use of double-sided tape

Fig. 19.9.3. Joint made with pressure-sensitive adhesive tape.

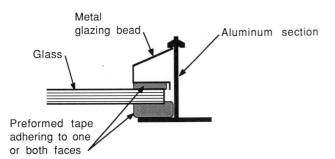

Fig. 19.9.1. Rubber gasket sealed by pressure from a zip-in strip.

a paper backing that is peeled off during installation. These tapes avoid the need for a caulking gun and the subsequent clean-up, but the joint must be designed so that the ribbon can be inserted. The ribbons are made from various polymers, such as polybutene and butyl rubber, and most of them incorporate a filler. Depending on the polymer and its method of curing, the tapes are either resilient—that is, like rubber—or nonresilient, that is, soft like a caulking compound. The *resilient tapes,* used mainly for window glazing (Fig. 19.9.2), are sometimes coated with a tacky rubber to provide some adhesion for easier installation. The *nonresilient tapes* are used mainly for sealing joints between walls and floors or ceilings, for sealing joints between external doors and windows and the surrounding walls, and for sealing around air conditioner units. They can also be used for glazing, but their softness requires a protective cover, which can be supplied by a bead of a compatible sealant from a caulking gun.

The other type are the *pressure-sensitive adhesive tapes,* which consist of a backing material with an adhesive on one side. The adhesive, which is either rubber-based or resin-based, adheres to most materials when a light pressure is applied. The transparent ad-

hesive tapes widely used in shops for wrapping parcels are of this type. Depending on the intended use, the backing material may be a transparent or pigmented polymer, such as cellophane, cellulose acetate, polyester, or vinyl; paper with or without fiber reinforcement; cloth; or aluminum foil.

These tapes have temporary uses during construction, for example, as masking tapes during painting, or for fixing temporary protective sheets of polyethylene. Their permanent uses are mostly for sealing joints between dry components, for example, gypsum drywall panels, bats of insulation, and sections of heating or air-conditioning ducts (Fig. 19.9.3). They are also wrapped around sprayed insulation on hot-water pipes and heating ducts as protection for the friable insulating material.

Adhesive tape can be fixed directly off the roll, but for taping ceilings and walls, an automatic taper with a long arm is useful and avoids the need for scaffolding.

19.10 WATERPROOFING MATERIALS FOR BASEMENTS AND ROOFS

The solid or semisolid hydrocarbons obtained from the distillation of petroleum or coal are usually called *asphalt* in America and *bitumen* in England (where asphalt means a mixture of bitumen and calcium carbonate). Similar naturally occurring materials have been used since antiquity where there was a local source of supply.

These materials are excellent for waterproofing and thus used extensively for basements, on-grade floors, and flat roofs (see Sec. 4.5). They can be liquified by heating and then laid to form a continuous layer that produces a waterproof membrane when it cools (see Sec. 4.9).

Other applications are bituminous paints and asphalt shingles. Bituminous paint consists of asphalt (bitumen) dissolved in a volatile solvent or suspended in water

Fig. 19.9.2. Window glazing with preformed sealing tape.

in an emulsion. It is used for waterproofing and for repairing bituminous flat roofs. Asphalt shingles (see Sec. 4.3) are made of heavy felt impregnated and coated with asphalt (bitumen).

A heavy polyethylene film, sealed at all overlaps between adjoining sheets, can be used for waterproofing below on-grade slabs, and even in basements, provided it can be protected against puncture (see Sec. 4.9). It cannot be used on roofs, however, because it is degraded by ultraviolet radiation.

In recent years, *elastomeric membranes* have been used to an increasing extent for flat roofs in place of asphalt (bitumen). They may be applied as fluids or as sheets of materials such as neoprene, butyl rubber, chlorinated polyethylene, or silicone rubber.

These materials can also be used on curved concrete roofs, such as shell structures, for which asphalts (bitumens) are unsuitable. They are less expensive, but also less durable, than copper sheet (see Sec. 11.6 and Fig. 11.6.1).

REFERENCES

19.1. *Munsell Book of Color*. Munsell Color Company, Baltimore, MD, 1983.
19.2. *IES Lighting Handbook*. Sixth Edition. Illuminating Engineering Society, New York, 1981. Reference Volume, pp. 5.4–5.8.
19.3. J. Hamilton: *Wallpaper*. H. M. Stationery Office, London, 1983. 48 pp.

SUGGESTIONS FOR FURTHER READING

A. E. Hurst: *Painting and Decorating*. Charles Griffin, London, 1963. 482 pp.
W. M. Morgan and J. R. Taylor: *Introduction to Paint Technology*. Oil and Colour Chemists' Association, London, 1976. 219 pp.
J. Boxall and J. A. von Fraunhofer: *Concise Paint Technology*. Elek, London, 1977. 214 pp.
A. G. Roberts: *Organic Coatings*. National Bureau of Standards, Building Science Series 7. U.S. Government Printing Office, Washington, 1968. 187 pp.
J. R. Panek and J. P. Cook: *Construction Sealants and Adhesives*. Wiley, New York, 1984. 348 pp.
A. Blaga and J. J. Beaudoin: Polymer Concrete. *Canadian Building Digest No. 242*. National Research Council, Ottawa, 1985. 4 pp.

20
Criteria for the Choice of Building Materials

The choice of building materials, which was very limited until the eighteenth century, has greatly increased and will continue to do so. Since any number of different materials are presently suitable for a particular building application, the designer must make a choice. Although cost is often a determining factor, particularly if the material is not to be visible, aesthetic considerations become important when a material occupies a prominent place in a building, and durability is an important aspect of aesthetics.

There are numerous sources of information on the properties of building materials, including the literature provided by manufacturers (see Sec. 20.5).

20.1 NATURAL AND MANUFACTURED MATERIALS

Natural materials, such as wood, stone, and mudbrick, are the oldest building materials. Almost as old are simple manufactured materials, such as hard-burnt bricks and iron, made by subjecting the raw materials to a high temperature. Products made by more complex processes are mostly of recent origin, and new materials are constantly being added to the list.

Fitness for the intended purpose remains the prime criterion, but cost, as remarked previously, is often a determining factor. Thus, the replacement of natural stone––the predominant material for important buildings in most countries until the eighteenth century––by brick and concrete was purely the result of their lower cost. Stone is today used mainly as a veneer where a good surface finish is required (see Sec. 12.6).

Although there is only a limited supply of some building materials, few are likely to disappear completely because the necessary raw materials are no longer available. Before that happens, an increase in price will exercise control over demand.

Lead was a common and relatively cheap material in Ancient Roman and Medieval times, and used extensively for a variety of purposes (see Sec. 11.7). Because of its increased cost, lead has since been replaced by other metals, by ceramics, and by plastics for most of its former uses, and consequently there is still an adequate supply of lead.

In the long term, a number of materials presently in common use will probably become exhausted, notably some metals and some varieties of stone, but other materials will adequately replace them. The raw materials for concrete, glass, bricks, and aluminum are available in very large quantities, although the cost may increase if less economic raw materials have to be used.

Some materials, such as wood and linseed oil, can be regenerated by suitable planting. In some countries, supplies of timber have been greatly reduced through the exploitation of virgin forests, but in others reforestation has kept pace with harvesting.

The amount of energy involved in obtaining building materials varies greatly from one to another. Very little is needed for the extraction of some natural materials. Thus, the energy required to quarry and cut marble is relatively small, but a great deal more is needed to transport it, say, from Italy to the American Middle West. Similarly, the energy required to transport Douglas fir grown in Oregon, say, to England must be added to the energy expended in felling the trees and converting them into planks.

The manufacture of bricks and cement requires an

appreciable amount of heat, usually produced by burning coal or oil. On the other hand, cement constitutes only 10 to 20 percent of concrete, and bricks are among the most durable of building materials; they rarely need replacement or repair during the life of a building, and they can sometimes be reused after a building is demolished.

Steel also requires a large amount of fossil fuel for extraction from iron ore, but it is a special case—a very strong material with an excellent strength/volume ratio. The highest energy user among the common building materials is aluminum (see Sec. 11.2).

In the late 1970s, when energy was in short supply in many countries, energy conservation in buildings was a major concern. Logically, this should encompass not merely a reduction in the use of energy required for heating and cooling buildings, but also a preference for materials and building processes that require as little energy as possible. Energy conservation is now viewed as a matter of cost, however, rather than as an ethical issue, and its effect is thus reflected in the price of materials rather than in a restraint on the employment of high-energy users. This still restricts the use of aluminum, which is the third most common element in the earth's crust, but nevertheless a relatively expensive material because of the large amount of energy required for its extraction.

The cost of labor is another major consideration in the choice of materials. Raw materials that are relatively cheap in themselves may be expensive to form. For example, the cost of the stone used in buildings today is mainly the cost of labor. Flat surfaces can be cut by methods that are much more efficient than those employed before the eighteenth century, but complex shapes still have to be cut with a mallet and chisel in a manner that does not differ greatly from that used in Ancient Egypt. By contrast, concrete can be cast into a mold without any cutting at all.

The rapid increase in the use of plastics is largely due to the ease with which they may be formed into complex shapes at low cost by mass production methods.

20.2 DURABILITY, MAINTENANCE, AND LIFE-CYCLE COSTING

Most building materials that do not require periodic maintenance show signs of becoming older. Natural stone and brick do so gracefully, and the old material may actually look better than the new; others, such as concrete and some plastics, acquire a "second-hand" look.

A few materials, however, retain their original appearance because they have a smooth surface of hard

and chemically inert glass. These include glazed tiles and terra cotta (see Sec. 15.1), porcelain enamel (see Sec. 10.8), and glass itself (see Sec. 17.1). These materials require no protection from the weather and very little cleaning if they are washed by clean rainwater.

On the other hand, most types of timber require protection if used out of doors, usually by paint (see Sec. 19.3), and paint requires periodic renewal. To make a proper comparison of cost, this periodic maintenance should be added to the initial cost to obtain the *life-cycle cost* (see Sec. 8.1).

A more expensive, but more durable, material may have a lower life-cycle cost. Public authorities and other long-term owners should make their choice of material on that basis. For a building contractor who erects houses for sale or for a private owner, however, it may make better economic sense to choose the cheaper material with the higher life-cycle cost. This keeps down the purchase price of the house, which may be the prime concern. The cost of the maintenance that needs to be done after a number of years may not fall on the original owner, moreover, since many people move frequently. Seven years is an approximate average period of ownership of one home in America, Western Europe, and Australia.

Thus the need for periodic maintenance is widely accepted if it keeps down the price of a house. Some home-owners may treat the need for repainting as an opportunity to change a color scheme, and the appearance of "newness" after painting is generally welcome.

During the eighteenth century, stone houses in London were gradually replaced by plastered and painted brick houses for economic reasons, and the custom spread to other parts of the world. Some of these houses had (and still have) a covenant that required the owner of the building to repaint it at specified (or shorter) intervals. These buildings are generally in good condition, and their appearance compares favorably with that of many stone or concrete buildings that have had no maintenance because the materials are considered durable. In fact, controlled maintenance may give better results than the use of "durable" materials.

One expects to have to repaint most timber and plaster surfaces from time to time, to renew varnish on metal and timber, and to replace broken glass occasionally. One does not expect to have to carry out costly maintenance on durable materials. Thus it is unacceptable for plated screws of ordinary steel to be used to fix nonferrous metals or stainless steel in locations where moisture is unavoidable, such as shower recesses. Contrary to an owner's expectations, the screws start rusting after a few years and have to be replaced.

20.3 TRADITION AND INNOVATION

Tradition has been a significant factor in the choice of materials, particularly for single-family houses. Buildings of stone or brick are traditional in many parts of Europe where the original forests were cut down long ago. In countries of the "New World"—such as the United States, Canada, and New Zealand—timber houses are common because of generous supplies of local timber.

The first place of settlement in Australia, Sydney Cove, lacked a supply of timber suitable for building construction, a fact that may have been largely responsible for the early development of brick manufacture. Today, most Australian single-family houses are built with a timber frame, but with a single-brick wall outside the timber frame (*brick-veneer*), so that they give the appearance of brick houses. The reasons for this compromise are probably traditional, rather than rational, even though the brick walls require less maintenance than timber siding (weatherboards) would and are more resistant to bush fires.

Once a tradition has been established, it becomes difficult to sell houses that do not conform to it, particularly to low-income earners. Traditional attitudes were at least partly responsible for the failure of a number of innovative building systems that were factory-produced in the 1940s and 1950s. Many of the system buildings were structurally and functionally sound and could have become economically competitive had they been produced in large numbers; however, they failed to find acceptance because they were too different from traditional houses.

Novelty is a desirable spur to progress, and the tendency to use new materials and new methods for existing materials is strongest in the design of commercial buildings and homes for the wealthy. This factor gradually influences the design of more traditional houses. Innovation should be based on economic and other rational grounds, however; it should not merely be motivated by the desire on the part of clients and their architects for the associated publicity.

It is possible to ascertain the strength and the thermal, acoustic and fire-resisting properties of materials from short-term laboratory tests, but determination of durability takes much longer because of the lack of reliable accelerated weathering and abrasion tests (see Sec. 8.5). Avoidable failures can occur if new materials and methods are used before adequate durability tests have been conducted. Once innovations have received favorable critical comment, they may establish themselves as a new fashion, and more buildings embodying them may be erected before reliable long-term durability tests are available. Some of the most expensive material failures have been the result of this train of events.

20.4 CONFLICTING FUNCTIONAL REQUIREMENTS

A single material can fulfill several functions. Prior to the eighteenth century, most important buildings were constructed with masonry walls that provided the structure, the fire protection, the sound insulation, a high thermal inertia, and some thermal insulation. Design usually followed empirical rules based on the structural requirement.

It is clearly an advantage to be able to use one material for a number of functional requirements, but it is often simpler and cheaper to use different materials for different functions.

Some functional requirements conflict. For example, sound insulation is almost proportional to mass, so that a heavy material is most useful for that purpose (see Sec. 9.2). Since the best thermal insulation is provided by entrapped air, however, thermal insulating materials are usually very light (see Sec. 6.3). Evidently, a material that is particularly good for *thermal* insulation would not be particularly suitable for *sound* insulation, and vice versa.

On the other hand, sound-insulating materials usually have a high thermal inertia (see Secs. 6.5 and 9.2), which is useful for some energy conservation strategies. Furthermore, some sound-absorbing materials have good thermal-insulating properties (see Secs. 6.3 and 9.2).

Most multistory buildings have a structural frame that frees the wall from their previous load-bearing role. It is therefore necessary to consider only thermal and sound insulation, moisture penetration, fire protection, and appearance. Each function can be provided separately by a single layer of one material. Thermal insulation, in particular, usually forms a soft internal layer of a "sandwich." In high-rise buildings, sound insulation is often not a major requirement for the upper external walls. Moisture penetration and thermal insulation need not normally be considered for partitions, and some partitions are not required to provide fire protection. The various functions, therefore, can usually be provided by a panel consisting of three or four layers. The structural frame allows the designer a much wider choice of materials than would be possible with loadbearing walls.

One particularly important function is the appearance of the visible surface, that is, the aesthetic quality of the material. It is important that this should not merely be satisfactory when the building is completed, but should remain so during its useful life. Durability and maintenance are important aspects of aesthetics.

Surfaces of stone occasionally deteriorate or become streaked with dirt as a result of faulty use of the material (see Sec. 12.5). Regrettably, concrete surfaces streaked with dirt because of incorrect detailing are a common occurrence (see Sec. 14.11 and Fig. 8.3.1). One possible solution is to paint the stone or concrete, but the paint must then be renewed at regular intervals. Where deterioration of stone or concrete is a possibility, it is better to substitute another surfacing material.

Concrete is an excellent building material—strong, durable (apart from its surface finish), fire-resistant, easily reinforced, easily formed into complex shapes and large masses, and cheap; it also provides high thermal inertia and good sound insulation. The durability of its surface finish, however, requires close attention. This has been ignored by some of the most renowned architects of the Modern Movement. Most of Le Corbusier's concrete buildings have weathered badly (for example, see Ref. 20.1), and the interior off-the-form concrete surfaces in the Sydney Opera House are beginning to look shabby because of dirt accumulation after less than 15 years in use.

Architectural historians tend to ignore problems of durability and maintenance; they are usually content to reproduce photographs taken shortly after the completion of a building, when its surfaces were new, even in books published fifty years later. The occupants and users of a building who have to live with the deterioration are unlikely to consider a building a masterpiece if the materials lack durability and cannot be properly maintained.

20.5 SOURCES OF INFORMATION

The number of readily available building materials and components has grown rapidly during the twentieth century and continues to grow. The best sources of information are the manufacturers themselves; most will readily supply technical information in great detail on request. This information is generally reliable in its positive aspects, since manufacturers and material suppliers who wish to remain in business will not knowingly give any information that is incorrect. Some suppliers will point out that their material cannot be used in certain ways; others prefer not to mention adverse information, and the architect or engineer has to infer its existence from the fact that appropriate positive statements are missing from a catalogue.

A number of publishers organize this trade literature in a standard format, classified and indexed, so that comparing materials and components can be readily compared. The most comprehensive of these compendia is the American publication, *Sweets' Catalogue.*

A great deal of information can be gathered from other literature of a periodic nature. This can be divided into several categories. The first consists of advertisements and short news items provided by manufacturers and suppliers. These are ordinarily sent to interested architects and engineers free of charge and include a card so that readers may write for further information on any items mentioned. These publications constitute, in fact, a regular update of the trade literature.

A second type of literature, the trade journal, is sold at a relatively modest price to individual subscribers and contains independently written articles that may contain critical comment on new materials and methods. The fact that these publications derive a substantial part of their income from advertisements usually does not restrain critical remarks on the materials advertised, but it may do so in some periodicals.

The third type is the journal that contains scientific papers, often of a highly specialized character. These journals may be published by professional societies or by scientific publishers; they do not normally carry any advertisements by manufacturers and suppliers of materials; and they have an editorial board of eminent specialists in the field to ensure that the papers published are factually correct and meet a high scientific standard. Their price is generally so high that libraries are the principal subscribers.

In addition, papers are continually being produced by industry associations and government research organizations. These may be published in the relevant journals or as special reports.

Industry associations are formed by manufacturers of similar materials to undertake research and promotion on a communal basis. For example, the Portland Cement Association is financed by the cement manufacturers of the United States and Canada for the purpose of promoting the use of cement and concrete, and undertaking research to extend our knowledge of these materials. The Cement and Concrete Association performs a similar function in Great Britain, and so does the Cement and Concrete Association of Australia. Industry associations exist for most major building material groups. Their professional staff have generally more independence than those of individual manufacturers, and they often have more money for research at their disposal.

Governmental research organizations—such as the Center for Building Technology of the U.S. National Bureau of Standards, the Institute for Research in Construction of the Canadian National Research Council, the (British) Building Research Establishment, and the Division of Building Research of the (Australian) Commonwealth Scientific and Industrial Research Organization—conduct research on building materials and on methods of using them. Their resources are spread over such a wide area, however, that some aspects are covered more thoroughly than others.

In most countries, building material standards are written by committees appointed by the local standards association. This function is performed by the Canadian Standards Association, the British Standards Institution, and the Standards Association of Australia. The American National Standards Institute, however, delegates this function mostly to professional societies, such as the American Society for Testing Materials, the American Concrete Institute, the American Institute for Timber Construction, and so on.

These committees consist of practicing engineers and architects, building research scientists, representatives of manufacturers, and technical staff of the sponsoring institution. Since the standards produced are submitted to public comment and usually undergo several reviews before they are published, they often represent a compromise between conflicting interests. They are revised from time to time in accordance with changes in manufacturing and professional practices.

Standard specifications are not merely important documents for regulating the manufacture and use of building materials; they also contain a great deal of interesting technical information about the materials and can be read with advantage in conjunction with textbooks. There are several hundred specifications for building materials, some of them accompanied by commentaries that give the technical background on which they are based.

Some materials are variable and require constant testing. For example, samples must be taken from every batch of concrete produced and tested for strength (see Sec. 14.4). The quality of other materials, such as steel, is easier to control, and the manufacturer's tests are usually accepted as adequate.

Strength, elastic deformation, thermal expansion and contraction, and fire resistance can be determined with considerable accuracy in the laboratory, and so can acoustic and thermal properties. Durability, however, can be ascertained accurately only from long-term tests and observations. As a rule, it is not economically feasible to wait for the completion of such tests, and new materials are therefore often used on the basis of theoretical forecasts and accelerated weathering tests (see Sec. 8.5). This decision is best left to architects and engineers with a long record of professional practice. Others can benefit from the experience gained from these innovations by asking for the location of buildings where new materials have been used and checking out their performance. If the material has performed satisfactorily, many manufacturers provide this information in their advertising literature.

20.6 THE CHOICE OF BUILDING MATERIAL

In the architecture of the Middle Ages and the Renaissance, choice was limited mainly to natural and locally available materials. Today, there is an *embarras de richesses* that will clearly continue to grow.

Traditional methods remain appropriate for some building types, however. The home ordinarily constitutes a family's largest investment, and it is much harder to sell if unfamiliar materials are used in its construction.

Cost remains a principal criterion of choice, particularly if a material will not be visible in the completed building. There is, for example, little difference between the performance of structural-steel frames and reinforced-concrete frames if they are properly designed. The cheaper of the two is usually selected, making due allowance for the effect of earlier or later completion time on cost and profitability.

Prior to 1950, steel frames were used for most highrise buildings because they usually cost less than reinforced-concrete frames. Since then, concrete has become more competitive, but this has not been a steady progress. Although the majority of tall buildings in Europe and Australia are now built with concrete frames, this is not the case in North America. The choice has thus varied with time and geographic location. It is not possible to predict now whether steel or concrete will have the cost advantage in ten years' time in New York, London, or Melbourne.

For visible materials, aesthetic considerations are often dominant, and as beauty is to a certain extent in the eye of the beholder, the choice varies from one designer to another, and from one client to another.

REFERENCES

20.1. Philippe Boudon: *Lived-in Architecture—Le Corbusier's Pessac Revisited*. Lund Humphries, London, 1972. 200 pp.

SUGGESTIONS FOR FURTHER READING

Forrest Wilson: *Building Materials Evaluation Handbook*. Van Nostrand Reinhold, New York, 1984. 358 pp.
Edward Allen: *Fundamentals of Building Construction—Materials and Methods*. Wiley, New York, 1985. 743 pp.
Caleb Hornbostel: *Materials for Architecture—An Encyclopedia Guide*. Reinhold, New York, 1981. 610 pp.
Harold J. Rosen and Philip M. Bennett: *Construction Materials Evaluation and Selection—A Systematic Approach*. Wiley, New York, 1979. 163 pp.

Glossary

Words in italics are cross-referenced to other glossary entries.

Absolute Humidity The mass of water vapor per unit volume of air.

Acid A chemical compound containing a nonmetal, hydrogen, and often oxygen as well, that neutralizes *bases* to form *salts*.

Alloy A substance with metallic properties that is composed of two or more elements which, after being mixed in the molten state, do not separate into distinct layers on solidifying. Most alloys consist of two or more metals; structural steel, a mixture of iron and carbon, is an exception.

Alumina Aluminum oxide.

Amorphous Not crystalline.

Annealing See *tempering*.

Attenuation Diminution or weakening, particularly of sound.

Average The sum of an assembly of numerical data divided by the number of data.

Base A substance that neutralizes an *acid*, forming a *salt* and water.

Beaufort Scale A scale for wind speed that ranges from 0 for complete calm to 12 for a hurricane (cyclone). The wind speed in km/h equals $3\,B^{1.5}$, where B is the Beaufort number of the wind.

Brittleness The property of lacking *ductility*. Brittle failure occurs by the rupture of interatomic bonds and occurs more readily in tension than in shear, or in diagonal shear due to compression. Hence, brittle materials often have a high compressive strength but low tensile strength. Brittle failure is typical of stone, concrete, brick, and other ceramics, but it also occurs in some metals, such as high-carbon steels and cast iron.

Capillary Action The action of a *capillary tube* when dipped in a bucket of water that causes the level in the tube to rise above that in the bucket as a result of surface tension.

Capillary Tube A tube with a very fine bore.

Carborundum The abrasive silicon carbide (SiC).

Cast Iron Iron with a carbon content between 1.8 and 4.5 percent.

Ceramics In the building industry, any material made from burned *clay*, such as brick, terra cotta, and ceramic tiles. In Materials Science and Solid-State Physics, compounds of metallic and nonmetallic elements, including natural stone, clay, and cement.

Clay A fine-grained soil consisting predominantly of hydrous aluminum silicate.

Concrete An artificial stone made from stone chips or gravel, sand, and a cement.

Conductance See *thermal transmittance*

Conduction See *thermal conduction*

Conductivity See *thermal conductivity*

Continental Climate The climate of the interior of a continent, which shows large seasonal variations as opposed, say, to the climate of a small island.

Control Joint A joint for controlling temperature and/or moisture movement; it may allow for expansion or contraction, or for both.

Convection See *thermal convection*

Corundum Aluminum oxide used as an abrasive.

Creep Time-dependent deformation resulting from a load.

Crystal A body whose atoms are arranged in a definite pattern, giving rise to characteristic crystal faces.

Curing A treatment to increase strength as a result of additional linkages being formed between molecules when an accelerator is added to a cold-setting resin or when a thermosetting plastic is heated above its critical temperature. *Also,* the increase in the strength of concrete resulting from the hydration of the cement, provided an adequate temperature and humidity are maintained.

Damp-Proof Course An impervious layer inserted into a pervious wall (such as a brick wall) to exclude water.

199

Deflection Deformation of a structural member due to bending.

Degree Day A unit employed for estimating the fuel consumption and specifying the heating load for a building in winter. For any one day when the temperature is below a specified value [usually 18°C (65°F) in America and 15°C (59°F) in Europe], there exist as many degree-days as the mean temperature for the day is below the specified value. The total for the winter is then compiled.

Dew Point The temperature at which air is fully saturated with water vapor so that condensation occurs if the humidity is increased or the temperature reduced.

Dressed Timber Timber that has been finished with a planing machine after being sawn to give it a smooth surface.

Dry Rot Timber decay caused by a fungus that flourishes only if the wood is damp.

Ductility The property of certain metals to undergo large permanent deformations at room temperature. The opposite of *brittleness*.

Efflorescence A deposit, usually white, formed on the surface of a brick, block, stone, or concrete wall, consisting of *salts* leached from the wall.

Elasticity The ability of a material to deform instantly under load and to resume its original form instantly when the load is removed.

Elastomer A synthetic material with rubberlike qualities.

Extrusion Producing a linear shape by pushing a billet of material through a die, a technique used for forming sections of aluminum and of various plastic materials.

Ferric Refers to a chemical compound of iron with a *valency* of 3.

Ferrous Refers to a chemical compound of iron with a *valency* of 2.

Finger Joint A joint formed between the ends of two pieces of material that are in line, made up of several meshing tongues or fingers of wood with a finger-jointing machine, and normally glued.

Flashing Sheet metal or plastic used to cover open joints in exterior construction to prevent ingress of water, for example, joints in roof valleys or parapets, or joints around window openings.

Fluid A material that flows—a liquid, vapor, or gas.

Flux A material used in soldering and brazing to keep the surfaces to be joined free from oxide films. The flux melts at a lower temperature than the solder. See also *luminous flux*.

Galvanizing The coating of steel or iron with zinc.

Gasket A piece of material or a fitting placed around a joint to make it airtight.

Halogen A generic term for the group of elements: fluorine (F), chlorine (Cl), bromine (Br), and iodine (I).

Halide A *salt* formed by a halogen and a metal. The best-known halide is common salt, NaCl.

Hardboard A board made from wood fibers, pressed together into a dense sheet, with little or no additional binder. See also *particle board*.

Hydraulic Cement A term used mainly in the eighteenth and nineteenth centuries to distinguish a true cement from hydrated lime. Cement hardens under water, but lime is washed out if submerged under water for a long period of time, because hydrated lime is water-soluble.

Hydraulics The science of fluid flow.

Infrared Radiation Radiation with wavelengths longer than 760 nm, that is, beyond the red end of visible light.

Lime A generic term for quicklime (CaO) and hydrated lime [Ca(OH)$_2$)].

Linseed Oil A vegetable oil obtained by crushing the seeds of flax. When exposed to air, it thickens and darkens as a result of oxidation and forms a tough skin.

Liquid A state of matter in which the shape of a given mass depends on the containing vessel but its volume (unlike that of a gas) does not.

Luminous Flux The light power from a light source, measured in lumen.

Mastic Originally the resin of the mastic tree, a small evergreen found near the Mediterranean; hence, a jointing compound that dries on the surface, but remains permanently plastic underneath.

Membrane A thin, impervious sheet.

Modulus of Elasticity The ratio of direct *stress* to direct *strain* in an *elastic* material; this is the (hypothetical) stress that would produce a unit strain.

Modulus of Rupture The nominal maximum tensile stress (calculated by assuming *elastic stress* distribution) in a material subjected to a bending test when the beam breaks in tension.

Moisture Movement The movement of moisture through a material, and hence the effect of moisture movement on the dimensions of the material. The drying of newly cast concrete and of timber after felling is called *shrinkage*. The moisture movement under load is called *creep*.

Monomer A chain molecule without cross linkages, as distinct from a *polymer*.

Oxide A chemical compound of oxygen and another element.

Parapet A portion of a wall that extends above roof level.

Particle Board A board made from wood fibers that are pressed together into a dense sheet using an appreciable amount of binder. See also *hardboard*.

Phase Diagram A diagram that shows temperature on the vertical axis and the composition of an *alloy* on the horizontal axis. It is used to illustrate the temperatures at which alloys made of any proportions of two or three elements exist in the liquid and the solid state, the temperatures at which transformations occur, and other features of an alloy system.

Plaster Any pasty material of mortarlike consistency used for covering the walls or ceilings of a building. The traditional plasters based on lime and gypsum are now rare, and portland cement, mixed with sand and water, is the common material for plastering.

Plaster of Paris The compound, calcium sulfate hemihydrate (CaSO$_4$·$\frac{1}{2}$H$_2$O), which is made from gypsum by heating it to drive off some some of its water.

Plasticity In Materials Science and in Rheology, the ability of a material, particularly a metal or a plastic, to deform at a constant stress without fracture. In concrete technology, the property of a concrete mix that can be easily placed in its mold without segregation.

Plastics A generic term for a number of materials that are easily formed into complex shapes during the manufacturing process. Most plastics are produced synthetically, and most contain carbon chains or rings. Plastics do not necessarily show plastic deformation prior to failure.

Polymer A large molecule formed from chain molecules (*monomers*) by cross linkages.

Pozzolana Originally a volcanic dust found in the slopes of Mount Vesuvius near Pozzuoli, which, when mixed with lime mortar, forms a *hydraulic cement*. It was used in Ancient Rome. Hence, any natural or artificial substance with pozzolanic properties.

Proof Stress The nominal stress (that is, load per unit of original cross-sectional area) that produces a specified permanent *strain,* usually 0.1 or 0.2 percent. This is specified for metals that exhibit significant *plasticity* without a marked *yield stress.*

Psychrometry The study of the properties of a mixture of air and water vapor.

Quenching Hardening of a material by rapid cooling from an elevated temperature, usually by immersion in oil or water.

Refractory Material A material that can withstand a very high temperature and is thus suitable for lining a furnace.

Relative Humidity The ratio of the amount of water vapor actually present in the air to that present at the same temperature in a water-saturated atmosphere, expressed as a percentage. See also *absolute humidity.*

Rheology The science of the flow of materials.

Salt A substance obtained by the reaction of an *acid* and a *base,* or by the displacement of the hydrogen of an acid by a metal. Most salts are *crystalline.* Common salt is sodium chloride (NaCl).

Sand A naturally occurring soil with a grain size from 10 mm (³⁄₈ in.) to 0.1 mm (0.004 in.). Most sands consist predominantly of *silica.*

Sarking A layer of boards or bituminous felt or plastic laid as undercovering for tiles and other roofing. Its main purpose is to prevent ingress of water in roofs laid to a low pitch.

Scarf Joint A joint formed between the ends of two pieces of material that are in line and tapered to form sloping surfaces that match; it may be glued or bolted.

Seasoning The drying of timber in the open air (natural seasoning) or in a kiln.

Set In mathematics, a group of different elements having at least one common characteristic. In materials science, the *strain* remaining after the removal of *stress.* In concrete technology, the initial stage of the chemical reaction between cement and water, when the concrete stiffens and loses the fluidity necessary to fill the mold.

Silica Silicon oxide (SiO_2).

Sprinkler Head A temperature-sensitive element that stops up pipes filled with water by means of a metal plug that melts, or a plastic plug containing liquid that bursts, at a predetermined temperature, usually 68°C (155°F). This is low enough to control a fire in its early stages by sprinkling water on it, but high enough to ensure that the system does not go off on a hot day without a fire.

Standard Deviation A measure of the spread of a *set* of *n* observations or measurements. If the *average* of a set of values, *x,* is x_a, the standard deviation is

$$s = \sqrt{\frac{\Sigma(x - x_a)^2}{n}}$$

It is necessary to square the variances (or departures from the average) and take the square root of their sum; otherwise the positive and negative variances would largely cancel out.

Steel An *alloy* of iron and carbon.

Strain A change in the dimensions or shape of a body per unit length or per unit angle. The strain usually considered is the direct strain, which is the elongation or shortening per unit length caused by a tensile or compressive *stress.*

Stress The internal force per unit area, considering an infinitesimally small part of a material. For simple tension and compression, stress is the force applied to the material, divided by its cross-sectional area.

Stress–strain diagram The diagram obtained by plotting the stresses produced in a test specimen by a load against the measured strains. It is used to assess the structural suitability of a material, since it shows its strength, its *elastic* and *plastic* deformation, and its *ductility* or *brittleness.*

Tempering Heating hardened steel below the *transformation temperature,* and then cooling it slowly to reduce its *brittleness* and improve its *ductility.* Annealing is a similar process in which the steel is heated above the *transformation temperature.*

Termite An insect that shuns light and is highly destructive to seasoned timber, especially soft wood. Also called white ants, termites occur only in warm climates.

Terra Cotta Burned clay units for ornamental work. Glazed terra cotta is often called "faience."

Thermal Conductance The same as *thermal transmittance.*

Thermal Conduction The process of heat transfer through a material whereby heat is transmitted from particle to particle, not as in *thermal convection* by movement of particles, nor by radiation.

Thermal Conductivity Rate of transfer of heat along a body by *thermal conduction.* Frequently called the "k-value," it may be expressed in metric or in British/American units.

Thermal Convection The transmission of heat by natural or forced motion of a liquid or a gas, that is, by movement of the particles in that medium, as opposed to *thermal conduction* or radiation.

Thermal Inertia The capacity of a material to store heat or cold. A material with high thermal inertia delays the response of a building to an external change of temperature.

Thermal Transmittance The amount of heat that passes through a unit area of a building material, of the thickness normally used in that type of building, as a result of a difference of 1° (C or F) between the two faces. Frequently called the "U-value," it may be expressed in metric or British/American units; it is also called "thermal conductance."

Ton, Tonne 1 long ton = 2240 lb; 1 short ton = 2000 lb; 1 metric ton (tonne) = 1000 kg = 0.984 long tons = 1.102 short tons. Also, 1 ton of refrigeration = 12,000 Btu per hour = 3517 W.

Transformation Temperature The temperature at which one *phase* of an *alloy* system changes to another phase.

Ultraviolet Radiation Radiation with wavelengths shorter than 390 nm, that is, beyond the violet end of visible light.

Valency The combining power of an atom. Thus, oxygen, which is bivalent, combines with two univalent hydrogen atoms to form water (H_2O), and two oxygen atoms combine with silicon (which has a valency of 4) to form *silica* (SiO_2).

Veneer A thin layer of material used as a facing.

Vicat Softening Point The temperature at which a standard needle penetrates into a *plastic* by a specified distance under a standard load.

Viscosity The internal friction caused by cohesion in fluids or in solids with flow characteristics.

Weatherometer A machine for the accelerated determination of the weather-resisting properties of materials (such as paints and plastics) by cycles imitating as closely as possible natural weathering conditions. Weatherometers can only be used for comparison between similar materials; they do not give an absolute value for durability.

White Ant Same as *termite*.

Wrought Iron Iron with a very low carbon content (less than 0.1 percent) made by a traditional process so that it has a fibrous structure.

Yield Stress The lowest stress at which *strain* increases without an increase of *stress* due to *plastic* deformation. It is easily measured in materials, such as structural steel, that have a pronounced yield stress. Most alloys do not show a distinct yield stress, and a *proof stress* is then specified.

A Note on the SI Metric System

There are three distinct systems of measurement in use at the present time. In customary British/American units, length is measured in feet and inches, mass and force in pounds, electrical energy in joules, heat energy in British thermal units, and temperature in degrees Fahrenheit.

In the old metric system, which is also still widely used, length is measured in meters, mass and force in grams, electric energy in joules, heat energy in calories, and temperature in degrees Celsius.

In the new SI system (*Système International d'Unités*), length is also measured in meters, mass in grams, electrical energy in joules, and temperature in degrees Celsius; however, force is measured in newtons and heat energy in joules.

In this book, all units are given in the SI metric system, followed by the customary British/American units in brackets. Conversion tables are therefore not required for reading this book. However, as the SI system is still not generally familiar, particularly in the United States, the following conversions may be helpful, especially for reading the references given at the end of each chapter if they happen to be in the "wrong" units.

Symbols for Large and Small Units

In the SI system, the large units are obtained by the prefixes kilo (one thousand, or 10^3), mega (one million, or 10^6), giga (one thousand million, or 10^9), and tera (one million million, or 10^{12}); for example:

$$1000 \text{ J} = 1 \times 10^3 \text{J} = 1 \text{ kJ (kilojoule)}$$
$$1000 \text{ kJ} = 1 \times 10^6 \text{J} = 1 \text{ MJ (megajoule)}$$

$$1000 \text{ MJ} = 1 \times 10^9 \text{J} = 1 \text{ GJ (gigajoule)}$$
$$1000 \text{ GJ} = 1 \times 10^{12} \text{J} = 1 \text{ TJ (terajoule)}$$

The increases are in increments of one thousand. There are no special names for the multiples 10 and 100, as in the old metric system.

Small units are obtained by the prefixed milli (one thousandth or 10^{-3}), micro (one millionth, or 10^{-6}), and nano (10^{-9}); for example:

$$0.001 \text{ m} = 1 \times 10^{-3}\text{m} = 1 \text{ mm (millimeter)}$$
$$0.001 \text{ mm} = 1 \times 10^{-6}\text{m} = 1 \text{ }\mu\text{m (micrometer)}$$
$$0.001 \text{ }\mu\text{m} = 1 \times 10^{-9}\text{m} = 1 \text{ nm (nanometer)}$$

The term "billion" should be avoided, as it means in America a multiple of 10^9, whereas in Europe and Australia it means a multiple of 10^{12}.

Temperature

In metric units, temperature is measured in degrees Celsius (°C); in customary British/American units, it is measured in degrees Fahrenheit (°F). They are related as follows:

$$0°C = 32°F \text{ and } 100°C = 212°F$$
$$°C = \tfrac{5}{9} (°F - 32)$$

In some thermal and all lighting calculations, temperature is expressed in degrees Kelvin, which refer to absolute zero. The degree sign is omitted for degrees Kelvin (K). Referred to absolute zero,

$$K = °C + 273.15$$

For temperature differences, only the relative size of the degree is important:

$$1 \text{ K} = 1°\text{C} = 1.8°\text{F}$$

Length

The metric unit for length is the meter (m). The gradations are as follows:

$$
\begin{aligned}
1 \text{ km} &= 1000 \text{ m} \\
1 \text{ m} &= 1000 \text{ mm} \\
1 \text{ mm} &= 1000 \mu\text{m} \\
1 \mu\text{m} &= 1000 \text{ nm}
\end{aligned}
$$

The wavelength of light and radiation is sometimes stated in a superseded measure: 1 angstrom = 0.1 nm.

The customary British/American units are the mile, the foot (ft), and the inch (in.):

$$1 \text{ mile} = 5280 \text{ ft}; \quad 1 \text{ ft} = 12 \text{ in.}$$

Thus,

$$
\begin{aligned}
1 \text{ mile} &= 1.609 \text{ km} \\
1 \text{ km} &= 0.62137 \text{ miles} \\
1 \text{ m} &= 3.281 \text{ ft} = 39.37 \text{ in.} \\
1 \text{ ft} &= 0.3048 \text{ m} \\
1 \text{ in.} &= 25.4 \text{ mm}
\end{aligned}
$$

Area

$$
\begin{aligned}
1 \text{ m}^2 &= 10.764 \text{ ft}^2 \\
1 \text{ ft}^2 &= 0.0929 \text{ m}^2
\end{aligned}
$$

One square meter = 10 square feet is a common approximation.

Volume and Capacity

$$
\begin{aligned}
1 \text{ m}^3 &= 35.315 \text{ ft}^3 \\
1 \text{ ft}^3 &= 0.02832 \text{ m}^3 \\
1 \text{ liter} &= 0.001 \text{ m}^3 = 0.220 \text{ Imperial gallons} \\
&= 0.264 \text{ U.S. gallons} \\
&= 1.057 \text{ U.S. quarts}
\end{aligned}
$$

Second Moment of Area (Moment of Inertia)

$$
\begin{aligned}
1 \text{ m}^4 &= 115.862 \text{ ft}^4 \\
1 \text{ ft}^4 &= 0.008\ 631 \text{ m}^4 \\
1 \text{ mm}^4 &= 2{,}402{,}510 \text{ in.}^4 \\
1 \text{ in.}^4 &= 416\ 231 \text{ mm}^4
\end{aligned}
$$

Mass

The metric unit is the gram (g). There are numerous British/American units; in this book, the pound (lb) and the grain are used.

$$
\begin{aligned}
1 \text{ kg} &= 1000 \text{ g} = 1{,}000{,}000{,}000{,}000 \text{ ng} \\
1 \text{ kg} &= 2.205 \text{ lb} \\
1 \text{ lb} &= 0.4536 \text{ kg} \\
1 \text{ g} &= 15.432 \text{ grain} \\
1 \text{ grain} &= 0.064\ 800 \text{ g}
\end{aligned}
$$

Density (Unit Weight of Materials)

Density is measured in kilograms per cubic meter or pounds per cubic foot. Conversions are as follows:

$$
\begin{aligned}
1 \text{ kg/m}^3 &= 0.064\ 243 \text{ lb/ft}^3 \\
1 \text{ lb/ft}^3 &= 16.018 \text{ kg/m}^3
\end{aligned}
$$

Time and Frequency

Time is accounted as follows:

$$
\begin{aligned}
1 \text{ hour} &= 60 \text{ minutes} = 3600 \text{ seconds} \\
1 \text{ day} &= 24 \text{ hours} = 86{,}400 \text{ seconds}
\end{aligned}
$$

Frequency is the inverse of time. It is measured in cycles per second. In SI units, this is called a hertz (Hz).

$$1 \text{ hertz} = 1 \text{ cycle per second} = 60 \text{ cycles per minute}$$

Speed and Velocity

In SI calculations, speed and velocity are given in meters per second or in kilometers per hour. In customary British/American units, velocity is stated in miles per hour or in feet per minute.

$$
\begin{aligned}
1 \text{ m/s} &= 196.85 \text{ ft/min} = 2.237 \text{ mph} = 3.6 \text{ km/h} \\
1 \text{ ft/min} &= 0.005\ 08 \text{ m/s} \\
1 \text{ mph} &= 0.447 \text{ m/s}
\end{aligned}
$$

Force, Pressure, and Stress

In British/American units, force is measured in pounds (lb) or kilopounds (kip). In this book, pressure and stress are measured in pounds per square inch (psi), kilopounds per square inch (ksi), or inches of mercury.

In the old metric units, force is measured in kilograms (kg), and pressure and stress in kilograms per square centimeter (kg/cm²) or millimeters of mercury.

In SI units, force is measured in newtons (N), and pressure and stress in pascals (Pa):

1 Pa = 1 N/m^2
1 N = 0.2248 lb
1 lb = 4.448 N
1 MN = 224.8 kip
1 kip = 4.448 kN
1 kPa = 0.295 inches of mercury
1 inch of mercury = 3386 Pa
1 kPa = 0.145 psi
1 psi = 6.895 kPa
1 MPa = 0.145 ksi
1 ksi = 6.895 MPa

Standard atmospheric pressure is 101.3 kPa = 14.7 psi = 760 mm mercury = 30 in. mercury.

Energy

All systems of measurement use joules (J) for electrical energy. Heat energy is also measured in joules in the SI system, but the old metric system uses calories (cal), and the customary British/American units employ British thermal units (Btu).

1 MJ = 1000 kJ = 1,000,000 J
1 kJ = 0.948 Btu = 0.239 kcal
1 Btu = 1.055 kJ

Another frequently employed unit is the kilowatt-hour:

1 kWh = 3.6 MJ

Power and Heat Flow

All systems of measurement use the watt (W) for electrical energy.

1 MW = 1000 kW = 1,000,000 W
1 W = 1 joule/second

A variety of other units are in use:

1 kW = 3421 Btu/h = 860 kcal/h = 239 cal/s
= 0.284 tons of refrigeration
= 1.341 British/American horsepower
= 1.360 metric horsepower
1 Btu/h = 0.293 W

Thermal Conductivity

This is measured in composite units:

1 W/mK = 6.933 Btu in./ft^{2}h °F
= 0.578 Btu/ft h °F
= 0.860 kcal/m h °C

Thermal Transmittance

This is measured in composite units:

1 W/m^{2}K = 0.1761 Btu/ft^{2}h °F
= 0.860 kcal/m^{2}h °C

Thermal Resistance

This is the reciprocal of thermal transmittance:

1 m^{2}K/W = 5.678 ft^{2}h °F/Btu
= 1.163 m^{2}h °C/kcal

Illuminance

The metric unit is the lux, and the (obsolete) foot unit is the footcandle.

1 lux = 0.0929 footcandles
1 footcandle = 10.76 lux

1 footcandle = 10 lux is a common approximation.

Luminance

The metric unit is candela per square meter (cd/m^2), and the (obsolete) metric units are the footlambert and candela per square foot.

1 cd/m^2 = 0.292 footlambert
= 0.093 candela per square foot

Sound Pressure

The decibel (db) is a logarithmic ratio, not an absolute unit. It becomes an absolute unit only when it is referred to a base. The customary base for sound pressure is the "threshold of hearing," which is taken as 20×10^{-6} Pa, and this becomes 0 db.

Index

The figures behind the entries are page numbers. Bold figures refer to major entries which may extend over more than one page.